Mastering Test-Driven Development with PHP 8

Building secure and reliable PHP 8 applications through TDD, design patterns, and functional data handling

Dr. Flávio Gomes da Silva Lisboa

bpb

www.bpbonline.com

First Edition 2025

Copyright © BPB Publications, India

ISBN: 978-93-65892-000

To View Complete
BPB Publications Catalogue
Scan the QR Code:

Dedicated to

*My beloved wife, **Maria**, and my dear daughter, **Koriander***

About the Author

Dr. Flávio Gomes da Silva Lisboa holds a PhD and a master's degree in social studies of science and technology from the Federal Technological University of Paraná. He holds a degree in computer science with a specialization in object-oriented programming and Java technology. Flávio is a certified software architect and engineer from Zend Technologies. He works as a technology analyst for the Brazilian Federal Data Processing Service (serpro), the largest public information technology company in Latin America, building and maintaining applications for cross-platform services.

At Serpro, Flávio coordinated a corporate program to promote free and open-source software, worked on the review of systems architecture for the Presidency of the Republic and the Ministry of Justice of Brazil, was head of the solution adaptation and mobility sector and architect of the ExpressoV3 project, and worked with support for the PHP programming language, behavior-oriented development, NoSQL databases, log analysis, and detection of bot attacks. He has experience in software development with emphasis for free and open-source software. FGSL is interested mainly in software architecture, area where he has experience in working with reuse, patterns, and frameworks.

He has been a speaker in PHP Conference Brazil for more than a decade and was honored by the event organization with a permanent room, alongside great members of the PHP Brazil community, as Elton Minetto, Guilherme Blanco, Ricardo Coelho, Rafael Dohms and Er Galvão. Flávio is also a professor at Centro Paula Souza, a network of colleges and technical schools, where he teaches systems analysis and design, web programming, and databases. Flávio is the author of the book Laminas Web Development, a complete guide about a PHP framework of the Linux Foundation. He also writes science fiction and in this segment, he has published the novels The One: the Solitude and the Harmony; Pandino, the Emperor: the Revenge of the One; and Freedom or Equality.

About the Reviewers

❖ **Mohamed A. Youssef** is a PHP developer with over 8 years of experience in back-end development, specializing in Symfony, Laravel, Magento, and OpenCart. He has worked on various web projects, focusing on server-side development, payment gateways, and XML integrations. He is also experienced in PHPUnit and **test-driven development** (**TDD**) to ensure code reliability and maintainability. Comfortable with HTML, CSS, JavaScript, and Linux environments, he enjoys building and optimizing web applications.

Aside from coding, Mohamed has a keen interest in reading and reviewing books, especially in history, technology, and digital trends. With a bachelor's degree in history from Cairo University, he appreciates both technical and historical perspectives in his reviews.

❖ **Sushil Kumar Gupta** is a seasoned senior software engineer with over 9 years of experience in developing scalable web applications using PHP, CodeIgniter, Laravel, Magento, and Shopify. He specializes in software redevelopment, API integrations, payment gateways, and CRM development, ensuring optimized performance and seamless user experiences.

Currently, he is a senior PHP developer at a fintech company, leading the development of a business loan system from scratch, focusing on security, scalability, and third-party financial integrations. Previously, at Addison IT Solutions, he played a key role in redeveloping healthcare software and led the homecare project, improving efficiency and system performance.

Sushil is also experienced in mentoring teams, conducting code reviews, and establishing best coding practices. His technical expertise extends to server management (Linux), MySQL, PostgreSQL, and API integrations. He holds an MBA in IT and a BCA, reflecting his strong academic foundation.

Passionate about technology and innovation, he enjoys tackling complex software challenges and continuously improving system performance. His contributions to the software development industry make him a valuable asset in any project requiring technical excellence and leadership.

Acknowledgement

I would like to express my sincere gratitude to all those who contributed to the completion of this book.

First and foremost, I extend my heartfelt appreciation to my fellow teachers and members of the PHP community in Brazil. Their recognition they have of my work have been a constant source of motivation.

I would like to extend my special thanks to the following individuals for their valuable input and contributions to this project: Anderson Fernandes Burnes, Daiana Alves, Eduardo Herbert Ribeiro Bona, Er Galvão Abbott, Felipe Augusto Rezende, Fernando Silva, Flávio Augusto da Silveira, Matheus Gontijo, Vítor Mattos and Wellton Costa de Oliveira. Your articles, classes and lectures contributed to many ideas I had and our meetings in events gave me valuable experiences to think about regarding a solid PHP education.

I am immensely grateful to BPB Publications for their guidance and expertise in bringing this book to fruition. Their support and assistance were invaluable in navigating the complexities of the publishing process.

I would also like to acknowledge the reviewers, technical experts, and editors who provided valuable feedback and contributed to the refinement of this manuscript. Their insights and suggestions have significantly enhanced the quality of the book.

Last but not least, I want to express my gratitude to the readers who have shown interest in my book. Your support and encouragement have been deeply appreciated.

Thank you to everyone who has played a part in making this book a reality.

Preface

Understanding the test-driven development approach is important for building quality applications. This book *Mastering Test-Driven Development with PHP 8* covers in a practical way the fundamentals necessary for a programmer to develop testable and secure PHP web applications.

Comprising 12 insightful chapters, this book covers a wide range of topics essential for creating web applications with the PHP programming language covered with testing and security mechanisms. We start with PHP fundamentals and test-driven development, providing a solid grounding in the basics. From there, we move towards object-oriented programming, exploring the implementation of this paradigm in PHP to read and write data stored in file system, relational and non-relational databases.

The book targets professionals with some experience in programming who intend or was requested to use PHP for backend. The book assumes readers know main web standards for web frontend, HTML and CSS. The book believes that the readers may have intermediate level knowledge of algorithms and data structures, requirements analysis and UML.

Through practical examples and an evolutionary approach, with heavy use of refactoring, this book takes the reader from the beginning through test-driven development, while showing the power of the PHP programming language to create easy-to-maintain web applications.

Chapter 1: Meeting and Installing PHP - This chapter of the book will cover the definition of PHP, how it works, and how we can create an environment to work with that programming language. We will start with an overview of the creation and evolution of PHP, then we will explain the structure of its community and how it is organized. We will also explain how to install PHP on a real machine with multiple options, from the simplest to the hardest way. Afterward, we will learn how to create a virtualized development environment for PHP. Finally, we will show how to prepare the environment for working with a test-driven development approach, which we will use in the next chapters. At the end of this chapter, you will be able to understand what is PHP and how to install it for developing backend applications.

Chapter 2: PHP Foundations - This chapter will cover the foundations of the PHP programming language. We will start by understanding PHP syntax and structural elements in comparison with C language. Then, we will learn the control-flow structures of

PHP in standard and alternative forms. We will also learn about data types, type-juggling, and operator precedence. Next, we will learn how to define functions and use built-in functions in PHP, along with PHP functions to manipulate cookies, sessions, HTML forms, and HTTP responses. By the end of this chapter, you will be able to understand the foundations of the PHP programming language. You will be able to recognize PHP flow control structures in their two forms.

Chapter 3: Function Driven Registration with File System Storage - This chapter of the book will cover the project and implementation of a book registration using function-oriented programming. We will start with the project presentation, which will serve as an exercise to learn PHP incrementally by refactoring an application. In this first version, the reader will learn how to code the registration with modularized code in functions and data storage in a file system. Every backend code produced from now on will be covered with tests. By the end of this chapter, you will be able to build a function driven PHP application. You will be able to use PHP to write and read data from text files in more than one format (plain text, CSV and JSON).

Chapter 4: Function Driven Registration with Relational Database Storage - This chapter of the book will cover refactoring of the book's registration application, replacing the file system storage with a relational database storage, using MySQL/MariaDB. This will be the first exercise of wide refactoring and the first step to think about the concept of decoupling. We will add the ability to read and write to database tables, making system storage configurable to work with both paradigms. At the end of this chapter, you will be able to build a function driven PHP application storing data in a relational database. You will be able to use PHP to create, recover, update and delete records from database tables.

Chapter 5: Function Driven Registration with Document Database Storage -This chapter of the book will cover a refactoring of the book registration application, replacing the relational database storage, using MySQL/MariaDB, with a document database storage based on MongoDB. We will add the ability to read and write to collections, widening the storage options of the application. By the end of this chapter, you will be able to build a function driven PHP application storing data in a document database. You will be able to use PHP to create, recover, update and delete records from collections in a MongoDB database.

Chapter 6: PHP OOP- This chapter will cover how to program object-oriented registration in PHP. We will start by learning how OOP techniques are implemented in the PHP programming language and how we replace uncoupled variables and functions with attributes (or properties) and methods encapsulated in classes. We will learn the foundations of object creation, cloning and comparison. We also will learn how to use the main reuse mechanism of object-oriented programming, class inheritance, and how to establish communication patterns using interfaces. Next, we will learn about the magic methods, the methods which are invoked in response to events. Finally, we will learn how to manipulate different relational databases with a standardized interface and how to handle exceptions and errors.

Chapter 7: Object-oriented Registration with File System Storage -This chapter of the book will cover how to refactor a function driven registration with file system storage for an object-oriented implementation. We will learn how to create classes and their methods from functions initially by converting the author recording in a plain text file to object-oriented mode. After this experience, we will refactor the recording in other file system formats. We will continue converting read, update and remove operations from functions to class methods. By the end of this chapter, you will be able to convert functions into methods and group them into classes. You will learn how to think about call semantics by having an actor performing an action rather than an action occurring without someone responsible for it.

Chapter 8: Object-oriented Registration with Relational Database Storage- This chapter will cover how to refactor a function driven registration with relational database storage for an object-oriented implementation. In this chapter, we will replace the use of the native MySQL driver with the **PHP Data Objects** (**PDO**) driver. We will learn what **object-relational mapping** (**ORM**) is, the architectural patterns of this approach and how to implement the two of them and using them to refactor the Librarian application. By the end of this chapter, you will be able to understand how to replace the use of native MySQL driver with the PDO driver. You will be able to understand ORM and ORM architectural patterns and how to use them for refactoring an application using a relational database.

Chapter 9: Object-oriented Registration with Document Database Storage- This chapter of the book will cover how to refactor a function-oriented database implementation from a document-oriented database to an object-oriented implementation using the Row Data Gateway design pattern. We will identify duplications and eliminate them, generalizing with abstract classes and enforcing patterns with interfaces. We will review the models we created, the user interface, and the request handling. By the end of this chapter, readers will be able to understand how to use Row Data Gateway pattern for document-oriented databases. You will be able to perform refactoring to eliminate duplication using abstract classes and enforce communication patterns using interfaces.

Chapter 10: Abstracting the Application Storage- This chapter of the book will cover the refactoring of the previous version of the book registration application and the creation of a new layer for decoupling the model layer from the storage paradigm. This change will be justified as a strategy to avoid a vendor lock-in and reducing the cost of a migration. This chapter will start covering what are design patterns and how to use them. Next, we will learn how to create a REST API for our application. After having implemented an API, we will learn how to generate a code coverage report. Then, we will follow with changes in the handling of the web pages, introducing an architecture pattern to separate the layout from the content. Finally, we will refactor the application with the Model-View-Controller pattern.

Chapter 11: Refactoring the Application with Secure Development- This chapter of the book will cover how to refactor PHP application by applying techniques to let it secure to reduce an attacker's chance of success. We will start talking about the relationship between secure development and secure code. We will learn about information resources about web application vulnerabilities and PHP vulnerabilities. After understanding these fundamentals, we will review the application's inputs, introducing filters and data validators. Next, we will review the data outputs, analyzing whether the application does not expose data that it should not. Finally, we will talk about the automated code analysis as a tool to help discover vulnerabilities.

Chapter 12: Authentication and Authorization- This chapter of the book will cover two topics of secure development. We will learn how to authenticate users using session-based and token-based authentication, as specified by the **JSON Web Token (JWT)** standard. We will also learn how to authorize users to perform specific operations within an application, using two different approaches, **access control list (ACL)** and **role-based authorization control (RBAC)**. In the latest version of the Librarian application, users will only be able to manipulate authors and books if they are authenticated and have permission to perform the operations. By the end of this chapter, you will be able to implement authentication and authorization in PHP applications. You will be able to authenticate users and persist the authentication data in the session or use a token in the JWT standard and use the application control layer to ensure that all non-public pages are only accessed by authenticated users.

Code Bundle and Coloured Images

Please follow the link to download the
Code Bundle and the *Coloured Images* of the book:

https://rebrand.ly/to9bb42

The code bundle for the book is also hosted on GitHub at
https://github.com/bpbpublications/Mastering-Test-Driven-Development-with-PHP-8.
In case there's an update to the code, it will be updated on the existing GitHub repository.

We have code bundles from our rich catalogue of books and videos available at
https://github.com/bpbpublications. Check them out!

Errata

We take immense pride in our work at BPB Publications and follow best practices to ensure the accuracy of our content to provide with an indulging reading experience to our subscribers. Our readers are our mirrors, and we use their inputs to reflect and improve upon human errors, if any, that may have occurred during the publishing processes involved. To let us maintain the quality and help us reach out to any readers who might be having difficulties due to any unforeseen errors, please write to us at :

errata@bpbonline.com

Your support, suggestions and feedbacks are highly appreciated by the BPB Publications' Family.

Did you know that BPB offers eBook versions of every book published, with PDF and ePub files available? You can upgrade to the eBook version at www.bpbonline. com and as a print book customer, you are entitled to a discount on the eBook copy. Get in touch with us at :

business@bpbonline.com for more details.

At **www.bpbonline.com**, you can also read a collection of free technical articles, sign up for a range of free newsletters, and receive exclusive discounts and offers on BPB books and eBooks.

Piracy

If you come across any illegal copies of our works in any form on the internet, we would be grateful if you would provide us with the location address or website name. Please contact us at **business@bpbonline.com** with a link to the material.

If you are interested in becoming an author

If there is a topic that you have expertise in, and you are interested in either writing or contributing to a book, please visit **www.bpbonline.com**. We have worked with thousands of developers and tech professionals, just like you, to help them share their insights with the global tech community. You can make a general application, apply for a specific hot topic that we are recruiting an author for, or submit your own idea.

Reviews

Please leave a review. Once you have read and used this book, why not leave a review on the site that you purchased it from? Potential readers can then see and use your unbiased opinion to make purchase decisions. We at BPB can understand what you think about our products, and our authors can see your feedback on their book. Thank you!

For more information about BPB, please visit **www.bpbonline.com**.

Join our book's Discord space

Join the book's Discord Workspace for Latest updates, Offers, Tech happenings around the world, New Release and Sessions with the Authors:

https://discord.bpbonline.com

Table of Contents

CHAPTER 1

Meeting and Installing PHP

Introduction

This chapter of the book will cover the definition of **Personal Home Page** (**PHP**), how it works, and how we can create an environment to work with that programming language. We will start with an overview of the creation and evolution of PHP, then we will explain the structure of its community and how it is organized. We will also explain how to install PHP on a real machine with multiple options, from the simplest to the hardest way. Afterwards, we will learn how to create a virtualized development environment for PHP. Finally, we will show how to prepare the environment for working with a test-driven development approach.

Structure

The chapter covers the following topics:

- PHP community and ecosystem
- Preparing PHP development environment
- Ways to install PHP
- Virtualized environment for PHP
- Test-driven environment for PHP

Objectives

By the end of this chapter, readers will be able to understand what is PHP and how to install it for developing backend applications. You will be able to quickly install a minimal development environment for PHP using the XAMPP package, but you will also be able to install it in other ways, both on real and virtual machines. Additionally, you will be able to prepare your environment to work with test-driven development.

PHP community and ecosystem

In this section, we will answer three fundamental questions about PHP, what it is, how it works, and how it is maintained. It will provide you with the most relevant knowledge to help you understand this concept.

Creation and ascension of PHP

In 1995, a Danish programmer named *Rasmus Lerdorf* published the source code of an interpreter he had created under the **General Public License (GPL)**, a free software license. In doing so, he allowed anyone to not only run the interpreter, but study, modify, and redistribute it, including modifications. The interpreter that *Rasmus* created was called **Personal Home Page tools**. This name reveals what *Rasmus* purpose was when he created the interpreter. He wanted a tool that would help him to create his web page.

Rasmus often says in his talks that the philosophy behind PHP is a programmatic approach to the web problem. This information is important because it shows that PHP knows what to focus on. It was not a language designed to solve any type of problem. Although today, it is possible to create PHP desktop applications or scripts for infrastructure automation, *Rasmus* designed it specifically to take advantage of the HTTP protocol. In 1995, to manipulate HTML form with two fields, *Rasmus* needed to write 63 lines in C language. The most concise alternative for him was the Perl language, with which he could write the same thing using 17 lines and the code was more readable for humans but *Rasmus* wanted an approach centered around HTML, which was a language designed for HTTP, a hypertext language for a hypertext protocol. So, he created a programming language that allowed him to write instructions to generate dynamic content within HTML tags.

By opening the source code of his interpreter, *Rasmus* got help making it more powerful. In fact, what he had produced in order to solve a personal problem attracted the interest of many people who saw enormous potential in the project for building dynamic websites. The first version of PHP had 14 source code files, collected in a single folder. Two years later, in 1997, the second version of PHP already had 68 files and its first subfolder. This second version was called **PHP/Forms Interpreter (PHP/FI)**. In 1997, the PHP documentation group was created, which grew in the following decades and built the documentation available at **https://www.php.net/docs.php**

In 1998, with the help of *Zeev Suraski* and *Andi Gutmans*, *Rasmus* released a third version of PHP with the support of object-oriented programming. Since then, the use of PHP increased rapidly, so that by 2004 more than 18 million domains were using it as their server-side programming language. Starting with the third version, PHP began to be distributed under the PHP license, but it remains free and open-source.

When *Zeev* and *Andi* began collaborating with *Rasmus*, they created a company called *Zend Technologies*, where Zend is the combination of the first two letters of their names. In PHP version four, the duo released the Zend engine, a compiler and runtime environment for PHP. With this engine, PHP gained greater performance because the scripts began to be compiled into blocks of machine language instructions called **opcodes**. PHP was not a Personal Home Page anymore, but a recursive acronym of PHP Hypertext Preprocessor.

Zend engine's architecture added compilation power while maintaining the ease of use that *Rasmus* wanted for PHP. Let us compare PHP architecture with Java architecture to understand it better. For printing the sentence *Hello, World!* using Java, you need to create a file with five lines and execute two commands, **javac** for compiling a **.java** file, generating a **.class** file with the bytecode, and **java** for running the **.class** file. For doing the same thing with PHP, you can create a **.php** file with one single line and you need to execute one only command, **php**. Zend engine compiles **.php** file generating opcode in memory for running that opcode.

The comparison between the two processes is shown in *Figure 1.1*:

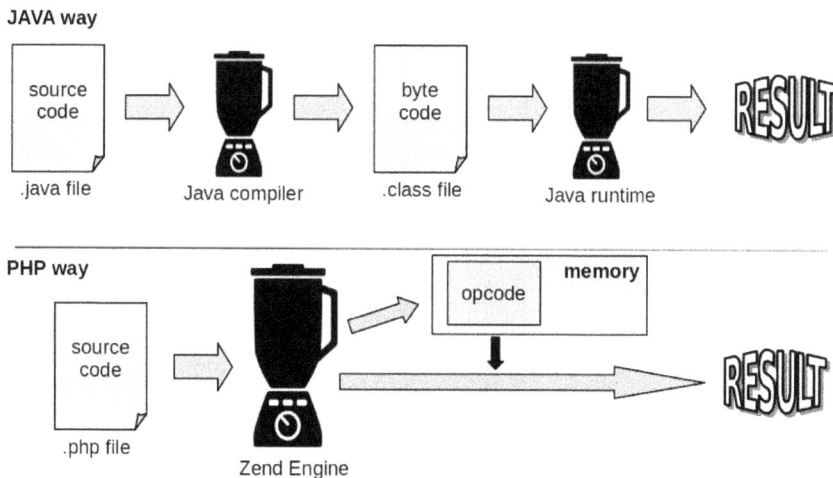

Figure 1.1: *Comparison between Java and PHP environments*

Over two decades, PHP has fully implemented support for object-oriented programming and complementary concepts like traits, always keeping the simplicity. In addition, it expanded its library of functions and integrations with other systems. PHP version eight is a much more complex system than *Rasmus Lerdorf's* small personal project and it also requires many people to maintain it.

Let us look at the community organization and the resources available for developers.

PHP ecosystem

PHP is written entirely in C language and it is currently maintained in a repository on GitHub for almost one thousand developers. If you are curious to know how the old versions of PHP were implemented, you can find them at the PHP Museum at **https://museum.php.net**. In addition to the development team, there is a team of documenters and translators. Guidelines for contributing to the documentation or translating it are available at **http://doc.php.net/tutorial**

PHP developers are currently working on evolving the language using **Requests for Comments** (**RFCs**). Each RFC contains a change that is discussed and then voted on by the group. If approved, it is implemented in the language. You can find out about how to create an RFC and which ones are being voted on, accepted, and implemented on the page **https://wiki.php.net/rfc**. The complete guidelines for contributing with PHP, including the explanation about the source code directory structure, are available at **https://github.com/php/php-src/blob/master/CONTRIBUTING.md**

Although it is not our goal here to learn how to modify PHP but rather how to use it to create applications using it, you may be interested in learning how to make changes to PHP. The first step to this is to find an issue at **https://github.com/php/php-src/issues** and resolve it. Remember you will have to program in C to do that.

PHP emerged and evolved through the collective contributions of numerous dedicated individuals. PHP developers keep the project active because they like it, not because they are paid to do so. They generally contribute to PHP outside of their working hours. To help maintain PHP, PHP Foundation was created, it brings together people and organizations that help support PHP. PHP Foundation receives monetary donations to maintain the PHP development infrastructure and the programming language itself. PHP Foundation is completely transparent and you can learn about its work at **https://thephp.foundation**

In addition to the community of PHP language developers, there is a much larger community of developers who use the PHP language to create web applications, desktop applications, and infrastructure automation scripts. This community has developed many widely used applications, such as database clients, content management systems, course management systems, and e-commerce platforms. In the next section, we will learn about several tools created to help PHP developers.

Once we have learned what PHP is, how it works, and how it is maintained, let us learn how to prepare a development environment for PHP.

Preparing PHP development environment

In this section, we will learn how to install a PHP development environment with the minimum requirements to create web applications that are capable of storing data in a relational database.

In 2004, almost half of Apache servers used the PHP integration module. The free and open web server Apache has become one of PHP's great partners over the years. Another great PHP partner is the MySQL database. The partnership with MySQL even generated a PHP client for the database, phpMyAdmin. This trio has become very popular under GNU/Linux operating system distributions. Thus, it was possible to develop and produce web applications using a stack of free and open-source code technologies. This stack made up of **Linux, Apache, MySQL, and PHP (LAMP)**.

Note: GNU is a recursive acronym for GNU is not Unix. Linux is the kernel of the operating system GNU.

Although the LAMP stack worked, it was not so trivial to install each of the software and integrate them. In 2002, recognizing this difficulty, two young Germans, *Kai Oswald Seidler* and *Kay Vogelgesang*, founded the Apache Friends project. This aimed to facilitate the installation of this technology stack. In fact, Apache Friends is not restricted to the Linux operating system. The project has Apache, MySQL, and PHP installation packages for Windows and MacOS as well. This set of packages is called **XAMPP**, where *X* can be any of the three supported operating systems.

Let us learn how to install XAMPP.

Installing XAMPP

You can get XAMPP from **https://www.apachefriends.org/download.html**. This page shows XAMPP installers grouped by operating system. There are generally three installers, for the three most recent stable versions of PHP. This is important information, XAMPP provides installers with stable versions. In the next section, we will see how to install PHP in the latest and unstable version, but for now, we will learn how to create a stable development environment. On the same XAMPP download page, there are links with instructions for installation on each operating system. The process is similar for all three operating systems, you download the installer, run it, and then start the Apache server and MySQL database.

Let us now look into the steps for installing XAMPP on a GNU/Linux distribution to demonstrate the installation process, as follows:

Note: Even if you do not use Linux, know that these procedures will be replicated in the section on creating the virtual development environment.

1. Download the XAMPP installer for PHP 8.2 from the Linux section of the page at **https://www.apachefriends.org/download.html,** as shown in *Figure 1.2*:

XAMPP for Linux 8.0.30, 8.1.25 & 8.2.12

Version		Checksum			Size
8.0.30 / PHP 8.0.30	What's Included?	md5	sha1	Download (64 bit)	151 Mb
8.1.25 / PHP 8.1.25	What's Included?	md5	sha1	Download (64 bit)	153 Mb
8.2.12 / PHP 8.2.12	What's Included?	md5	sha1	Download (64 bit)	151 Mb

Requirements   More Downloads

Figure 1.2: XAMPP installers for Linux with PHP from 8.0 to 8.2

2. Open the terminal in the **Downloads** folder and run the installer according to the following commands:

```
$ sudo chmod 755 xampp-linux-x64-8.2.12-0-installer.run
$ sudo ./xampp-linux-x64-8.2.12-0-installer.run
```

   Note: For Windows, it is enough to click on the installer file.

3. Then, the splash screen will appear as shown in in *Figure 1.3*:

Welcome to XAMPP!

XAMPP is an easy to install Apache distribution
containing MySQL, PHP and Perl

Figure 1.3: Splash screen of XAMPP installer for Linux

4. A few seconds later, the **XAMPP Setup Wizard** window will open, as shown in *Figure 1.4*. From there, just click on the **next** button on each screen that appears:

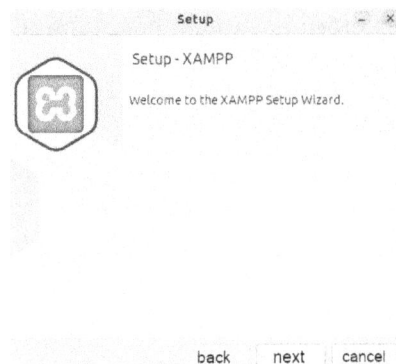

Figure 1.4: First step of XAMPP installation with the setup wizard

5. The **Setup** wizard will start unpacking XAMPP files in the **/opt** directory, by default, and will show the progress of the operation as shown in *Figure 1.5*:

Figure 1.5: XAMPP installation progress

6. When the installation is completed, the **Setup** wizard will show a screen as shown in *Figure 1.6*:

Note: If the Launch XAMPP option is already checked, Click the Finish button.

Figure 1.6: End of XAMPP installation

7. Finally, after the **Setup** wizard closes, the XAMPP Control Panel, refer to *Figure 1.7*, will be opened. XAMPP Control Panel is a program that allows you to manage the web serve r and database server:

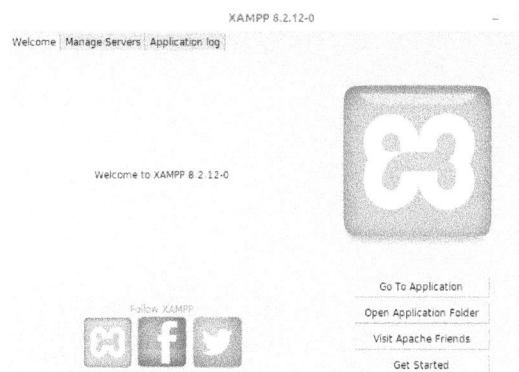

Figure 1.7: XAMPP Control Panel

Before using the XAMPP Control Panel, let us learn how can you start this program after closing the window. The XAMPP Control Panel in the Linux distribution is located in the **/opt/lampp** directory. To start it, you need to grant the execute permission the first time the following command:

```
sudo chmod 755 manager-linux-x64.run
```

Then, run it like the following command:

```
$ sudo ./manager-linux-x64.run
```

Note: In Windows, the control panel is in the C:\xampp folder. You can start it by clicking on the xampp-control.exe file.

You can also run XAMPP from the command line. Just type **./lampp** in the **/opt/lampp** directory and you will see all the options for actions you can perform.

Well, for starting the servers using the control panel, you must click on the **Manage Servers** tab. The window will change for the screen as shown in *Figure 1.8*.

You can see that there are three servers available, **MySQL Database**, **ProFTPD**, and **Apache Web Server**. Yes, XAMPP also comes with an FTP server to help you transfer files from your local machine to the production server. But here, we are only interested in Apache and MySQL servers.

Initially, the servers are in the **Stopped** state. To start a specific server, you click on it and then select the **Start** button on the right. To start all servers, you can click on the **Start All** button at the bottom.

Refer to the following figure:

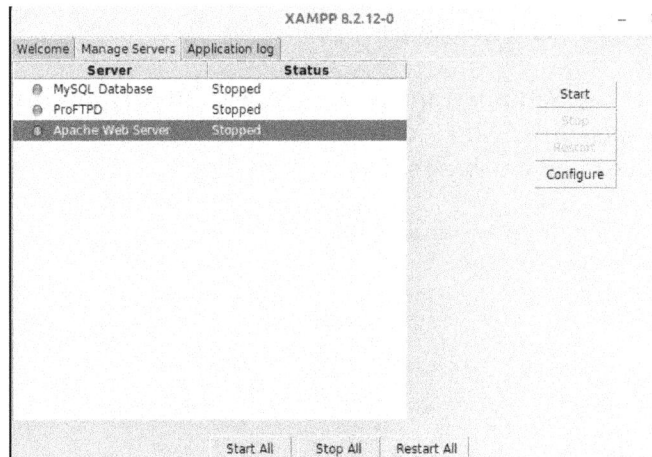

Figure 1.8: XAMPP Manage Servers tab

It is expected that the server or servers will change their state to running after you click on **Start** or **Start All**, respectively. If XAMPP is unable to start the server, one of the reasons might be that there is another software listening on the same port. In this case, there are three of the following options available:

- You must shut down the other application that is using the same port.
- You must modify the configuration of the other application so that it uses another port.
- You must modify the XAMPP server configuration so that it uses another port.

In order to change a server's port in the XAMPP control panel, you must select the server in the **Manage Servers** tab and click on the **Configure** button. A window will open where you can enter another port number. *Figure 1.9* shows an example of the window for changing the **Apache Web Server** configuration. In addition to changing the port, you can also open the configuration file and log files.

After you have made the necessary port adjustments, you can start the **Apache Web Server** and the **MySQL Database** server. Now, we can write PHP code capable of generating dynamic web pages and accessing a relational database.

Refer to the following figure:

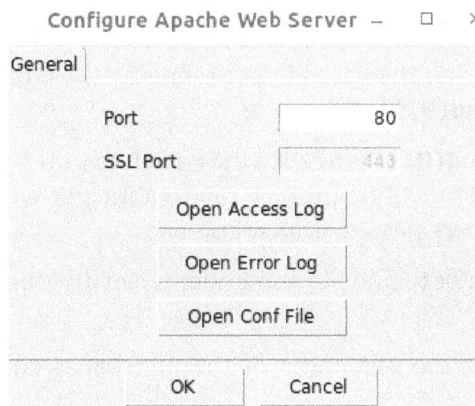

Figure 1.9: Changing the port for Apache Web Server

Let us now explore the XAMPP development environment.

Note: The servers continue to run even if you close the XAMPP window. To turn them off, you need to click on the Stop button or Stop All button.

Exploring XAMPP environment

Before displaying a web page generated with PHP code, let us run PHP code through the terminal. As we said in the section on the history of PHP, this programming language can be used to create automation scripts for infrastructure. Thus, you can create PHP scripts that run without needing to integrate with a web server.

Let us create our first PHP script file. Create a file called **hellosomeone.php** in a directory of your choice. Fill the file with the following content:

```php
<?php
$someone = ( rand(0,9) % 2 == 0 ? 'Universe' : 'World' );
echo "Hello $someone!";
```

After saving the file, run it using the XAMPP PHP interpreter, as follows:

```
$ /opt/lampp/bin/php hellosomeone.php
```

In Windows, we will type:

```
$ c:\xampp\php\php.exe hellosomeone.php
```

The output will be the text **Hello World**. If it does not appear, then **Hello Universe** will appear. Let us look at the following explanation and understand why we can have two different outputs:

- The first line has a tag **<?php**, which delimits the beginning of the PHP code. We will talk more specifically about this in the web page example later.

- The first statement creates a variable called **$someone**. All variables in PHP start with **$**, so it is very easy to identify variables in PHP code.

- The value assigned to the variable **$someone** by the = operator is conditioned by the expression **rand(0,9) % 2 == 0**.

- The expression **rand(0,9)** is a call to the **rand** function, by passing two arguments, **0** and **9**. The **rand** function returns a random integer whose value is in the range between the numbers passed as an argument.

- We use the **%** operator to find the remainder when dividing the result of **rand(0,9)** by **2**.

- We check whether the remainder of the division is equal to zero by using the equality operator **==**.

If the remainder of the division is equal to zero, the **$someone** variable receives the value to the right of the **?** operator, which represents the truth of the condition. If the remainder of the division is non-zero, the variable receives the value to the right of the **:** operator, which represents the falsehood of the condition. The combination of operators **?** and **:** is called a **ternary conditional operator**.

Finally, the **echo** command prints the expression to its right to standard output, in this case, the terminal.

The elements will be discussed in more detail in the *Chapter 2, PHP Foundations*. For now, we just need a little PHP code to produce some results. In this example, we had to create the **hellosomeone.php** file with a PHP code snippet that could be interpreted. However, it is possible to execute PHP statements without creating a file. When we invoke PHP with the **-r** argument, we can pass a language instruction to be executed immediately.

Following statement will print **Hello World** in the terminal:

```
$ php -r "echo 'Hello World!';"
```

You will know all the arguments to run PHP on the command line by calling the PHP interpreter with the **--help** or **-h** argument. Now, let us move on to generating HTML page with PHP, or we can generate a part of an HTML page with PHP because a web page can have static and dynamic parts.

You can start by creating a file called **myfirstpage.php** inside the **/opt/lampp/htdocs** directory (or **c:\xampp\htdocs**, on Windows). The **htdocs** directory is the Apache root web directory in XAMPP. The content of **myfirstpage.php**, must be as follows:

```
<!DOCTYPE html>
<html>
<body>
<?php
$someone = ( rand(0,9) % 2 == 0 ? 'Universe' : 'World' );
echo "Hello, $someone!";
?>
</body>
</html>
```

The **<?php** and **?>** tags are the delimiters of the PHP code within the HTML code. They inform the web server the block should be delegated for PHP interpretation. When a file has the PHP code, only the opening tag is needed, as we did in the **hellosomeone.php** file. But if the file has HTML and PHP code, it is necessary to use opening and closing tags.

Let us see what results this file produces to understand PHP processing with a web server.

If you invoke **http://localhost/myfirstpage.php** in your favorite web browser, you will get a page with the phrase **Hello World** or **Hello Universe**. If you open the page source code in the browser you will not see PHP code, but only the HTML. PHP code was processed by the PHP interpreter, at the request of the Apache Web Server.

Figure 1.10 illustrates the process of generating dynamic content with PHP, considering our file in a production environment, with a computer or smartphone making an HTTP request to a server in some cloud computing environment. HTTP protocol is very simple, you request a file and if it exists and you have permission, the web server sends it to you. But you can configure the web server to delegate the interpretation of a file type to another program. In this case, the web server does not return the requested file, but rather a new file generated by this program. This is what happens in Apache when the PHP module is activated. Files with the **.php** extension are not returned directly by Apache. They are interpreted by PHP, which processes the block of code delimited by the **<?php** and **?>** tags. The processing result replaces the PHP code blocks with HTML code and a new document is returned by Apache to the requesting client.

Refer to the following figure:

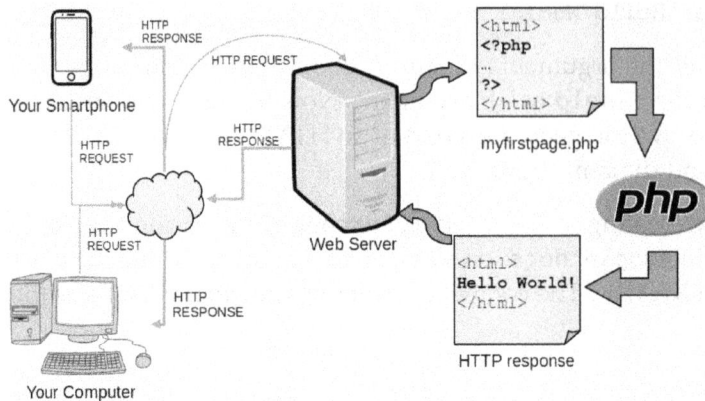

Figure 1.10: How web servers produce new HTML documents with PHP

You have learned how to install XAMPP and how to start programming in PHP with this environment. You must be eager to manipulate the MySQL database but do not worry as we will do it soon. Let us talk about other options for installing PHP besides XAMPP.

Installing PHP

XAMPP typically provides the latest stable versions of PHP. You can, however, install any version of PHP. In fact, you can install several versions of PHP on the same machine. As we said earlier, PHP is a program written in C language. To install PHP, you can download the source code and use a C compiler to generate the interpreter.

Installing PHP from compressed source code

One of the ways to obtain PHP source code is at **https://www.php.net/downloads**. On this page, you will find PHP compressed in **tar.gz**, **tar.bz2**, and **tar.xz** formats. For each version of PHP, there is a hyperlink called **Windows downloads**, where you can find the PHP compiled for Windows and compressed in zip, format that is, for Windows, PHP is ready to use. but let us consider that we are on a Linux machine and downloaded the PHP version 8.3.3 file in **tar.gz** format.

Refer to the following steps to install PHP from the source code:

1. The first step is to decompress the file and access the created directory.

   ```
   $ tar zxvf php-8.3.3.tar.gz
   ```

2. The second step is to run the configure program to generate the make file. For a production environment, we run configure without arguments, as follows:

   ```
   $ cd php-8.3.3
   $ ./configure
   ```

Note: If ./configure is not found, you must run ./buildconf command before.

For a development environment, where we need to debug, it is desirable to run configure with the **--enable-debug** argument, as follows:

```
$ ./configure –enable-debug
```

You may get the following error while running configure:

```
configure: error: The pkg-config script could not be found or is too
old.
```

If this occurs, you need to install the **pkg-config** program, which should be available in the operating system's package installer. For example, for Debian-based systems, we can install **pkg-config** as follows:

```
$ sudo apt install pkg-config
```

After installing **pkg-config**, however, another error may occur when trying to repeat the **configure** command:

```
No package 'libxml-2.0' found
```

If this occurs, you need to install the **libxml2-dev** library, which should be available in the operating system's package installer. For example, for Debian-based systems, we can install **libxml2-dev** as follows:

```
$ sudo apt install libxml2-dev
```

After installing **libxml2-dev**, however, another error may occur when trying to repeat the **configure** as follows:

```
No package 'sqlite3' found
```

If this occurs, you need to install **sqlite3** and **libsqlite3-dev** libraries, which should be available in the operating system's package installer. For example, for Debian-based systems, we can install **sqlite3** and **libsqlite3-dev** as follows:

```
$ sudo apt install sqlite3 libsqlite3-dev
```

Finally, after resolving these dependencies, you can run the **configure** command successfully. The last sentence of the configure command output should be the following:

```
Thank you for using PHP.
```

3. The third step is to run the **make** program to process **Make** file. You can create a job for each job of your processor using the **-j** argument. In the following example, we run the **make** command on a 4-core processor:

```
$ make -j4
```

Note: The number after -j should match the number of CPU cores available.

4. The fourth step is optional but recommended for evaluating the quality of the PHP build, especially if the version is a release candidate. It involves running the **make TEST** command, for running the all tests for all PHP-enabled functionalities and extensions. Considering a 4-core processor, we can run this command as follows:

```
$ make TEST_PHP_ARGS=-j4 test
```

At the end of the run, you can store the test results in a file.

Note: PHP has more than 18 thousand of tests.

5. Finally, you can run the **make install** command to generate the PHP interpreter:

```
$ make install
```

The **make install** command tells you where you are installing each PHP component, providing output as shown in the following code, with the installation target of each PHP component:

```
Installing shared extensions:      /usr/local/lib/php/extensions/
debug-non-zts-20230831/
Installing PHP CLI binary:         /usr/local/bin/
Installing PHP CLI man page:       /usr/local/php/man/man1/
Installing phpdbg binary:          /usr/local/bin/
Installing phpdbg man page:        /usr/local/php/man/man1/
Installing PHP CGI binary:         /usr/local/bin/
Installing PHP CGI man page:       /usr/local/php/man/man1/
Installing build environment:      /usr/local/lib/php/build/
Installing header files:           /usr/local/include/php/
Installing helper programs:        /usr/local/bin/
   program: phpize
   program: php-config
Installing man pages:              /usr/local/php/man/man1/
   page: phpize.1
   page: php-config.1
Installing PDO headers:            /usr/local/include/php/ext/pdo/
```

You can check the installed PHP version with the command:

```
$ php -version
```

Note: You may want to install PHP in a different directory than the default. Just tell the `configure` command in the directory with the `--prefix` argument. In fact, you can determine the location of all PHP components. To find out the configuration customization options, use call `./configure --help`.

Installing PHP from GitHub repository

Another way to obtain PHP source code is to clone the PHP GitHub repository. To do this, you need to install the Git version control system. It is available for installation at: **https://git-scm.com/downloads**. With Git installed, you can clone the PHP repository as follows:

```
$ git clone https://github.com/php/php-src.git
```

This command will, after some time, create the **php-src** directory. Inside the **php-src** directory, you can verify that your clone is set to the master branch using the **git status** command.

```
$ cd php-src
$ git status
```

You need to switch to the branch of the version you want to build. In this case, we will switch to the version 8.3.4 branch using the **git checkout** command.

```
$ git checkout PHP-8.3.4
```

From here, the installation steps are the same as we did in the previous section starting with the **configure** command.

The **https://www.php.net/downloads** page only shows files from stable versions of PHP. With the Git repository, you can install development and therefore unstable versions. These two options are the most exciting for installing PHP.

Installing PHP from package management systems

The most convenient way to install PHP and its extensions in GNU\Linux is through package management systems. For example, to install PHP on Debian-based Linux systems, you use the **Advanced Packaging Tool** (**APT**), as follows:

```
$ sudo apt install php
```

For Fedora-based Linux systems, you can use two packages manager, according to Fedora version. Before Fedora 22, you must use **Yellowdog Update, Modified** (**YUM**), as follows:

```
$ sudo yum install php
```

As of Fedora 22, you must use **Dandified YUM** (**DNF**), as follows:

```
$ sudo dnf install php
```

It is important to know that the core of PHP and its dependencies, the extensions, are separate packages. So, when you install the **php** package, it only contains the interpreter core. Depending on the functions you need, you will have to install other packages. For example, if you need access to the MySQL database on a Debian-based system, you will need to run the following command:

```
$ sudo apt install php-mysql
```

You will know if you need to install a specific package if you try to use a certain function and get an error as follows:

```
Fatal error: Uncaught Error: Call to undefined function...
```

With the package manager, you can install any PHP extension you need with a single command. In the next section we will learn how to install a PHP extension when you have installed PHP by compiling the source code from the compressed file or Git repository clone.

Installing PHP extensions from source code

If you look again at the output of the **make install** command which we showed in the section on installing from the compressed archive, you will see that there is a mention of a helper program called **phpize**. This program compiles extensions for PHP.

The source code for PHP extensions is located in the **ext** subdirectory. To compile an extension, you must access the extension's subdirectory within **ext** and run **phpize**. For example, to compile the **gd** extension, we run the following commands from the PHP source code **root** directory:

```
$ cd ext
$ cd gd
$ phpize
```

The output of this command will be something, as follows:

```
Configuring for:
PHP Api Version:         20230831
Zend Module Api No:      20230831
Zend Extension Api No:   420230831
```

After running **phpize**, you must configure the extension installation with the **configure** command, as follows:

```
$ ./configure
```

Occasionally, when running the configure program, you may be warned that a dependency is missing for the extension to be installed, as in the case of the **gd** extension. The warning is as follows:

```
configure: error: Package requirements (libpng) were not met:
No package 'libpng' found
```

In order to proceed with the extension installation, you must install the required dependency. This can be done by compiling the source code, which is the most exciting way, or by the operating system's package management system. In the example of the

gd extension, on a Debian-based system, we need to install the **libpng-dev** package as follows:

```
$ sudo apt install libpng-dev
```

With the dependency installed, you can successfully run **configure** again. After running it, you must continue executing the make and make install commands. Optionally, you can run the following:

make TEST before **make install**.

After installing the extension, you need to enable it. In the example of the **gd** extension on Linux, a **gd.so** file was created in **ext/gd/modules**. Let us copy this file to the extension's directory of our PHP installation. You can now ask how to know which directory this is. Well, this information was given at the end of the PHP installation, but you can retrieve it at any time with the **php -i** command. The value of the **extension_dir** directive is where PHP extensions are looked for by the interpreter. In our example, **extension_dir** has the value **/usr/local/lib/php/extensions/debug-non-zts-20230831**. So, we would do the following to make the **gd** extension ready to use:

```
$ cd ext/gd/modules
$ cp gd.so /usr/local/lib/php/extensions/debug-non-zts-20230831
```

Alternatively, you can create a symbolic link to the extension on the target instead of copying it but this is only viable if you do not delete the PHP source code directory later.

When an extension file is in **extension_dir**, this means that PHP can find that extension, but it does not mean that it will use it. For PHP to use the extension, it must be enabled in the configuration file, **php.ini**. To find out where the **php.ini** file used by the PHP installation is, you use the **php -i** command. The information will be on a line as follows:

```
Configuration File (php.ini) Path => /usr/local/lib
```

The **php.ini** file path is determined by the configure command, in the PHP installation, through the **--with-config-file-path** argument.

You can create an empty **php.ini** file in the location configured by PHP and fill it with the directives you want to change. In the example of our Linux installation, we can create the file as follows:

```
$ touch /usr/local/lib/php.ini
```

You can copy all directive blocks displayed by **php -i** that begin with the row **Directive => Local Value => Master Value**. **Master Value** is defined by PHP compilation. **Local Value** is the value that is actually being used by PHP. **Local Value** can be determined by the **php.ini** file, by the web server directives, or by the **ini_set** function. Currently, **Local Value** and **Master Value** are the same.

After you paste the directive blocks, you must delete the initial row. Rows that are configured as no value must be discarded, as well as lines in which there are sentences with spaces between words. The rest must be in the format **key=value**. For example, refer to the following row:

```
allow_url_fopen => On => On
```

The example shown above should be changed to the following assignment:

```
allow_url_fopen=On
```

However, there are other rows, as follows:

```
ctype functions => enabled
```

Rows like the one above where the words to the left of the arrow are separated by a space and not a dash must be deleted.

Some essential notes for the **php.ini** file are as follows:

- Special characters such as &, HTML tags, and sentences with spaces between words must be delimited with apostrophes. For example: **arg_separator.input='&'**.

- The on value can be replaced by one and the off value can be replaced by zero.

- If you want to let comments in the **php.ini**, you need to add a **#** at the beginning of the row.

After you create the file, it will be used by PHP. In case it is being used with a web server; you will need to restart the server.

After creating the **php.ini** file, you must try to use the function of the extension you just installed, but you can still receive the following error:

```
Fatal error: Uncaught Error: Call to undefined function...
```

This is because you have to enable the extension in the **php.ini** file. For example, to enable the **gd** extension we installed, we add the following line to the **php.ini** file:

```
extension=gd.so
```

As the extension directory is already configured by the **extension_dir** directive, PHP knows where to find the extension file.

After enabling the extension, you can use it smoothly. In the example given above, we can call a function from the **gd** extension, as follows:

```
$ php -r "print_r(gd_info());"
```

The output will be like the code as follows:

```
Array
(
    [GD Version] => bundled (2.1.0 compatible)
    [FreeType Support] =>
    [GIF Read Support] => 1
```

```
        [GIF Create Support] => 1
        [JPEG Support] =>
        [PNG Support] => 1
        [WBMP Support] => 1
        [XPM Support] =>
        [XBM Support] => 1
        [WebP Support] =>
        [BMP Support] => 1
        [AVIF Support] =>
        [TGA Read Support] => 1
        [JIS-mapped Japanese Font Support] =>
)
```

In the previous example, we used the **print_r** function to transform the array returned by the **gd_info** function into text, and thus be able to display it.

Of course, all this work to enable the extension could have been avoided if we had already ordered this in the installation configuration.

A very useful piece of information is that if you enable the readline extension, you can run PHP in iterative mode, using the **-a** argument, as follows:

$ php -a

The output for this command will be as the following prompt:

Interactive shell

php >

In iterative mode, each instruction or block of instructions is executed as soon as its typing is completed. Iterative mode is very useful for quickly understanding how an instruction works, without having to create a file to be interpreted. It can also be used to do small tasks.

Let us repeat a previous example in iterative mode, as follows:

php > $someone = (rand(0,9) % 2 == 0 ? 'Universe' : 'World');
php > echo "Hello $someone!";

After knowing the various ways to install PHP and its extensions, let us prepare the development environment that we will use in the next chapters.

Virtualized environment for PHP

We want to ensure that all exercises proposed from now on are performed by everyone who reads this book. Therefore, we will use a virtual development environment, so that everyone works with the same configuration. After completing the course in this book, you can experiment with building different environments. Let us use a virtual machine through *Oracle VirtualBox*. You can get VirtualBox from **https://www.virtualbox.org/wiki/ Downloads**. In this book, we will use VirtualBox 7.0. The detailed instructions for installing VirtualBox for several operating systems are available at **https://www.virtualbox.org/ manual/UserManual.html#installation**.

Before starting VirtualBox, we need to download the image of the operating system that we are going to install virtually. In this book, we will use the Debian operating system in version 12. You get Debian from **https://www.debian.org/download**. In this book, we will use release 12.5, but you can safely use a higher release if it is available.

Creating virtual machine

After downloading the Debian image, open VirtualBox. The home window will be as shown in *Figure 1.11*:

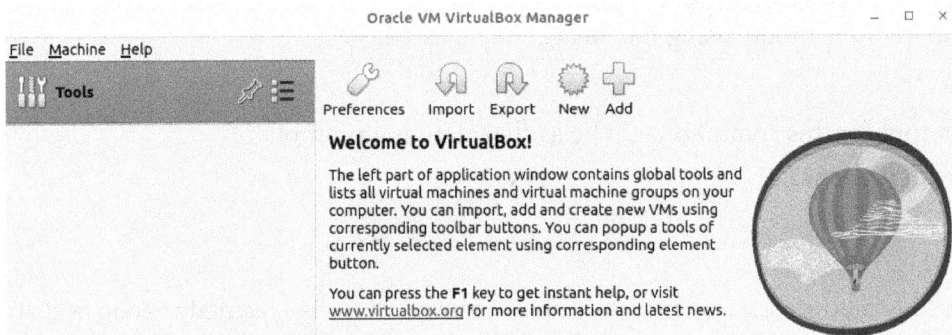

Figure 1.11: *VirtualBox home window*

Let us create our virtual machine in just a few steps, as follows:

1. In order to create a new virtual machine, you have two options as follows:

    a. Click on the **New** icon in the right part of the window.

    b. Click on **Machine | New** in the top menu, refer to *Figure 1.12*:

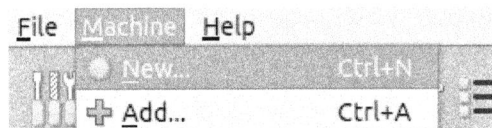

Figure 1.12: *New Machine menu*

2. The VirtualBox will open the window for creating a new image, refer to *Figure 1.13*. It will automatically select a directory to store the virtual machines, **Folder** field. You must select **Linux** in the **Type** field and **Debian 12 Bookworm** in the **Version** field:

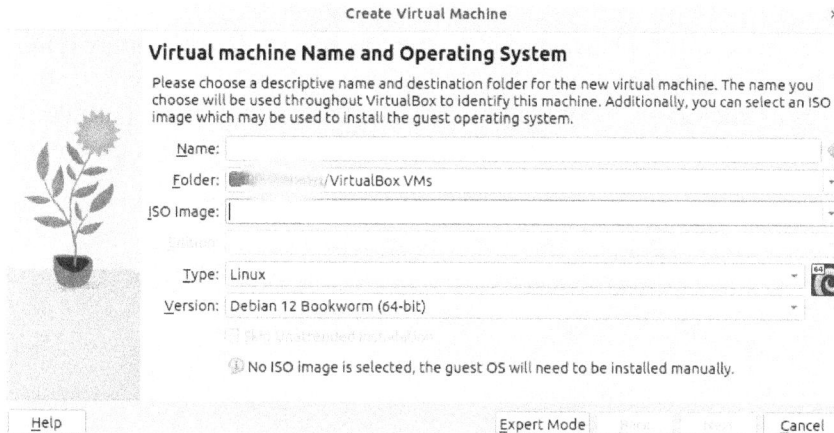

Figure 1.13: *Create a virtual machine*

3. You need to select the image file. Click on **ISO Image** | **Other**. Refer to *Figure 1.14*:

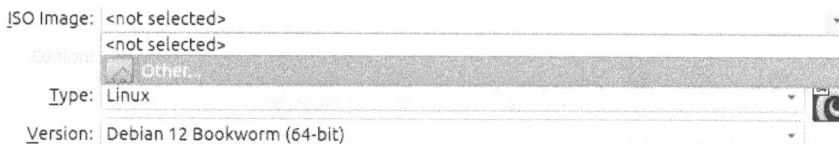

Figure 1.14: *Select ISO Image*

> **Note: International Organization for Standardization (ISO) here is related to ISO 9660 file system.**

4. The file manager window will open, and you can navigate to the directory where you downloaded the Debian image. Select it by clicking on the file. The **ISO Image** field will be filled in with the path to the image file.

Refer to *Figure 1.15*:

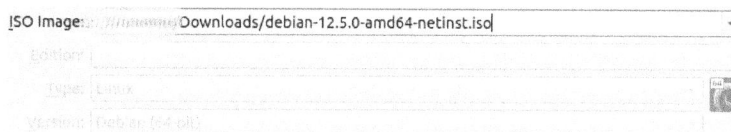

Figure 1.15: *Debian ISO image selected*

5. The virtual machine needs a name. Let us call it **Debian12.5**, as shown in *Figure 1.16*:

Name: Debian12.5

Figure 1.16: Virtual machine name

6. Now, the **Next** button is enabled, and you can click on it.

7. The next window is **Unattended Guest OS Install Setup** as shown in *Figure 1.17*. Here, we will define a user for the operating system. By default, the username comes as **vboxuser**. At this point, you need to set that user's password and, more importantly, remember it later. After doing this, you can click on the **Next** button.

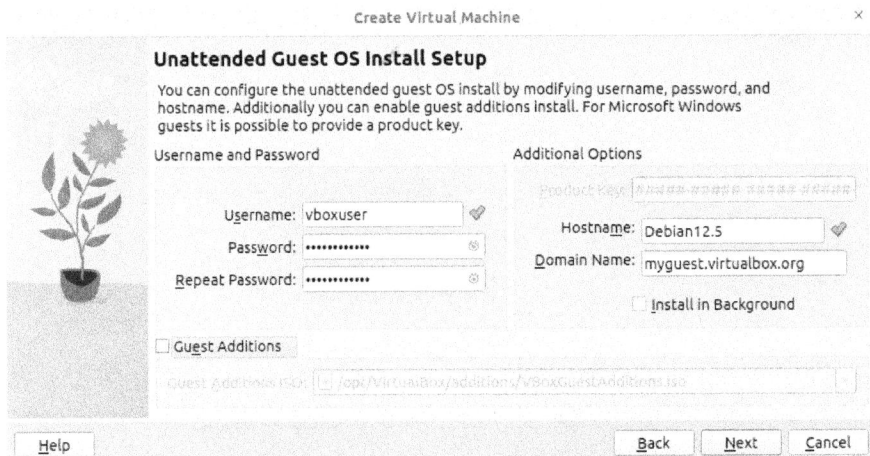

Figure 1.17: Username and password

8. In the next window, you can configure the base memory and processors of your virtual machine. In the environment used to produce this book, based on a physical machine with 8GB of memory, a 1TB disk, and a 2.4GHz Intel Core i5 processor, we configured a base memory of 5GB and 4 CPUs, as shown in *Figure 1.18*. After configuring these items, you can click on the **Next** button.

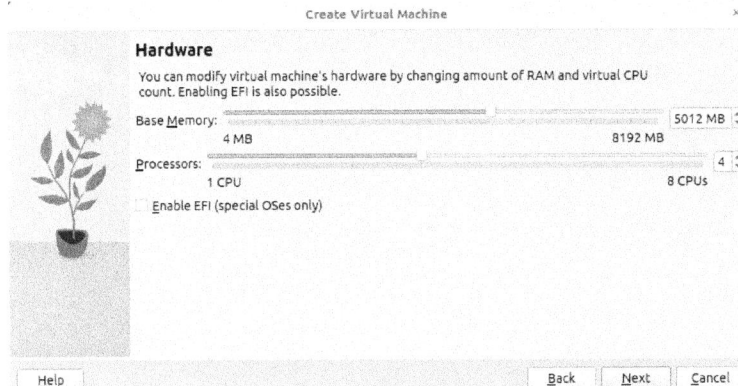

Figure 1.18: Hardware configuration for virtual machine

9. In the next window, decide whether to use a virtual hard disk or not, and whether you create a new disk or use an existing one. We will create a new disk with 20GB, as shown in *Figure 1.19*. After selecting the **Create a Virtual Hard Disk Now** option, click on the **Next** button.

Figure 1.19: *Virtual hard disk configuration for virtual machine*

10. The next window will show a summary of the virtual machine configuration, and at this point, you can go back to fix something. If everything is okay, click on the **Finish** button.

The virtual machine is created, with the Debian operating system image is ready for the installation. The virtual machine will be listed on the left side of the window with the **Powered Off** status. If you need to modify the machine's configuration, you can right-click on it and choose the **Settings...** item, as you can see in *Figure 1.20*. Alternatively, you can go to **Machine | Settings** in the top menu.

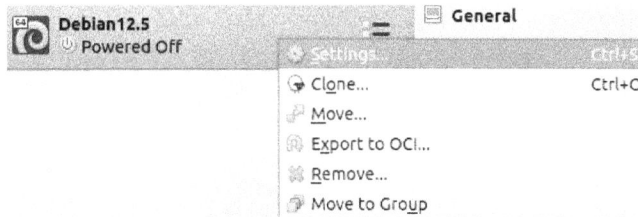

Figure 1.20: *Virtual machine settings*

In the next section, we will install Debian.

Installing operating system in virtual machine

Let us now look into the two steps for installing Debian12.5 in this virtual machine, as follows:

1. Select the **Debian12.5** machine and click on the **Start** button on the right side. The virtual machine will change to **Running** status. Debian will start its installer, initially checking the network connection to be able to download packages. Once the connection is confirmed, the installer will start downloading packages, this process will take some time.

2. When the installation finishes, you will see the login screen as shown in *Figure 1.21*, with the username-defined when you were creating the virtual machine as shown in *Figure 1.17*. Click on the username (**vboxuser** in our example) and the system will ask for the password.

Now, with the virtual operating system installed, let us prepare our development environment for the exercises we will do.

Refer to the following figure:

Figure 1.21: Debian 12 login screen

After logging in and closing the welcome splash screen, you will arrive at the Debian home screen as shown in *Figure 1.22*. In the top left corner is the **Activities** menu. When you click on it, Debian opens, a search box will appear for you to search for programs by name, and at the bottom of the screen, a square formed by six dots will allow you to browse all installed programs.

There must be three programs installed in Debian that are essential for our work, these three programs are as follows:

*   Firefox, which is a web browser.
*   Nautilus, which is a graphical file manager.
*   Terminal, which is the command line interface.

The icons for Firefox and Nautilus are highlighted by default in the bottom menu of the program search. You can install Konsole as an alternative for the terminal if this one is not available.

Refer to the following figure:

Figure 1.22: Debian 12 home screen

Test-driven environment for PHP

We will meet the requirements for installing the PHP testing framework and then demonstrate how it will be used, introducing the basic procedures of test-driven development.

Meeting requirements for PHPUnit

If you have not installed XAMPP yet, now is the time. You will follow the steps described in the *Installing XAMPP* section on the Debian virtual machine. From now on, all references we make to the operating system will be relative to the virtual machine we created.

There is one important detail you should note. The XAMPP installation guidelines assume that your user has administrator permissions. However, **vboxuser** has no such permission, so we need to grant these permissions. When you enter the password for **vboxuser** during the virtual machine creation, this password is also used for the root user. Let us change the session to the root user and add the **vboxuser** to the /`etc/sudoers` file.

Refer to the following steps:

1. Change to the root user with the **su** command by using the same password as you have configured for the **vboxuser**, as follows:

   ```
   $ su
   ```

2. Install the Vim editor and open **/etc/sudoers** file, as follows:

    ```
    $ apt install vim
    $ vim /etc/sudoers
    ```

3. Search for the following rows, as follows:

    ```
    # User privilege specification
    root   ALL=(ALL:ALL) ALL
    ```

4. Add the following row after the previous rows by using *Insert* key, as follows:

    ```
    vboxuser ALL=(ALL:ALL) ALL
    ```

5. Save and quit the file with **wq!** command (forced write and quit).

6. Change the root user to **vboxuser** again by using the following command:

    ```
    $ exit
    ```

Now, proceed with running the XAMPP installer following the instructions provided in the *Installing XAMPP* section.

Once XAMPP is installed and your user can administer the system, let us prepare our PHP development environment to work with test-driven development. Start by installing the dependency manager for PHP, Composer. With Composer, we can easily install various components written in PHP, in any version we want. We will use the Composer to install PHPUnit, the PHP testing framework.

First, we will install Composer in three steps, as follows:

1. Download Composer at version 2.7.2 (**composer.phar** file):

    ```
    $ wget http://getcomposer.org/download/2.7.2/composer.phar
    ```

2. Move it to a directory in the operating system's search path:

    ```
    $ sudo mv composer.phar /usr/bin/composer
    ```

3. Grant the permission to run the **composer** file.

    ```
    $ sudo chmod 755 /usr/bin/composer
    ```

If you try to run **composer** with the version argument then, you will receive the following error message:

```
/usr/bin/env: php: No such file or directory
```

This is because the Composer is a PHP program compressed into a single file (**.phar**) and it depends to be executed on the PHP interpreter. Although, a PHP interpreter exists in the XAMPP executable directory, it is not in the operating system's search path. So, let us put it there. In fact, we will create a symbolic link to the PHP interpreter in a directory where the operating system searches for programs. Let us make this using the **ln** command, as follows:

```
$ sudo ln -s /opt/lampp/bin/php /usr/bin/php
```

After creating the symbolic link, you can run the PHP interpreter from any directory as shown in the following example:

```
$ php --version
PHP 8.2.12 (cli) (built: Nov 25 2023 08:09:53) (NTS)
Copyright (c) The PHP Group
Zend Engine v4.2.12, Copyright (c) Zend Technologies
```

Accordingly, you can run Composer by using the following command:

```
$ composer --version
Composer version 2.7.2 2024-03-11 17:12:18
PHP version 8.2.12 (/usr/bin/php)
Run the "diagnose" command to get more detailed diagnostics output.
```

While it is satisfactory to have an instance of PHP and an instance of Composer on our workstation, it is convenient to have an instance of PHPUnit for each software project. Tests are an integral part of the software, similar to functional code and documentation. In fact, tests are also documentation, but a very special documentation, they show how the system really works.

The procedure we will adopt from now on will be the following, we will install PHPUnit as a dependency within each project. There will not be a global instance of PHPUnit serving multiple projects. Now, let us create a small example project to demonstrate how we will use PHPUnit.

Steps to test-driven development

Let us create a small program to extract square root, using Eudoxo's algorithm. Let us create a directory called **squareroot** for our program with the **mkdir** command, as follows:

```
$ mkdir squareroot
```

Inside the **squareroot** directory, we will practice test-driven development by following the steps:

1. Typically, the first thing you would do is implement Eudoxus's algorithm to extract the root and solve the problem but we will not do that. In test-driven development, you start by writing a test. This way, you document what the program is expected to do.

2. Let us install PHPUnit so we can use it to run the test we will write. We will do this with the Composer, as follows:

    ```
    $ composer require phpunit/phpunit
    ```

3. You will see the following question appear:

The package you required is recommended to be placed in require-dev (because it is tagged as "testing") but you did not use --dev.

Do you want to re-run the command with --dev? [yes]?

This question is asked because PHPUnit is categorized as a development dependency and Composer wants to make sure of this because we did not say that we want a development dependency. You can answer yes.

4. Composer's required command downloads the requested component and records the version used in the **composer.json** file. If the file does not exist, it creates it. In our case, the content of the file will be as follows:

```
{
    "require-dev": {
        "phpunit/phpunit": "^11.0"
    }
}
```

5. Let us now generate the PHPUnit configuration file by using the **--generate-configuration** argument. We will adopt the default value for the configuration, so just type enter until the end, as follows:

```
$ vendor/bin/phpunit --generate-configuration
PHPUnit 11.0.6 by Sebastian Bergmann and contributors.

Generating phpunit.xml in [YOUR DIRECTORY]/squareroot

Bootstrap script (relative to path shown above; default: vendor/
autoload.php):
Tests directory (relative to path shown above; default: tests):
Source directory (relative to path shown above; default: src):
Cache directory (relative to path shown above; default: .phpunit.
cache):

Generated phpunit.xml in [YOUR DIRECTORY]/squareroot.
Make sure to exclude the .phpunit.cache directory from version
control.
```

According to the adopted configuration, PHPUnit will run tests in the **tests** directory, looking for source code files in the **src** directory. Let us create the **src** and **tests** directories, as follows:

```
$ mkdir src
$ mkdir tests
```

6. Let us now create a **test** class, in the **tests** directory, in a file called **SquareRootTest.php**. You can use an editor of your choice to create the file. If you are not comfortable with vi or vim, you can use nano but, if you want a graphical text editor, you can install **gedit**, as follows:

```
$ sudo apt install gedit
```

7. Later we will install a more powerful source code editor, but for now, a simple editor is enough for us. The **SquareRootTest.class** file will have the following content:

```php
<?php
use PHPUnit\Framework\TestCase;

class SquareRootTest extends TestCase {
public function testExtraction()
{
        $this->assertEquals(12,square_root(144));
}
}
```

The **SquareRootTest** class contains a method prefixed with the test which executes an assertion. The assertion contains something we expect the program to do. In this case, we expect that the **square_root** function returns **12** when it receives **144** as an argument.

You can save the file and run PHPUnit, as follows:

```
$ vendor/bin/phpunit
```

8. The output should be as follows:

```
PHPUnit 11.0.6 by Sebastian Bergmann and contributors.

Runtime:       PHP 8.2.12
Configuration: [YOUR DIRECTORY]/squareroot/phpunit.xml

E 1 / 1 (100%)

Time: 00:00.017, Memory: 8.00 MB

There was 1 error:

1) SquareRootTest::testExtraction
Error: Call to undefined function square_root()
```

```
[YOUR DIRECTORY]/squareroot/tests/SquareRootTest.php:7
```

ERRORS!
Tests: 1, Assertions: 0, Errors: 1.

You have now completed the first step of test-driven development; you have created a test that fails. It may seem strange to celebrate a failure but consider that we have a mechanism that checks whether our program meets a requirement in a particular case.

In test-driven development, you are guided by the tests. You start by writing down what you expect to happen and the test will tell you what you need to do to achieve it. On our first failure, the test said it failed because the **square_root** function was not defined. So, let us define it now.

9. Let us create the **functions.php** file inside **src** directory with the following content:

```php
<?php
function square_root($number)
{
return $number;
}
```

We have implemented the **square_root** function, but without the correct algorithm, in fact, without any algorithm at all. This is intentional so that we can now see the execution of the assertion.

10. For the **functions.php** file to be found by the test class, we need to configure the loading of this file. We will do this by adding the following snippet to the **composer.json** file:

```
"autoload" : {
"files" : ["src/functions.php"]
}
```

This snippet tells the Composer that the **functions.php** file should be loaded automatically with each request. But it is not enough to add this snippet. You need to ask the composer to recreate your auto-loading class with the following command:

```
$ composer dumpautoload
```

11. Let us run PHPUnit again. This time the output will be as follows:

```
There was 1 failure:

1) SquareRootTest::testExtraction
Failed asserting that 144 matches expected 12.

[YOUR DIRECTORY]/squareroot/tests/SquareRootTest.php:7

FAILURES!
Tests: 1, Assertions: 1, Failures: 1.
```

This time PHPUnit was able to execute the assertion because it found the function definition. However, the test still fails because the function does not return the expected value. Now, let us move on to the second step of test-driven development, making the program pass the test.

12. Change the contents of the **functions.php** file to the following:

```php
<?php
function square_root($number, $iterations = 100)
{
    $p = $number;
    $n = $iterations;

    $x = ((1 + $p)/2);

    for ($i=1;$i<$n;$i++){
            $x = ((($p/$x) + $x)/2);
    }
    return $x;
}
```

Note: The square_root function runs with several iterations set to 100 by default but it can be called with any number of iterations. Do not worry now because we will learn more about functions in the next chapter.

13. Let us run PHPUnit again. This time the output will be as follows:

```
There was 1 risky test:

1) SquareRootTest::testExtraction
This test does not define a code coverage target but is expected to
do so
```

```
[YOUR DIRECTORY]/squareroot/tests/SquareRootTest.php:5
```

```
OK, but there were issues!
Tests: 1, Assertions: 1, Risky: 1.
```

14. Our code has now passed the test but PHPUnit states that there is a risk related to test coverage. This occurs because we do not explicitly inform the test which code it should cover. Let us add the following annotation to say that the test should only cover the **square_root** function, as follows:

```
/**
@covers \square_root
**/
class SquareRootTest extends TestCase {
public function testExtraction()
{
        $this->assertEquals(12,square_root(144));
}
}
```

15. Let us run PHPUnit again. This time the output will be as follows:

```
There was 1 PHPUnit test runner deprecation:


1) Metadata found in doc-comment for class SquareRootTest. Metadata
in doc-comments is deprecated and will no longer be supported in
PHPUnit 12. Update your test code to use attributes instead.


OK, but there were issues!
Tests: 1, Assertions: 1, Deprecations: 1.
```

The risk warning is gone, but now there is a deprecation warning. This warning is about the change of annotations for attributes that will occur in PHPUnit 12 but we are using version 11, you can ignore these messages. If you update PHPUnit to version 12, just replace the annotation block with the following attribute:

```
#[CoversFunction('square_root')]
```

Well, now we have a code that works, and whose operation is guaranteed by a test. The third step of test-driven development is to refactor the code, improving it but we will leave this step to practice with the exercises in the next chapters.

The files that were created in this chapter are available in the **chapter01** folder of the book repository.

Conclusion

In this chapter, we covered how PHP community and ecosystem were formed and how they are organized. We covered the preparation of a PHP development environment using XAMPP and several ways to install PHP. We covered the creation of a virtualized environment for PHP using VirtualBox with a Debian image. Finally, we covered the preparation of a test-driven development environment with PHPUnit.

In the next chapter, we will learn about PHP foundations, using the test-driven development approach.

Points to remember

- PHP is an interpreter written in C language.
- Although originally an interpreter, PHP compiles its code in memory through the Zend engine.
- PHP is free and open-source software.
- There are several ways to install PHP.
- XAMPP is a package with a set of software for developing in PHP that has installers for various operating systems.
- PHPUnit allows you to create tests for PHP programs and better than that, create programs from tests.

Exercises

1. Create other assertions in the SquareRootTest class to test different numbers of iterations.

2. Check the minimum number of iterations required for the test not to fail. For example, you can test an assertion with ten iterations, as follows:

   $this->assertEquals(12,square_root(144,10));

Join our book's Discord space

Join the book's Discord Workspace for Latest updates, Offers, Tech happenings around the world, New Release and Sessions with the Authors:

https://discord.bpbonline.com

CHAPTER 2
PHP Foundations

Introduction

This chapter will cover the foundations of the PHP programming language. We will start by understanding PHP syntax and structural elements in comparison with C language. Then, we will learn the control-flow structures of PHP in standard and alternative forms. We will also learn about data types, type juggling, and operator precedence. Next, we will learn how to define functions and use built-in functions in PHP, along with PHP functions to manipulate cookies, sessions, HTML forms, and HTTP responses.

Structure

The chapter covers the following topics:

- PHP syntax and structural elements
- Control-flow structures
- Data types and operators
- Functions
- Built-in file system and array functions
- Cookies and sessions

- Handling HTML forms
- Handling multiple views

Objectives

By the end of this chapter, you will be able to understand the foundations of the PHP programming language. You will be able to recognize PHP flow control structures in their two forms. You will know how to use file system and array functions, and in addition, you will know how to define your functions. You will also learn how to manipulate cookies, sessions, and HTML forms, as well as manipulate the HTTP response.

PHP syntax and structural elements

In the previous chapter, we read that the PHP interpreter is written in C language. We also saw that *Rasmus Lerdorf*, creator of PHP, shows in his lectures that his language is more concise than the C language. So, to discuss the syntax and structural elements of PHP, let us make a comparison with the C language.

Let us start with a program that does a sum and displays the result in the terminal. We will show the code and explain it in sequence. Let us create a file called **piecesofapie.c** with the following content:

```c
#include <stdio.h>

void main()
{
    float pieces;

    pieces = 0.33 + 0.33 + 0.33;

    printf("We have %.2f of a pie\n",pieces);
}
```

This program can be compiled on Debian Linux with GCC, as shown in the following:

```
$ gcc piecesofapie.c -o piecesofapie
```

GCC can be installed on Debian, as shown in the following:

```
$ sudo apt install gcc
```

Let us understand the **piecesofapie.c** program. The C language is extremely modularized. To run a program, you are required to declare at least one function, the **main** function. It is the starting point of a C program. This **main** function contains three instructions, as follows:

- The first one declares a variable of type **float**.
- The second one assigns a sum to that variable.
- The third one prints the value of this variable in the terminal.

In order to print from a C program, you need to import the **stdio.h** library. Without it, the **printf** function does not work.

Now, let us write a PHP program that does the same action. Create a file called **piecesofapie.php** with the following content:

```php
<?php
$pieces = 0.33 + 0.33 + 0.33;

echo "We have $pieces of a pie\n";
```

As we have seen previously, all PHP code must be preceded by an opening tag. This feature is due to *Rasmus'* project of inserting PHP code inside HTML pages. While the use of the opening tag is mandatory in PHP, on the other hand, this language does not require the definition of a function to write a program. The PHP program contains two instructions, as follows:

- The first one assigns a sum to **$pie** variable.
- The second one prints the value of this variable in the terminal.

As you can see, you do not need a placeholder to insert a variable value inside a text to print it while using the **echo** command in PHP. But PHP also has a **printf** function. The instruction with **echo** command could be replaced by the following command:

```php
printf("We have %.2f of a pie\n",$pieces);
```

However, when using **echo**, we do not need to format the **$pie** variable so that it has exactly two decimal places.

Comparing the C program with the PHP program, we can see that the instructions end with a semicolon in both. Forgetting the semicolon is a frequent mistake in both languages.

Another common detail between languages is the use of meta commands within a text to be printed. In this case, the **\n** meta command informs that after printing the text, a new line must be started. The program will print the text, and the terminal prompt will be displayed like the text shown in the following:

```
We have 0.99 of a pie
$
```

Without **\n**, the following prompt would appear to the right of the text:

```
We have 0.99 of a pie$
```

One of the differences between the two codes is that the PHP program does not declare the variable before assigning a value to it. While the C language is statically typed, PHP is dynamically typed. In PHP, the type of variable is defined by the assigned value. Furthermore, as seen in the previous chapter, in PHP, all variables begin with a dollar sign.

The other difference is the method of printing. In C, the **printf** function takes two arguments. The first argument is text with a placeholder that defines the format of the variable passed as the second argument. In PHP, the **echo** command receives a text with the variable itself in the position where it should be printed.

PHP's syntax is similar to the C language, but PHP is more concise and readable. Let us learn more about the similarities and differences between C and PHP languages in the next sections.

In addition to the semicolon, something common between C and PHP, we can identify the following structural elements of the PHP programming language: variables, constants, expressions, operators, control structures, and functions. Let us start with control-flow structures.

Control-flow structures

We can divide the control-flow structures into four categories: Decision structures, repetition structures, repeated function call structures, and jumping structures. Let us learn how to use each one of these structures.

Making decisions with if and else statements

Decision structures define code blocks that are executed depending on a condition. You can have one or more code blocks within a decision structure, according to the conditions that you need to control. We will begin with the if...else structure. An if...else structure has two code blocks. The first block is executed if the defined condition is true. Otherwise, the second block is executed. As we did in the last section, we will make a comparison between a C implementation and a PHP implementation. We will write a program that says if a random integer number is even or odd.

First, we will create a file named **evenorodd.c**, with the following content:

```c
#include <stdlib.h>
#include <stdio.h>

void main() {
    int r = rand();

    if (r % 2 == 0) {
        printf("%d is even\n",r);
    } else {
```

```
        printf("%d is odd\n",r);
    }
}
```

The instructions of this C program are as follows:

- Declare an integer variable **r** and set it with **rand** function which requires **stdlib.h**. This function returns a random integer number until 2,147,483,647.

- Check **if** the rest of **r** divided by **2** is equal to **0**.

- If **r** is equal to **0**, print a message saying that **r** is even.

- If **r** is different from **0**, print a message saying that **r** is odd.

Now, let us see the equivalent program in PHP. Let us create a file called **evenorodd.php** with the following content:

```
<?php
$r = rand(0,2147483647);

if ($r % 2 == 0) {
    echo "$r is even\n";
} else {
    echo "$r is odd\n";
}
```

The PHP implementation is shorter because we do not need to import two libraries and define a **main** function. While the C **rand** function uses a maximum value defined by the **RAND_MAX** constant, the PHP **rand** function receives the maximum value as a second argument. These are the main differences. On the other hand, the decision structure is the same, and you have a condition between parentheses after the **if** keyword and two code blocks delimited by curly braces. There is another syntax feature that C and PHP have in common: curly braces as code block delimiters.

The conditions in C and PHP also share a common syntax. The operator for the rest of a division is a percentage, and the equal operator is a double equal sign. This last feature is a common source of mistakes because it is easy to forget one equal sign, and then you make an assignment instead of a comparison. Let us see one example of this kind of mistake. While being with our compared programming, we will create a file called **equalmistake.c**, with the following content:

```
#include <stdlib.h>
#include <stdio.h>

void main() {
    int r = 0;
```

```
    if (r = 0) {
            printf("This text never will be printed\n");
    } else {
            printf("This text always will be printed\n");
    }
}
```

If you compile and run this program, the result will be the text **This text always will be printed**. This is because the expression **r = 0** is not a comparison but an assignment. The decision structure evaluates the result of the expression, which in this case is zero, and zero is treated as false in C. Thus, the condition is not satisfied, and the else code block is executed.

This problem can also occur in PHP because the syntax is similar. PHP also uses the equals sign for assignment and the double equals sign for equality comparison. Let us see the content of a file called **equalmistake.php** with the PHP implementation for the previous C program, as follows:

```
<?php
$r = 0;

if ($r = 0) {
        echo "This text never will be printed\n";
} else {
        echo "This text always will be printed\n";
}
```

In both C and PHP, the else block is not mandatory. If there is nothing to do if the condition is not satisfied, there is no point in having an **else** block. When there is something to be done, it is possible to dispense with the **else** block, assuming a result as the default. As an example, let us refactor the program **evenorodd.c** into a file called **evenorodd2.c**, removing the else block, as shown in the following:

```
#include <stdlib.h>
#include <stdio.h>
#include <string.h>

void main() {
        int r = rand();
        char kind[4] = "odd";

        if (r % 2 == 0) {
```

```
            strcpy("even",kind);
    }
    printf("%d is %s\n",r,kind);
}
```

In this new implementation, we create a variable called **kind**, which is an array of four characters. This variable initially receives the value **odd** and is only changed if the condition is satisfied. Thus, we only have one instruction with a call to the **printf** function.

The C language does not have the string data type. When it is necessary to manipulate strings, we use character arrays. Therefore, to change the kind value, we cannot use the assignment operator, as it is necessary to assign a value to each character in the array. So, to use the assignment operator to change the content of **kind** from **odd** to **even**, we would have to write the following instructions:

```
kind[0] = 'e';kind[1] = 'v';kind[2] = 'e';kind[3] = 'n';
```

With this approach, the more characters we have, the more instructions we have to write. The C **string** library has the **strcpy** function, which allows you to assign a string value to an array of characters.

PHP has the string data type. Thus, the PHP version for implementation without an else block eliminates the use of a function to assign a new value to the **$kind** variable. It also eliminates the need to import three libraries. The **evenorodd2.php** program code is mentioned in the following:

```php
<?php
$r = rand(0,2147483647);

$kind = 'odd';

if ($r % 2 == 0) {
    $kind = 'even';
}
echo "$r is $kind\n";
```

Avoiding the use of else can make the code more readable by focusing on what changes when the decision structure condition is met.

Note: Readability is a fundamental characteristic of program maintenance. There is no guarantee that the person who made the program will be available to modify it when necessary. The maintenance of a program must be independent of its creator.

Alternative if and else statements

Now, let us talk about the alternative syntax for the if...else control structure. In the C language, we work with a file that contains only instructions from the C language. PHP, in turn, was created to be inserted into HTML files. When we use control structures based on C syntax within HTML code, they may not be very clear, as in the example of the following **evenoroddweb.php** file:

```
<!doctype html>
<html>
<body>
<p>
<?php
$r = rand(0,2147483647);

if ($r % 2 == 0) {
?>
<span style="color:blue">
<?php
      echo "$r is even\n";
} else {
?>
<span style="color:red">
<?php
      echo "$r is odd\n";
}
?>
</span>
</p>
</body>
</html>
```

This HTML document shows a random integer within a paragraph for each request, with the detail of using the color blue for even numbers and red for odd numbers through CSS.

This is an opportune time to introduce a useful PHP feature for developers: the built-in server. You do not need to move the **evenoroddweb.php** file to the **htdocs** directory to be able to run it with Apache. You can use a web server built into PHP to run it where it is. We do this with the following command:

```
php -S localhost:8008
```

The **-S** argument tells PHP that we want to raise a server at the address and port specified on the right. In this case, we are setting up a server on the local machine on port **8008**. It does not necessarily need to be on port **8008**, and you can use any free port. However, if you use port **8008**, you can see the web page at **http://localhost:8008/evenoroddweb.php**.

You can reload the page multiple times and see not just the different numbers but also numbers with different colors. When you understand what the **evenoroddweb.php** file does, let us get back to the code. Notice that we used the opening tags three times to insert PHP code into the HTML page. This example shows that PHP control structure can be visually fragmented in an HTML page. If there are several control structures, one inside the other, it can be difficult to know where each one ends since closing the code block of all control structures is a curly brace, as we will see later.

Let us use an alternative syntax for the if...else structure in a file called **evenoroddweb2. php**. The content of the file will be as follows:

```
<!doctype html>
<html>
<body>
<p>
<?php
$r = rand(0,2147483647);

if ($r % 2 == 0):
?>
<span style="color:blue">
<?php
    echo "$r is even\n";
else:
?>
<span style="color:red">
<?php
    echo "$r is odd\n";
endif;
?>
</span>
</p>
</body>
</html>
```

In the alternative syntax, we do not use curly braces to delimit blocks of code. Closing the code block is done by combining the word end with the keyword that starts the control structure. As we start the structure with **if**, then we close it with **endif**. Furthermore, the **if** condition must be followed by a colon, just like the word **else**. Finally, the closing word, **endif**, is treated as a statement that requires a semicolon.

As you can see, the use of this alternative form may be motivated by readability.

Making decisions with many conditions to evaluate

A program can have several conditions to be evaluated. In the following example, code in the **manyconditionswithifelse.php** file, the program simulates the invocation of a function based on a letter that the user passes as an argument:

```php
<?php
$letter = $argv[1] ?? 'x';

if ($letter == 'a'){
      echo 'archive';
} else if ($letter == 'b') {
      echo 'brief';
} else if ($letter == 'c') {
      echo 'create';
} else if ($letter == 'd') {
      echo 'delete';
} else if ($letter == 'e') {
      echo 'extract';
} else if ($letter == 'f') {
      echo 'format';
} else {
      echo 'command not found';
}
echo "\n";
```

The variable **$argv** is an array with the arguments passed through the command line. The first element is the file name, so we use the second element (index **1**). The operator **??** is the null coalescing operator. It evaluates the expression to its left and checks that it exists and is not null. If it exists and is not null, the operator returns the expression itself. Otherwise, it will return the value to its right. This way, we can guarantee that there is always a value to be evaluated, even if the user does not type any letters.

For example, if you call the program by using the following command:

```
php manyconditionswithifelse.php c
```

The result will be the text **create**.

Note: You can always code something that works but is more complicated to read. In Chapter   02 **of the book repository, there is a file called** manyconditionswithifelsestreetfighterstyle.php **which shows an inadequate implementation using the street fighter style anti-pattern. It is as if your code was hit by a hadouken.**

This   time, we did not show the C version, but you can find the many conditionswithifelse.c **file and the next C versions for PHP programs in** Chapter 02 **of the book repository.**

As you can see, this type of decision chain repeats the if and else expressions and the equality comparison for each value to be checked. There is, however, a control structure more suited to this situation. There is a control structure more suited to this situation. If you need to check multiple conditions for a variable using equality comparison, you can use the **switch** control structure.

Let us create the **manyconditionswithswitch.php** file and implement the same simulation using the **switch** control structure, as shown in the following:

```php
<?php
$letter = $argv[1] ?? 'x';

switch ($letter){
    case 'a':
        echo 'archive'; break;
    case 'b':
        echo 'brief'; break;
    case 'c':
        echo 'create'; break;
    case 'd':
        echo 'delete'; break;
    case 'e':
        echo 'extract'; break;
    case 'f':
        echo 'format'; break;
    default:
        echo 'command not found';
}
echo "\n";
```

As you can see, in the **switch** structure, we mention the variable to be checked once. Each case statement contains the block of code to be executed for a given value. There is one very important detail: if a **case** statement does not end with a **break** statement, PHP will continue checking other cases until it finds a **break** statement. The **default** statement is executed if no case satisfies the equality condition and is not terminated with a **break** statement. This is why all cases end with a break in this example; otherwise, in addition to printing the name of the function, the phrase **command not found** would be printed in a clear contradiction.

Although we have only one instruction in our example, you can have several instructions inside a case. The initial delimiter of a case is the colon, and the final delimiter is the **break** statement, as we said before.

The if...else and switch structures are suitable for holding blocks of code that carry out multiple instructions. but if the multiple conditions are limited to returning a value, you can use the **match** structure. Let us rewrite the previous program in the **manyconditionswithmatch.php**, as shown in the following:

```php
<?php
$letter = $argv[1] ?? 'x';


echo match($letter) {
        'a' => 'archive',
        'b' => 'brief',
        'c' => 'create',
        'd' => 'delete',
        'e' => 'extract',
        'f' => 'format',
        default => 'command not found'
};
echo "\n";
```

As you can see, the **match** structure offers a more concise way of coding if the goal is to select a value to return. There is a similar implementation to using an array, but we will see this later in the section on variable types. Now, let us talk about repetition structures.

Repetition structures

Repetition structures or loops define code blocks that are executed while a condition is true. PHP has four structures of this type. To explain how the repetition structures work, let us repeat the increment of a value to a variable until that value exceeds a threshold. Let us increase the **$sum** variable by **101** while its value is less than **5000**.

We will begin with the **while** structure. This structure tests a condition before executing a block of code. We will implement our **while** example in the **whileexample.php** file, as shown in the following:

```php
<?php

$sum = 0;
$iteractions = 0;

while ($sum < 5000) {
        $sum+=101;
        $iteractions++;
}
echo "\$sum is $sum after $iteractions iteractions\n";
```

We also increment a **$iterations** variable to know how many times the block is executed until the condition is no longer satisfied.

PHP has the same concise sum operators as C. Instead of writing **$sum = $sum + 101**, we just write **$sum+=101**. Instead of writing **$iteractions = $iteractions + 1**, we write **$iteractions++**.

Note: The while structure has an alternative syntax, more appropriate to be used when PHP is inserted into HTML. You can find an example of the alternative while syntax in the whileexamplealternative.php file in the Chapter 02 directory of the book repository. There you will also find the whileexample.c file with the C language version.

The second type of repetition structure is the do...while structure. This structure tests a condition after executing a block of code. We will implement our do...while example in the **dowhileexample.php** file. The content for this is shown in the following:

```php
<?php

$sum = 0;
$iteractions = 0;

do {
        $sum+=101;
        $iteractions++;
} while ($sum < 5000);
echo "\$sum is $sum after $iteractions iteractions\n";
```

Note: In the do...while structure, the condition is terminated with a semicolon. In the Chapter 02 directory of the book repository, you will find the `dowhileexample.c` file with the C language version.

In order to make the difference between while and do while clear, let us modify the increment example, starting with the **$sum** variable with **5000**. The `whileanddowhilecomparison.c` file will count how many iterations each repetition structure will make. Let us look at the following implementation:

```php
<?php

$sum = 5000; $iteractions = 0;

do {
    $sum+=101;
    $iteractions++;
} while ($sum < 5000);
echo "\$sum is $sum after $iteractions iteractions\n";

$sum = 5000; $iteractions = 0;

while ($sum < 5000) {
    $sum+=101;
    $iteractions++;
}
echo "\$sum is $sum after $iteractions iteractions\n";
```

When running this program, the output will be as follows:

$sum is 5101 after 1 iteractions
$sum is 5000 after 0 iteractions

The condition is not satisfied for either of the two repetition structures, but since do...while only testing the condition after executing the block of code, it does at least one iteration.

Note: As you can see from the variable assignment of `whileanddowhilecomparison.php`, you can have more than one statement on the same line. This can be convenient as long as it does not impair readability.

The last repetition structure we will look at in this section is the **for** structure. In a while and do...while structures, we have to initialize variables before the structure and make increments within the code block. The **for** structure allows you to initialize variables, test conditions, and define increments in a single line. Next, in the **forexample.php** file, we rewrite the sum example from this section using the **for** structure, as shown in the following:

```php
<?php

for ($sum=0,$iteractions=0;$sum < 5000;$iteractions++) {
      $sum+=101;
}
echo "\$sum is $sum after $iteractions iteractions\n";
```

As you can see, there are three elements in the opening of the **for** structure placed in parentheses, as follows:

- Variables with their initial values.

- The condition for the repetition to continue.

- The increment to be made to a control variable.

Note: In the Chapter 02 directory of the book repository, you will find the forexample.c file with the C language version.

There is still one last repetition structure, foreach, but we will get to know it after learning about the array data type.

Repeated calls to functions based on ticks

The **declare** function can be used for three different purposes: defining the character encoding, defining whether control of argument and return types of functions will be mandatory, and defining an action to be performed in response to an event. Let us talk about the third purpose.

In PHP, you can define an action to be repeated for every *n* statement that is executed, where *n* is an integer number greater than zero. To do this, we use the **declare** structure combined with the **register_tick_function** function. The procedure is as follows:

- You define the number of ticks to call a function. A tick is an event caused by a statement.

- You define a function to be called for every number of ticks defined by the declared structure.

- You tell PHP that this function must be executed with the **register_tick_function** function.

Let us take an example, with the file **declareticksample.php**, of a function called every four ticks.

```php
<?php
declare(ticks=4);

$GLOBALS['counter'] = 0;
```

```php
function tickHandler()
{
	$GLOBALS['counter']++;
}


register_tick_function('tickHandler');

$ticks = 0;
while ($GLOBALS['counter'] < 1000) {
	echo "one\n";
	echo "two\n";
	$ticks+=3;
}
echo "$ticks ticks\n";
echo $GLOBALS['counter'] . " calls to tickHandler\n";
```

The last lines of this program's output will be the following:

2997 ticks

1000 calls to tickHandler

As you can see, the **tickHandler** function is called at every iteration of the while loop. However, this call was programmed outside the loop. It is important to say that all instructions executed after calling the **register_tick_function** function are counted. So, although we counted the ticks inside the loop, there are also ticks generated before and after.

The **$GLOBALS** identifier is a global visibility array. We used it because we needed a variable that was visible inside and outside the **tickHandler** function.

Jumping to another section of a program

In 1968, in a paper submitted to *Communications of the ACM*, *Edsger W. Dijkstra* argued that the quality of programmers was a decreasing function of the density of *goto* statements in the programs they produced. *Dijkstra* claimed that goto had disastrous effects and should be abolished.

The C language already had the **goto** statement when PHP was created, but this statement was only incorporated into PHP in version 5.3. The delay in introducing **goto** in PHP was precisely due to the controversy of this declaration. but when it was finally introduced, it was done with restrictions.

The **goto** statement can be useful for exiting a chain of control structures, avoiding unnecessary execution of instructions. In the following example, in the **gotoexample.php** file, we see how to escape a **while** structure within a **for** structure:

```php
<?php
for ($i=0;$i<1000;$i++){
    $j=0;
    while ($j<1000){
        echo "i = $i and j = $j\n";
        if ($i == 42){
            goto endgame;
        }
        $j++;
    }
}
endgame:
echo "That's all folks!\n";
```

In this example, when the variable **$i** takes the value of **42**, the program flow is diverted to the instruction following the **endgame** label.

In PHP, you can only use **goto** exit control structures, never to enter them. This is a big difference between PHP and the C language. In the C language, we can use **goto** in order to divert the flow to any part of a program, which can be dangerous. In the following example, from the **gotoharmfulexample.c** file, we have a jump into a structure that causes an infinite loop. You will never see the sentence **That's all folks** to be printed with the following code:

```c
#include <stdio.h>

void main() {
    int i,j;

    for (i=0;i<1000;i++){
backtogame:
        j=0;
        while (j<1000){
            printf("i = %d and j = %d\n",i,j);
            j++;
        }
    }
    goto backtogame;
```

```
        printf("That's all folks!\n");
}
```

In PHP, such an attempt would result in a fatal error with a warning that **goto** into the loop or switch statement is not allowed. As you can see in PHP, **goto** is not harmful, **goto** was never the problem; the problem is the programmer.

Data types and operators

PHP is a weakly and dynamically typed language. It is weakly typed because you can change the type of a variable throughout a program multiple time. PHP is dynamically typed because it is not necessary to declare variables with their type. Just assign a value to an identifier, and the type is determined by the value.

In order to explain the fundamental types of PHP variables, as well as expressions and operators, we will use PHPUnit to write some tests. In this section, we will use the **DataTypesTest** class that is in the **chapter02/tests** directory of our repository. You can run the tests successfully for this class with PHPUnit and confirm that they pass the assertions. You can find a **datatypestest.c** file in the **Chapter 02** directory with the C language version for the variables handled by **DataTypesTest** class for comparison.

Integer

Let us start with the method that tests the integer PHP type. Refer to the following code for the **DataTypesTest->testInteger** method:

```
public function testInteger()
{
        $unluckyNumber = 13;
        $daysInAYear = 365;
        $byte = 0b1000;
        $sixteen = 0o20;
        $blue = 0x0000FF;

        $this->assertEquals('integer',gettype($unluckyNumber));
        $this->assertTrue(gettype($daysInAYear) == 'integer');
        $this->assertEquals(8,$byte);
        $this->assertEquals(16,$sixteen);
        $this->assertEquals(255,$blue);
}
```

Let us understand what the **testInteger** method does:

- It creates two integer type variables, **$unluckyNumber**, and **$daysInAYear**, assigning numbers without fractional parts to identifiers.

- It creates the integer type variable **$byte** by associating the binary number **1000**, which is equal to **8**. Binaries are identified in PHP with the prefix **0b**.

- It creates the integer type variable **$sixteen** by associating the octal number **20**, which is equal to **16**. Octals are identified in PHP with the prefix **0o**.

- It creates the integer type variable **$blue** by associating the hexadecimal number **FF**, which is equal to **255**. Hexadecimal is identified in PHP with the prefix **0x**.

- It checks with the **assertEquals** method, whether the **gettype** function returns **string** for the **$unluckyNumber** variable. The **gettype** function returns the type of the variable passed as an argument.

- It checks with the **assertTrue** method, whether the **gettype** function returns **string** for the **$dayInAYear** variable. The comparison made with the **==** operator is the same as that carried out by the **assertEquals** method.

- Finally, the test checks whether the binary, octal, and hexadecimal variables are equal to their respective decimal values.

In the C language, you can define an integer type variable with different ranges using the **short**, **long**, and **unsigned** modifiers, as shown in the following example code snippet:

```
unsigned int unluckyNumber = 13;
int daysInAYear = 365;
short int byte = 0b1000;
long int blue = 0x0000FF;
```

In PHP, there are no modifiers for the integer type. You can store positive and negative integer numbers in a range of two billion. You can check the maximum and minimum values for integers on the current platform using the constants **PHP_INT_MAX** and **PHP_INT_MIN**, respectively.

You may ask what happens if you do an operation whose result is outside the range of the **integer** type, such as calculating the following maximum limit twice:

```
$integerOutOfLimit = 2 * PHP_INT_MAX;
```

An error does not occur in this case. What happens is that the variable **$integerOutOfLimit** assumes the type **float**, a type that we will learn about in the upcoming section.

Floating point

Now, let us look at the method that tests the float PHP type. The code for the **DataTypesTest->testFloat** method is mentioned in the following:

```php
public function testFloat()
{
        $pi = 3.1415926;
        $piecesOfAPizza = 8.0;
        $piecesOfACake = (float) 4;
        $avogadro = 6.02214076e23;
        $nano = 1E-9;

        $this->assertEquals('double',gettype($pi));
        $this->assertEquals('double',gettype($piecesOfAPizza));
        $this->assertEquals('double',gettype($piecesOfACake));
        $this->assertEquals('double',gettype($avogadro));
        $this->assertEquals('double',gettype($nano));
}
```

Let us understand what the **testFloat** method does:

- It creates the float type variable **$pi** by assigning a number with a fractional part.

- It creates the float type variable **$piecesOfAPizza**, showing that a zero after the decimal point is enough to define a real number.

- It creates the float type variable **$piecesOfACake** using the casting operator. If four were assigned directly, the variable would be an integer. But by placing the float type in parentheses before the variable, we convert the integer value to float.

- It creates the float type variable **$avogadro** using scientific notation. The expression *6.02214076e23* is like writing *6.02214076 x 10^{23}*.

- It creates the float type variable **$nano** using scientific notation. The expression *1E-9* is like writing *1 x 10^{-9}*.

- Finally, we use the **assertEquals** method to check the type of variables. The **gettype** function returns **double** for all. This is not a mistake. In PHP, there is no difference between **float** and **double** as there is in the C language. In PHP, there is a single type of variable for real numbers: **float**. When casting, you use the word **float**, but the **gettype** function returns **double**.

You can store positive and negative real numbers in a range of approximately *1.8 X 10^{308}*. You may ask what happens if you do an operation whose result is outside the **float** type range, such as calculating twice the float limit, as shown in the following:

```php
$maxFloat = 1.8E308;
$floatOutOfLimit = 2 * $maxFloat;
```

No error will occur in this case. If you print the value of **$floatOutOfLimit**, the result will be INF from infinity. Let us see what will happen if you do some operation with the INF value, like dividing it in half, as follows:

```
$halfInfinite = $floatOutOfLimit / 2;
```

No error occurs in this case because it is a defined operation. If you print the value of **$halfInfinite**, the result is INF.

In order to check whether a variable has an infinite value, you can use the **is_infinite** function.

If you do an undefined operation, like taking the square root of a negative number or dividing infinity by infinity, as shown in the following:

```
$infiniteDivision = $floatOutOfLimit / $floatOutOfLimit;
```

The result will be **Not a Number** (**NAN**).

Let us see what happens if you do an operation with a NAN, like dividing it in half, as shown in the following:

```
$halfOfANAN = $infiniteDivision / 2;
```

$halfOfANAN will be a NAN too. To check whether a variable has the value NAN, you can use the **is_nan** function.

Chars and strings

Now, let us look at the method that tests the string PHP type. The code for the **DataTypesTest->testString** method is mentioned in the following:

```
    public function testString()
    {
            $letter = 'a';
            $word = 'alphabet';
            $aguy = 'john jonah jameson';
            $anotherguy = "john jonah jameson";
            $sentencewithsinglequotes = '$letter is the first letter of the
$word';
            $sentencewithdoublequotes = "$letter is the first letter of the
$word";

            $this->assertEquals('string',gettype($letter));
            $this->assertTrue(gettype($word) == 'string');
            $this->assertEquals($aguy,$anotherguy);
            $this->assertStringContainsString('word',$sentencewithsinglequ
```

```
otes);
            $this->assertStringContainsString('alphabet',$sentencewithdoub
lequotes);
    }
```

Let us understand what the **testString** method does:

- It creates the single character variable **$letter** by assigning a character between single quotes.

- It creates the multiple-character variable **$letter** by assigning a character chain between single quotes.

- It assigns the same text to two different variables, **$aguy**, and **$anotherguy**, with the difference that single quotes are used in the first one and double quotes in the second one.

- It creates the variable **$sentencewithsinglequotes** by assigning text in single quotes that contain the names of two variables (**$letter** and **$word**).

- It creates the variable **$sentencewithdoublequotes** by assigning text in double quotes that contain the names of the same two variables above.

- It uses **assertEquals** to verify that the **$letter** variable, containing a single character, is of type **string**.

- It checks with **assertTrue** that the variable **$word**, which contains several characters, is a **string**.

- It verifies that the variables **$aguy** and **$anotherguy**, which received the same text between different quotes, are the same for PHP.

- It checks that the variable **$sentencewithsinglequotes** contains the word, which seems obvious.

- It checks that the variable **$sentencewithdoublequotes** contains the word **alphabet**, which may not be obvious.

An important feature of the PHP string type is the possibility of automatically converting variable names into their respective values. When you assign text to a variable using single quotes, you tell PHP that the contents of the variable are exactly what you wrote, which is the case with **$sentencewithsinglequotes**. When you assign text to a variable using double quotes, you tell PHP that the variable names mentioned in that text should be replaced with the variable values, which is the case with **$sentencewithdoublequotes**.

If there are no variable names in a text, that is, there are no identifiers preceded by **$**, there is no difference between using single and double quotes, which is the case in the comparison between the variables **$aguy** and **$anotherguy**. But it is recommended that you do not use double quotes to define text without variables so that your intention is clearer to the code reader.

There is still an important feature about the string type in PHP, but we will talk about it in the arrays section because it is more convenient. Let us now move on to the Boolean type.

Boolean

Now, let us look at the method that tests the Boolean PHP type. Following is the code for the **DataTypesTest->testBoolean** method:

```
public function testBoolean()
{
        $theEarthIsRound = true;
        $theEarthIsFlat = false;

        $this->assertTrue($theEarthIsRound);
        $this->assertNotTrue($theEarthIsFlat);
        $this->assertEquals(true,1);
        $this->assertEquals(true,2999);
        $this->assertEquals(true,'a');
        $this->assertEquals(true,'alphabet');
        $this->assertEquals(false,0);
        $this->assertEquals(false,'');
}
```

Let us understand what the **testBoolean** method does:

- It creates the Boolean variable **$theEarthIsRound** with the value **true**.
- It creates the Boolean variable **$theEarthIsFlat** with the value **false**.
- It checks with the **assertTrue** method that creates the Boolean variable **$theEarthIsRound** is equal to **true**.
- It checks with the **assertNotTrue** method that creates the Boolean variable **$theEarthIsFlat** equals to **false**.
- It checks that **1** is equal to **true**.
- It checks that **2999** is equal to **true**.
- It checks that a single character is equal to **true**.
- It checks that a string is equal to **true**.
- It checks that the number zero is equal to **false**.
- It checks that an empty string is equal to **false**.

Any non-zero number is considered true in PHP, as is any non-empty string.

You can write Boolean keywords in several ways, **true** and **false**, **True** and **False**, **TRUE** and **FALSE**. However, it is recommended that you follow the pattern and type words the same way throughout the program. Item 2.5 of **PHP standards recommendations (PSR)-12** recommends that keywords in PHP be written in lowercase letters.

> **Note: They are documents published by the PHP Framework Interop Group (PHP-FIG). The PSRs that deal with coding standards are 1 (Basic Coding Standard) and 12 (Extended Coding Style guide).**

Constants and enumerations

You use variables in a program to store values that can change during the program's execution but if a variable never changes value, it is not a variable but a constant.

For example, we created a **$pi** variable in **DataTypesTest->testFloat** method. However, this variable will never change its value because it is a mathematical constant. It is more appropriate in this case to use the **define** function to define a PI constant, as shown in the following:

```
define('PI',3.1415926);
```

Constants created with the **define** function have a global scope. They are visible to any class function or method. Constants can store all the types we have covered so far, in addition to the object and array types. As you have seen, the define function expects two arguments: the constant name and its value. The constant name is a string and must be written in upper case. Some examples of definitions of string and Boolean constants are mentioned in the following:

```
define('ENVIRONMENT','test');
define('ENABLE_DEBUG',true);
```

The **DataTypesTest->testConstant** method shows how we refer to defined constants, as shown in the following code:

```
    public function testConstant()
    {
        $this->assertEquals(3.1415926, PI);
        $this->assertEquals('test', ENVIRONMENT);
        $this->assertTrue(ENABLE_DEBUG);
}
```

You can find out if a constant has been defined using the **defined()** function.

Constants can be used to define values of limited options, such as states of a process. For example, if a process has three states, running, blocked, and ready, we could define three integer constants, as shown in the following:

```
define('PROCESS_RUNNING',0);
define('PROCESS_BLOCKED',1);
```

```
define('PROCESS_READY',2);
```

However, there is a more suitable structure for this situation in which we enumerate values for a limited number of options, the **enum** structure. We can represent the states of a process with an **enum**, as shown in the following example:

```
enum Process {
        case Running;
        case Blocked;
        case Ready;
}
```

The **DataTypesTest->testEnumeration** method illustrates how we assign and check values of an **enum** type, as shown in the following:

```
    public function testEnumeration()
    {
            $state = Process::Running;
            $this->assertEquals(Process::Running, $state);
            $state = Process::Blocked;
            $this->assertTrue(Process::Blocked == $state);
            $state = Process::Ready;
            $this->assertEquals(Process::Ready, $state);
    }
```

All cases of an **enum** can be represented as a string using the **name** property. For example, **Process::Running->name** returns the string **Running**. This is a read-only property. You cannot change cases of an **enum** type.

NULL type

The types of variables we have covered so far allow for more than one value. The NULL type, however, only allows a single value: **null**. The NULL type can be a useful value when there is no value to return.

For example, we look for a record in an employee table to extract an employee's salary, which is a float value. However, we did not find the record. Without a record, there is no field. We cannot return a zero of type float because there is no field, and returning a zero would mean that the salary is zero but if we return null, we did not find the salary.

In PHP, comparisons can be done by value only or by value and type. We will learn more about this in the section on operators, but at this point, it is important to clarify how the null value is compared to other values.

There are two states that a variable can assume that can be confused with null: **empty** and **unset**. Notice that we are not discussing types but states. There is no **empty** type or **unset** type. These are states that a variable can assume and that are checked with operators or functions. In the **DataTypesTest->testNull** method, we make some comparisons to show the relationship between the **null** value and the **empty** and **unset** states, as shown in the following:

```
public function testNull()
{
        $goal = null;
        $this->assertEquals('NULL',gettype($goal));
        $this->assertNull($goal);
        $this->assertTrue($goal == null);
        $this->assertTrue(is_null($goal));
        $this->assertFalse(is_null(0));
        $this->assertFalse(is_null(''));
        $this->assertFalse(is_null(false));
        $this->assertTrue(is_null($notDefined));
        $this->assertEquals(null,$goal);
        $this->assertEquals(null, 0);
        $this->assertEquals(null,'');
        $this->assertEquals(null,false);
        $this->assertEquals(null,$notDefined);
        $this->assertTrue(empty($goal));
        $this->assertTrue(empty(0));
        $this->assertTrue(empty(''));
        $this->assertTrue(empty(false));
        $this->assertTrue(empty($notDefined));
        $this->assertFalse(isset($goal));
        $this->assertFalse(isset($notDefined));
}
```

Let us understand what the **testNull** method does:

- It creates the null variable **$goal**.

- It checks that the type of the null variable **$goal** is **NULL** (in upper case).

- It checks that the **$goal** variable is null with the **assertNull** method.

- It checks that the **$goal** variable is null using the **==** operator.

- It verifies that the **is_null** function returns **true** for the **$goal** variable.

- It verifies that the **is_null** function returns **false** for the number zero, which means that zero is not equal to **null**.

- It checks that the **is_null** function returns **false** for an empty string, which means that an empty string is not equal to **null**.

- It verifies that the **is_null** function returns **false** for the Boolean value false, which means that false is not equal to **null**.

- It verifies that the **is_null** function returns true for a variable that has not been defined, which means that an undefined value is equal to **null**.

- It checks that the **$goal** variable is equal to the null value with the **assertEquals** method.

- It checks that null equal zero with the **assertEquals** method, which contradicts the return of the **is_null** function.

- It checks that null is equal to an empty string with the **assertEquals** method, which contradicts the return of the **is_null** function.

- It checks that null is equal to false with the **assertEquals** method, which contradicts the return of the **is_null** function.

- It checks that null is equal to an undefined variable, which has the same result as the **is_null** function.

- It verifies that the **empty** function returns **true** for the null variable **$goal**.

- It verifies that the **empty** function returns **true** for zero.

- It verifies that the **empty** function returns **true** for an empty string.

- It verifies that the **empty** function returns **true** to **false**.

- It verifies that the **empty** function returns **true** for an undefined variable.

- It verifies that the **isset** function returns **false** for a null variable.

- It checks that the **isset** function returns **false** for an undefined variable.

From the assertions of the **testNull** method, we can verify that a null variable is empty and unset. However, the same assertions leave us in doubt about the equivalence of the null value with zero, with the Boolean false, and with an empty string. The **is_null** function appears to make a different comparison than the **assertEquals** method. This seems confusing because at one time, null and zero are the same, and at another, they are not. Let us explain this.

Well, you may remember that in the Boolean type section, we showed with **assertEquals** that zero and the empty string were equal to false. The same **assertEquals** method says that zero and the empty string are equal to null. The **assertEquals** method makes comparisons using the == operator, which compares values. This is something important to understand.

In PHP, you can compare only values or values and types. When you do a comparison with the == operator, you are only comparing the values. The **is_null** function, in turn, does not just compare the value. It checks whether the variable type is **NULL**. This is why the results are different.

Using the **is_null** function for the **$goal** variable is equivalent to using the following expression:

```
$goal == null && gettype($goal) == 'NULL';
```

In PHP, you have the possibility of returning different types in the same function, so it is necessary to compare not only values but also the type of the variable.

In the section on expressions and operators, we will talk about the different types of comparison. However, before that, let us talk about dynamic variable creation and variable destruction.

Variable variables and destruction of variables

PHP's weak and dynamic typing allows you to do type-juggling, like this code in the file **typejugglingexample.php**, in the **Chapter 02** folder:

```php
$weakButDynamic = 1;
echo 'First, $weakButDynamic is ' . gettype($weakButDynamic) . "\n";
$weakButDynamic = 1.618;
echo 'Now, $weakButDynamic is ' . gettype($weakButDynamic) . "\n";
$weakButDynamic = "some text";
echo 'Now, $weakButDynamic is ' . gettype($weakButDynamic) . "\n";
$weakButDynamic = false;
echo 'Now, $weakButDynamic is ' . gettype($weakButDynamic) . "\n";
$weakButDynamic = null;
echo 'Now, $weakButDynamic is ' . gettype($weakButDynamic) . "\n";
$weakButDynamic = 2;
echo 'Now, $weakButDynamic is ' . gettype($weakButDynamic) . " again\n";
```

As you can see, we assign values of different types to the same variable, changing its type several times. The following output of this program shows how the variable type changes:

```
First, $weakButDynamic is integer
Now, $weakButDynamic is double
Now, $weakButDynamic is string
Now, $weakButDynamic is boolean
Now, $weakButDynamic is NULL
Now, $weakButDynamic is integer again
```

This flexibility allows you to reuse variables that would otherwise be discarded because they are tied to a type and avoids unnecessary allocation of memory space. but there is another flexibility in PHP that, if misused, can easily consume more memory: **variable variables**.

A variable variable is a variable whose name is defined by another variable. It is a powerful feature of PHP that allows you to dynamically create variables at runtime.

We will show an example of the dynamic creation of ten variables to illustrate how variable variables work. In the **variablevariablesexample.php** file, we change the value of the variable **$name** ten times to create ten variables of type integer, with different values.

```php
<?php
for($i=0;$i<10;$i++){
        $name = 'twopower' . $i;
        $$name = pow(2,$i);
        echo "$name = {$$name} \n";
}
```

Note that we have an assignment to an identifier preceded by two-dollar signs (**$$name**). The first dollar sign tells the interpreter that what follows is a variable name. The second dollar sign tells the interpreter that the variable name is inside another variable.

In the first iteration, **$name** is equal to **twopower0**. Thus, the following instruction is used:

```php
$$name = pow(2,$i);
```

The previous instruction is equivalent to writing the following instruction:

```php
$twopower0 = pow(2,0);
```

The output of the **variablevariablesexample.php** program shows that from one variable, **$name**, we created ten new variables, as shown in the following:

```
twopower0 = 1
twopower1 = 2
twopower2 = 4
twopower3 = 8
twopower4 = 16
twopower5 = 32
twopower6 = 64
twopower7 = 128
twopower8 = 256
twopower9 = 512
```

It can very easily become dangerous. By using variable variables, you can quickly occupy a large amount of memory with a few lines of code. The program in the **fillingthememory.php** file shows how to quickly exhaust available memory by combining variables with an infinite loop, which does not last infinitely. Observe the following small program:

```
$i = 0;
while (true) {
     $newVariable = "variable$i";
     $$newVariable = $i;
     $i++;
     echo 'Allocated memory: ' . memory_get_usage() . " bytes\n";
}
```

The **fillingmemory.php** program creates entire variables and displays the memory used by PHP for each new variable created with the **memory_get_usage()** function. You can run this program for a while and stop it to see how much memory has been occupied since the program started. If you leave it running indefinitely, your computer may freeze, and then you will have to restart it, so do not delay in stopping the program. To give you a reference, in six seconds of execution, we recorded an increase in occupied memory from 393816 bytes to 316529392 bytes. This means that it only took six seconds for the memory allocation to increase by more than 800%.

With great power comes great responsibility. If you can create variables dynamically, you should destroy them when you no longer need them. You can destroy a variable in PHP at any time using the **unset** function. In the **destroyingvariables.php** file, we rewrote the program that creates entire variables, destroying the variable right after displaying the occupied memory. Let us see how this example uses an **unset** function:

```
$i = 0;
while (true) {
     $newVariable = "variable$i";
     $$newVariable = $i;
     $i++;
     echo 'Allocated memory: ' . memory_get_usage() . " bytes\n";
     unset($$newVariable);
}
```

After ten seconds of execution, this program went from 393864 occupied bytes to just 393896 bytes, a change of just 32 bytes. This shows how easy it is to free up memory in PHP programs.

Arithmetic expressions and operators

We can define an expression in PHP as a combination of variables, constants, and operators that results in a value. This value must be a valid type in PHP. We already know most types of variables and how to define constants. Now, let us understand how operators work in PHP. In this section, we will use the **OperatorsTest** class that is in the **chapter02/tests** directory of the book repository.

The **OperatorsTest->testArithmetic** method shows how we use PHP's arithmetic operators, as shown in the following:

```
public function testArithmetic()
{
        $number1 = 8;
        $number2 = 3;

        $this->assertEquals(11, $number1 + $number2);
        $this->assertEquals(5, $number1 - $number2);
        $this->assertEquals(-5, $number2 - $number1);
        $this->assertEquals(24, $number1 * $number2);
        $this->assertEquals(2.67, round($number1 / $number2,2));
        $this->assertEquals(2, $number1 % $number2);

}
```

In the **OperatorsTest->testArithmetic** method, we add, subtract, multiply, and divide two integer variables. When dividing, the result is of type float, and we use the round function to round this result to two decimal places. The remainder of integer division is given by the **%** operator, which we already used in the section on decision structures.

If you try to divide by zero, PHP will throw an exception. An exception is an object with information about an error. An exception can be made to avoid interrupting the program. In the following example of **OperatorsTest->DivisionByZero** method, we catch the **DivisionByZeroError** exception using the try...catch structure. In this structure, the **try** block contains the section where we expect an error to occur, while the **catch** block contains the section to handle this error. In this case, when division by zero causes the error, we check if the exception error message contains the string **Division by zero**, as shown in the following:

```
public function testDivisionByZero()
{
        try {
                $impossibleValue = 2/0;
        } catch (DivisionByZeroError $e) {
                $this->assertStringContainsString('Division by
zero',$e->getMessage());
        }
}
```

Arithmetic operators allow us to talk about automatic type conversion in PHP. As long as the types have compatible values, PHP automatically converts the values of variables based on the operators. If the operation is arithmetic, PHP will attempt to convert non-numeric operators to numbers. In the following example of the **OperatorsTest->testTypeConversion** method, we perform the four arithmetic operations using an integer variable and a string variable:

```php
public function testTypeConversion()
{
        $number1 = 1;
        $number2 = "1";

        $this->assertEquals(2, $number1 + $number2);
        $this->assertEquals(0, $number1 - $number2);
        $this->assertEquals(1, $number1 * $number2);
        $this->assertEquals(1, $number1 / $number2);

}
```

PHP converts the string 1 to the integer 1 because the values are compatible. This conversion is a feature of PHP's weak typing. In a strongly typed language such as Python, a sum of an integer and a string would result in an error, as shown in the following example:

```
>>> number1 = 1
>>> number2 = "1"
>>> number1 + number2
Traceback (most recent call last):
  File "<stdin>", line 1, in <module>
TypeError: unsupported operand type(s) for +: 'int' and 'str'
```

Python does not automatically convert variables. You need to do explicit conversions. In the example we showed, it would be necessary to convert the string variable into an integer, as shown in the following:

```
>>> number1 + int(number2)
```

JavaScript, in turn, does automatic type conversion, but it is not as consistent as PHP. In the following example, we see that JavaScript converts the same variables to different types in addition and subtraction operations:

```
> number1 = 1;
1
> number2 = "1";
'1'
> number1 + number2;
'11'
```

```
> number1 - number2;
0
```

PHP is not as demanding as Python in using operators, but it is consistent in its results, unlike JavaScript.

In addition to the basic arithmetic operators, PHP has increment and decrement operators. In the **OperatorsTest->testIncrementDecrement** method, we illustrate the use of these operators:

```
public function testIncrementDecrement()
{
        $number = 1;

        $this->assertEquals(2, ++$number);
        $this->assertEquals(1, --$number);
        $number+=2;
        $this->assertEquals(3, $number);
        $number-=3;
        $this->assertEquals(0, $number);
}
```

Increment and decrement operators shorten addition and subtraction expressions. In the **testIncrementDecrement** function, let us see the following examples of operators:

- **++$number** is equal to **$number = $number + 1**.
- **--$number** is equal to **$number = $number - 1**.
- **$number+=2** is equal to **$number = $number + 2**.
- **$number-=3** is equal to **$number = $number - 3**.

In this example, you may consider the operator's position strange when incrementing and decrementing a unit. Since you have been paying close attention to all the examples, you may have remembered that we incremented a **$iterations** variable by one in the section on repetition structures. When we did this, we placed the operator to the right of the variable, as shown in the following:

```
$iteractions++;
```

You must have noticed that we placed the operator to the left of the variable in the **testIncrementDecrement** method. The reason is the order in which operations take place. When you place the operator on the right, PHP returns the variable value first and then increments/decrements it. When you place the operator on the left, PHP increments/decrements the variable first and then returns its value. If we used the operator on the right in the test, it would fail because we would compare the variable's value before the increment/decrement.

Logical expressions and operators

Logical operators are essential for constructing expressions whose result is true or false. The following **OperatorsTest->testLogic** method illustrates the use of logical operators whose operands are Boolean variables or expressions:

```php
public function testLogic()
{
        $sentence1 = true;
        $sentence2 = false;
        $sentence3 = true;
        $sentence4 = false;

        $this->assertTrue($sentence1);
        $this->assertFalse($sentence2);
        $this->assertTrue(!$sentence2);
        $this->assertFalse(!$sentence1);
        $this->assertTrue($sentence1 && $sentence3);
        $this->assertFalse($sentence1 && $sentence2);
        $this->assertFalse($sentence2 && $sentence4);
        $this->assertTrue($sentence1 || $sentence2);
        $this->assertTrue($sentence1 || $sentence3);
        $this->assertFalse($sentence2 || $sentence4);
        $this->assertTrue($sentence1 xor $sentence2);
        $this->assertFalse($sentence1 xor $sentence3);
        $this->assertFalse($sentence2 xor $sentence4);
}
```

We can observe four Boolean operators in this method, as follows:

- The NOT operator is represented by the character (**!**). This operator returns the opposite Boolean value of the variable to its right. What is true becomes false, and what is false becomes true.

- The AND operator returns true if both operands are true. Otherwise, it returns false. This operator is represented by the characters **&&**, which are the same ones used in the C language. But it is also possible to use the keyword **and**.

- The OR operator returns true if at least one of the operands is true. It returns false only if both are false. This operator is represented by the characters **||**, which are the same as those used in the C language. However, it is also possible to use the keyword **or**.

- The XOR operator returns true if only one of the operands is true. This operator is represented by the keyword **xor**.

Comparison expressions and operators

Boolean values can be generated from comparisons. The following **OperatorsTest->testComparison** method illustrates the use of comparison operators whose operands can be variables of different types:

```php
public function testComparison()
{
        $nothing = 0;
        $one = 1;
        $oneDotZero = 1.0;
        $neon = 10;
        $starTrekIsCool = true;
        $lifeIsEasy = false;

        $this->assertTrue($one == $oneDotZero);
        $this->assertFalse($one != $oneDotZero);
        $this->assertTrue($one != $neon);
        $this->assertTrue($one < $neon);
        $this->assertTrue($one >= $oneDotZero);
        $this->assertTrue($oneDotZero <= $neon);
        $this->assertTrue($neon > $one);
        $this->assertTrue($one == $starTrekIsCool);
        $this->assertFalse($one === $starTrekIsCool);
        $this->assertTrue($one !== $oneDotZero);
        $this->assertTrue($nothing == $lifeIsEasy);
        $this->assertFalse($nothing === $lifeIsEasy);
        $this->assertTrue($nothing !== $lifeIsEasy);
}
```

From the assertions of the **testComparison** method, we can observe the following:

- The **==** operator only checks the equality of values, so for this operator, the integer **1** is equal to float **1.0**, just as the integer **1** is equal to the Boolean **true**.

- The **===** operator checks the equality of values and types, so for this operator, the integer **1** is not equal to the float **1.0**, just as the integer **1** is not equal to the Boolean **true**.

- The **!=** operator only checks the inequality of values, so for this operator, is false to state that **1** is different from **1.0**.

- The **!==** operator checks the inequality of values and types, so for this operator, it is true to state that **1** is different from **1.0**.

Comparisons with the greater than (`>`), less than (`<`), greater than or equal to (`<=`), and less than or equal to (`>=`) operators are made by value only. Therefore, for the expression:

```
$one > $lifeIsEasy
```

The result is true because PHP converts the operands into numbers before comparing.

Functions

In a program, you may have to repeat the same set of instructions, in the same sequence, at different times. To avoid the explicit repetition of instructions, which, in addition to generating larger files, makes programs more complicated to read, there are subroutines. Subroutines are blocks of code that can be invoked from any part of a program. Subroutines arise naturally from checking that there is code replication in a program.

Some subroutines return values, called **functions,** and subroutines that do not return values are called **procedures**. In PHP, both types of subroutines are implemented with the same block of code identified by the **function** keyword. Functions are more frequent than procedures because you generally send data to be processed and want a result. An example of a function that receives a number and returns its triple is given in the following:

```
function triple($number)
{
        return 3 * $number;
}
```

The **triple** function is implemented in the **FunctionsTest.php** file, in the **chapter02/ tests** directory, and is tested in this file by the **assertEquals** method, as follows:

```
$this->assertEquals(6, triple(2));
```

The **triple** function does not define the argument type or return type. The variable **$number** can be an integer or float. However, you can try to do an absurd operation by calling the **triple** function with a string argument, as follows:

```
triple('sheep');
```

The function will accept any type of variable as an argument. The following error will occur in the arithmetic operation within the function:

TypeError: Unsupported operand types: string * int

This error occurs because PHP cannot convert a string variable to a numeric variable if there is no number contained in the variable.

A PHP function can return different types of variables, just as it can receive them. The following **getOddInTheWord** function returns a string value if it finds an odd number in a sentence or **false** if it does not:

```
function getOddInTheWord($word)
{
```

```
        $length = strlen($word);
        for ($i=0;$i<$length;$i++){
                $letter = (int) $word[$i];
                if ($letter % 2 != 0){
                        return $word[$i];
                }
        }
        return false;
}
```

Just like in the C language, in PHP, internally, a string is an array of characters. This is why you can access a specific character from a string in the form of an element of an array. The expression **$word[$i]** is the **$i** character of the variable **$word**.

The possibility of receiving and returning different types of variables in a function is standard PHP behavior. This behavior can be modified by activating strict mode, with the **declare** function, as shown in the following:

```
declare(strict_types=1);
```

When used to enable strict mode, the **declare** function must be the first statement in a PHP file. Strict mode enables argument and return type checking of class functions and methods in PHP. This only works if you declare both argument and return types.

Let us rewrite the two previous functions, **triple** and **getOddInTheWord**, in the **StrictFunctionsTest.php** file in the **chapter02/tests** directory. The strict version of **triple** will be the **strictTriple** function.

```
function strictTriple(int $number):int
{
        return 3 * $number;
}
```

Note that we defined that **strictTriple** accepts only one integer argument and must necessarily return an integer, return type is defined after the colon. If you try to call **strictTriple** by passing a non-integer number, as follows:

```
strictTriple(3.14);
```

The result will be an error, as follows:

TypeError: strictTriple(): Argument #1 ($number) must be of type int, float given

It does not matter that the operation within the function admits numbers of different types. From the moment the argument has a declared type, and strict mode is turned on, the function must receive an argument of the declared type.

Strict mode eliminates the possibility of a function returning more than one type. So, the strict version of **getOddInTheWord** has to replace false with an empty string, as shown in the following:

```php
function getStrictOddInTheWord(string $word):string
{
        $length = strlen($word);
        for ($i=0;$i<$length;$i++){
                $letter = (int) $word[$i];
                if ($letter % 2 != 0){
                        return $word[$i];
                }
        }
        return '';
}
```

PHP has a vast library of functions. Some are a part of the core of the language, such as string and math functions, and others are available in PHP extensions. In the next section, we will talk about some functions that are built into the core of PHP. However, before that, let us see an interesting feature of PHP: variable functions.

A variable function is a variable that is used as a function. You can assign the name of a function to a variable and then invoke that variable as if it were a function. Let us illustrate this with the **testVariableFunctions** method of the **SpecialFunctionsTest** class, as follows:

```php
        public function testVariableFunctions()
        {
                $operation = 'sin';
                $this->assertEquals(round(sqrt(2)/2,2),
round($operation(deg2rad(45)),2));
                $operation = 'cos';
                $this->assertEquals(round(sqrt(2)/2,2),
round($operation(deg2rad(45)),2));
                $operation = 'tan';
                $this->assertEquals(1, round($operation(deg2rad(45))));
        }
```

Let us understand what this method does:

- It assigns the **$operation** variable the name of a PHP mathematical function, **sin**, which is the function for calculating the sine of an angle.

- It makes an equality assertion, checking whether half the square root of **2** is equal to the return of **$operation(deg2rad(45))**.

- The **sqrt** function is the PHP function for extracting square roots. We do not need the **square_root** function implemented in *Chapter 1, Meeting and Installing PHP*.

- The **deg2rad** function converts the value of an angle from degrees to radians. This is necessary because PHP's trigonometric functions work with radians and not degrees.

- When you place parentheses immediately after the name of a variable, PHP understands that you want to call the function whose name is contained in that variable. So, calling **$operation(deg2rad(45))**, the first time is the same as calling **sin(deg2rad(45))**.

- We use the round function to round the compared values to two decimal places to avoid differences in less significant decimal places.

- Then, we change the value of the **$operation**, in sequence, to **cos** (cosine function) and **tan** (tangent function) and make the assertions.

Variable functions are variables that point to functions, just as variable variables are variables that point to other variables.

Note: The `SpecialFunctionsTest.php` file is available at the `chapter02/test` directory, as well as the other test class files mentioned in this chapter.

Built-in file system and array functions

In this section, we will talk about some functions built into the PHP core related to the file system and array manipulation. We will also take the opportunity to talk about two types of variables that we did not cover in the section on variables: resource and array.

File system

Eventually, in a program, you will need to manipulate the file system. Your program may need to read or write files, create and remove directories, copy files from one directory to another, and search for files in a directory. PHP has a powerful collection of functions for these tasks.

In order to introduce file system functions, let us attempt an example where we create, write to, and read a file. This first example is in the **FilesystemTest.php** file in the **chapter02** directory:

```
public function testCreateSaveAndReadFileLineByLine()
{
    $path = __DIR__;
    $this->assertTrue(file_exists($path));
    $fileName = $path . DIRECTORY_SEPARATOR . 'filexample.txt';
    if (!file_exists($fileName)){
```

```
                    $handle = fopen($fileName,'a');
                    $this->assertEquals('resource',gettype($handle));
                    fwrite($handle, str_pad("The mouse ate the king of
Rome's clothes,\n",80,' '));
                    fwrite($handle, str_pad("so the king of Rome said he
had new clothes.",80,' '));
                    fclose($handle);
            }
            $content = '';
            $handle = fopen($fileName,'r');
            while (!feof($handle)){
                    $content .= fread($handle,80);
            }
            fclose($handle);
            $this->assertNotEquals('resource',gettype($handle));
            $this->assertStringContainsString('mouse',$content);
            $this->assertTrue(str_contains($content,'king'));
            $this->assertFalse(str_contains($content,'queen'));
            $this->assertStringContainsString('Rome',$content);
            $this->assertTrue(str_contains($content,'clothes'));
            $this->assertFalse(str_contains($content,'Romulus'));
            unlink($fileName);
    }
```

Let us understand what the **testCreateSaveAndReadFileLineByLine** method does:

- First, we assign to the variable **$path** the content of the magic constant **__DIR__**, which contains the directory of the current file. **Magic constants** are identifiers preceded and followed by a double dash that contain constant values for a given context. In the example, **__DIR__** will be constant within files in the same directory but will change the value for a file in another directory.

- We check that the directory contained in the **$path** variable exists with the **file_exists** function, which checks the existence of files and directories.

- We define in the **$fileName** variable the full path to the file we want to create using the **DIRECTORY_SEPARATOR** constant to generate the directory bar of the operating system where PHP is running. So, this code works for any operating system.

- We open the **filexample.txt** file with the **fopen** function. The second argument of the function is the opening mode. A mode means that the file must be open for writing, and the pointer must be positioned at the beginning of the file. In this mode, if the file does not exist, PHP creates it.

- The **fopen** function returns a variable of type resource. This type of variable holds a reference to an external resource, in this case, to a file.

- We write two sets of 80 characters to the file. The **fwrite** function writes several characters to the file referred to by the resource type variable. The **str_pad** function pads a string with a given character until it is the desired length.

- We open the file again using **fopen** function with **r** mode. This mode opens the file read-only and positions the pointer at the beginning of the file.

- We read the file every 80 characters with the **fread** function until the end. When the file pointer reaches the end, the **feof** function returns true.

- Some programming languages use the same sum operator to concatenate texts. This is not the case with PHP, which uses the dot for this. To concatenate a text with the content of a variable, storing the concatenated content in it, we use the **.=** operator which, in the example given, would be equivalent to writing:

  ```
  $content = $content . fread($handle,80);
  ```

- You can find out if a variable of type resource is still connected to an external resource using the **gettype** function. If the variable has lost connection to the resource, the **gettype** function will return **resource(closed)** instead of just **resource**.

- We check that the words in the text we recorded are present in the read text. Some assertions use the **str_contains** function to check whether a word is contained within the text.

- Finally, we destroy the **filexample.php** file using the **unlink** function. You may recognize that unlinking is a nice way of saying that you are destroying something.

Even with the succinctness of PHP, you might consider that it took many lines of code to write and read a file with just two lines of text. The **testCreateSaveAndReadFileLineByLine** method approach is more appropriate for files with dozens or hundreds of lines. If you want to read files whose content is no longer than a paragraph, there is a simpler approach.

The **FilesystemTest.php** file also contains the **testCreateSaveAndReadFileAtOnce** method. This method presents an example of writing and reading files without using a resource variable and with just two functions.

Let us understand what the **testCreateSaveAndReadFileAtOnce** method does:

- The first three instructions are the same as the previous method.

- The first difference is how we define the text to be recorded. Instead of fragmenting the text inline to save it, we define the text as a single block using PHP's heredoc syntax. In this syntax, you define an identifier (text, in this case) to delimit a block of text and enter the text as you want it to be interpreted. This means that line breaks will be saved as line breaks and tabs will be saved as tabs.

- We write the text at once with the **file_put_contents** function. This function creates the destination file if it does not exist.

- We read the file contents at once with the **file_get_contents** function.

- We destroyed the file in the same gentle way.

With these two approaches, you learn the essentials of file manipulation in PHP.

Note: There should be no trailing spaces of the heredoc block identifier. Trailing spaces will cause a syntax error: unexpected token "<<".

Arrays

We have been mentioning arrays since the section on decision structures. We postpone the formal presentation of this type of data so that we can talk about the foreach repetition structure and the array functions in a single section, including the use of closures. Furthermore, we need to tell the truth about the data array type: it is not an array.

What we call an array in PHP is a powerful data map. For a comparison, in Python, we have two distinct data structures, lists and dictionaries. The following snippet shows how a list and a dictionary are different types in Python:

```
>>> list = ['apple','banana','cranberries']
>>> list[0]
'apple'
>>> glossary = { 'salty':'something with salt','sweet':'something with
sugar'}
>>> glossary['sweet']
'something with sugar'
>>> type(list)
<class 'list'>
>>> type(glossary)
<class 'dict'>
```

Note that in Python, the list has a numeric index, an integer starting at zero. This index is not declared but automatically assigned by the order of the elements. The dictionary, in turn, is a structure of key-value pairs where the key is a text. A list in Python is created with square brackets, whereas a dictionary is created with curly braces.

Well, in PHP, there is no such thing as a list type and a dictionary type. The array type plays both roles. The example we showed in Python would be implemented in PHP, as follows:

```
php > $list = ['apple','banana','cranberries'];
php > $list[0];
php > echo $list[0];
```

```
apple
php > $glossary = ['salty'=>'something with salt','sweet'=>'something with
sugar'];
php > echo $glossary['sweet'];
something with sugar
php > echo gettype($list);
array
php > echo gettype($glossary);
array
```

The array type in PHP is a variable that connects keys with values. Keys can be integers or strings. Values can be any valid type in PHP. Each key-value pair is an element of the array. If you do not explicitly define the key to an array element, PHP assumes it is an integer, equal to the last integer used as the key plus one.

In the following code in the **ArrayTest.php** file, we show an example of creating a list with the individual creation of elements to illustrate the automatic assignment of sequential indexes:

```
public function testCreateList()
{
        $list = ['apple','banana','cranberries'];
        $this->assertIsArray($list);
        $this->assertEquals('banana',$list[1]);
        $list = [];
        $list[] = 'apple';
        $list[] = 'banana';
        $list[] = 'cranberries';
        $this->assertEquals('banana',$list[1]);
}
```

In the **ArrayTest->testCreateList** method, we can verify that the second element created automatically receives the index **1**. You can see that to create an element of a list, simply assign a value to the array variable followed by square brackets.

An alternative way to create an array is to use the **array** function. The variable **$list**, in the previous example, could have been created it as shown in the following:

```
$list = array();
```

In the following **ArrayTest->testCreateDictionary** method, we have an example of an array with text-type keys, which is the equivalent of Python's dictionary type:

```
public function testCreateDictionary()
{
        $aliens = [
```

```
                    'Clark Kent' => 'Krypton',
                    'Jonn Jonzz' => 'Mars',
                    'Koriander'  => 'Tamaran',
                    'Lar Gand'   => 'Daxam'
            ];
            $this->assertIsArray($aliens);
            $this->assertArrayHasKey('Koriander',$aliens);
        }
```

Previously, we discussed a repetition structure only when we covered the array data type. Now, we will fulfill this promise by explaining how the foreach repetition structure works.

For arrays that contain lists, foreach is used to assign each variable the value of the current element in that iteration. In the **ArrayTest->testListForeach** method, we see an example, as follows:

```
        public function testListForeach()
        {
            $pigs = ['Fifer','Fiddler','Practical'];
            $this->assertCount(3,$pigs);
            foreach($pigs as $pig){
                $this->assertIsString($pig);
            }
        }
```

In the **testListForeach** example, at each iteration, an element of the **$pigs** array is assigned to the **$pig** variable. We do not need to define a counter in foreach or a stopping criterion. This repeating structure loops through all the elements of an array.

You can see that we use an **assertCount** method comparing the array with the number **3**. This method checks the number of elements in the array, which, in this case, is **3**. You can also check the number of elements in an array using the **count** function.

Note: Although a string is internally an array of characters, you cannot use the count function to count how many characters are in a string. If you try to do this, you will receive an error. To do this, you use the strlen function. You can see an example of this function in the test classes in the functions section.

For arrays that contain dictionaries, you may need to manipulate not just the values but also the keys. To do this, foreach allows you to assign the element's key to one variable and the element's value to another variable. The distinction between a key and a value is determined by their order in relation to the **=>** sign. What is on the left is a key, and on the right is the value. In the following **ArrayTest->testDictionaryForeach** method, we see an example, as follows:

```php
public function testDictionaryForeach()
{
        $heroes = [
                'Bruce' => 'Batman',
                'Clark' => 'Superman',
                'Diana' => 'Wonder Woman'
        ];
        foreach($heroes as $realName => $heroName){
                $this->assertTrue(array_key_exists($realName,$heroes));
                $this->assertTrue(in_array($heroName,$heroes));
        }
}
```

In this example, the key to the current element of the **$heroes** array is assigned to the variable **$realName**, while the value of the element is assigned to the variable **$heroName**. We use the **array_key_exists** function to check if a key exists in the array and the **in_array** function to check if a value exists in the array.

We knew the **match** decision structure when we talked about control-flow structures. Now it is the moment to see an alternative for that structure using an array. You know that a PHP array can be used as a dictionary. Let us create the **manyconditionswitharray.php** file with the following content:

```php
<?php
$letter = $argv[1] ?? 'x';

$commands = [
        'a' => 'archive',
        'b' => 'brief',
        'c' => 'create',
        'd' => 'delete',
        'e' => 'extract',
        'f' => 'format',
        'x' => 'command not found'
];

echo $commands[$letter];
echo "\n";
```

We created this file without testing so you can compare it directly to the **manyconditionswithmatch.php** file.

As we already said, array values can be any valid PHP type. This means that an array element can have another array as its value, which in turn can have elements that have another array as its value, and so on. That is, arrays can be multidimensional.

In the following example, we show the creation of two arrays, **$autobots** and **$decepticons**, that are used to form a third array (**$transformers**):

```
php > $autobots = ['Optimus Prime', 'Bumblebee', 'Jazz', 'Ironhide'];
php > $decepticons = ['Megatron', 'Starscream', 'Soundwave', 'Shockwave'];
php > $transformers = [$autobots, $decepticons];
php > echo $transformers[1][2];
```

Output:

Soundwave

The first pair of brackets with index **1** refers to the second element of the first dimension of the array. The second pair of brackets with index **2** refers to the third element of the second dimension of the array. Remember that indices start at zero.

Now, to finish our introduction to arrays, let us discuss two subjects simultaneously: the use of anonymous functions, or closures, and the use of callback functions. Next, in the **ArrayTest->testCallbackFunction** method, we have the following example of how to repeat the same operation for each element of an array:

```
public function testCallbackFunction()
{
        $callback = function(&$value,$key) {
                $value = 'Black ' . $value;
        };
        $characters = ['Adam', 'Canary', 'Vulcan'];
        array_walk($characters, $callback);
        $this->assertEquals('Black Adam', $characters[0]);
        $this->assertEquals('Black Canary', $characters[1]);
        $this->assertEquals('Black Vulcan', $characters[2]);
}
```

Let us understand what the **testCallbackFunction** method does:

- First, we define an **anonymous function**, which is a function without a name. It needs to be assigned to a variable to be used later. This variable becomes invocable.

- Note that the anonymous function assigned to the **$callback** variable takes two arguments, **$value** and **$key**. The **$value** argument is preceded by the **&** character. The function modifies the variable $value, concatenating the string **Black** at its beginning.

- We define a list with some names for the **$characters** variable.

- We call the **array_walk** function, passing the **$characters** array and the **$callback** anonymous function as arguments.

- The **array_walk** function executes the function passed as a second argument (**callback** function) for each element of the array passed as a first argument.

- The **array_walk** function does not require an anonymous function. You can pass the name of any function as a string.

- The **array_walk** function will loop, calling the **callback** function for each element in the array. The **callback** function takes as arguments the value and key of the current array element, respectively.

- If you want the **callback** function to modify the value of the array element, you have to indicate that the first argument of the function must be passed by reference. This is why there is an **&** character before the **$value**. This character indicates that you are not modifying a local variable, but the reference to an external variable.

- Thus, after executing **array_walk**, all **$characters** elements are preceded by **Black**.

The same mass modification of array elements can be done with foreach. The following code indicates a version with foreach in the **ArrayTest->testNoCallbackFunction** method:

```php
public function testNoCallbackFunction()
    {
        $characters = ['Adam', 'Canary', 'Vulcan'];
        foreach($characters as $key => $value){
            $characters[$key] = 'Black ' . $value;
        }
        $this->assertEquals('Black Adam', $characters[0]);
        $this->assertEquals('Black Canary', $characters[1]);
        $this->assertEquals('Black Vulcan', $characters[2]);
    }
```

Some special PHP variables are arrays, and these are superglobal variables. You have already seen one of them, **$GLOBALS**.

In PHP, there are two scopes of variables: local and global. Variables created within class functions and methods are only visible in the respective functions and methods. Variables created outside of functions and methods are visible globally. Superglobal variables are global visibility variables that are pre-defined. We will learn about these variables in the next sections, approaching important elements for web pages.

Cookies and sessions

In order to create or modify cookies with PHP, we use the **setcookies** function. In the following example, we will create a cookie on one page and read its content on another page.

Let us create the **cookies01.php** file to create a cookie called **country**:

```php
<?php
setcookie('country','wonderland');
?>
I have put a cookie into your browser. Click <a href="cookies02.php">here</a> to see its content.
```

Next, let us create the **cookies02.php** file to show the value of the cookie, as follows:

```php
<?php
$content = $_COOKIE['country'];
?>
The cookie is <?=$content?>!
```

You can test this example by starting the PHP server embedded in the directory of the **cookies01.php** and **cookies02.php** files, as shown in the following:

```
php -S localhost:8000
```

Port **8000** is a suggestion; you can use any free port. If you use **8000**, as in the example, you can test cookie usage by calling **localhost:8000/cookies01.php** in your favorite browser. You can click on the link on the first page and see the cookie value on the second page.

As you can see, cookies created with **setcookie** can be retrieved with the **$_COOKIE** superglobal array. The cookie name is the key to the array, which, in this case, works like a dictionary. Cookies are stored in the local machine, and they are sent with the HTTP request. PHP updates **$_COOKIE** with each request.

Note: The setcookie function must be called before the HTTP response. Never write code that sends content to the client before calling a setcookie function.

We start with cookies because they are rejected by many people. Every day, millions of people around the world reject cookies because they help collect personal data. Sessions do not have this rejection problem, although they are victims of destruction, like cookies. Well, if you did not believe this justification, it does not matter because we already talked about cookies first, so we can now talk about sessions.

Session data is stored in PHP in the superglobal variable **$_SESSION**. In the following example, we will store a value in the session on one page and try to read it on another page. Trying is the appropriate word because this example will serve to clarify the nature of the session.

Let us create the **nosession01.php** file to store a string in the **$_SESSION** array, as follows:

```php
<?php
$_SESSION['box'] = 'jewel';
?>
I have put a jewel into the box. Click <a href="nosession02.php">here</a>
to see the jewel.
```

Next, let us create the **nosession02.php** file to show the value of the session variable, as follows:

```php
<?php
$boxContent = $_SESSION['box'];
?>
The box has a <?=$boxContent?>!
```

If you are using an **8000** port, you can test session usage by calling **http://localhost:8000/ nosession01.php** in your favorite browser. You click on the link on the first page where you will see the following error in the server log:

PHP Warning: Undefined global variable $_SESSION

Let us understand what it means to be not defined in PHP. This warning can suggest that **$_SESSION** is not already defined. Well, it is defined if a session is started. The HTTP protocol is session less. Applications that use HTTP must implement a session. Data lifetime in HTTP is the response time to a request. Data from one request is not transmitted to another request via HTTP. So, it is normal for a variable created in one request to not exist in another. For the state of this variable to be preserved, we need to start a session, which means informing that there will be an area on the server to store data created in a request so that it is available for other requests.

In PHP, a session is started by the **session_start** function. Let us redo the previous example using this function and create the **session01.php** file to store a string in the **$_SESSION** array, as follows:

```php
<?php
session_start();
$_SESSION['box'] = 'jewel';
?>
I have put a jewel into the box. Click <a href="session02.php">here</a> to
see the jewel.
```

Next, let us create the **session02.php** file to show the value of the session variable, as follows:

```php
<?php
session_start();
$boxContent = $_SESSION['box'];
```

```
?>
```
The box has a <?=$boxContent?>!

If you are using an 8000 port, you can test session usage by calling **http://localhost:8000/session01.php** in your favorite browser. You click the link on the first page and find a jewel inside the box this time.

Note that both files, **session01.php** and **session02.php** call the **session_start** function. It can suggest that the **session_start** function must be invoked in each PHP file, but it is not true. It means that the **session_start** function must be called with each request to create or maintain the created session. A PHP file can be a part of another PHP file, which calls the **session_start** function. Therefore, it does not need to be called in each file, as long as it is guaranteed to be called for each HTTP request.

Handling HTML forms

Arrays are also used in manipulating HTML forms in PHP. In this section, we will see how the superglobal variable **$_POST** is used to read data sent by the POST method of the HTTP protocol.

Let us create the **form.html** file with the following content:

```
<!doctype html>
<html>
<body>
<form action="page.php" method="post">
Word of the day: <input type="text" name="word">
<input type="submit" value="send">
</form>
</body>
</html>
```

The **form.html** file defines an HTML page with a form that has only a text field and a button to send form data to the **page.php** file using the HTTP POST method.

Next, let us create the **page.php** file with the following content:

```
<!doctype html>
<html>
<body>
<p>
The word of the day is <?=$_POST['word']?>
<p>
<a href="form.html">Go back to the form</a>
```

```
</body>
</html>
```

If you are using an **8000** port, you can test HTTP POST usage by calling **http://localhost:8000/ form.html** in your favorite browser. You fill in the text field and click on the button send. The **page.php** file is requested and shows your word.

Handling multiple views

An HTTP response has a content type that is defined by the **Content-Type** header. This header and any others can be set by the HTTP **header** function. In the following example, we show how the same content can be displayed in two different formats: HTML and JSON.

Let us create the **multipleviews.php** file with the following content:

```php
<?php
$type = $_GET['type'] ?? 'text/html';
$type = $type == 'json' ? 'application/json' : $type;
header('Content-Type:' . $type);
echo '{"message" :  "How do you see this content now?"}';
```

This file attempts to read the type parameter sent by the HTTP GET method. If the parameter is not found, the **$type** variable receives **'text/html'**. In other words, the default is to display content in HTML. If the type parameter is found and equals JSON, the **$type** variable is set to **application/json**. The **$type** variable is used as the value of the **Content-Type** header.

If you are using an **8000** port, you can test the HTML view by calling **http://localhost:8000/ multipleviews.php** in your favorite browser. The output is shown in the following:

{"message" : "How do you see this content now?"}

You can test the JSON view by calling **http://localhost:8000/multipleviews.php?type=json** in your favorite browser. The output will be different according to the browser.

This example was very simple, but there is no reason to worry because you will make other exercises with different types of views for response data. This is only the beginning.

Conclusion

In this chapter, we covered the foundations of the PHP programming language. We also covered PHP syntax and structural elements in comparison with C language, along with the control-flow structures of PHP in standard and alternative forms. We discussed data types, type juggling, operators, and expressions. We explored function definition and some built-in functions in PHP and covered PHP functions to manipulate cookies, sessions, HTML forms, and HTTP responses.

In the next chapter, we are going to learn how to build a function driven registration with the file system.

Points to remember

- PHP is a weak and dynamically typed language.

- PHP has a syntax similar to the C language.

- PHP has alternative flow control structures that are more appropriate for data presentation files such as HTML pages.

- PHP performs type conversion based on operations, as long as there is compatibility.

- PHP can control the type of arguments and returns of functions and methods.

- PHP has an extensive library of functions.

- The array data type is a data map that can be used as a list or dictionary.

Exercises

1. Change the last statement of the getStrictOddInTheWord function in the StrictFunctionsTest.php file to return a false and run PHPUnit to see the result.

2. Remove the session_start function call in sessions02.php. Check if $_SESSIONS['box'] returns any value after this change.

3. Change the superglobal variable $_POST in the form.php and page.php files to $_GET and change the method attribute of the form tag to GET.

Join our book's Discord space

Join the book's Discord Workspace for Latest updates, Offers, Tech happenings around the world, New Release and Sessions with the Authors:

https://discord.bpbonline.com

CHAPTER 3
Function Driven Registration with File System Storage

Introduction

This chapter of the book will cover the project and implementation of a book registration using function-oriented programming. We will start with the project presentation, which will serve as an exercise to learn PHP incrementally by refactoring an application. In this first version, the reader will learn how to code the registration with modularized code in functions and data storage in a file system. Every backend code produced from now on will be covered with tests.

Structure

The chapter covers the following topics:

- Project of book registration
- Saving data to the file system
- Reading data from the file system
- Updating data in the file system
- Removing data from the file system
- Creating the web pages

Objectives

By the end of this chapter, readers will be able to build a function driven PHP application. You will be able to use PHP to write and read data from text files in more than one format (plain text, **comma-separated value (CSV)**, and **JavaScript Object Notation (JSON)**). You will know how to import a PHP file into another PHP file and how to use Composer to import a file without having to indicate its path every time.

Project of book registration

The problem that will serve as our exercise until the last chapter is controlling a collection of books. We need to store and retrieve two sets of data, that is, books and their authors. Our initial project consists of a PHP application that writes and reads these data sets to the file system. The datasets we will manipulate are made up of attributes of different types.

The author's dataset consists of the following:

- **code**: Integer with a maximum value of 9999
- **last_name**: String with a maximum of 20 characters
- **middle_name**: String with a maximum of 20 characters
- **first_name**: String with a maximum of 20 characters

The book's dataset consists of the following:

- **code**: Integer with a maximum value of 9999
- **title**: String a maximum of 80 characters
- **author_code**: Integer with a maximum value of 9999

We will divide our system into two main parts, which we will call view and logic. The view part consists of the interface and presentation of data to the user. The logic part consists of data processing.

Figure 3.1 shows a **Unified Modeling Language (UML)** component diagram with the components designed for each of these parts of the system. This diagram shows the data flow and component dependency. Arrows labelled dispatch indicate that one component is invoking another and sometimes sending data. This flow, when it occurs between components of the view category, illustrates navigation between HTML pages. Arrows labelled use indicate that a component depends on another to function. In this case, all logic components depend on the **book.functions.php** functions file. This, in turn, depends on the **book.config.php** configuration file.

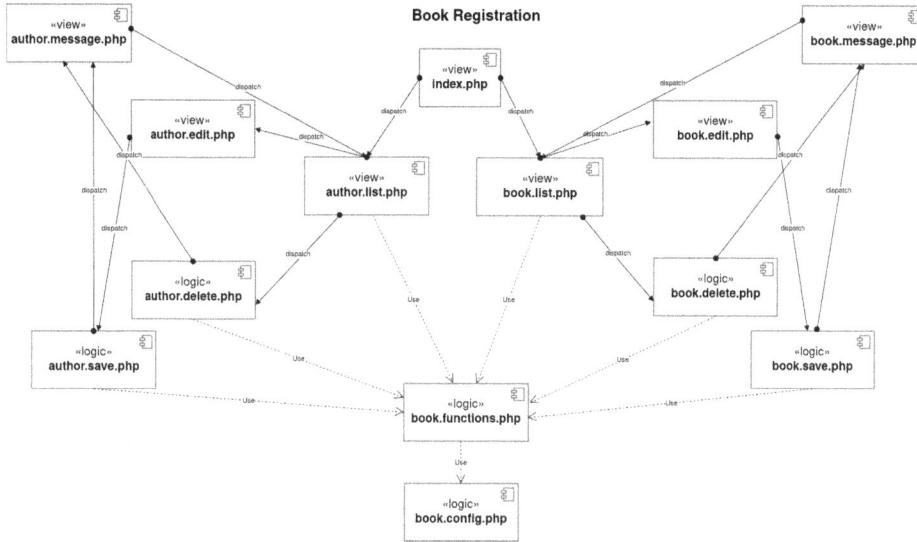

Figure 3.1: Component diagram of the registration book system

Now, let us describe the roles and responsibilities of each component of our system:

- The **index.php** file is the entry point for our application. From there, the user chooses whether to manipulate author or book data.

- The **index.php** file can invoke the **author.list.php** file to display the list of registered authors or the **book.list.php** file to display the list of registered books. These two files have a link for **index.php**, so the user can always go back to the home page.

- From the page displayed by **author.list.php** or by **book.list.php**, the user can perform three operations: Create a new record, change an existing record, or remove a record.

- To create or change records, the user uses the form displayed by the **author.edit. php** or **book.edit.php** files.

- The files **author.edit.php** and **book.edit.php** respectively invoke **author. save.php** and **book.save.php** to write the record to the file system.

- The **author.delete.php** and **book.delete.php** files remove records from the file system.

- After a write or remove operation, the user is taken to the page generated by **author.message.php** or **book.message.php**. This page tells you whether the previous operation was successful and displays a link to the listing page for that data collection.

- The logic for writing and reading the file system is contained in the **book. functions.php** file.

- The **book.config.php** file defines the location of the files that contain author and book data and the format in which the data is stored.

Our system has a fundamental restriction: the author code in the book record must exist in the author record.

The construction of our system, which we will call the **librarian**, will begin with the logic part of the system. As to reading records, we need them to exist. We will start by implementing record writing. We will do this in the next section using the **test-driven development** (**TDD**) approach.

Saving data to file system

Let us create a directory called **librarian**. Inside it, let us install PHPUnit using Composer, as follows:

```
$ mkdir librarian
$ cd librarian
$ composer require phpunit/phpunit
```

The first step in TDD is to create a test that fails. This step is taken by writing what we want to happen before writing the code that makes it happen.

In order, we need an author before recording a book, so let us write the test for recording an author record. We need to generate the configuration for PHPUnit.

Run the following command in the **librarian** directory:

```
$ vendor/bin/phpunit -generate-configuration
```

You will keep the default values for all options except the **src** directory. Instead of **src**, this item will be **/**, as our project's source code files will be in the root of the **librarian** directory.

After configuring PHPUnit, we will create the **tests** directory and, within it, the **StorageTest.php** file, as follows:

```
$ mkdir tests
$ cd tests
$ touch StorageTest.php
```

Note: You can edit your files with any text editor because PHP does not depend on a specific editor. However, an editor with specific features for programming makes work more productive. We suggest using Visual Studio Code, which is available for Windows, MacOS, and several Linux distributions, including Debian from our virtual machine. You can get Visual Studio Code for free at https://code.visualstudio.com. Specific documentation for using PHP with Visual Studio Code is available at https://code.visualstudio.com/docs/languages/php

The **StorageTest** class will contain all read and write tests for the Librarian system. As we already said in the chapter objectives, we will record and read in various formats. Initially, we will record in plain text.

Saving data in plain text

Let us fill the **StorageTest.php** file with the following content:

```php
<?php
use PHPUnit\Framework\TestCase;

class StorageTest extends TestCase
{
        public function testSaveAuthorInPlainText()
        {
                $this->assertTrue(saveAuthorInPlainText('Wells','Herbert','George'));
        }
}
```

Our intention is to know whether a record with the author **Wells**, **Herbert**, and **George** was written to a plain text file.

When creating the test, we define the data we want to send. In this case, the function arguments and the return type. In this case, a Boolean, to be evaluated by the **assertTrue** method.

As you have noticed, the **savePlainText** function does not exist. There is no need to worry because this absence does not matter at this point. The first concern is writing the test. When writing a test, the requirement is documented of what the expected behavior of a program is.

As we said, the first step in TDD is to write a test that fails. You may question what the point of a failed test is. This test tells you what you have to do to stop it from failing. When we run the test right now, the output will be as follows:

There was 1 error:

1) StorageTest::testSaveAuthorInPlainText
Error: Call to undefined function saveAuthorInPlainText()

Note: The test tells you what you need to do. It says that the saveAuthorInPlainText function is not defined, so you need to define it. Test error messages should be considered as guidance for development.

In the first step of TDD, you define what you want to happen. In other words, you write a requirement in the form of a source code. In the second step of TDD, you define how this requirement will be met; that is, you write the source code that makes the test work.

According to the test guidance and our component diagram, we will create the **saveAuthorInPlainText** function in the **book.functions.php** file, as follows:

```php
function saveAuthorInPlainText($lastName, $middleName, $firstName)
{
    $filepath = getConfig()['author_filepath'] . DIRECTORY_SEPARATOR .
'authors.txt';
    $handle = fopen($filepath,'a+');
    fseek($handle, -65, SEEK_END);
    $row = fread($handle, 65);
    $code = (int) substr($row, 0, 4);
    $code++;
    $row = str_pad($code, 4, ' ', STR_PAD_LEFT) . str_pad($lastName, 20, '
', STR_PAD_LEFT) .
    str_pad($middleName, 20, ' ', STR_PAD_LEFT) . str_pad($firstName, 20, '
', STR_PAD_LEFT) . "\n";
    fwrite($handle, $row);
    fclose($handle);
    $handle = fopen($filepath,'r');
    $found = false;
    fseek($handle, -65, SEEK_END);
    $currentRow = fread($handle, 65);
    $found = ($currentRow == $row);
    fclose($handle);
    return $found;
}
```

We know what the **saveAuthorInPlainText** function does, but let us understand how it does, as follows:

- It opens a file in **a+** mode. This mode creates the file if it does not exist and opens it for writing and reading, placing the pointer for writing at the end of the file.

- It uses **fseek** function for reading the last **65** bytes. The constant **SEEK_END** places the pointer for reading at the end of the file, and a negative number moves back the number of bytes from the informed position.

- It reads the last line of the file to extract the author code contained in the first **4** characters and increments this code by one unit.

- It formats a line to be recorded with **4** spaces for the code, **20** spaces for each other attribute, and an end-of-line character, totaling **65** bytes.

- The formatted line is written, and the file is closed.

- It opens the file in **r** mode, that is, read-only, and looks for the last line recorded using the **fseek** function. We place the file pointer **65** bytes before the end. It is the same action performed to generate a new code.

- If the line read is the same as the line formatted for writing, the function returns true.

If you run PHPUnit now, you will still receive an undefined function call error because the**book.functions.php** file is not automatically loaded by the test class.

We need to add an attribute to the **composer.json** file so that the **book.functions.php** file is loaded in every request since it is a dependency of all of our application's logic files. Add the **autoload** attribute with the **files** mechanism, as shown in the following excerpt:

```
"autoload" : {
    "files": ["book.functions.php"]
}
```

After modifying the **composer.json** file, you need to run a command to generate the **autoload** file, as follows:

```
$ composer dumpautoload
```

After generating the autoload file, when calling PHPUnit again, you will encounter a new error, as follows:

```
There was 1 error:
```

```
1) StorageTest::testSaveAuthorInPlainText
Error: Call to undefined function getConfig()
```

This error message shows that this time, the **StorageTest** class encountered the **saveAuthorInTextPlain** function. However, it did not find the **getConfig** function because we have not created this function yet. Let us create it in the **book.functions.php** file, as follows:

```
function getConfig()
{
    return require 'book.config.php';
}
```

The **require** command imports the specified file into the current file, as if you copied the contents of the file and pasted it onto that line. If this command is repeated, it will import the file again. If you have a situation where an imported file does not change its content and you want to import the content only one time, then you must use the **require_once** command. The require and **require_once** commands check the existence of the file and cause a fatal error if it does not exist. There is another pair of commands, that is, **include** and **include_once**, which do not check for existence, do not cause an error and can be used if the import is unnecessary.

You may question the need for a function that only has one statement. You may ask why we do not put this statement directly in the **saveAuthorInPlainText** function. The reason for having a separate function to retrieve the contents of the configuration file is to keep the location and structure of the configuration decoupled from the rest of the application. All functions that need configuration data will have to read the file, without a single function to return the configuration. If the configuration file changes the directory, name, or data format, we will have to change lines of code throughout the application. With an exclusive function to return the configuration, we reduce the change to a single point.

Creating the **getConfig** function is not enough. If you run the test right after creating this function, you will receive the following error:

```
1) StorageTest::testSaveAuthorInPlainText
Error: Failed opening required 'book.config.php' (include_path='.:/opt/
lampp/lib/php')
```

We need to create **book.config.php** file.

PHP looks for the file not only in the path defined by autoloading but in the directories defined by PHP's **include_path** directive. Let us create **book.config.php** file.

Its contents will be as follows:

```php
<?php
return [
        'author_filepath' => dirname(__FILE__)
];
```

The **author** file directory will be the same directory as the **book.config.php** file, so we can use the **dirname** function to extract the directory name from the magic constant **__FILE__**. We do not use the magic constant **__DIR__** because it returns the directory of the file that initiated the call, and as **book.config.php** will be called by others, this would cause an error.

Finally, after creating the configuration file, you can run PHPUnit, and the test will pass successfully, although with a warning, as follows:

```
There was 1 risky test:

1) StorageTest::testSaveAuthorInPlainText
This test does not define a code coverage target but is expected to do so

[YOUR DIRECTORY/librarian/tests/StorageTest.php:10

OK, but there were issues!
Tests: 1, Assertions: 1, Risky: 1.
```

The second step of TDD is now completed. You made your code pass the test. Now, we can move on to the third step, which is refactoring the code to make it better.

First, however, let us resolve the warning that PHPUnit displayed. Since our system does not have any classes, we cannot indicate a code coverage target. So let us put the **@ coversNothing** annotation before the **testSaveAuthorInPlainText** method, as follows:

```
/**
* @coversNothing
*/
```

When you run PHPUnit again, you will be warned about the deprecation of the **@ coversNothing** annotation and its deprecation in PHPUnit 12, as follows:

```
There was 1 PHPUnit test runner deprecation:
```

1) Metadata found in doc-comment for method StorageTest::testSaveAuthorInPlainText(). Metadata in doc-comments is deprecated and will no longer be supported in PHPUnit 12. Update your test code to use attributes instead.

To ensure that our tests are compatible with both versions, we will keep the annotation block but add the **CoversNothing** attribute as follows:

```
#[CoversNothing()]
```

This attribute must be imported at the beginning of the file, as follows:

```
use PHPUnit\Framework\Attributes\CoversNothing;
```

Now, when running PHPUnit, you have a test passing successfully and with no risks identified, as follows:

OK (1 test, 1 assertion)

Another adjustment we will make to the test is to follow the principle of always returning to the initial state. If you run the test three times, you will see that the **authors.txt** file will have three lines, and each time you rotate, a line will be added. This means that our test has a different state each time it is run.

Note: In a test, what is done must be undone. This means that the final state of a test must be the same as the initial state.

Therefore, we will add two lines to the end of the **saveAuthorInPlainText** method, deleting the **authors.txt** file, as follows:

```
$filepath = getConfig()['author_filepath'] . DIRECTORY_SEPARATOR . 'authors.
txt';
unlink($filepath);
```

If you run the test now, the **authors.txt** file will be deleted. It will only exist while the test is running.

You noticed that we had to directly mention the author's data file name in two different places, the function that writes the author and the test method.

Note: The recording function is tightly coupled with a file name: `authors.txt`, but if we want to change the file name, then we will have to change this function and, in all places, where this file is used. This is not appropriate. It is best if the file name is part of the configuration.

Let us modify the configuration so that we have the full path to the file and its name.

First, let us change the **books.config.php** file, replacing the line as follows:

```
'author_filepath' => dirname(__FILE__)
```

For this line, as follows:

```
'author_plaintext_filepath' => dirname(__FILE__) . DIRECTORY_SEPARATOR .
'authors.txt'
```

Next, we will replace the **saveAuthorInPlainText** function with the following line:

```
$filepath = getConfig()['author_filepath'] . DIRECTORY_SEPARATOR . 'authors.
txt';
```

For this line, as follows:

```
$filepath = getConfig()['author_plaintext_filepath'];
```

Finally, in the **testSaveAuthorInPlainText** method, we will replace the line as follows:

```
$filepath = getConfig()['author_filepath'] . DIRECTORY_SEPARATOR . 'authors.
txt';
```

for this line, as follows:

```
$filepath = getConfig()['author_plaintext_filepath'];
```

You can successfully run the tests after these changes. Now, the function and the tests are decoupled from common configuration data.

Note: Configuration data must be defined in only one place for being used in many places.

We completed the third step of TDD. We will refactor our code so that it continues to do what it did before but in a better way.

In the next section, we will implement it using tests and recording authors in CSV format.

Saving data in CSV format

CSV identifies a file format where values are separated by commas. In fact, we can use other characters as separators, and we will use a colon for our application.

Let us add the following test method to **StorageTest** class:

```
/**
* @coversNothing
*/
#[CoversNothing()]
public function testSaveAuthorInCSV()
{
        $this->assertTrue(saveAuthorInCSV('Wells','Herbert','George'));
        $filepath = getConfig()['author_csv_filepath'];
        unlink($filepath);
}
```

To make it clear how to disable the test coverage warning for PHPUnit in any version, this time we show what the **@coversNothing** annotation and the **CoversNothing** attribute will be before the test method. We will omit this in the next code snippets.

This test will fail when you run it for the first time, with the following error message:

Error: Call to undefined function saveAuthorInCSV()

Let us create the **saveAuthorInCsv** function in the **book.functions.php** file, as follows:

```
function saveAuthorInCSV($lastName, $middleName, $firstName)
{
    $filepath = getConfig()['author_csv_filepath'];
    $handle = fopen($filepath,'a+');
    $code = 0;
    while (!feof($handle)){
        $row = fgetcsv($handle, null, ';');
        $code = $row[0] ?? $code;
    }
    $code++;
    $fields = [
        str_pad($code, 4, ' ', STR_PAD_LEFT),
        str_pad($lastName, 20,' ', STR_PAD_LEFT),
        str_pad($middleName, 20, ' ', STR_PAD_LEFT),
        str_pad($firstName, 20, ' ', STR_PAD_LEFT)
    ];
    fputcsv($handle, $fields, ';');
    fclose($handle);
    $handle = fopen($filepath,'r');
```

```
    $found = false;
    $currentCode = 0;
    while (!feof($handle)) {
        $currentRow = fgetcsv($handle, null, ';');
        $currentCode = $currentRow[0] ?? $currentCode;
    }
    $found = ((int) $currentCode == $code);
    fclose($handle);
    return $found;
}
```

We know what the **saveAuthorInCSV** function does, but let us understand how it does it, as follows:

- It opens a file in **a+** mode. It is the same as the previous function.

- It iterates through the lines of the file, reading each line with the **fgetcsv** function, which extracts the line's content into an indexed array. With each line read, it tries to read the code field. If the code field does not exist, it keeps the last value read.

- It increments the code by one unit.

- It creates an array with the attributes to be written. We maintain the lengths used in the plain text file function.

- The array is written to the file by the **fputcsv** function if the file is closed.

- It opens the file in **r** mode, read-only, and iterates through the lines of the file until the end, reading each line with **fgetcsv** function and storing the author code.

- If the last author code is equal to the author code written by **fputcsv** function, the **saveAuthorInCSV** function returns **true**.

We have changed the reading strategy with respect to the plain text file. In the plain text file, we locate the last record by counting the bytes from the end of the file. This works because our records have a fixed length, but although we have maintained the formatting for the fields when writing the CSV file, we do not necessarily need to do this, as the **fgetcsv** function can read lines of different length until it finds the end-of-line character.

If you try to run the tests now, the **testSaveAuthorInCSV** test will fail because you need to add the following line to the configuration file:

```
'author_csv_filepath' => dirname(__FILE__) . DIRECTORY_SEPARATOR . 'authors.
csv'
```

Now, you can run the tests successfully. If you want to see the contents of the author's file, just comment out the unlink function line in the test method and run a few times. With three executions, for example, the **authors.csv** file will be as follows:

```
"    1";"            Wells";"            Herbert";"            George"
"    2";"            Wells";"            Herbert";"            George"
"    3";"            Wells";"            Herbert";"            George"
```

Note: The `fputcsv` function does not write the fields just by concatenating the separator (colon in this case). It surrounds the value of each field with double quotation marks.

To complete this section, we have to practice refactoring. The idea is to always try to improve something after it is working.

First, we make it work, then we make it work better. You cannot improve what is not working.

Robert Martin states in his book *Clean Code* that *duplication may be the root of all evil in software*. With this warning in mind, let us eliminate some duplication in our functions.

First, let us replace the integer **65** used in the **saveAuthorInPlainText** function with a constant, **AUTHOR_ROW_LENGTH**. We will define this constant at the beginning of this should come together

```
const AUTHOR_ROW_LENGTH = 65;
```

After defining the constant, replace every occurrence of **65** with **AUTHOR_ROW_LENGTH** and run the tests to check if everything keeps working. Be careful with the **fseek** function because the value is negative in the second argument, so it will be **-AUTHOR_ROW_LENGTH**.

Next, we will replace the direct call to the **str_pad** function with a function called **formatField**, which will encapsulate the former and reduce the number of arguments needed to two.

Following is the **formatField** function code:

```
function formatField($field, int $length)
{
    return str_pad($field, $length, ' ', STR_PAD_LEFT);
}
```

After declaring this function, we will replace each call of **str_pad** in **saveAuthorInPlainText** and **saveAuthorInCSV** functions by **formatField**. For example, the following line in **saveAuthorInPlainText** function:

```
    $row = str_pad($code, 4, ' ', STR_PAD_LEFT) . str_pad($lastName, 20, '
', STR_PAD_LEFT) .
    str_pad($middleName, 20, ' ', STR_PAD_LEFT) . str_pad($firstName, 20, '
', STR_PAD_LEFT) . "\n";
```

This will be as follows:

```
$row = formatField($code, 4) . formatField($lastName, 20) .
formatField($middleName, 20) . formatField($firstName, 20) . "\n";
```

Note: The replacement made the code more readable. You can run the tests successfully after the changes because the functions keep doing the same things.

The third step of TDD is completed. We will refactor our code so that it continues to do what it did before, but in a better way. A better way can mean an optimization of a process or a structure improvement that helps to maintain the source code.

In the next section, we will implement it using tests and recording authors in JSON format.

Saving data in JSON format

JSON is a lightweight data-interchange format that has become a standard for data transmission in web applications.

Let us add the following test method to **StorageTest** class:

```php
public function testSaveAuthorInJSON()
{
    $this->assertTrue(saveAuthorInJSON('Wells','Herbert','George'));
    $filepath = getConfig()['author_json_filepath'];
    unlink($filepath);
}
```

Of course, as the first step of TDD, when running this test, it will fail because the **saveAuthorInJSON** method does not exist. Let us implement this method in the **book. functions.php** file, as follows:

```php
function saveAuthorInJSON($lastName, $middleName, $firstName)
{
    $filepath = getConfig()['author_json_filepath'];
    $handle = fopen($filepath,'a');
    fclose($handle);
    $json = json_decode(file_get_contents($filepath));
    if ($json == NULL){
        $json = [];
    }
    $code = 0;
    foreach ($json as $row) {
        $code = $row->code;
    }
    $code++;
    $dict = [
        'code' => $code,
```

```
            'last_name'   => $lastName,
            'middle_name' => $middleName,
            'first_name'  =>  $firstName
    ];
    $json[] = $dict;
    $text = json_encode($json);
    file_put_contents($filepath, $text);
    $json = json_decode(file_get_contents($filepath));
    $found = false;
    $currentCode = 0;
    foreach ($json as $row) {
        $currentCode = $row->code;
    }
    $found = ($currentCode == $code);
    return $found;
}
```

We know what the **saveAuthorInCSV** function does, but let us understand how it does it, as follows:

- It opens a file in **a** mode and closes it immediately. The **a** mode creates the file if it does not exist and opens it for writing. We do this to ensure the file exists.

- It reads the entire contents of the file using the **file_get_contents** function. The content read is assigned to the **$json** variable, after to be decoded with the **json_decode** function. The **json_decode** function transforms JSON string into PHP compatible type. JSON format defines arrays and objects, so a JSON string can be decoded into an array or an object from **StdClass** class.

- The **authors.json** file must contain an array of objects. So, the **saveAuthorInCSV** function uses the foreach repetition structure to iterate over this array and read all the objects, retrieving the author's code until we reach the last element.

- It increments the code by one unit.

- It creates an array with the attributes to be written. This time, we do not worry about the lengths of the attributes because we are not breaking lines.

- The new author is added to the array of existing authors, and the entire array, converted to JSON by the **json_encode** function, is written to the **authors.json** file.

- It reads the content of the file again, converting it to an array of objects and iterating over this array until the last element, storing the author code for each iteration.

- If the last author code is equal to the author code written by the **file_put_contents** function, the **saveAuthorInJSON** function returns true.

The test will continue to fail until you add the path configuration for the JSON file in the **book.config.php** file, as follows:

```
'author_json_filepath' => dirname(__FILE__) . DIRECTORY_SEPARATOR .
'authors.json'
```

Now that we have a properly tested implementation of recording authors in three different formats, let us implement the reading functions to retrieve the data from any author using their code.

Reading data from the file system

There are two read operations we need to implement. Reading a single record to change it and reading a set of records to list them. For each format, we will initially implement reading a single record using the code as a search key. After that, we will implement the reading of a set of records.

Reading plain text data

For testing the reading of a single record from the **authors.txt** file, we will add the following test method to the **StorageTest** class:

```
public function testReadAuthorInPlainText()
{
    saveAuthorInPlainText('Von Goethe','Wolfgang','Johann');
    saveAuthorInPlainText('Fitzgerald','Scott','Francis');
    saveAuthorInPlainText('Doyle','Arthur','Conan');
    $author = readAuthorInPlainTextByCode(2);
    $this->assertEquals('Scott',$author['middle_name']);
    $filepath = getConfig()['author_plaintext_filepath'];
    unlink($filepath);
}
```

The **testReadAuthorInPlainText** method adds three records to the plain text file and checks whether the middle name of the second record is **Scott**.

The test will fail if you run it now, as the **readAuthorInPlainTextByCode** function does not exist.

Let us implement it in the **book.functions.php** file, as follows:

```
function readAuthorInPlainTextByCode(int $code)
{
```

```
$filepath = getConfig()['author_plaintext_filepath'];
$handle = fopen($filepath,'r');
$author = [];
while(!feof($handle)){
    $row = fread($handle, AUTHOR_ROW_LENGTH);
    $readCode = (int) substr($row,0,4);
    if ($readCode == $code){
        $author = [
            'code' => $code,
            'last_name' => trim(substr($row,4,10)),
            'middle_name' => trim(substr($row,15,10)),
            'first_name' => trim(substr($row,25,10))
        ];
        break;
    }
}
fclose($handle);
return $author;
}
```

Note: The `readAuthorInPlainTextByCode` function returns an array with author attributes, removing all leading and trailing spaces from the string attributes. Also note that as soon as we find the author, we stop reading the file, using the break statement. Now, you can run the tests successfully again.

Next, for testing the reading of a set of records from the **authors.txt** file, we will add the following test method to the **StorageTest** class:

```
public function testReadAuthorsInPlainText()
{
    saveAuthorInPlainText('Shelley','Wollstonecraft','Mary');
    saveAuthorInPlainText('Christie','Mary','Agatha');
    saveAuthorInPlainText('Lispector','Pinkhasivna','Chaya');
    $authors = readAuthorsInPlainText();
    $this->assertCount(3,$authors);
    $this->assertEquals('Agatha',$authors[1]['first_name']);
    $filepath = getConfig()['author_plaintext_filepath'];
    unlink($filepath);
}
```

In this test, we include three authors with the **saveAuthorInPlainText** method, then read all the authors with the **readAuthorsInPlainText** method. We check if the **$authors** array returned by the function has three elements and if the second element (with index **1**) has **Agatha** as its first name.

This test will fail because the **readAuthorsInPlainText** function does not exist. Let us create it in the **book.functions.php** file as follows:

```php
function readAuthorsInPlainText()
{
    $filepath = getConfig()['author_plaintext_filepath'];
    $handle = fopen($filepath,'r');
    $authors = [];
    while(!feof($handle)){
        $row = fread($handle, AUTHOR_ROW_LENGTH);
        $author = [
            'code' => (int) substr($row,0,4),
            'last_name' => trim(substr($row,4,20)),
            'middle_name' => trim(substr($row,25,20)),
            'first_name' => trim(substr($row,45,20))
        ];
        if ($author['code'] != 0) {
            $authors[] = $author;
        }
    }
    fclose($handle);
    return $authors;
}
```

While the **readAuthorInPlainTextByCode** function returns one-dimensional array, the **readAuthorsInPlainText** function returns multidimensional array.

Reading CSV data

For testing the reading of a single record from the **authors.csv** file, we will add the following test method to the **StorageTest** class:

```php
public function testReadAuthorInCSV()
{
    saveAuthorInCSV('Von Goethe','Wolfgang','Johann');
    saveAuthorInCSV('Fitzgerald','Scott','Francis');
    saveAuthorInCSV('Doyle','Arthur','Conan');
```

```
        $author = readAuthorInCSVByCode(2);
        $this->assertEquals('Scott',$author['middle_name']);
        $filepath = getConfig()['author_csv_filepath'];
        unlink($filepath);
    }
```

This test requires creating the following function in **book.functions.php**:

```
function readAuthorInCSVByCode(int $code)
{
    $filepath = getConfig()['author_csv_filepath'];
    $handle = fopen($filepath,'r');
    $author = [];
    while(!feof($handle)){
        $row = fgetcsv($handle, null, ';');
        $readCode = (int) is_array($row) && isset($row[0]) ? $row[0] : 0;
        if ($readCode == $code){
            $author = [
                'code' => $code,
                'last_name' => trim($row[1]),
                'middle_name' => trim($row[2]),
                'first_name' => trim($row[3]),
            ];
            break;
        }
    }
    fclose($handle);
    return $author;
}
```

Note: When reading the line, we check if the read content is an array with the is_array function and if the first element exists with the isset function. This is a procedure to avoid errors if the line content is not in CSV format.

Next, for testing the reading of the set of records from the **authors.csv** file, we will add the following test method to **StorageTest** class:

```
    public function testReadAuthorInCSV()
    {
        saveAuthorInCSV('Von Goethe','Wolfgang','Johann');
        saveAuthorInCSV('Fitzgerald','Scott','Francis');
        saveAuthorInCSV('Doyle','Arthur','Conan');
```

```
        $author = readAuthorInCSVByCode(2);
        $this->assertEquals('Scott',$author['middle_name']);
        $filepath = getConfig()['author_csv_filepath'];
        unlink($filepath);
    }
```

This test requires creating the following function in **book.functions.php**:

```
function readAuthorsInCSV()
{
    $filepath = getConfig()['author_csv_filepath'];
    $handle = fopen($filepath,'r');
    $authors = [];
    while(!feof($handle)){
        $row = fgetcsv($handle, null, ';');
        if (!is_array($row) || count($row) != 4) continue;
        $author = [
            'code' => (int) $row[0],
            'last_name' => trim($row[1]),
            'middle_name' => trim($row[2]),
            'first_name' => trim($row[3]),
        ];
        $authors[] = $author;
    }
    fclose($handle);
    return $authors;
}
```

After reading the file line with the **fgetcsv** function, we will check if the result is an array and if this array has four elements. Otherwise, we skip to the next iteration. This procedure avoids errors when reading the end of the file.

Reading JSON data

For testing the reading of a single record from the **authors.json** file, we will add the following test method to the **StorageTest** class:

```
    public function testReadAuthorInJSON()
    {
        saveAuthorInJSON('Von Goethe','Wolfgang','Johann');
        saveAuthorInJSON('Fitzgerald','Scott','Francis');
        saveAuthorInJSON('Doyle','Arthur','Conan');
        $author = readAuthorInJSONByCode(2);
```

```
        $this->assertEquals('Scott',$author['middle_name']);
        $filepath = getConfig()['author_json_filepath'];
        unlink($filepath);
    }
```

This test requires creating the following function in **book.functions.php**:

```
function readAuthorInJSONByCode(int $code)
{
    $filepath = getConfig()['author_json_filepath'];
    $content = file_get_contents($filepath);
    $authors = json_decode($content);
    foreach($authors as $author) {
        if ((int) $author->code == $code) {
            return (array) $author;
        }
    }
    return [];
}
```

This method is shorter than plain text and CSV reading partners because the **json_decode** function returns an object that is interchangeable with an array. Using the casting operator, we convert the object to an array without having to deal with each attribute.

Next, for testing the reading of a set of records from the **authors.json** file, we will add the test method to the **StorageTest** class.

This test requires creating the following function in **book.functions.php**:

```
    public function testReadAuthorsInJSON()
    {
        saveAuthorInJSON('Shelley','Wollstonecraft','Mary');
        saveAuthorInJSON('Christie','Mary','Agatha');
        saveAuthorInJSON('Lispector','Pinkhasivna','Chaya');
        $authors = readAuthorsInJSON();
        $this->assertCount(3,$authors);
        $this->assertEquals('Agatha',$authors[1]['first_name']);
        $filepath = getConfig()['author_json_filepath'];
        unlink($filepath);
    }
```

This test requires creating the following function in **book.functions.php**:

```
function readAuthorsInJSON()
{
```

```
$filepath = getConfig()['author_json_filepath'];
$content = file_get_contents($filepath);
$authors = json_decode($content);
foreach($authors as $index => $author) {
    $authors[$index] = (array) $author;
}
return $authors;
}
```

Now that we have tested functions for reading authors, let us implement the update functions.

Updating data in file system

First of all, let us understand how updating records in a text file will work in our application.

So far, you have learned that we have functions for opening files, closing files, reading content from files, and writing content to files. When writing content to plain text and CSV files, we use the **fwrite** and **fputcsv** functions. You may have noticed that the arguments of these functions basically tell you what will be written to which file. This is enough to append data to the end of a file. We cannot inform through these functions that we want to modify a line that has the code with a certain value. In fact, text file write functions are not designed to modify a specific part of a file but only to add content. These text files are not databases, which we will cover in *Chapter 4, Function Driven Registration with Relational Database Storage*.

In a text file, when a record is changed, we do not overwrite the existing data in the current file. We copy the previous and subsequent records to a new file, writing a record with the modified data between them.

Figure 3.2 illustrates the process. Thus, our update functions will not modify the existing file but will produce a new file with the modified record:

UPDATING ROWS IN A TEXT FILE

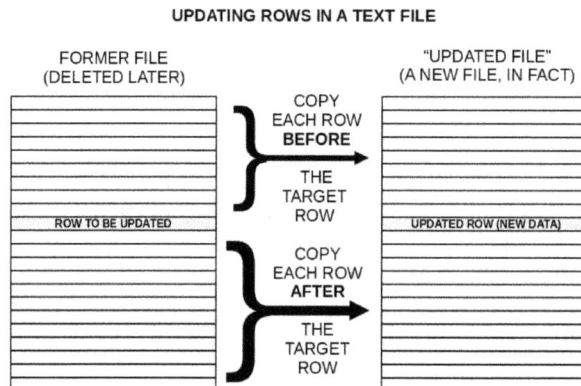

Figure 3.2: Updating a text file

Updating plain text data

Let us add the following test method to the **StorageTest** class:

```
public function testUpdateAuthorInPlainText()
{
    saveAuthorInPlainText('Maupassant','de','Guy');
    saveAuthorInPlainText('Saint-Exupéry','de','Antoine');
    saveAuthorInPlainText('Balzac','de','Honoré');
    $author = readAuthorInPlainTextByCode(1);
    $this->assertEquals('Guy',$author['first_name']);
    updateAuthorInPlainText(1,[
        'last_name' => 'Raspe',
        'middle_name' => 'Erich',
        'first_name' => 'Rudolf'
    ]);
    $author = readAuthorInPlainTextByCode(1);
    $this->assertEquals('Rudolf',$author['first_name']);
    $filepath = getConfig()['author_plaintext_filepath'];
    unlink($filepath);
}
```

This test adds three authors to the **authors.txt** file, modifies the first author, and checks their first name before and after the change. This test requires creating the following function in **book.functions.php**:

```
function updateAuthorInPlainText(int $code, array $data)
{
    $sourcePath = getConfig()['author_plaintext_filepath'];
    $targetPath = str_replace('.txt','.tmp',$sourcePath);
    $sourceHandle = fopen($sourcePath,'r');
    $targetHandle = fopen($targetPath,'w');
    $changed = false;
    while(!feof($sourceHandle)){
        $row = fread($sourceHandle, AUTHOR_ROW_LENGTH);
        $readCode = (int) substr($row,0,4);
        if ($readCode == $code){
            $author = [
                'code' => $code,
                'last_name' => trim(substr($row,4,20)),
```

```
                'middle_name' => trim(substr($row,25,20)),
                'first_name' => trim(substr($row,45,20))
            ];
            foreach($data as $key => $value){
                $author[$key] = $value;
            }
            $row = formatField($code,4) . formatField($author['last_
name'],20) .
            formatField($author['middle_name'],20) .
formatField($author['first_name'],20) . "\n";
            $changed = true;
        }
        fwrite($targetHandle,$row,AUTHOR_ROW_LENGTH);
    }
    fclose($sourceHandle);
    fclose($targetHandle);
    unlink($sourcePath);
    copy($targetPath,$sourcePath);
    unlink($targetPath);
    return $changed;
}
```

First, we read each line from **authors.txt** and save it to the authors.tmp, replacing the line to be updated by the new data. Next, we delete the authors.txt file and copy the **authors. tmp** file as **authors.txt** and finally delete the **authors.tmp** file.

Updating CSV data

Let us add the following test method to the **StorageTest** class:

```
public function testUpdateAuthorInCSV()
{
    saveAuthorInCSV('Maupassant','de','Guy');
    saveAuthorInCSV('Saint-Exupéry','de','Antoine');
    saveAuthorInCSV('Balzac','de','Honoré');
    $author = readAuthorInCSVByCode(1);
    $this->assertEquals('Guy',$author['first_name']);
    updateAuthorInCSV(1,[
        'last_name' => 'Raspe',
        'middle_name' => 'Erich',
```

```
            'first_name' => 'Rudolf'
        ]);
        $author = readAuthorInCSVByCode(1);
        $this->assertEquals('Rudolf',$author['first_name']);
        $filepath = getConfig()['author_csv_filepath'];
        unlink($filepath);
    }
```

This test requires creating the following function in **book.functions.php**:

```
function updateAuthorInCSV(int $code, array $data)
{
    $sourcePath = getConfig()['author_csv_filepath'];
    $targetPath = str_replace('.csv','.tmp',$sourcePath);
    $sourceHandle = fopen($sourcePath,'r');
    $targetHandle = fopen($targetPath,'w');
    $changed = false;
    while(!feof($sourceHandle)){
        $row = fgetcsv($sourceHandle, null, ';');
        if (!is_array($row) || count($row) != 4) continue;
        $readCode = (int) $row[0];
        if ($readCode == $code){
            $author = [
                'code' => $code,
                'last_name' => trim($row[1]),
                'middle_name' => trim($row[2]),
                'first_name' => trim($row[3]),
            ];
            foreach($data as $key => $value){
                $author[$key] = $value;
            }
            $row = [
                formatField($code,4),
                formatField($author['last_name'],4,20),
                formatField($author['middle_name'],20),
                formatField($author['first_name'],20)
            ];
            $changed = true;
        }
```

```
        fputcsv($targetHandle,$row,';');
    }
    fclose($sourceHandle);
    fclose($targetHandle);
    unlink($sourcePath);
    copy($targetPath,$sourcePath);
    unlink($targetPath);
    return $changed;
}
```

The implementation of the update in CSV format does not bring any major news.

Updating JSON data

Let us add the following test method to the **StorageTest** class:

```
public function testUpdateAuthorInJSON()
{
    saveAuthorInJSON('Maupassant','de','Guy');
    saveAuthorInJSON('Saint-Exupéry','de','Antoine');
    saveAuthorInJSON('Balzac','de','Honoré');
    $author = readAuthorInJSONByCode(1);
    $this->assertEquals('Guy',$author['first_name']);
    updateAuthorInJSON(1,[
        'last_name' => 'Raspe',
        'middle_name' => 'Erich',
        'first_name' => 'Rudolf'
    ]);
    $author = readAuthorInJSONByCode(1);
    $this->assertEquals('Rudolf',$author['first_name']);
    $filepath = getConfig()['author_json_filepath'];
    unlink($filepath);
}
```

This test requires creating the following function in **book.functions.php**:

```
function updateAuthorInJSON(int $code, array $data)
{
    $sourcePath = getConfig()['author_json_filepath'];
    $content = file_get_contents($sourcePath);
    $authors = json_decode($content);
```

```
$changed = false;
foreach($authors as $index => $author) {
    if ((int) $author->code == $code) {
        foreach($data as $key => $value){
            $author->$key = $value;
        }
        $authors[$index] = $author;
    }
}
$targetPath = str_replace('.json','.tmp',$sourcePath);
file_put_contents($targetPath,json_encode($authors));
unlink($sourcePath);
copy($targetPath,$sourcePath);
unlink($targetPath);
return $changed;
}
```

We have finished implementing the update in three data formats that we are using. Now, let us implement the part that usually always works the first time, that is, deleting records.

Removing data from file system

The process to delete records in a text file is very similar to the process to update records. *Figure 3.3* illustrates the process:

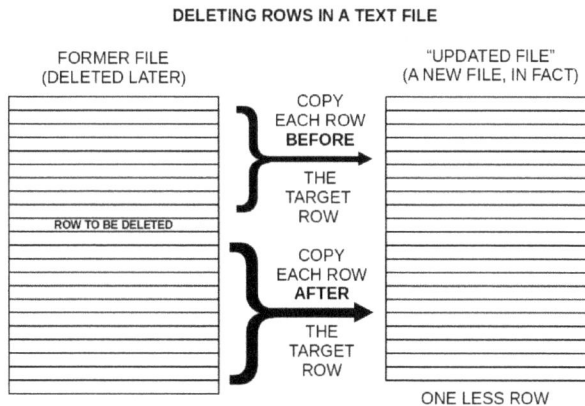

Figure 3.3: Removing a row from the text file

As you can see, when a record is deleted, we do not erase the existing data in the current file. We copy the previous and subsequent records to a new file and ignore the record selected for deletion.

Removing plain text data

Let us add the following test method to the **StorageTest** class:

```
public function testDeleteAuthorInPlainText()
{
    saveAuthorInPlainText('Assis','de','Machado');
    saveAuthorInPlainText('Alencar','de','José');
    saveAuthorInPlainText('Queiroz','de','Rachel');
    $author = readAuthorInPlainTextByCode(2);
    $this->assertEquals('Alencar',$author['last_name']);
    deleteAuthorInPlainText(2);
    $author = readAuthorInPlainTextByCode(2);
    $this->assertEmpty($author);
    $filepath = getConfig()['author_plaintext_filepath'];
    unlink($filepath);
}
```

The read function returns an empty array if it does not find the record. So, we use the **assertEmpty** method to check if the array is empty.

This test requires creating the following function in **book.functions.php**:

```
function deleteAuthorInPlainText(int $code)
{
    $sourcePath = getConfig()['author_plaintext_filepath'];
    $targetPath = str_replace('.txt','.tmp',$sourcePath);
    $sourceHandle = fopen($sourcePath,'r');
    $targetHandle = fopen($targetPath,'w');
    $changed = false;
    while(!feof($sourceHandle)){
        $row = fread($sourceHandle, AUTHOR_ROW_LENGTH);
        $readCode = (int) substr($row,0,4);
        if ($readCode == $code) {
            $changed = true;
            continue;
        }
        fwrite($targetHandle,$row,AUTHOR_ROW_LENGTH);
    }
    fclose($sourceHandle);
    fclose($targetHandle);
```

```
        unlink($sourcePath);
        copy($targetPath,$sourcePath);
        unlink($targetPath);
        return $changed;
}
```

Removing CSV data

Let us add the following test method to **StorageTest** class:

```
    public function testDeleteAuthorInCSV()
    {
        saveAuthorInCSV('Assis','de','Machado');
        saveAuthorInCSV('Alencar','de','José');
        saveAuthorInCSV('Queiroz','de','Rachel');
        $author = readAuthorInCSVByCode(2);
        $this->assertEquals('Alencar',$author['last_name']);
        deleteAuthorInCSV(2);
        $author = readAuthorInCSVByCode(2);
        $this->assertEmpty($author);
        $filepath = getConfig()['author_csv_filepath'];
        unlink($filepath);
    }
```

This test requires creating the following function in **book.functions.php**:

```
function deleteAuthorInCSV(int $code)
{
    $sourcePath = getConfig()['author_csv_filepath'];
    $targetPath = str_replace('.csv','.tmp',$sourcePath);
    $sourceHandle = fopen($sourcePath,'r');
    $targetHandle = fopen($targetPath,'w');
    $changed = false;
    while(!feof($sourceHandle)){
        $row = fgetcsv($sourceHandle, null, ';');
        if (!is_array($row) || count($row) != 4) continue;
        $readCode = (int) $row[0];
        if ($readCode == $code){
            $changed = true;
            continue;
```

```
        }
        fputcsv($targetHandle,$row,';');
    }
    fclose($sourceHandle);
    fclose($targetHandle);
    unlink($sourcePath);
    copy($targetPath,$sourcePath);
    unlink($targetPath);
    return $changed;
}
```

Removing JSON data

Let us add the following test method to the **StorageTest** class:

```
public function testDeleteAuthorInJSON()
{
    saveAuthorInJSON('Assis','de','Machado');
    saveAuthorInJSON('Alencar','de','José');
    saveAuthorInJSON('Queiroz','de','Rachel');
    $author = readAuthorInJSONByCode(2);
    $this->assertEquals('Alencar',$author['last_name']);
    deleteAuthorInJSON(2);
    $author = readAuthorInJSONByCode(2);
    $this->assertEmpty($author);
    $filepath = getConfig()['author_json_filepath'];
    unlink($filepath);
}
```

This test requires creating the following function in **book.functions.php**:

```
function deleteAuthorInJSON(int $code)
{
    $sourcePath = getConfig()['author_json_filepath'];
    $content = file_get_contents($sourcePath);
    $authors = json_decode($content);
    $changed = false;
    foreach($authors as $index => $author) {
        if ((int) $author->code == $code) {
            unset($authors[$index]);
```

```
        }
    }
    $targetPath = str_replace('.json','.tmp',$sourcePath);
    file_put_contents($targetPath,json_encode($authors));
    unlink($sourcePath);
    copy($targetPath,$sourcePath);
    unlink($targetPath);
    return $changed;
}
```

Therefore, with test coverage, we implemented all operations for creating, retrieving, updating, and removing records in three text file formats. You can refute this by stating that we did not do all the operations because we did not implement writing, reading, updating, and removing books. This implementation is like the one we did for the authors and the code can be accessed from the provided GitHub link.

Our next step is to build the user interface, which consists of our application's web pages.

Creating web pages

We will build our user interface by simulating the path a user will take to access the system, create the first author, change its name, and then delete it.

Creating homepage

Let us start building the user interface from the home page of our application. Continuing with our TDD practice, let us create a test to check if the homepage exists and if it has the content we expect. The interface tests will be created in the **ViewTest.php** file in the same directory as **StorageTest.php**, that is, the **tests** directory.

Let us implement the following method in the **StorageTest** class to test the homepage:

```
    public function testIndex()
    {
        $path = realpath(__DIR__ . '/../');
        $descriptorspec = array(
            0 => ["pipe", "r"],
            1 => ["pipe", "w"],
            2 => ["file", "/dev/null", "a"]
          );
        $process = proc_open('nohup php -S localhost:8008
&',$descriptorspec,$path);
```

```
    $rest = new Rest();
    $response = $rest->doGet([],'localhost:8008/index.php',200);
    $this->assertStringContainsString('Librarian',$response);
    proc_terminate($process);
}
```

Let us understand what the **testIndex** method does, as follows:

- Using the **proc_open** method starts a background process for the built-in PHP server. The **$descriptorspec** variable is a descriptor of the process execution configuration. The first element of this array is **standard input (stdin)**, open for **read-only (r)**. The second element is **standard output (stdout)**, open for **writing (w)**. The third element is the **error output (stderr)**, open for writing in the form of **addition (a)**. The **proc_open** function returns a variable of type resource.

- The **nohup** command is used is used to prevent the locking of the terminal because the server runs expecting requests. The **&** character is used to indicate running in the background.

- An object of the **Rest** class is instantiated to make an HTTP GET request to the homepage.

- The method checks whether the page contains the text **Librarian**.

- Finally, the method kills the process using the **proc_terminate** function.

On the first attempt, there will be an error because the test method will not find the **Rest** class. This class belongs to a library that we can install with Composer, as follows:

$ composer require fgsl/rest

After installing the component, you need to declare its namespace at the top of the **ViewTest.php** file, as follows:

use Fgsl\Rest\Rest;

On the second attempt, the method will fail because the page does not exist. You will probably see a message with error 404, which is the HTTP status for document not found. Let us then create the **index.php** file, which is our homepage. Its content will be as follows:

```
<!doctype html>
<html>
<head>
<title>Librarian</title>
</head>
<body>
<h1>Librarian</h1>
<ul>
```

```
<li><a href="author.list.php">Authors</a></li>
<li><a href="book.list.php">Books</a></li>
</ul>
</body>
</html>
```

With the page created, the **testIndex** method will be executed successfully.

Let us remember the third step of TDD, the refactoring step, when we improve the code that is working. Let us resume this step now because it is an opportune moment. When testing an HTML page, we can check its content using the XPath query language. This language allows you to browse elements of HTML and XML documents. With XPath, we can check if the page has the structure we expect.

Note: The XPath specifications are available at https://www.w3.org/TR/xpath

With XPath, we can check, for example, whether the first anchor element in the unordered list on the **index.php** page has the value **Authors**. Let us add the following statements to the **testIndex** method:

```
$doc = new DomDocument();
$doc->loadHTML($response);
$xpath = new DOMXpath($doc);
$elements = $xpath->query("/html/body/ul");
$this->assertEquals('Authors',$elements[0]->childNodes[1]-
>nodeValue);
```

Let us understand what these instructions do, as follows:

- The **DomDocument** class serves to represent the content of an HTML or XML file as a hierarchy of objects using the **Document Object Model (DOM)**. The **loadHTML** method loads HTML content and converts its structure to an object.

- The **DOMXpath** class creates a search object for a **DOMDocument** object. The **DOMXpath** query method allows you to search for one or more elements of the document, returning an object or an array of objects.

- The child elements of an HTML or XML element (tag) in the DOM are retrieved by the **childNodes** attribute. The value of an element (the text between the tags) is retrieved by the **nodeValue** attribute.

Note: If the HTML is not well formed, the loadHTML method will probably fail.

As a final improvement to the **testIndex** method, we will move the call to the **proc_terminate** function to just after the call to the **Rest::doGet** method. We do not need to keep the web server process active after we make the request.

Creating the listing page

Let us add the following test method to the **ViewTest** class:

```
public function testListAuthors()
{
    saveAuthor('Márquez','García','Gabriel');
    saveAuthor('Borges','Luis','Jorge');
    saveAuthor('Llosa','Vargas','Mario');
    $process = $this->startPHPServer();
    $rest = new Rest();
    $response = $rest->doGet([],'localhost:8008/author.list.php',200);
    proc_terminate($process);
    $doc = new DomDocument();
    $doc->loadHTML($response);
    $xpath = new DOMXpath($doc);
    $elements = $xpath->query("/html/body/h1");
    $this->assertEquals('Authors',$elements[0]->childNodes[0]-
>nodeValue);
    $this->assertStringContainsString('Jorge Luis Borges',$response);
    unlink(getPathForFile('author'));
}
```

Let us understand what the **testListAuthors** method does, as follows:

- It saves three authors by calling the **saveAuthor** method.
- It starts the built-in PHP web server and makes a request to the author listing page.
- It checks whether there is an **h1** element with the value **Authors**, specifically the first node.
- It checks if the page has the text **Jorge Luis Borges**, which is the full name of one of the three added authors.
- It removes the author's file, using the path provided by **getPathForFile** function.

On the first attempt, there will be an error because the test method will not find the **saveAuthor** method. Let us implement it in **book.functions.php**, as follows:

```
function saveAuthor($lastName, $middleName, $firstName)
{
    $fileFormat = getConfig()['file_format'];

    $saved = false;
```

```php
switch($fileFormat){
    case 'txt':
        $saved = saveAuthorInPlainText($lastName, $middleName,
$firstName);
        break;
    case 'csv':
        $saved = saveAuthorInCSV($lastName, $middleName, $firstName);
        break;
    case 'json':
        $saved = saveAuthorInJSON($lastName, $middleName, $firstName);
}
    return $saved;
}
```

The **saveAuthor** function is a proxy to the specific record writing functions. You also can see that on the second attempt, there will be an error because the **file_format key** was not found in the **book.config.php** file. Let us add this key, setting it to **txt**, as follows:

```php
'file_format' => 'txt'
```

On the third attempt, the test method will fail because the method **startPHPServer** does not exist. Let us implement it in the **ViewTest** class, as follows:

```php
private function startPHPServer()
{
    $path = realpath(__DIR__ . '/../');
    $descriptorspec = array(
        0 => ["pipe", "r"],
        1 => ["pipe", "w"],
        2 => ["file", "/dev/null", "a"]
    );
    return proc_open('nohup php -S localhost:8008
&',$descriptorspec,$path);
}
```

The **startPHPServer** method will avoid repeating these instructions to start the built-in PHP web server, an operation we will do in all user interface test methods. Replace the web server startup instructions in the **testIndex** method with the call to the **startPHPServer** method. The **test** method will become smaller, and we will avoid code repetition.

In the fourth attempt, the test method will fail because the page does not exist. You will probably see a message with error 404, which is the HTTP status for document not found. Let us then create the **author.list.php** file. Its content will be as follows:

```
<!doctype html>
<html>
<head>
<title>Librarian</title>
</head>
<body>
<h1>Authors</h1>
<a href="author.edit.php">Add an author</a>
<table>
<thead>
<tr>
<th>code</th>
<th>name</th>
<th>action</th>
</tr>
</thead>
<tbody>
<?=listAuthorsInTable()?>
</tbody>
</table>
</body>
</html>
```

In the fifth attempt, the method will fail because it does not find **Jorge Luis Borges** on the page. In fact, none of the authors are on the page, but you must have noticed a call to the **listAuthorsInTable** function in the **author.list.php** file. The aim of this function is to generate an HTML table with the registered authors. Let us implement it in the **book.functions.php** file, as follows:

```
function listAuthorsInTable()
{
    $fileFormat = getConfig()['file_format'];
    $authors = [];
    switch($fileFormat){
        case 'txt':
            $authors = readAuthorsInPlainText();
            break;
        case 'csv':
            $authors = readAuthorsInCSV();
            break;
```

```
        case 'json':
            $authors = readAuthorsInJSON();
    }
    $html = '';
    foreach($authors as $author){
        $html.='<tr>';
        $html.='<td><a href="author.edit.php?code=' . $author['code'] .
'">' . $author['code'] . '</a><td>';
        $html.="<td>{$author['first_name']} {$author['middle_name']}
{$author['last_name']}<td>";
        $html.='<td><a href="author.delete.php?code=' . $author['code'] .
'">remove</a><td>';
        $html.='</tr>';
    }
    return $html;
}
```

As you can see, this function reads the authors from the configured file and generates an HTML block with table rows. In the sixth attempt, the method will fail again, stating that it does not find **Jorge Luis Borges** on the page. The test method will show the HTML page content, and now you will see that the page ends in the **tbody** tag and not in the **html** tag. It happens because the page rendering is interrupted when calling the **listAuthorsInTable** function because the **author.list.php** file does not find it. It does not find it because it did not import the Composer **autoload** file. We need to add the following lines at the beginning of the **author.list.php** file:

```php
<?php
require 'vendor/autoload.php';
?>
```

In the seventh attempt, the method will fail because the function **getPathForFile** does not exists. Let us implement in **book.functions.php**, as follows:

```php
function getPathForFile(string $entity)
{
    $fileFormat = getConfig()['file_format'];

    $path = '';
    switch($fileFormat){
        case 'txt':
```

```
            $path = getConfig()[$entity . '_plaintext_filepath'];
            break;
        case 'csv':
            $path = getConfig()[$entity . '_csv_filepath'];
            break;
        case 'json':
            $path = getConfig()[$entity . '_json_filepath'];
    }
    return $path;
}
```

After this, the **testListAuthors** method will run successfully.

Creating edition form

Let us add the following test method to **ViewTest** class:

```
public function testNewAuthor()
{
    $process = $this->startPHPServer();
    $rest = new Rest();
    $response = $rest->doGet([],'localhost:8008/author.edit.php',200);
    proc_terminate($process);
    $doc = new DomDocument();
    $doc->loadHTML($response);
    $xpath = new DOMXpath($doc);
    $nodeList = $xpath->query('//input[@type="text"]');
    $this->assertEquals(3,$nodeList->length);
    $node = $nodeList->item(0);
    $this->assertEmpty($node->nodeValue);
}
```

In this test method, we checked if the author's edit page has three **input** elements of type **text** and if the first element has no value. This test requires creating **author.edit.php** file as follows:

```
<!doctype html>
<html>
<head>
<title>Librarian</title>
</head>
<body>
```

```
<h1>Author</h1>
<form method="post" action="author.save.php">
<label for="first_name">First name:</label>
<input type="text" name="first_name"><br/>
<label for="middle_name">Middle name:</label>
<input type="text" name="middle_name"><br/>
<label for="last_name">Last name:</label>
<input type="text" name="last_name"><br/>
<input type="submit" value="save">
</form>
</body>
</html>
```

The **testNewAuthor** method tests the scenario where the user is going to add a new author, so the form is empty. Now, let us create the **testEditAuthor** method to test the scenario in which the user will change data for a registered author. The **testEditAuthor** method must be as follows:

```
    public function testEditAuthor()
    {
        saveAuthor('Sharma','Lakshmi','Raj');
        $process = $this->startPHPServer();
        $rest = new Rest();
        $response = $rest->doGet([],'localhost:8008/author.edit.
php?code=1',200);
         proc_terminate($process);
        $doc = new DomDocument();
        $doc->loadHTML($response);
        $xpath = new DOMXpath($doc);
        $nodeList = $xpath->query('//input[@type="text"]');
        $this->assertEquals(3,$nodeList->length);
        $node = $nodeList->item(0);
        $this->assertEquals('Raj',$node->getAttributeValue('value'));
        unlink(getPathForFile('author'));
    }
```

This test will fail because the input field for the author's first name is empty.

We need to implement instructions in the **author.edit.php** file to retrieve author data from the code.

First, let us add the following block of instructions to the beginning of the **author.edit.php** file:

```php
<?php
require 'vendor/autoload.php';
$code = $_GET['code'] ?? 0;
$author = getAuthorByCode($code);
?>
```

If you run the tests again, with just this modification, the **testNewAuthor** and **testEditAuthor** methods will show an error in the **loadHTML** method of the **DomDocument** class. This occurs because the **getAuthorByCode** function does not exist, and the HTML page defined by the **author.edit.php** file is not rendered.

Let us implement the **getAuthorByCode** function in the **book.functions.php** file, as follows:

```php
function getAuthorByCode($code)
{
    $fileFormat = getConfig()['file_format'];

    $author = [];
    switch($fileFormat){
        case 'txt':
            $author = readAuthorInPlainTextByCode($code);
            break;
        case 'csv':
            $author = readAuthorInCSVByCode($code);
            break;
        case 'json':
            $author = readAuthorInJSONByCode($code);
    }
    if (empty($author)){
        $author = [
            'first_name' => '',
            'middle_name' => '',
            'last_name' => ''
        ];
    }
    return $author;
}
```

If you run the tests again, you will have the impression that everything has gotten worse because the other tests that were working will fail. The problem is that, when calling the **getAuthorByCode** method and testing to include a new author, an error occurs because the authors file does not exist. It is only created when an author is added. So, we need to ensure that the author's file exists before trying to read its contents. To do this, we will create the prepareFile function in the **book.functions.php** file, as follows:

```php
function prepareFile(string $entity)
{
    $path = getPathForFile($entity);
    if (!file_exists($path)){
        $handle = fopen($path,'w');
        fclose($handle);
    }
}
```

The **prepareFile** function checks whether the file exists. If it does not exist, it creates a file with no content. We will call this function in the **author.edit.php** file, before reading the author, as follows:

```php
<?php
require 'vendor/autoload.php';
$code = $_GET['code'] ?? 0;
prepareFile('author');
$author = getAuthorByCode($code);
?>
```

If you run the tests again, the assertion will say that the first text box does not contain the value **Raj** because we do not associate author attributes with form fields. We need to modify the HTML form, and it will be as follows:

```html
<form method="post" action="author.save.php">
<label for="first_name">First name:</label>
<input type="text" name="first_name" value="<?=$author['first_name']?>"><br/>
<label for="middle_name">Middle name:</label>
<input type="text" name="middle_name" value="<?=$author['middle_
name']?>"><br/>
<label for="last_name">Last name:</label>
<input type="text" name="last_name" value="<?=$author['last_name']?>"><br/>
<input type="submit" value="save">
</form>
```

We use PHP's short syntax to associate the author's name with the value attribute of the input element. With this change, all tests will finally run successfully, but not for long time because we have not finished our author registration yet.

Saving records from data sent by form

Let us add the following test method to **ViewTest** class:

```
public function testSaveAuthor()
{
    $data = [
        'first_name' => 'Fyodor',
        'middle_name' => 'Mikhailovich',
        'last_name' => 'Dostoevsky'
    ];
    $process = $this->startPHPServer();
    $rest = new Rest();
    $response = $rest->doPost($data, [],'localhost:8008/author.save.
php',302);
     proc_terminate($process);
    $this->assertStringContainsString('Record saved
successfully!',$response);
    unlink(getPathForFile('author'));
}
```

This test simulates sending data through an HTML form using the HTTP POST method. When running the test, it will fail because the **author.save.php** file does not exist. Let us create it with this content, as follows:

```php
<?php
require 'vendor/autoload.php';
$firstName = $_POST['first_name'] ?? null;
$middleName = $_POST['middle_name'] ?? null;
$lastName = $_POST['last_name'] ?? null;
$message = 'The record has not been recorded';
if ($firstName == null || $middleName == null || $lastName == null){
    $message = 'No data, no recording';
} else if (saveAuthor($lastName,$middleName,$firstName)) {
    $message = 'Record saved successfully!';
}
header('location: author.message.php?message=' . base64_encode($message));
```

Let us understand what the **author.save.php** does, as follows:

- It attempts to read data sent via HTTP POST.
- If there is data, it writes this data to a text file.

- It redirects to another page using the header function, sending the message encoded in **base64**.

Now, the test will fail because the **author.message.php** file does not exist. Let us create it with the following content:

```
<!doctype html>
<html>
<head>
<title>Librarian</title>
</head>
<body>
<p><?=base64_decode($_GET['message'] ?? 'no message')?></p>
<a href="author.list.php">Authors</a>
</body>
</html>
```

With this change, all tests will finally run successfully. We have only tested the scenario where a user adds an author. We need to test the scenario where a user updates an author. Let us create a test method in the **ViewTest** class to add an author and change their last name by simulating submitting an HTML form via HTTP POST. This method will be as follows:

```
    public function testUpdateAuthor()
    {
        $data = [
            'first_name' => 'Boris',
            'middle_name' => 'Leonidovich',
            'last_name' => 'Pasternak'
        ];
        saveAuthor($data['last_name'],$data['middle_name'],$data['first_
name']);
        $data['code'] = 1;
        $data['last_name'] = 'Neigauz';
        $process = $this->startPHPServer();
        $rest = new Rest();
        $response = $rest->doPost($data, [],'localhost:8008/author.save.
php',302);
      proc_terminate($process);
        $this->assertStringContainsString('Record updated
successfully!',$response);
        $author = getAuthorByCode(1);
```

```
        $this->assertEquals('Neigauz',$author['last_name']);
        unlink(getPathForFile('author'));
    }
```

It will fail on the first try because neither the form nor the recording script is prepared for a record change.

First, let us add a hidden input field to the author form in the **author.edit.php** file, immediately after the last name field, as follows:

fsff

As you can see, this hidden field will store the author code. The second step is to modify the **author.save.php** file so that it retrieves an existing record and modifies it. This file will be as follows:

```php
<?php
require 'vendor/autoload.php';
$code = $_POST['code'] ?? 0;
$firstName = $_POST['first_name'] ?? null;
$middleName = $_POST['middle_name'] ?? null;
$lastName = $_POST['last_name'] ?? null;
$message = 'The record has not been recorded';
if ($firstName == null || $middleName == null || $lastName == null){
    $message = 'No data, no recording';
}
if ($code == 0 && saveAuthor($lastName,$middleName,$firstName)) {
    $message = 'Record saved successfully!';
}
if ($code <> 0 && updateAuthor($code,$lastName,$middleName,$firstName)) {
    $message = 'Record updated successfully!';
}
header('location: author.message.php?message=' . base64_encode($message));
```

The test will still fail because we need to implement the **updateAuthor** function in the **book.functions.php** file, as follows:

```php
function updateAuthor($code, $lastName, $middleName, $firstName)
{
    $fileFormat = getConfig()['file_format'];

    $data = [
        'last_name' => $lastName,
        'middle_name' => $middleName,
```

```
        'first_name' => $firstName
    ];


    $saved = false;
    switch($fileFormat){
        case 'txt':
            $saved = updateAuthorInPlainText($code, $data);
            break;
        case 'csv':
            $saved = updateAuthorInCSV($code, $data);
            break;
        case 'json':
            $saved = updateAuthorInJSON($code, $data);
    }
    return $saved;
}
```

With this change, all tests ran successfully again. Let us finish our registration implementing the removal of authors.

Removing record

Let us add the following test method to the **ViewTest** class:

```
    public function testDeleteAuthor()
    {
        $data = [
            'first_name' => 'Vladimir',
            'middle_name' => 'Vladimirovich',
            'last_name' => 'Nabokov'
        ];
        saveAuthor($data['last_name'],$data['middle_name'],$data['first_
name']);
        $process = $this->startPHPServer();
        $rest = new Rest();
        $response = $rest->doGet([],'localhost:8008/author.delete.
php?code=1',302);
        proc_terminate($process);
        $this->assertStringContainsString('Record deleted
successfully!',$response);
```

```
    $author = getAuthorByCode(1);
    $this->assertEmpty($author['last_name']);
    unlink(getPathForFile('author'));
}
```

As we know, the test will fail the first time. It will fail because the **author.delete.php** file does not exist.

Let us create it with the following content:

```php
<?php
require 'vendor/autoload.php';
$code = $_GET['code'] ?? 0;
$message = 'The record has not been deleted';
if ($code == 0){
    $message = 'It cannot delete what does not exist';
}
if ($code <> 0 && deleteAuthor($code)) {
    $message = 'Record deleted successfully!';
}
header('location: author.message.php?message=' . base64_encode($message));
```

In the second attempt, the test will still fail because the **deleteAuthor** function does not exist. Let us implement it in the **book.functions.php** file as follows:

```php
function deleteAuthor($code)
{
    $fileFormat = getConfig()['file_format'];

    $deleted = false;
    switch($fileFormat){
        case 'txt':
            $deleted = deleteAuthorInPlainText($code);
            break;
        case 'csv':
            $deleted = deleteAuthorInCSV($code);
            break;
        case 'json':
            $deleted = deleteAuthorInJSON($code);
    }
    return $deleted;
}
```

Now, the tests will run successfully, but before closing, since we are discussing removing records, it is worth remembering that we did not test the listing page without records. If we did not do this, the listing page would have a problem when trying to read records from a file that does not exist because it is only created when the first record is written. The solution is simple: just add the **prepareFile** function to the beginning of the **author. list.php** file, as follows:

```
require 'vendor/autoload.php';
$code = $_GET['code'] ?? 0;
prepareFile('author');
$author = getAuthorByCode($code);
?>
```

Now, our author registration is complete. You can start the web server and browse the pages we created from testing, including changing, listing, and deleting authors.

You can find the implementation for book registration in the **chapter03** directory of our repository. You will see that it is very similar to author registration.

Conclusion

In this chapter, we covered how to build a function driven PHP application. We covered the use of PHP to write and read data from text files in more than one format (plain text, CSV, and JSON). We discussed how to import a PHP file into another PHP file and how to use Composer to import a file without having to indicate its path every time.

In the next chapter, we are going to learn about how to build a function driven registration with storage in a relational database.

Points to remember

- You can read and write text files line by line using the fopen, fread, frwrite, and fclose functions.

- You can read and write the complete contents of a text file using the file_get_contents and file_put_contents functions.

- The fgetcsv and fputcsv functions respectively read and write a line in a file in CSV format.

- Changing and deleting records in a text file involves creating a new file.

- PHP can start operating system processes with proc_open and kill them with proc_terminate.

- The DomDocument and DOMXpath classes allow, respectively, loading HTML documents and searching for elements with the XPath query language.

Exercises

In the file book.config.php, replace any of the occurrences of dirname(__FILE__) by __DIR__, run the tests, and observe the error message. Undo this action and perform the following:

1. Analyze the functions in the book.functions.php file and identify which are tolerant to the failure of the file to be handled. Add code to these functions that prevents this type of failure.

2. Check for code that repeats between functions and create new functions to reduce repetitions.

Join our book's Discord space

Join the book's Discord Workspace for Latest updates, Offers, Tech happenings around the world, New Release and Sessions with the Authors:

https://discord.bpbonline.com

CHAPTER 4

Function Driven Registration with Relational Database Storage

Introduction

This chapter of the book will cover a refactoring of the book registration application, replacing the file system storage with a **relational database** (**RDB**) storage, using MySQL/MariaDB. This will be the first exercise of wide refactoring and the first step to thinking about the concept of decoupling. We will add the ability to read and write to database tables, making system storage configurable to work with both paradigms.

Structure

The chapter covers the following topics:

- Creating database and tables with MySQL
- Refactoring test classes and functions file
- Saving data to tables
- Reading data from tables
- Updating data to tables
- Removing data from tables
- Reviewing code

Objectives

By the end of this chapter, you will be able to build a function driven PHP application storing data in RDB. You will also be able to use PHP to create, recover, update, and delete records from database tables.

Creating database and tables with MySQL

We will modify the librarian project so that it can connect to RDB without losing the possibility of reading and writing data in text files. The database management system we will be using is MySQL. As we are using XAMPP, we will also use MariaDB, a fork of MySQL.

Let us model the datasets from the previous chapter as two tables. *Figure 4.1* illustrates **authors** and **books** tables related by author code. This **code** is the primary key in the **authors** table and a foreign key in the **books** table. For each record in the **authors** table, we can have *n* records in the **books** table.

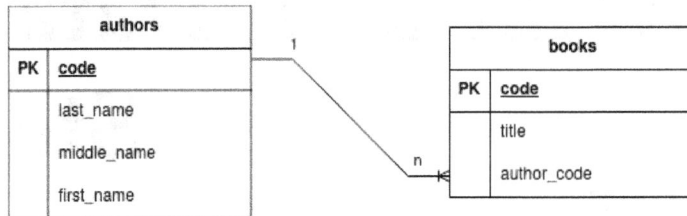

Figure 4.1: Physical data model diagram of the librarian database

In order to create these tables, we will use the phpMyAdmin web client available through XAMPP and follow the steps:

1. Start the Apache and MySQL servers and access **http://localhost** in your preferred browser. You will see a page like the one in *Figure 4.2*.

2. Click on the **phpMyAdmin** link at the top of the page.

Figure 4.2: XAMPP homepage at localhost

3. By default, the MariaDB root user in XAMPP does not have a password, so the link leads directly to the **phpMyAdmin** home page, as shown in *Figure 4.3*, without requiring a password. This can be easily changed with the help of the XAMPP security command.

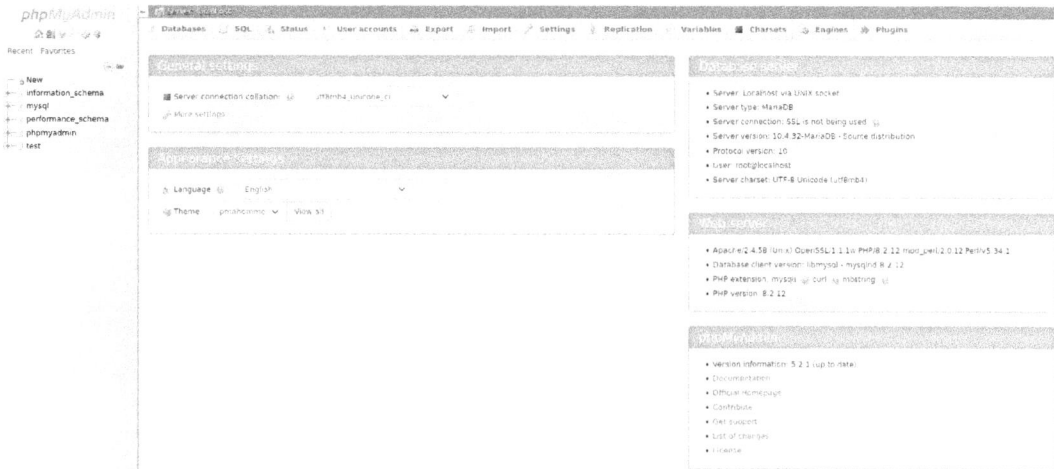

Figure 4.3: phpMyAdmin homepage

4. If you click on the **Databases** tab in the top menu of the page, the frame on the right will change and display a form for creating a database, as shown in *Figure 4.4*.

5. Let us fill in the blank name field with the **librarian** and click on the **Create** button. The character encoding is configured by default to a set of UTF-8, so we will have many characters available to register our authors and books.

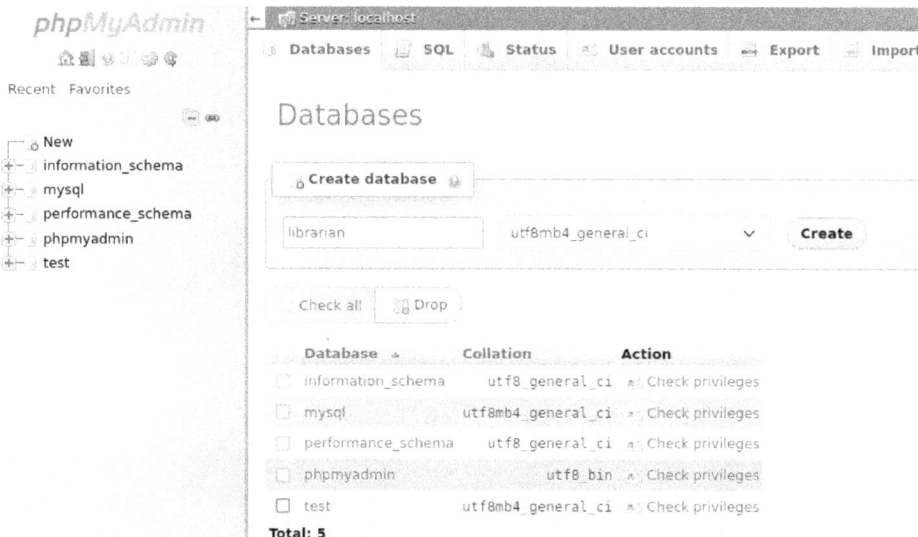

Figure 4.4: Create database in phpMyAdmin

6. After clicking the **Create** button, the database is created and you can see it in the database tree on the left. The frame on the right changes to a table creation form. Refer to *Figure 4.5*.

7. Now, we will fill in the **Table name** field with `authors`, our independent table, and put **4** in the **Number of columns** field.

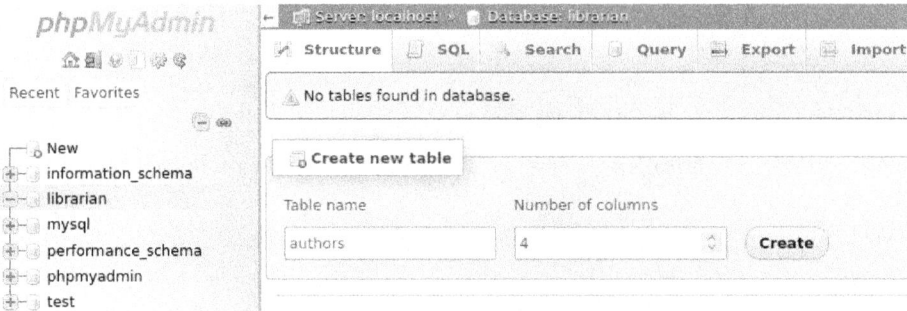

Figure 4.5: Create new table in phpMyAdmin

8. After clicking the **Create** button, the right frame changes to display the table field definition form, as shown in *Figure 4.6*. In this form, we will define the `code` field with type **INT** and we will configure it as the table's primary key, with auto-increment, that is, its value will be automatically generated in an arithmetic progression of reason 1. The fields `last_name`, `middle_name`, and `first_name` will be configured with the **VARCHAR** type with size **20**, according to the specification.

9. After defining the fields, we click on the **Save** button at the bottom to create the table.

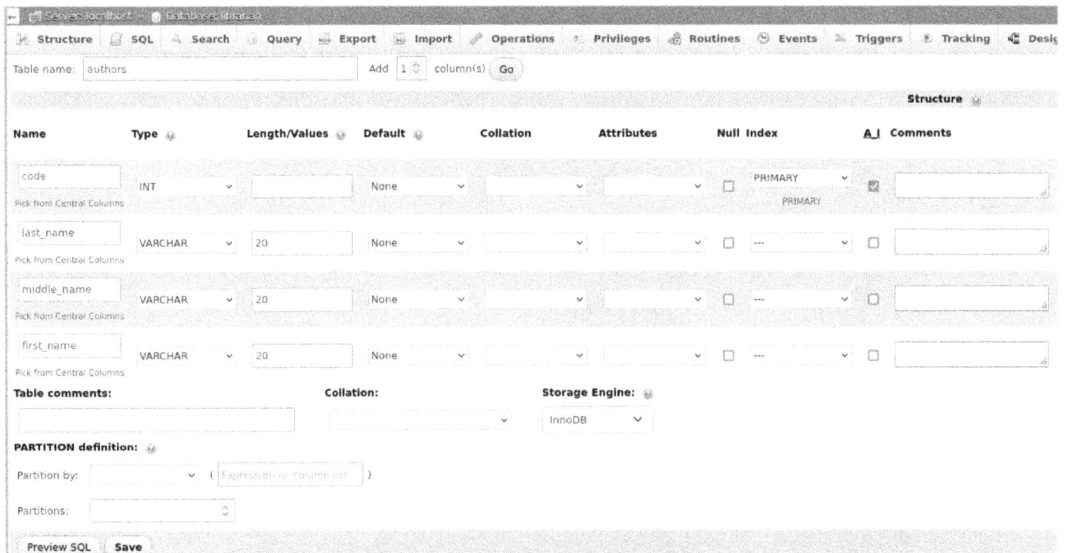

Figure 4.6: Authors table structure

10. There is one detail that may not be obvious. When selecting the **PRIMARY** option for the **code** field, a window titled **Add index** opens, as shown in *Figure 4.7*. It shows the configuration of the primary key, which can be simple or composite.

11. In the case of the **authors** table, the key is simple, consisting of just one field. Just click the **Go** button in that window when it opens.

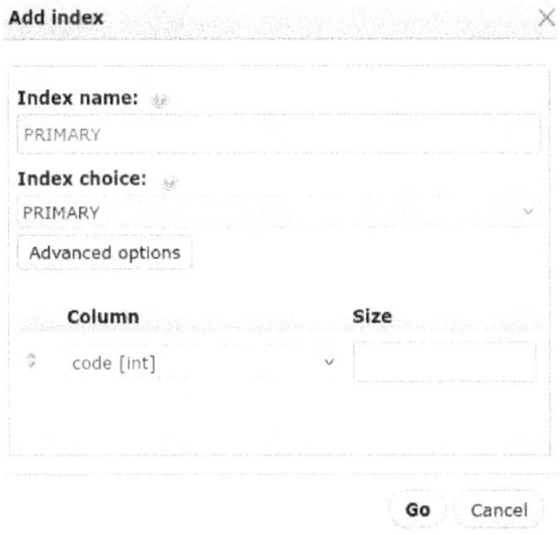

Figure 4.7: Primary key definition in phpMyAdmin

12. After creating the **authors** table, we will create the **books** table. After a database is created, it appears as a node in the tree structure in the left frame. Inside the **librarian** node, you will see a **New** node, which allows you to create a new table, as shown in *Figure 4.8*. Click this node to create the **books** table.

Figure 4.8: Librarian database and node to create a new table

13. After clicking the **Create** node, the right frame changes to display the table field definition form, as shown in *Figure 4.9*. Write **books**, without apostrophes in the **Table name** field. In this form, we will define the **code** field with type **INT** and configure it as the table's primary key, with auto-increment, as we did in the **authors** table.

14. The field **last_name**, and title will be configured with the **VARCHAR** type with size **80**, and the field **author_code** will be configured with the **INT** var type, according to the specification we made in the previous chapter. In the **author_ code** field, the relationship key between **authors** and **books** will be configured as an **INDEX**.

Note: In a real system, making the title length 80 maybe show errors in case of the title of the book is too long. Usually we use 255 to be sure saving the whole title correctly.

After defining the fields, we click on the **Save** button at the bottom to create the table, as shown in the following figure:

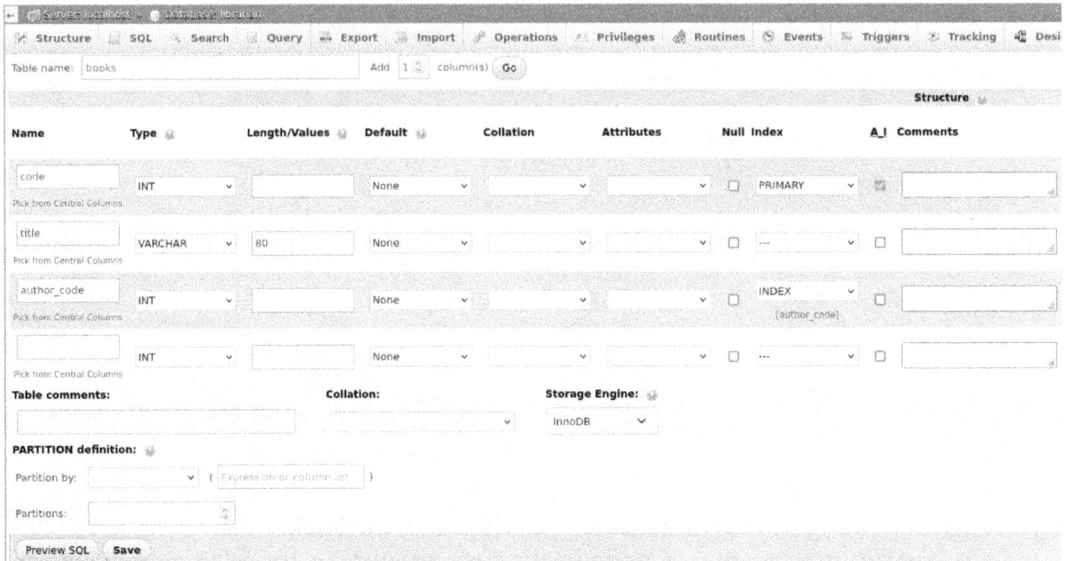

Figure 4.9: Books table structure

15. There is one detail that may not be obvious. When selecting the **INDEX** option for the **code** field, a window titled **Add index** opens, as shown in *Figure 4.10*. It shows the configuration of the index, including its name. You do not need to fill the **Index name** field in this form, because phpMyAdmin will create a default name. Just click the **Go** button in that window when it opens.

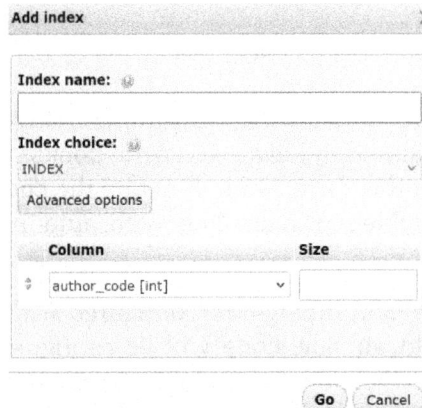

Figure 4.10: Index definition in phpMyAdmin

16. After creating the tables, let us create the relationship between them. In the left box, there is a **Designer** tab. Click it and the tables will be displayed in a physical model, which shows the fields and their data types. Then, click on the **Create relationship** item in the left menu.

Refer to the following figure for a better understanding:

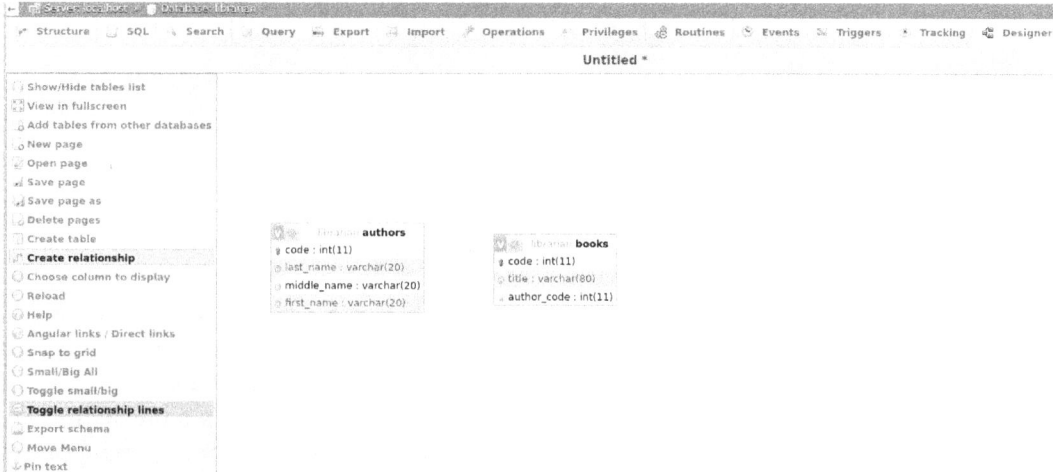

Figure 4.11: *Creating a relationship with phpMyAdmin Designer*

We will create a relationship between the two tables in a few steps, as follows:

1. The first step to defining the relationship is to select the referenced key, as shown in *Figure 4.12*. Click on the **code** field in the **authors** table.

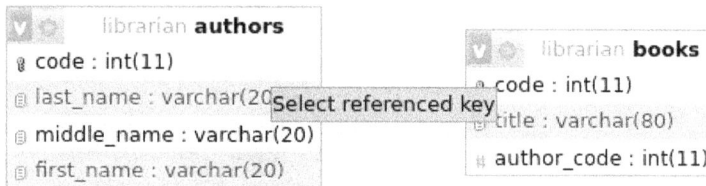

Figure 4.12: *Selecting referenced key*

2. Then, to define the relationship is to select the foreign key, as shown in *Figure 4.13*. Click on the **author_code** field in the **books** table.

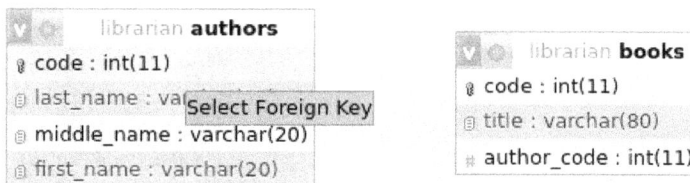

Figure 4.13: *Selecting foreign key*

3. After defining the referenced key and foreign key, the phpMyAdmin Designer opens a window to define the relationship's actions if the referenced key is deleted or changed, as shown in *Figure 4.14*:

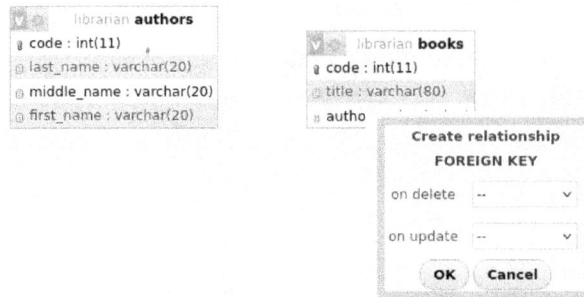

Figure 4.14: Selecting foreign key

4. Now, let us select the **CASCADE** option in the **on delete** and **on update** fields, as shown in *Figure 4.15*. This means that if a record is changed in the **authors** table, the value of the referenced key will be changed in the **books** table where it is a foreign key. And if a record is removed from the **authors** table, all records in the **books** table related to it will be deleted. In the file system implementation, we do not have this functionality. For example, if an author is removed from the **authors.txt** file, their books in the **books.txt** file will remain there.

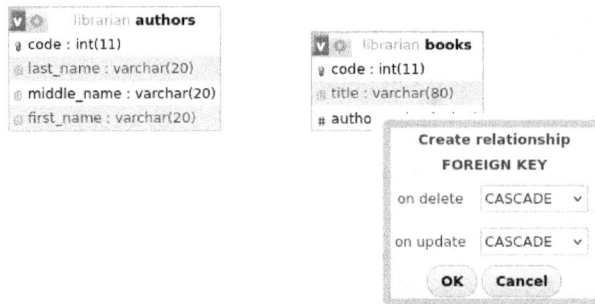

Figure 4.15: Setting CASCADE on delete and on update

After defining the relationship, phpMyAdmin Designer displays the two tables connected by a line, which goes from the code field in the **authors** table to the **author_code** field in the **books** table, as shown in *Figure 4.16*. We are ready to write and read from the **librarian** database.

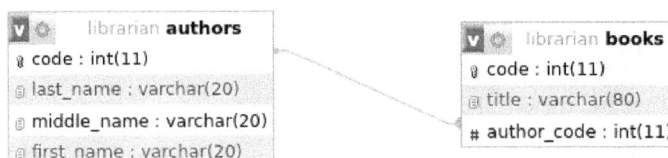

Figure 4.16: Relationship between authors and books tables

Refactoring test classes and functions file

Robert Cecil Martin, in his book *Clean Code*, advises us to pause and reflect on the new design of every few lines of code we write. If we are extremely focused on solving a problem with lines of code, we can end up creating another problem, which is managing the code we write. Constantly refactoring code is important to keep it readable, not only for others but for us. We need to try to keep small units of code that are quickly understandable. So, before starting to implement data persistence in our application using a RDB, let us reorganize the code base we have, which already has a considerable degree of complexity.

First of all, let us do some refactoring to avoid problems with starting PHP's built-in web server. It may be that, when running the tests, they eventually fail if the HTTP request is sent before the server is ready to respond. So let us modify the function that starts the server process so that it waits a second before returning. This means that the following line of the **ViewTest->startPHPServer** method:

```
return proc_open('nohup php -S localhost:8008 &',$descriptorspec,$path);
```

This line should be replaced by three lines, as follows:

```
$process = proc_open('nohup php -S localhost:8008
&',$descriptorspec,$path);
sleep(1);
return $process;
```

The second step is to prevent tests from destroying data files. As you noted in the previous chapter, we delete files at the end of each test, so that the next test always starts with a new file. However, we cannot mix test data with the data we use to develop an application. So, let us modify the test classes to make a copy of the text files and restore them at the end of test processing. Since each test class needs to do this, we should create an abstract class with backup and restore methods and have the **ViewTest** and **StorageTest** classes inherit these methods.

Let us create the **src** directory inside the **Librarian**. Inside **src**, we will create the **Test** directory. Inside the **Test**, we will create the **AbstractBackupTest.php** file, with the following content:

```
<?php
namespace Librarian\Test;

use PHPUnit\Framework\TestCase;

abstract class AbstractBackupTest extends TestCase
{
    public static function setUpBeforeClass(): void
    {
```

```
        $bookPath = getPathForFile('book');
        $authorPath = getPathForFile('author');
        if (file_exists($bookPath)){
            copy($bookPath,$bookPath . '.bkp');
            unlink($bookPath);
        }
        if (file_exists($authorPath)){
            copy($authorPath,$authorPath . '.bkp');
            unlink($authorPath);
        }
    }

    public static function tearDownAfterClass(): void
    {
        $bookPath = getPathForFile('book');
        $authorPath = getPathForFile('author');
        if (file_exists($bookPath . '.bkp')){
            copy($bookPath . '.bkp', $bookPath);
            unlink($bookPath . '.bkp');
        }
        if (file_exists($authorPath . '.bkp')){
            copy($authorPath . '.bkp', $authorPath);
            unlink($authorPath . '.bkp');
        }
    }
}
```

As you can observe, the **AbstractBackupTest** extends the **TestCase** class from **PHPUnit**, which means that **AbstractBackupTest** inherits every non-private attribute and method from **TestCase**. In addition, **AbstractBackupTest** implements the following methods:

- **setUpBeforeClass**: This method is executed once before all test methods in the class. In this case, it copies the text files of **authors** and **books** with the **.bkp** extension, if they exist.

- **tearDownAfterClass**: This method is executed once all test methods of the class have been executed. In this case, it restores the data files from the copies with **.bkp** extension and then deletes the copies.

For the **AbstractBackupTest** class to be found, we need to add the mapping between **namespace** and directory in the **composer.json** file. The **autoload** attribute will be as follows:

```
"autoload" : {
    "files": ["book.functions.php"],
    "psr-4": {
        "Librarian\\": "src/"
    }
},
```

After changing the **composer.json** file, you need to recreate the **autoload** class with the following command:

composer dumpautoload

Next, we change the **StorageTest** and **ViewTest** classes, so that they extend **AbstractBackupTest** instead of **TestCase**.

The **StorageTest** declaration will be as follows:

```
class StorageTest extends AbstractBackupTest
```

The **ViewTest** declaration will be as follows:

```
class ViewTest extends AbstractBackupTest
```

In both class files, the following statement should be replaced:

```
use PHPUnit\Framework\TestCase;
```

The previous statement should be replaced by the following:

```
use Librarian\Test\AbstractBackupTest;
```

The tests should continue to run successfully with these changes. Now, let us modify our application's function file, **book.functions.php**. We will extract the following specific functions to manipulate the plain text, CSV, and JSON formats to other files:

- **txt.functions.php**
- **csv.functions.php**
- **json.functions.php**

After extracting the functions, we will import the new files at the beginning of the **book. functions.php** file, as follows:

```
<?php
const AUTHOR_ROW_LENGTH = 65;
const BOOK_ROW_LENGTH = 89;

require_once 'txt.functions.php';
require_once 'csv.functions.php';
require_once 'json.functions.php';
```

Just as we divided the file system functions into three distinct files, let us divide the **StorageTest** class into three distinct test classes, as follows:

- **TxtTest**, with plain text tests.
- **CSVTest**, with CSV tests.
- **JSONTest** with JSON tests.

These three classes will inherit from **AbstractBackupTest**, and after they are created, the **StorageTest** class will be eliminated. The private method **StorageTest->deleteBookAndAuthors** must be moved to **AbstractBackupTest** class as a protected method.

The tests should continue to run successfully after these changes. We did not create any new functionality; we just reorganized our code.

Now, we can start implementing persistence in RDB.

Saving data to tables

Let us create the **DatabaseTest** class in the **test** directory, as we did with the other test classes. The initial structure of the class will be as the following declaration:

```php
<?php
use PHPUnit\Framework\TestCase;
use PHPUnit\Framework\Attributes\CoversNothing;


class DatabaseTest extends TestCase
{
}
```

Next, let us create a test in this class to know whether a record with the author *Herbert*, *George*, and *Wells* was saved to the **authors** table in the **librarian** database, as follows:

```php
    public function testSaveAuthorInDatabase()
    {
        $this->assertTrue(saveAuthorInDatabase('Wells','Herbert','George'));
    }
```

This test will fail because the **saveAuthorInDatabase** function does not exist. Now, we will create it in a file called **database.functions.php**, in the root directory of our application. The function will be as follows:

```php
function saveAuthorInDatabase($lastName, $middleName, $firstName)
{
    $stmt = $mysqli->prepare("INSERT INTO authors(last_name,middle_
```

```
name,first_name) VALUES (?, ?, ?)");
    $stmt->bind_param('sss', $lastName, $middleName, $firstName);
    return $stmt->execute();
}
```

The three instructions in this function do the following actions:

- The first instruction prepares a SQL **INSERT** statement for the **authors** table.

- The second instruction associates the function arguments with the table fields, in the order in which they were specified in the statement.

- The third instruction sends the statement with the associated arguments to be executed by the database. If successful, true is returned.

Note: The first argument of bind_param method uses i for int, d for float, s for string, and b for blob (a variable which will be sent in packets).

If you try to run the test, it still complains that the function does not exist. It is because you need to import the **database.functions.php** file into the **book.functions.php** file, with the following instruction:

```
require_once 'database.functions.php';
```

With this change, the test will display the following error:

```
Error: Call to a member function prepare() on null
```

The error message tells us that we are trying to call a method from something that is not an object. Indeed, the **$mysqli** variable did not receive any value. This variable needs to receive an object that establishes a connection to the librarian database. As this connection will be used in all database operations, we will not create it directly within the **saveAuthorInDatabase** function but will obtain it from another function. So, before calling the method prepare, we will add the following instructions:

```
$mysqli = getConnection();
```

Just adding this statement will not make the test run successfully. We need to implement this function, which will return an object of the **mysqli** class, which encapsulates operations for MySQL and Maria DB databases. We will implement this in the **database. functions.php** file, as follows:

```
function getConnection()
{
    $db = getConfig()['db'];
    return new mysqli($db['host'], $db['username'], $db['password'],
$db['database']);
}
```

For the **getConnection** function to work, we need to define the **db** key in the **book. config.php** configuration file, as follows:

```
'db' => [
    'host' => 'localhost',
    'username' => 'root',
    'password' => '',
    'database' => 'librarian'
]
```

Note: In our exercise, we are using the root user configured by XAMPP without a password. This can be tolerated in development, but never use the root user in production and never use a user without a password.

Despite the configuration, the following error will still occur if you have not started the database server:

mysqli_sql_exception: Connection refused

After starting the database, the test will finally pass, and an author will be successfully added to the **authors** table. Note that unlike text files, we do not need to worry about generating the author code, as the table already provides that. We do not need to read the last record to be able to increment the code. This responsibility lies with the table.

You should remember that in the last chapter, we said that we would follow the principle of always returning to the initial state. So, we need to restore the table to the initial state, before the test. Let us add the following statement to the **testSaveAuthorInDatabase** method:

```
$this->truncateTable('authors');
```

This method will delete all records from the table and reset the auto-increment counter. We have to implement this method. Let us use it as a private method:

```
private function truncateTable(string $table)
{
    $mysqli = getConnection();
    $mysqli->query('DELETE FROM ' . $table);
    $mysqli->query('ALTER TABLE ' . $table . ' AUTO_INCREMENT = 1');
}
```

We will use this method in each author test so that the table is always empty for the next test.

Reading data from tables

Since we have implemented author recording using tests, we now have data to read and can create read tests. Let us implement the following test method in the **DatabaseTest** class:

```
public function testReadAuthorInDatabase()
{
    saveAuthorInDatabase('Von Goethe','Wolfgang','Johann');
    saveAuthorInDatabase('Fitzgerald','Scott','Francis');
    saveAuthorInDatabase('Doyle','Arthur','Conan');
    $author = readAuthorInDatabaseByCode(2);
    $this->assertEquals('Scott',$author['middle_name']);
    $this->truncateTable('authors');
}
```

As you might expect, this test will fail on the first try because the **readAuthorDatabaseByCode** function does not exist. So, let us implement it in the **database.functions.php** file as follows:

```
function readAuthorInDatabaseByCode(int $code)
{
    $mysqli = getConnection();
    $result = $mysqli->query('SELECT * FROM authors WHERE code = ' .
$code);
    if ($result === false){
        return [];
    }
    return $result->fetch_assoc();
}
```

The function shown above does the following:

- It obtains the object from the **mysqli** class that establishes the connection to the database.

- It invokes the query method of the **mySQL** class to execute a SQL **SELECT** command.

- If no records are found, the **query** method returns **false** and the function returns an empty array.

- If at least one record is found, the result of the **query** method is an object of the **mysqli_result** class, which allows you to retrieve the records.

- The function invokes **the fetch_assoc** method of the **mysqli_result** class to obtain one only record in the form of an associative array, or dictionary, with field names as array keys.

After testing the reading of one author, we will implement a test to read a set of authors. Let us create the following test method in the **DatabaseTest** class:

```
public function testReadAuthorsInDatabase()
{
    saveAuthorInDatabase('Shelley','Wollstonecraft','Mary');
    saveAuthorInDatabase('Christie','Mary','Agatha');
    saveAuthorInDatabase('Lispector','Pinkhasivna','Chaya');
    $authors = readAuthorsInDatabase();
    $this->assertCount(3,$authors);
    $this->assertEquals('Agatha',$authors[1]['first_name']);
    $this->truncateTable('authors');
}
```

You know that this test will fail because **readAuthorsInDatabase** function does not exist. So, let us create it in the **book.functions.php**, as follows:

```
function readAuthorsInDatabase()
{
    $mysqli = getConnection();
    $result = $mysqli->query('SELECT * FROM authors');
    if ($result === false){
        return [];
    }
    return $result->fetch_all(MYSQLI_ASSOC);
}
```

Following are the two differences between this function and the previous function, which read one record:

- It executes a SQL **SELECT** command without a **WHERE** clause, which means that all table records will be returned by the database.

- It uses the **fetch_all** method, which returns a set of records. The **MYSQLI_ASSOC** constant is used to return associative arrays. The default behavior of **fetch_all** is to return an array with numeric indexes.

You should have observed that the number of lines for implementing the reading of records using a RDB is less than the number of lines we use to read records from text files. The database encapsulates the complexity we have to deal with when directly manipulating the file system.

Now that we have utilized writing and reading, let us implement updating.

Updating data to the tables

With data persisted in the database, in addition to reading it, we can change it. Let us implement the following test method in the **DatabaseTest** class:

```
public function testUpdateAuthorInDatabase()
{
    saveAuthorInDatabase('Maupassant','de','Guy');
    saveAuthorInDatabase('Saint-Exupéry','de','Antoine');
    saveAuthorInDatabase('Balzac','de','Honoré');
    $author = readAuthorInDatabaseByCode(1);
    $this->assertEquals('Guy',$author['first_name']);
    updateAuthorInDatabase(1,[
        'last_name' => 'Raspe',
        'middle_name' => 'Erich',
        'first_name' => 'Rudolf'
    ]);
    $author = readAuthorInDatabaseByCode(1);
    $this->assertEquals('Rudolf',$author['first_name']);
    $this->truncateTable('authors');
}
```

As you might expect, this test will fail on the first try because the **updateAuthorInDatabase** function does not exist. So, let us implement it in the **database.functions.php** file as follows:

```
function updateAuthorInDatabase(int $code, array $data)
{
    $mysqli = getConnection();
    $placeholders = '';
    $types = '';
    $values = [];
    foreach($data as $field => $value){
        $placeholders .= $field . ' = ?,';
        $types .= 's';
        $values[] = $value;
    }
    $placeholders = substr($placeholders,0,strlen($placeholders)-1);
    $stmt = $mysqli->prepare('UPDATE authors SET ' . $placeholders . '
WHERE code = ?');
```

```
    $stmt->bind_param($types, ...$values);
    return $stmt->execute();
}
```

Let us understand what the **updateAuthorInDatabase** function does:

- It iterates over the **$data** array received as an argument, changing the value of three variables: **$placeholders**, **$types**, and **$values**.

- **The $placeholders** variable is the concatenation of the value assignments to the fields, but in place of the values, we use the question mark as a placeholder.

- The **$types** variable is the concatenation of the data types of the fields to be changed, in the format expected by the **$stmt->bind_param** method.

- The **$values** variable is the array with the values to be changed.

- At the end of the iteration, the function removes the last character from the **$placeholders** variable, so that there is no comma at the end.

- The function prepares an SQL **UPDATE** command using the field names provided by the **$placeholders** variable.

- The function assigns values to fields using the **bind_param** method. Since we do not know how many fields will change, we use the **...** operator to pass the **$values** array as a variable set of arguments.

- The last instruction sends the statement with the associated arguments to be executed by the database. If successful, **true** is returned.

We create, retrieve, and update records in the **authors** table. Now, let us delete records.

Removing data from tables

Now we will complete the **create, read, update, and delete** (**CRUD**) of our registry based on a RDB. We started with the letter C (create), writing data to the database. Then we implemented the letter R (read), reading data from the database. In the third step we did the U (update), changing data written to the database. We finish with the D (delete), deleting data written to the database.

Let us implement the following test method in the **DatabaseTest** class:

```
    public function testDeleteAuthorInDatabase()
    {
        saveAuthorInDatabase('Assis','de','Machado');
        saveAuthorInDatabase('Alencar','de','José');
        saveAuthorInDatabase('Queiroz','de','Rachel');
        $author = readAuthorInDatabaseByCode(2);
        $this->assertEquals('Alencar',$author['last_name']);
```

```
        deleteAuthorInDatabase(2);
        $author = readAuthorInDatabaseByCode(2);
        $this->assertEmpty($author);
        $this->truncateTable('authors');
    }
```

This test will fail on the first try because the **deleteAuthorInDatabase** function does not exist. So, let us implement it in the **database.functions.php** file as follows:

```
function deleteAuthorInDatabase(int $code)
{
    $mysqli = getConnection();
    $stmt = $mysqli->prepare('DELETE FROM authors WHERE code = ?');
    $stmt->bind_param('i', $code);
    return $stmt->execute();
}
```

Using the database, in comparison with the plain text storage, we reduced the number of instructions to delete a record from 20 to 4. With the **deleteAuthorInDatabase** function, we completed the author registration operations. Now, let us review our code so that the application's web interface starts using the database.

Reviewing code

After practicing the first two steps of **test-driven development** (**TDD**) in the previous sections, now we will use the third step, which is refactoring the code to improve it. We will make two improvements: A reduction in test execution time and the expansion of the web interface test coverage using databases and other text file options, in addition to plain text.

Reducing runtime of tests

You may have noticed that **PHPUnit** runtime increased considerably after we implemented the **ViewTest** class, which starts and stops the built-in PHP web server multiple times. This occurs because there is a one-second delay to ensure that the server is ready to respond to requests. This delay occurs with each request test.

All tests in the **ViewTest** class need the web server. So, instead of starting and stopping the server with each test, let us start it before the first test and end it after the last test. You may already suspect that we will do this by using the **setUpBeforeClass** and **tearDownAfterClass** methods, which we learned to use in this chapter.

Let us add a **static** attribute to the **ViewTest** class, to keep the server process within the class's visibility scope:

```
    private static $process;
```

Let us implement the **setUpBeforeClass** method, starting the web server and storing the process in the static variable **$process,** as follows:

```
public static function setUpBeforeClass(): void
{
    self::$process = self::startPHPServer();
}
```

We are calling the **startPHPServer** method with the **self** keyword instead of **$this**. We do this because we are in a static method, in class scope, so we cannot use **$this** which is object scope. But we also need to modify the **startPHPServer** method as it will now be called in the class scope. Thus, the signature of this method is as follows:

```
private function startPHPServer()
```

This way, the method can only be called by an instance of the class, with the **$this** keyword. We cannot use **$this** in a static method, only **self**. So, we add the **static** identifier to the **startPHPServer** method, so that it can be called with **self**. The signature will be as follows:

```
private static function startPHPServer()
```

In order to terminate the server process, let us implement the **tearDownAfterClass** method, as follows:

```
public static function tearDownAfterClass():void
{
    proc_terminate(self::$process);
}
```

Now, we can eliminate all lines with the following instruction:

```
$process = $this->startPHPServer();
```

We can use the following instruction as well:

```
proc_terminate($process);
```

After these changes, you can run **PHPUnit** again and you will notice that it runs faster. Now, there is only a one-second pause for the entire **ViewTest** class. We made the tests faster and reduced the number of lines by two times the number of tests.

Testing web interface with a database

After creating tests for database operations, we will test the web interface integrated with the database. We could do this by overriding the plain text file storage configuration for database. But if we do this, we will be reducing our test coverage, which was already not complete, because we did not test the web interface with CSV and JSON files. It would be appropriate for us to test the web interface with all storage options.

You should remember that we have implemented a procedure to separate the text files used for development from the text files used by the **PHPUnit** tests. We backup the text files, if they exist, and after we recovered them. For avoiding the destruction of development data from the database, we will create a test copy of the database. Using phpMyAdmin, you can create a copy of the **librarian** database using the **Copy database to** form, available in the **Operations** tab, as shown in *Figure 4.17*. Let us name the copy **librarian_test** after clicking the **Go** button, located on the right of the form. The copy of the database appears in the database tree in the left frame.

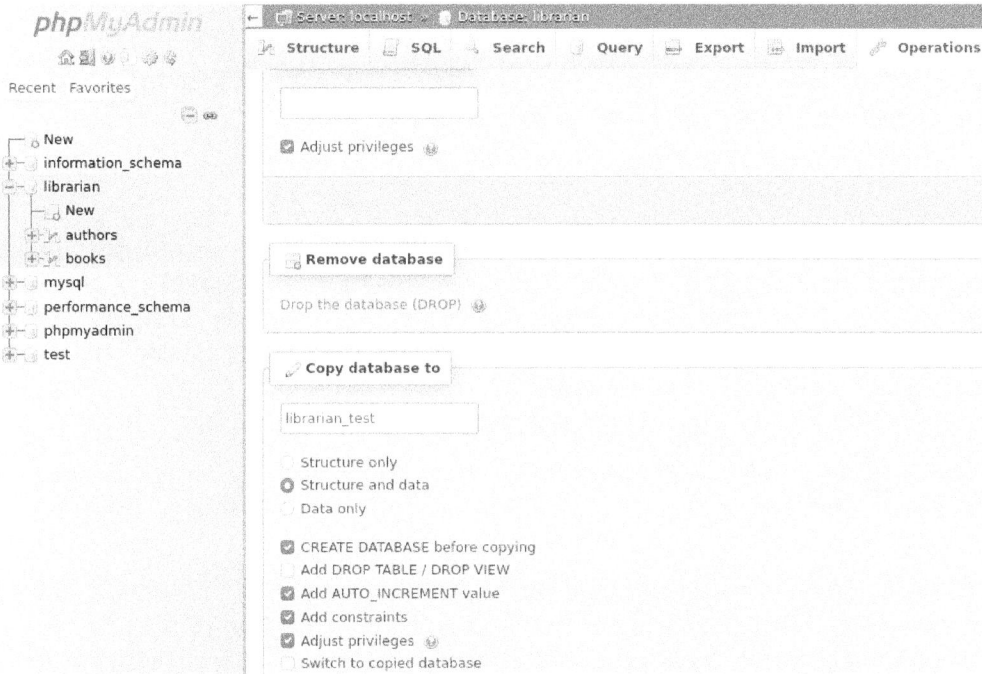

Figure 4.17: Copying a database in phpMyAdmin

Now, you may ask how the tests will connect to the **librarian_test** test database if the configuration file is pointing to the librarian development database. An alternative is to edit the file and manually change the name of the database when browsing the application using a browser and change it again before running the tests but this alternative is laborious and depends on our memory. Let us do something more automatic and safer, refer to the following steps:

1. The first step is to implement a function in the **book.functions.php** file to change the contents of the configuration file, as follows:

```
function replaceConfigFileContent(string $search, string $replace)
{
    $configPath = dirname(__FILE__) . DIRECTORY_SEPARATOR . 'book.
config.php';
```

```
$content = file_get_contents($configPath);
$content = str_replace($search, $replace, $content);
file_put_contents($configPath, $content);
}
```

2. We will call this function in the **ViewTest::setupBeforeClass** method, as follows:

```
replaceConfigFileContent("'database' => 'librarian'","'database' =>
'librarian_test'");
```

3. Next, we will call **replaceConfigFileContent** function in the **ViewTest::testDownAfterClass** method, as follows:

```
replaceConfigFileContent("'database' => 'librarian_test'","'database'
=> 'librarian'");
```

Now, when you run the tests, the **ViewTest** class will use the **librarian_test** database and not the **librarian** database. Let us replicate this in the **DatabaseTest** class so that it also uses the **librarian_test** database. Simply implement the **setUpBeforeClass** and **tearDownAfterClass** methods by calling the **replaceConfigFileContent** function, according to the **ViewTest** class example.

Well, despite this change, the **DatabaseTest** class effectively tests the test database, but the **ViewTest** class does not. The **ViewTest** class tests storage in a plain text file, according to the **file_format** setting. Let us change this by using the same strategy adopted to use the test database, as follows:

1. We will give a more appropriate name to the configuration that will determine the origin and destination of the data. Let us modify the **file_format** configuration key in **the book.config.php** file to **storage_format** and the **$fileFormat** variable to **$storageFormat**.

2. The second step is to replace all occurrences of the **file_format** key in the **book. functions.php** file with **storage_format**.

3. We will add the following statement to the **ViewTest::setUpBeforeClass** method:

```
replaceConfigFileContent("'storage_format' => 'txt'","'storage_
format' => 'rdb'");
```

4. Add the following statement to the **ViewTest::tearDownAfterClass** method:

```
replaceConfigFileContent("'storage_format' => 'rdb'","'storage_
format' => 'txt'");
```

Until now, these changes will only cause errors, as the read and write functions used by the web interface do not use the **rdb** configuration key yet.

5. Add a case to the switch structure of the **saveAuthor** function in the **book.functions.php** file, as follows:

```
        break;
    case 'rdb':
        $saved = saveAuthorInDatabase($lastName, $middleName,
$firstName);
```

6. Add a case to the switch structure of the **listAuthorsInTable** function in the **book.functions.php** file, as follows:

```
        break;
    case 'rdb':
        $authors = readAuthorsInDatabase();
```

7. Add a case to the switch structure of the **getAuthorByCode** function in the **book.functions.php** file, as follows:

```
        break;
    case 'rdb':
        $author = readAuthorInDatabaseByCode($code);
```

8. Add a case to the switch structure of the **updateAuthor** function in the **book.functions.php** file, as follows:

```
        break;
    case 'rdb':
        $saved = updateAuthorInDatabase($code, $data);
```

9. Add a case to the switch structure of the **deleteAuthor** function in the **book.functions.php** file, as follows:

```
        break;
    case 'rdb':
        $deleted = deleteAuthorInDatabase($code);
```

You might imagine that we can now run the tests, but we still have problems. Remember that we created a procedure to ensure that the text file existed before any records were created. This procedure is directly coupled to our web interface in the **author.list.php** and **author.edit.php** files. This is the call to the **prepareFile** function.

10. Now, we will remove this coupling by deleting the **prepareFile** function call on these two files. Next, we will add a call to this function for each case of **getAuthorByCode** and **listAuthorsInTable** functions that read text files.

Let us see an example. The following case is from the **getAuthorByCode** function for reading an author in a plain text file:

```
case 'txt':
    $author = readAuthorInPlainTextByCode($code);
    break;
```

It will be as follows:

```
case 'txt':
    prepareFile('author');
    $author = readAuthorInPlainTextByCode($code);
    break;
```

Note that we destroy the text files at the end of each test of **ViewTest** class. Now, we need to clear the table. We want to have the ability to test the web interface with all the storage formats. So, we will create a function that can delete a text file or clear a database table according to the configuration. Let us implement the **clearEntity** function in the **book.functions.php** file, as follows:

```
function clearEntity(string $entity)
{
    $storageFormat = getConfig()['storage_format'];

    $path = '';
    switch($storageFormat){
        case 'txt':
        case 'csv':
        case 'json':
            unlink(getPathForFile($entity));
            break;
        case 'rdb':
            truncateTable($entity . 's');
    }
}
```

As you may remember, if you do not put a break in the case of a switch, PHP continues executing the next cases. Therefore, as the procedure for plain text, CSV and JSON files are the same, we do not need to repeat the instruction. You may have noticed that the **truncateTable** function does not exist. We need to implement it in the **database.functions.php** file since it is a function that affects the database. We already have the implementation of this function. Just move the **truncateTable** method from the **DatabaseTest** class to the **database. functions.php** file and remove the private identifier. Next, we need to replace all calls to the **truncateTable** method in **DatabaseTest** class with a call to the **TruncateTable** function. For example, take a look at the following code:

```
$this->truncateTable('authors');
```

It will be as follows:

```
truncateTable('authors');
```

11. So, the next step is to remove the calls to the unlink function in the **ViewTest** class and replace them with calls to the **clearEntity** function.

Let us give an example. Look at the following instruction:

```
unlink(getPathForFile('author'));
```

It will be replaced by the following:

```
clearEntity('author');
```

Finally, after all these steps, we are ready to successfully run the tests with the web interface accessing the database.

Expanding test coverage

After creating tests for database operations, we will test the web interface integrated with the database. We could do this by overriding the plain text file storage configuration for the database. But if we do this, we will be reducing our test coverage, which was already not complete because we did not test the web interface with CSV and JSON files. It would be appropriate for us to test the web interface with all storage options.

Let us do this expansion of test coverage with a few steps, as follows:

1. Create four copies of the **ViewTest** class named **ViewTxtTest**, **ViewCSVTest**, **ViewJSONTest**, and **ViewDatabaseTest**. Then, delete the **ViewTest** class.

   Note: Copying a class means copying the file where the class is declared. Deleting a class means deleting the file where the class is declared. These operations consider the good practice that there is one class per file.

2. As the default configuration is plain text storage, the **ViewTxtTest** class does not need to modify the configuration file. So, in this class, the **setupBeforeClass** method will be as follows:

   ```
   public static function setUpBeforeClass(): void
   {
       self::$process = self::startPHPServer();
   }
   ```

   The **ViewTxtTest::tearDownAfterClass** method will be as follows:

   ```
   public static function tearDownAfterClass():void
   {
   ```

```
        proc_terminate(self::$process);
    }
```

3. In the **ViewCSVTest** class, you will need to modify the configuration file. So, the **setupBeforeClass** method will be as follows:

```
public static function setUpBeforeClass(): void
{
    self::$process = self::startPHPServer();
    replaceConfigFileContent("'storage_format' =>
'txt'","'storage_format' => 'csv'");
}
```

And the **ViewCSVTest::tearDownAfterClass** method will look like this:

```
public static function tearDownAfterClass():void
{
    proc_terminate(self::$process);
    replaceConfigFileContent("'storage_format' =>
'csv'","'storage_format' => 'txt'");
}
```

4. In the **ViewJSONTest** class, you will also need to modify the configuration file. So, the **setupBeforeClass** method will be as follows:

```
public static function setUpBeforeClass(): void
{
    self::$process = self::startPHPServer();
    replaceConfigFileContent("'storage_format' =>
'txt'","'storage_format' => 'json'");
}
```

The **ViewCSVTest::tearDownAfterClass** method will be as follows:

```
public static function tearDownAfterClass():void
{
    proc_terminate(self::$process);
    replaceConfigFileContent("'storage_format' =>
'json'","'storage_format' => 'txt'");
}
```

It is not necessary to change the **setUpBeforeClass** and **tearDownAfterClass** methods of the **ViewDatabaseTest** class because they already change the configuration file for reading and writing to the database.

You may have missed your book registration, but there is no need to worry. You can find the implementation for book registration in the **chapter04** directory of our repository. You will see that it is very similar.

Conclusion

In this chapter, we covered how to refactor the book registration application, replacing the file system storage with a RDB storage, using MySQL/MariaDB. We covered an exercise of wide refactoring and an important step to think about the concept of decoupling. We covered the addition of the ability to read and write to database tables, making system storage configurable to work with both paradigms.

In the next chapter, we are going to learn about how to build a function driven registration with document database storage.

Points to remember

- phpMyAdmin is a graphical tool for creating databases, tables, and relationships for MySQL and MariaDB. This tool is free and open-source software shipped with XAMPP, but it can be installed separately.

- One of the ways to connect to a MYSQL or MariaDB database is by using the PHP mysqli extension.

- The mysqli class has several methods for reading and writing data from a MySQL or MariaDB database by using the SQL.

Exercise

1. The readAuthorInDatabaseByCode and readAuthorsInDatabase functions have several of the same lines. Modify these functions so that one calls the other and there are no repetitions.

   Tip: Add an argument to the readAuthorsInDatabase function.

Join our book's Discord space

Join the book's Discord Workspace for Latest updates, Offers, Tech happenings around the world, New Release and Sessions with the Authors:

https://discord.bpbonline.com

CHAPTER 5

Function Driven Registration with Document Database Storage

Introduction

This chapter of the book will cover a refactoring of the book registration application, replacing the **relational database** (**RDB**) storage, using MySQL/MariaDB, with a document database storage based on MongoDB. We will add the ability to read and write to collections, widening the storage options of the application.

Structure

The chapter covers the following topics:

- Installing MongoDB and PHP support for MongoDB
- Saving documents to collections
- Reading documents from collections
- Updating documents to collections
- Removing documents from collections
- Testing web interface with storage in MongoDB

Objectives

By the end of this chapter, you will be able to build a function driven PHP application storing data in a document database. You will be able to use PHP to **create, read, update and delete** (CRUD) records from collections in a MongoDB database.

Installing MongoDB and PHP support for MongoDB

MongoDB is a document-oriented database with a free and open-source distribution. It is part of a category of databases called NoSQL that do not use the **Structured Query Language** (**SQL**). MongoDB has its own query language. First, you need to install MongoDB. As you are using a virtual environment based on Debian, you should follow the instructions available at the following link:

https://www.mongodb.com/docs/manual/tutorial/install-mongodb-on-debian/#std-label-install-mdb-community-debian

To start the MongoDB server on Debian, use the following command:

```
$ sudo systemctl start mongod
```

To check if the server is running, use the status argument of the **systemctl** command, as follows:

```
$ sudo systemctl status mongod
```

You must see an output like **(active (running))** if MongoDB was started successfully.

To shut down the MongoDb server, use the following command:

```
$ sudo systemctl stop mongod
```

In a RDB or SQL, we have data organized as records in tables and there is a possibility of establishing relationships between tables. In a MongoDB database, we have **Binary JSON** (**BSON**) documents gathered into collections. BSON is a binary representation of JSON documents.

The BSON specification is documented in the following link:

http://bsonspec.org.

PHP has a driver for MongoDB, installable via the **PHP Extension Community Library** (**PECL**). PECL is a part of the **PHP Extension and Application Repository** (**PEAR**). To use PECL, you need to install PEAR. On Debian-based systems, you install PEAR as follows:

```
$ sudo apt install php-pear
```

PEAR is a component distribution system written in PHP. PECL is a PHP extension installer. PECL needs to compile the source code of the extensions, so it is necessary to install the development package for PHP, as follows:

```
$ sudo apt install php-dev
```

With PECL installed, you can use it to install the PHP driver for MongoDB, as follows:

```
$ sudo pecl install mongodb
```

During MongoDB driver installation, PECL will prompt for configuration options. Let us do a default installation, so you can type **ENTER** for all questions, therefore, PECL will assume the default values.

After installing the MongoDB driver, let us install the **PHP Library for MongoDB** (**PHPLIB**) using Composer, as follows:

```
$ composer install mongodb/mongodb
```

In a RDB management system, we need to create the database and tables before inserting data into them. In MongoDB, the database and collection are created when we insert the first document. We can go straight to implementing author recording in MongoDB.

Saving documents to collections

Let us create the **CollectionTest** class in the **test** directory, as follows:

```
<?php
use PHPUnit\Framework\TestCase;
use PHPUnit\Framework\Attributes\CoversNothing;


class CollectionTest extends TestCase
{
}
```

This class will contain tests for operations on documents from the **authors** and **books** collections of the MongoDB **librarian** database. Let us copy the **setUpBeforeClass** and **tearDownAfterClass** from **DatabaseTest** class to switch to the test database. This way we can have, as in the case of the RDB, a development base and a testing base.

Let us start implementing a test to include an author document, as follows:

```
    public function testSaveAuthorInCollection()
    {
        $this->assertTrue(saveAuthorInCollection('Wells','Herbert','George'));
        dropCollection('authors');
    }
```

This test will fail because the **saveAuthorInCollection** function does not exist. Let us implement it in the **collection.functions.php** file, as follows:

```php
function saveAuthorInCollection($lastName, $middleName, $firstName)
{
    $database = getMongoDbConnection();
    $insertOneResult = $database->authors->insertOne([
        'code' => $database->authors->countDocuments() + 1,
        'last_name' => $lastName,
        'middle_name' => $middleName,
        'first_name' => $firstName
    ]);
    return $insertOneResult->getInsertedCount() == 1;
}
```

The **saveAuthorInCollection** function does the following:

- It gets through **getMongoDbConnection** function, an object that connects to the MongoDB database.

- It uses the **insertOne** method to write a BSON document using an array to send the data. The associative array, or dictionary, is interchangeable with the BSON document which is a JSON object.

- It returns **true** if the included documents count equals **1**.

Note that we use the countDocuments method of the Collection class to generate the value of the code field. The next code is the number of documents in the collection plus one.

For the **saveAuthorInCollection** function to work, we need to create the **getMongoDbConnection** function. Let us implement it in the same **collection. functions.php** file, as follows:

```php
function getMongoDbConnection()
{
    $database = getConfig()['db']['database'];
    $mongo = new MongoDB\Client("mongodb://localhost:27017");
    return $mongo->$database;
}
```

The **getMongoDbConnection** function does the following:

- It retrieves the database name from the configuration file, which is the same as that used for the RDB.

- It creates an instance of **MongoDB\Client**, connecting to the default MongoDB port, 27017. There is no username and password for authentication, by default.

- It returns the database object, based on the name defined in the configuration file.

Note: You can create a user to authenticate against a database using the mongosh program. The MongoDb\Client has a second optional argument for sending authentication parameters. You can find the reference about it at the following link:

https://www.mongodb.com/docs/php-library/current/reference/method/ MongoDBClient__construct

If you think it is enough and try to run the tests, you will see the following error message:

```
Error: Call to undefined function saveAuthorInCollection()
```

This is because it is not enough to create the **collection.functions.php** file. We need to import it into the **book.functions.php** file, as follows:

```
require_once 'collection.functions.php';
```

There will still be an error when running the tests because the **dropCollection** function does not exist. Let us implement it in the **collection.functions.php** file, as follows:

```
function dropCollection(string $collectionName)
{
    $database = getMongoDbConnection();
    $collection = $database->$collectionName;
    $collection->drop();
}
```

Now, we can run the tests successfully. The **CollectionTest->saveAuthorInCollection** method creates the **librarian_test** database, the authors collection and inserts a BSON document with *H. G. Wells'* data into it. After confirming the inclusion, the method destroys the collection to return to the initial state, so that the next test starts from an empty collection.

Now that we can write documents, let us implement document reading.

Reading documents from collections

Let us start reading tests with the reading of one only document from a collection. Let us implement the following method in the **CollectionTest** class:

```
public function testReadAuthorInCollection()
{
    saveAuthorInCollection('Von Goethe','Wolfgang','Johann');
    saveAuthorInCollection('Fitzgerald','Scott','Francis');
```

```
saveAuthorInCollection('Doyle','Arthur','Conan');
$author = readAuthorInCollectionByCode(2);
$this->assertEquals('Scott',$author['middle_name']);
dropCollection('authors');
    }
```

Note: This difference between the RDB and the document-based database. In the second case, the database and collection are created on demand, when the first document is inserted.

This test will fail because the **readAuthorInCollectionByCode** function does not exist. Let us implement it in the **collection.functions.php** file, as follows:

```
function readAuthorInCollectionByCode(int $code)
{
    $database = getMongoDbConnection();
    $result = $database->authors->findOne(['code' => $code]);
    if (is_null($result)){
        return [];
    }
    return $result;
}
```

The **findOne** method returns a document that matches the filter defined by an array. In this case, we filter by the code field.

After testing the reading of one document, we will test the reading of several, with the **testReadAuthorsInCollection** method, as follows:

```
public function testReadAuthorsInCollection()
{
    saveAuthorInCollection('Shelley','Wollstonecraft','Mary');
    saveAuthorInCollection('Christie','Mary','Agatha');
    saveAuthorInCollection('Lispector','Pinkhasivna','Chaya');
    $authors = readAuthorsInCollection();
    $this->assertCount(3,$authors);
    $this->assertEquals('Agatha',$authors[1]['first_name']);
    dropCollection('authors');
}
```

This test will fail because the **readAuthorsInCollection** function does not exist. Let us implement it in the **collection.functions.php** file, as follows:

```
function readAuthorsInCollection()
{
    $database = getMongoDbConnection();
    $result = $database->authors->find();
    if (is_null($result)){
        return [];
    }
    return $result->toArray();
}
```

The **find** method of the **Collection** class returns an iterable object of the **cursor** class, from which we can extract a list of objects. The **toArray** method transforms the list of objects into an array.

Note: There are two relevant things about the find method. The first is that this method has an optional argument to filter the results. The second is that an iterable object in PHP implements the Iterator interface. Elements from Iterator implementations can be extracted with the foreach structure. In this case, the toArray method encapsulates this extraction.

Now, the read tests will run successfully, and we can implement the update test.

Updating documents to collections

Let us implement the following test method in the **CollectionTest** class:

```
    public function testUpdateAuthorInCollection()
    {
        saveAuthorInCollection('Maupassant','de','Guy');
        saveAuthorInCollection('Saint-Exupéry','de','Antoine');
        saveAuthorInCollection('Balzac','de','Honoré');
        $author = readAuthorInCollectionByCode(1);
        $this->assertEquals('Guy',$author['first_name']);
        updateAuthorInCollection(1,[
            'last_name' => 'Raspe',
            'middle_name' => 'Erich',
            'first_name' => 'Rudolf'
        ]);
        $author = readAuthorInCollectionByCode(1);
        $this->assertEquals('Rudolf',$author['first_name']);
        dropCollection('authors');
    }
```

This test will fail because the **updateAuthorInCollection** function does not exist. Let us create it in the **collection.functions.php** file, as follows:

```php
function updateAuthorInCollection(int $code, array $data)
{
    $database = getMongoDbConnection();
    $result = $database->authors->updateOne(
        ['code' => $code],
        ['$set' => $data]
    );
    return $result->getModifiedCount() == 1;
}
```

Unlike the SQL database, we do not need to do concatenation to generate the update expression. We pass the array of data to be changed directly to the **$set** key of the **updateOne** method. To find out if the update was successful, we check if the **getModifiedCount** method returns as one.

Now, the read tests will run successfully, and we can implement the delete test.

Removing documents from collections

Let us implement the following test method in the **CollectionTest** class:

```php
    public function testDeleteAuthorInCollection()
    {
        saveAuthorInCollection('Assis','de','Machado');
        saveAuthorInCollection('Alencar','de','José');
        saveAuthorInCollection('Queiroz','de','Rachel');
        $author = readAuthorInCollectionByCode(2);
        $this->assertEquals('Alencar',$author['last_name']);
        deleteAuthorInCollection(2);
        $author = readAuthorInCollectionByCode(2);
        $this->assertEmpty($author);
        dropCollection('authors');
    }
```

This test will fail because the **deleteAuthorInCollection** function does not exist. Let us create it in the **collection.functions.php** file, as follows:

```php
function deleteAuthorInCollection(int $code)
{
    $database = getMongoDbConnection();
```

```
    $result = $database->authors->deleteOne(['code' => $code]);
    return $result->getDeletedCount() == 1;
}
```

The **deleteOne** method deletes a document that matches the filter defined by an array. In this case, we filter by the code field. To find out if the delete was successful, we check if the **getDeletedCount** method returns **1**. Now the tests will pass, and we can review our code.

Testing web interface with storage in MongoDB

We will test the interface with storage in MongoDb. For this, we will create a new test class but avoiding code replication.

To create this new class, following are the steps:

1. Copy the **ViewDatabaseTest** class as **ViewCollectionTest**;

2. Change the **ViewCollectionTest** parent class from **AbstractBackupTest** to **ViewDatabaseTest**, as follows:

   ```
   class ViewCollectionTest extends ViewDatabaseTest
   ```

3. Remove the static private attribute **$process** from **ViewCollectionTest**.

4. Remove all **ViewCollectionTest** methods except **setUpBeforeClass** and **tearDownAfterClass**.

5. Change the following line of **ViewCollectionTest::setUpBeforeClass**:

   ```
   replaceConfigFileContent("'storage_format' => 'txt'","'storage_format' => 'rdb'");
   ```

   for this, as follows:

   ```
   replaceConfigFileContent("'storage_format' => 'txt'","'storage_format' => 'ddb'");
   ```

6. Change the following line in **ViewCollectionTest::tearDownAfterClass**:

   ```
   replaceConfigFileContent("'storage_format' => 'rdb'","'storage_format' => 'txt'");
   ```

   for this, as follows:

   ```
   replaceConfigFileContent("'storage_format' => 'ddb'","'storage_format' => 'txt'");
   ```

7. Change the **ViewDatabaseTest::$process** attribute from private to protected, as follows:

   ```
   protected static $process;
   ```

8. Change the private static method **ViewDatabaseTest::startPHPServer** to protected, as follows:

```
protected static function startPHPServer()
```

Note: A protected method is visible by child classes but is not accessible outside the class. Only the class itself or its children can execute protected methods.

With these eight steps, we can create an extension or child class of **ViewDatabaseTest**, which tests the interface using MongoDB as storage, but this class still will not work because the functions in the **book.functions.php** file do not deal with the **ddb** value for the **storage_format** configuration.

Adding support to MongoDB in functions

Let us review the functions in the **book.functions.php** file, adding treatment for the **storage_format** configuration with a value of **ddb**.

Following are the steps:

1. Let us start by adding the following case to the **saveAuthor** function's switch structure:

```
        break;
    case 'ddb':
        $saved = saveAuthorInCollection($lastName, $middleName,
$firstName);
```

2. Add the following case to the **listAuthorsInTable** function's switch structure:

```
        break;
    case 'ddb':
        $authors = readAuthorsInCollection();
```

3. Add the following case to the **readAuthorsInCollectionByCode** function's switch structure:

```
        break;
    case 'ddb':
        $author = readAuthorInCollectionByCode($code);
```

4. Add the following case to the **updateAuthor** function's switch structure:

```
        break;
    case 'ddb':
        $saved = updateAuthorInCollection($code, $data);
```

5. Add the following case to the **deleteAuthor** function's switch structure:

```
            break;
    case 'ddb':
        $deleted = deleteAuthorInCollection($code);
```

After these changes, you can run the tests but they will fail with the following message:

Message: Class "ViewDatabaseTest" not found

You will note that the error occurs in the **ViewCollectionTest** class, which inherits **ViewDatabaseTest**. This error occurs because **PHPUnit** only loads the file of the class it is testing at that moment. Our test classes are not **autoloadable** by Composer, as there is no configuration in the **composer.json** file for this. But we are not going to create this configuration yet. For now, let us resolve the **ViewCollectionTest** class problem by adding the following import statement before defining the class:

require_once 'ViewDatabaseTest.php';

With this change, tests can be run successfully.

Conclusion

In this chapter, we covered how to refactor the book registration application, adding the option to store data in a document database based on MongoDB.

In the next chapter, we are going to learn about the foundations of object-oriented programming in PHP.

Points to remember

- To create a MongoDB database, it is necessary to start the MongoDB server, in Debian, it is the mongod service.

- In MongoDB, collections and banks are created when the first document is added.

- There is no relationship between collections in MongoDB like there is between tables in a SQL database.

Exercises

1. Note that the functions in the collection.functions.php file always start with the same statement. Refactor these functions to eliminate this initial line.

2. Implement book registration, following the example of author registration.

   Tip: A variable that contains an object can be replaced by calling a function that returns the same object.

Join our book's Discord space

Join the book's Discord Workspace for Latest updates, Offers, Tech happenings around the world, New Release and Sessions with the Authors:

https://discord.bpbonline.com

CHAPTER 6

PHP OOP

Introduction

This chapter will cover how to program object-oriented in PHP. We will start by learning how **object-oriented programming** (**OOP**) techniques are implemented in the PHP programming language and how we replace variables and functions with attributes and methods. We will learn the foundations of object creation, cloning and comparison. We also will learn how to use the main reuse mechanism of OOP, class inheritance, and how to establish communication patterns using interfaces. Next, we will learn about the magic methods, the methods which are invoked in response to events. Finally, we will learn how to manipulate different relational databases with a standardized interface and how to handle exceptions and errors.

Structure

The chapter covers the following topics:

- OOP techniques
- Handling databases with PHP Data Objects
- Handling exceptions and errors

Objectives

By the end of this chapter, readers will be able to define classes and their members and use them to program with maximum code reuse. You will understand the difference between object creation and object cloning and how to compare objects. You will be able to use interfaces to establish communication patterns between objects. You will also learn how to use the main reuse mechanism of OOP, inheritance, and the complementary mechanism, traits. In addition, you will also learn how objects react to events through magical methods. Finally, using the **PHP Data Objects** (**PDO**) extension, you will be able to implement access to a relational database without creating technology lock-in with a specific vendor.

OOP techniques

We will first discuss the members of a class, which are attributes and methods. Next, we will explain how objects are created, cloned, and compared. We will learn how to standardize communication between objects using interfaces and we will learn about the object-oriented reuse mechanism, inheritance. Finally, we will learn about a specific PHP implementation, and magic methods.

Classes, attributes, and methods

In the book, *The Object Primer, Scott Ambler* defines class as a software abstraction of an object. This is not very enlightening if you do not know what an object is. Additionally, it is not clearer when we read that *Scott* defines an object as a software construct that mirrors a concept in the real world.

Let us try to improve this. A class is the abstraction of the actor of an action or the cause of an effect. In the particular universe of computer programming, a class is also a unit of reuse, like a function. A function, in turn, is an abstraction of an action or effect. However, in the real world, actions do not happen alone, just like effects. An actor performs actions, and cause effects. Class is the recognition that actions are the responsibility of someone or something.

In OOP, a class is a definition. As a definition, a class can exist on a sheet of paper or in a digital file. Once defined, the class exists indefinitely in the medium in which it is persisted. An object, in turn, is the materialization of the class in the computer's memory. An object exists only as long as the computer is on. It needs to be created explicitly and can be destroyed at any time.

A class has two types of members: attributes and methods. Essentially, attributes are variables and methods are functions. In addition to the different names, they have a person responsible. To refer to an attribute, it is necessary to mention the class or object to which it belongs. The same applies to methods. **Instance attributes** are variables of a specific object. **Class attributes** are variables shared by the objects of a class.

Let us create a class to understand these concepts. Since we are using the test-driven approach, let us create a test. Let us create the **AuthorTest** class with a **testAuthorInstantiation** method, as follows:

```php
<?php
use PHPUnit\Framework\TestCase;
class AuthorTest extends TestCase
{
    public function testAuthorInstantiation()
    {
        $author = new Author();
        $author->setFirstName('Camilo');
        $author->setMiddleName('Castelo');
        $author->setLastName('Branco');

        $this->assertEquals('Camilo', $author->getFirstName());
        $this->assertEquals('Castelo', $author->getMiddleName());
        $this->assertEquals('Branco', $author->getLastName());
    }
}
```

Let us understand what we are doing in the **AuthorTest->testAuthorInstantiation** method, as follows:

- First, we create an instance of the **Author** class using the **new** operator. Instance is another name for an object, related to the fact that the object is ephemeral and can only last for an instant.

- Next, we invoke methods to modify object attributes. This category of methods is called **setter**.

- Finally, we make assertions by comparing the values we send for modification with the return of methods that read object attributes. This category of methods is called **getter**.

Note: The $author variable is not the object, but a reference to the object. Different variables can point to the same object.

We do not always need to run all the tests. You can indicate a specific test class to run by passing its file name as an argument. To run just the **AuthorTest** class, we execute the following command:

```
$ vendor/bin/phpunit tests/AuthorTest.php
```

When running this test class, we will have the following result:

```
1) AuthorTest::testAuthorInstantiation
Error: Class "Author" not found
```

Of course, the **Author** class does not exist. We need to create it. Let us understand where it must be created.

In *Chapter 4, Function Driven Registration with Relational Database Storage,* we created **src** directory to accommodate an abstract class for tests that needed to backup text files and restore them later. This **src** directory will be the home for our application's classes. In the same chapter, we configured Composer to autoload classes whose namespace started with **Librarian** from files located in the **src** directory. This autoloading follows the PSR-4 specification of the **PHP Frameworks Interoperability Group** (**PHP-FIG**).

A namespace is a unique identifier to which we can associate class names. Namespaces were created to avoid class name collisions, that is, classes with the same name. We can have class names that are the same as long as they are defined in different namespaces. For example, we can have an **Adapter** class that implements the same design pattern for authentication and an **Adapter** class that implements the same pattern for databases. The first can be in the **Authentication** namespace and the other in the **Database** namespace. And both can be used in the same PHP file, as long as at least one receives a nickname to distinguish it from the other.

The following code snippet illustrates this example:

```
use Authentication\Adapter;
use Database\Adapter as DatabaseAdapter;
$authenticationAdapter = new Adapter();
$databaseAdapter = new DatabaseAdapter;
```

Namespaces can have as many levels as necessary. PSR-4 establishes a correspondence between namespace levels and directory levels, so that each namespace corresponds to a directory and the last to the class file. In the case of our application, the **Librarian** namespace points to the **src** directory. From there, sub namespaces correspond to subdirectories of **src**. This is why the **Librarian\Test\AbstractBackupTest** namespace corresponds to the **src/Test/AbstractBackupTest.php** file.

Let us create a **Model** subdirectory inside **src**. Inside this **Model**, we will create the **Author.php** file, as follows:

```
<?php
namespace Librarian\Model;
class Author
{
}
```

Note: The directory is called Model because it will contain the models of our business, in this case, authors and books.

We created the **Author** class, then we can run the **AuthorTest** class again. We can run it, but the **class not found** error will continue. This is because we must define the namespace of the class we want to use. When PHP encounters the **Author** class name, it checks whether there is a namespace in the file for the class and attempts to load it according to the configured rules,in this case, configured by Composer. If there is no namespace defined for the class, it is treated as if it were in the root namespace. To resolve the **class not found** error, we need to add the following statement at the beginning of the **AuthorTest.php** file, before the class definition, as follows:

```
use Librarian\Model\Author;
```

With this change, when running the **AuthorTest** class again, we have a new error:

```
1) AuthorTest::testAuthorInstantiation
Error: Call to undefined method Librarian\Model\Author::setFirstName()
```

This error occurs because the **Author** class does not have the **setFirstName** method. Let us implement it as follows:

```
    public function setFirstName()
    {
    }
```

The error will repeat with the **setMiddleName** and **setLastName** methods. Let us implement them following the **setFirstName** example. After implementing these three methods in the Author class, **AuthorTest** will display the following error:

```
1) AuthorTest::testAuthorInstantiation
Error: Call to undefined method Librarian\Model\Author::getFirstName()
```

To resolve this error, we create the method in the **Author** class, as follows:

```
    public function getFirstName()
    {
    }
```

Now, when running the test, we have a new type of error, as follows:

```
1) AuthorTest::testAuthorInstantiation
Failed asserting that null matches expected 'Camilo'.
```

Now, we have an error in the assertion, because the **getFirstName** method does not return the string **'Camilo'**. Let us modify the **getFirstName** method so that it returns the value of an attribute, as follows:

```
    public function getFirstName()
    {
        return $this->firstName;
    }
```

Note: The $this keyword refers to the class instance, the current object.

After this change, when running the test, we have a failure, as follows:

1) AuthorTest::testAuthorInstantiation

Failed asserting that null matches expected 'Camilo'.

This message means that **$this->firstName** is null. It is null because no value was previously associated with it. We should associate a value with the **$this->firstName** attribute with the **setFirstName** method. Let us modify it as follows:

```
public function setFirstName(string $firstName)
{
    $this->firstName = $firstName;
}
```

Now, the **setFirstName** method assigns the received argument to the **$this->firstName** attribute. However, unlike variables, attributes must be declared. So, at the beginning of the class block, we will add the **$this->firstName** attribute declaration, as follows:

```
private string $firstName;
```

When we declare the attribute, we do not use the **$this** keyword. It is only used within methods. Note that we declared the **$this->firstName** attribute as private. This means that only the class itself can read and write this attribute.

Now the test will pass the assertion that tests the **getFirstName** method, but will fail the others. Following the example of the **getFirstName** and **setFirstName** methods, let us implement the other methods of the **Author** class. There will, however, be a message related to the test's code coverage:

1) AuthorTest::testAuthorInstantiation

This test does not define a code coverage target but is expected to do so

We need to tell which class is being covered by the test class. Before declaring the **AuthorTest** class, we will add a note block and an attribute, so that the test class is compatible with versions of PHPUnit 12 and earlier.

Refer to the following code:

```
/**
 * @covers Author
 */
#[CoversClass(Author::class)]
```

The **CoversClass** attribute requires the namespace to be declared, as follows:

```
use PHPUnit\Framework\Attributes\CoversClass;
```

Now the **Author** class will successfully pass the test without warnings.

Object creation, cloning and comparison

An object can be created, in PHP, by two operators: **new** and **clone**. We have already used the **new** operator several times. It creates a new object from the class specified to the right of the operator. The **clone** operator, in turn, creates a copy of an existing object. The **new** operator generates an object from a class. The **clone** operator generates an object from another object. What does not create a new object is assigning a variable of type object to another variable. The **new** and **clone** operators do not return the object itself, but a reference to it.

Let us create a test in the **AuthorTest** class to illustrate the difference between the ways of creating objects in PHP and explain how the comparison between objects works, as follows:

```php
public function testAuthorCloning()
{
    $author = new Author();
    $author->setFirstName('Federico');
    $author->setMiddleName('Garcia');
    $author->setLastName('Lorca');
    $authorCopy = $author;
    $authorClone = clone $author;
    $this->assertEquals($author->getFirstName(),$authorCopy-
>getFirstName());
    $this->assertEquals($author->getFirstName(),$authorClone-
>getFirstName());
    $this->assertEquals($author, $authorCopy);
    $this->assertEquals($author, $authorClone);
    $this->assertTrue($author == $authorCopy);
    $this->assertTrue($author == $authorClone);
    $this->assertTrue($author === $authorCopy);
    $this->assertFalse($author === $authorClone);
    $this->assertEquals(spl_object_hash($author), spl_object_
hash($authorCopy));
    $this->assertNotEquals(spl_object_hash($author), spl_object_
hash($authorClone));
}
```

The explanation of what the **AuthorTest->testAuthorCloning** method does is as follows:

- It creates an instance of the **Author** class, assign it to the **$author** variable and fills in its attributes.

- It stores a copy of the reference to the created object in another variable, **$authorCopy**.

- It creates a clone of the object and associates this clone with the **$authorClone** variable.

- It verifies that both the **$author** variable and the **$authorCopy** variable return the same author's first name. This is because both variables refer to the same object.

- It verifies that both the **$author** variable and the **$authorClone** variable return the same author's first name. This is because the object clone has the same data as the cloned object.

- When we compare the **$author** variable with **$authorCopy** and **$authorClone** using the **assertEquals** method, the result is true. Comparison with **assertEquals** is equivalent to using **assertTrue** to check the result of comparison with the equality operator (**==**). The equality operator compares only attribute values.

- When we compare the variables **$author** and **$authorCopy** using the identity operator (**===**), the result is true because both variables refer to the same object.

- When we compare the variables **$author** and **$authorClone** using the identity operator, the result is false because the variables refer to different objects. The identity operator not only compares attribute values, but also the object's unique identifier.

- The **spl_object_hash** function returns a unique identifier for an object. When we use it with the **$author** and **$authorCopy** variables, we verify that they are the same object.

- When we use the **spl_object_hash** function with the **$author** and **$authorClone** variables, we see that they are different objects.

Note: While spl_object_hash returns a unique string for an object, spl_object_id returns a unique integer for an object.

Interfaces

In their book, *Design Patterns*, Erich Gamma and his fellows state the following principle: *program to an interface, not an implementation*. This statement occurs when they are discussing reducing dependency between objects. Interfaces serve to create communication patterns. If two objects use the same communication pattern, one can be replaced by the other. More specifically, if two objects have the same method, with the same arguments and return the same type of data, then they become interchangeable.

Interfaces also serve to make different objects, from different classes, have common behaviors. In our business, authors and books have codes. Reading and writing code are a common behavior between the **Author** and **Book** classes. Therefore, we will create an interface for the code reading and writing methods and implement this interface in the **Author** and **Book** classes. An interface is like a class devoid of attributes and method implementation. An interface only has the method signature, which defines the data that will be received and what will be returned. Let us create **CodeInterface** interface, as follows:

```php
<?php
namespace Librarian\Model;
interface CodeInterface
{
    public function setCode(int $code);
    public function getCode(): int;
}
```

As we discussed, the namespace corresponds to the directory path where the class file is located. This also applies to interfaces. Thus, since the namespace of the **CodeInterface** interface is **Librarian\Model**, the **CodeInterface.php** file is in the **Model** subdirectory of the **src** directory, which maps to the **Librarian** namespace.

The **CodeInterface** interface defines a **setCode** method, which takes one argument and returns nothing, and a **getCode** method, which takes nothing and returns an integer. An interface alone is useless. It needs to be implemented by a class. Let us change the declaration of the **Author** class so that it implements the **CodeInterface** interface, as follows:

```php
class Author implements CodeInterface
```

If we run the **AuthorTest** class after this change to the **Author** class, we will be informed of the following error by **PHPUnit**:

```
PHP Fatal error:  Class Librarian\Model\Author contains 2 abstract methods
and must therefore be declared abstract or implement the remaining
methods (Librarian\Model\CodeInterface::setCode, Librarian\Model\
CodeInterface::getCode)
```

This message shows that an interface works like a contract that guarantees that certain methods will be implemented. Since the class declaration says that it implements a certain interface, the class is obliged to implement the methods of that interface. That said, let us implement the **CodeInterface** interface methods in the **Author** class. The steps are as follows:

1. First, let us create the **$code** private attribute, as follows:

    ```php
    private int $code;
    ```

2. Next, let us create the public **setCode** method, as follows:

    ```php
    public function setCode(int $code)
    {
    ```

```
        $this->code = $code;
    }
```

3. Finally, let us create the public **getCode** method, as follows:

```
    public function getCode(): int
    {
        return $this->code;
    }
```

With this change, the **AuthorTest** class runs successfully again. Note that the signature of the method implemented in the class must be exactly the same as what is declared in the interface. If you forget to put the type in the argument or return, you will see a fatal error message, because the contract was not fulfilled.

As we already said, the **CodeInterface** interface must also be implemented by the **Book** class. This class has not been created yet and we will create it now. The beginning of the **Book.php** file will have the following lines:

```
<?php
namespace Librarian\Model;
class Book implements CodeInterface
```

Compared to the **Author** class, the **Book** class has something new in the declaration of its attributes, as we can see in the following lines:

```
    private int $code;
    private string $title;
    private Author $author;
```

Note that one of the attributes is an object of the **Author** class. Just as the **books** table is dependent on the **authors** table, the **Book** class is dependent on the **Author** class.

We will not show the methods for reading and writing these attributes as there is no need. You can implement these methods by comparing them with the **Author** class since they follow a pattern. However, we will present the code to test the **Book** class.

We will create the **BookTest** class, as follows:

```
<?php
use PHPUnit\Framework\TestCase;
use PHPUnit\Framework\Attributes\CoversClass;
use Librarian\Model\Author;
use Librarian\Model\Book;


/**
 * @covers Book
```

```
*/
#[CoversClass(Book::class)]
class BookTest extends TestCase
{
    public function testBookInstantiation()
    {
        $author = new Author();
        $author->setFirstName('José');
        $author->setMiddleName('Emílio');
        $author->setLastName('Pacheco');
        $book = new Book();
        $book->setTitle('El viento distante');
        $book->setAuthor($author);
        $this->assertEquals('El viento distante', $book->getTitle());
        $this->assertEquals('Pacheco', $book->getAuthor()->getLastName());
    }
}
```

As you can see, the **BookTest->testBookInstantiation** method performs the following actions:

1. It creates an instance of the **Author** class.
2. It creates an instance of the **Book** class.
3. It configures the attributes of the **Book** instance using the modifier methods.
4. It checks whether the object has retained the title and last name of the author.

You can see that we invoke the **getLastName** method from the **getAuthor** method. We do not need to assign an object to a variable just to invoke a method. If a method returns an object, we can call a method on that object directly from the method that returns it.

At this point, you notice that the **Author** and **Book** classes have lines of code repeated between them. The declaration of the **$code** attribute and the implementation of the **setCode** and **getCode** methods are exactly the same. We discussed that a class can also be a reuse unit and in the next section, we will demonstrate this by eliminating the repetition we created between the **Author** and **Book** classes.

Inheritance

In his book *Clean Code, Robert Cecil Martin* states that *duplication may the root of all evil in software*. Duplicate code means more than one place to fix it when something is wrong.

David Thomas and *Andrew Hunt*, in their book *The Pragmatic Programmer*, state that it is necessary to follow the **Don't Repeat Yourself** (**DRY**) principle to have code that is easy to understand and maintain. If there are sets of instructions that are used in different places in a program, they should not be repeated in each of those places. They should be isolated into reusable, referenceable blocks of code.

Functions are blocks of reusable code. Instead of repeating the same set of instructions in several parts of a program, you write just one line, which is the function call. The function prevents you from having to change various points in the program when the set of instructions it contains needs to be corrected or improved. Functions are reuse units.

In OOP, the class is a unit of reuse. While a function allows you to reuse only behavior, a class allows you to reuse data and behavior. Code reuse with classes is governed by a technique called **inheritance**. Inheritance in OOP is a metaphor for genetic inheritance, in which children inherit characteristics from their parents. A class that reuses code from another is a child class. A class that has code reused by another is a parent class.

When developing software, you may notice that two or more classes have duplicate attributes and methods. The procedure, in this case, is to move the duplicate attributes and methods to another class, from which the first ones will inherit. This class, which brings together common data and behavior, will generally not be instantiated directly. In this case, it has a special identifier, so that it is just a reuse unit and not an instance generator. This identifier is the **abstract** keyword, which is used in the class declaration. A class defined with the **abstract** keyword is an abstract class.

It is important to clarify two points about inheritance and instance generation, as follows:

- Any class can inherit attributes and methods from another, whether abstract or not.

- Abstract classes do not generate instances. You cannot use the **new** operator with an abstract class.

That said, let us eliminate code duplication between the **Author** and **Book** classes by creating an **abstract class** called **AbstractCode**. This class will define the attribute and methods common to both classes. The implementation of this class will be as follows:

```php
<?php
namespace Librarian\Model;
abstract class AbstractCode implements CodeInterface
{
    protected int $code;

    public function setCode(int $code)
    {
        $this->code = $code;
```

```
    }

    public function getCode(): int
    {
        return $this->code;
    }
}
```

Note that **AbstractCode** implements the **CodeInterface** interface. Therefore, the **Author** and **Book** classes no longer need to explicitly implement this interface, as they will inherit it through **AbstractCode**.

Also, note that the **$code** attribute, which was defined as private in the **Author** and **Book** classes, is defined as protected in the **AbstractCode** class. We discussed, when we created the **AbstractBackupTest** class. Private attributes are not inherited. If you want an attribute to be inherited, but do not want it to be public, it must be declared protected.

Let us remove the **$code** attribute and the **setCode** and **getCode** methods from the **Author** and **Book** classes. Next, let us change the declaration of these classes so that they inherit from **AbstractCode**.

The Author class declaration will look be as follows:

```
class Author extends AbstractCode
```

The **Book** class declaration will be as follows:

```
class Book extends AbstractCode
```

You can run the tests successfully after these changes. No functionality has been modified. Using inheritance only eliminated code duplication. Now, if there is any change to be made related to the code attribute and its methods, there is only one file to be modified and not two.

In *Figure 6.1*, we can see **Unified Modeling Language (UML)** class diagram that summarizes the relationship between the interface and the classes we create the following:

- The **AbstractCode** class declares the **$code** attribute and implements the **CodeInterface** interface, defining the behavior of the **setCode** and **getCode** methods.

- The **Author** and **Book** classes inherit the **$code** attribute and the **setCode** and **getCode** methods from the **AbstractCode** class.

- The **Book** class has a compositional relationship with the **Author** class, because a book needs an author to exist.

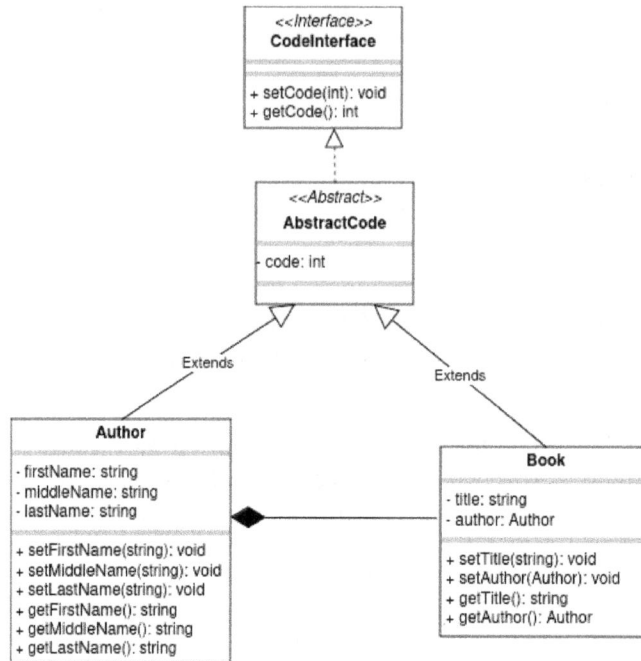

Figure 6.1: *Class diagram with implementation, inheritance and composition*

A class can be inherited by multiple classes. On the other hand, in PHP specifically, a class can only have one parent. This is what we call simple inheritance.

Some programming languages, such as C++ and Python, have multiple inheritance, that is, they allow a class to inherit attributes and methods from multiple classes. Multiple inheritance can become complicated when parent classes have attributes or methods with the same name. It is to avoid this confusion about the origin of inherited members that languages like PHP and Java do not implement multiple inheritance.

By avoiding the confusion of multiple inheritance, we end up losing some of the reuse power of classes. Without being able to inherit from more than one class, we will inevitably copy and paste code, generating duplication.

To get around the limitation of simple inheritance, PHP implements a construct called **trait**. As the name suggests, it is a block of code that defines a characteristic. Traits are better metaphors of genetic inheritance for programming, because in genetic inheritance a child does not inherit all the characteristics of one of the parents, but some characteristics of each of them.

Traits look like classes, but they cannot be instantiated. They can only be used. A class can use multiple traits and a trait can be used by multiple classes.

Let us take an example, implementing the reusable code of the **AbstractCode** class as a trait. First, let us create a test class called **TraitTest** with a **testTrait** method, as follows:

```php
class TraitTest extends TestCase
{
    public function testTrait()
    {
        $traitUser = new TraitUser();
        $traitUser->setCode(42);

        $this->assertEquals(42, $traitUser->getCode());
    }
}
```

Of course, this test will fail because TraitUser does not exist. Let us create it as follows:

```php
<?php
namespace Librarian\Model;
class TraitUser implements CodeInterface
{
    use CodeTrait;
}
```

Note that the **TraitUser** class implements the **CodeInterface** interface. This means that it needs to implement the **setCode** and **getCode** methods. These methods are implemented in **CodeTrait**, so the **TraitUser** class can use **CodeTrait** to fulfill the contract with **CodeInterface**.

 Note: In PHP, a class can extends only one class, but it can use multiples traits.

TraitTest will not work yet. If you run the test case at this point, you will be presented with the following error message:

```
PHP Fatal error:  Trait "Librarian\Model\CodeTrait" not found
```

This happens because **CodeTrait** does not exist yet. A trait is searched for in the same way as a class. The name of the trait is prefixed to the namespace of the file where it is located and the **autoloader** tries to find it from the established rules, in this case, from the rules in the **composer.json** file.

Let us create **CodeTrait**, as follows:

```php
<?php
namespace Librarian\Model;
trait CodeTrait
{
    protected int $code;
```

```php
    public function setCode(int $code)
    {
        $this->code = $code;
    }

    public function getCode(): int
    {
        return $this->code;
    }
}
```

Now, the **TraitTest** class will run successfully.

Magic methods

Typically, the programmer explicitly invokes an object method. There are some special methods, which are executed when events occur. They are, therefore, event-oriented methods. These methods are called **magic methods** in PHP and follow the pattern of always starting with two dashes.

The most common magic method is the **constructor**. The constructor is a method called when the object is created with the new operator. The constructor allows the object to receive arguments upon its creation. So, you can set attribute values or inject dependencies into an object. In PHP, the constructor method is called **__construct**.

Let us create the **AuthorTest->testAuthorConstructor** method to illustrate the use of the constructor, as follows:

```php
    public function testAuthorConstructor()
    {
        $author = new Author('Richard', 'Brinsley', 'Sheridan');
        $this->assertEquals('Richard', $author->getFirstName());
        $this->assertEquals('Brinsley', $author->getMiddleName());
        $this->assertEquals('Sheridan', $author->getLastName());
    }
```

Note that we are passing the author names in parentheses after the class name and then checking to see if the attributes match those values. Running this test will result in the following error:

1) AuthorTest::testAuthorConstructor

Error: Typed property Librarian\Model\Author::$firstName must not be accessed before initialization

This message means that the **Author->firstName** attribute did not receive any initial valu
because we have not implemented the constructor method yet.

Let us implement it as follows:

```
    public function __construct(string $firstName = '', string $middleName =
'', string $lastName = '')
    {
        $this->firstName = $firstName;
        $this->middleName = $middleName;
        $this->lastName = $lastName;
    }
```

Note that we assign default values to the constructor arguments so that they are optional.

A magical method that is not very common in use is the **destructor**. The destructor is
a method called when the object is destroyed, when it is removed from the computer's
memory. In PHP the destructor method is called **__destruct**. Let us create the **AuthorTest-
>testAuthorDestructor** method to illustrate the use of the destructor, as follows:

```
    public function testAuthorDestructor()
    {
        $author = new Author('Ana', 'Maria', 'Machado');
        $objectId = spl_object_id($author);
        unset($author);
        $output = shell_exec('grep "php: object ' . $objectId . ' was
destroyed" /var/log/syslog');
        $this->assertStringContainsString($objectId, $output);
    }
```

In this test, we create an object and store its unique identifier. We then destroy it and
check if there is a record in the system log that the object was destroyed. The **shell_exec**
function allows you to execute operating system commands and capture the output of
those commands. Of course, this test will fail because the **Author** class does not have a
destructor method that does this recording.

Let us implement it as follows:

```
    public function __destruct()
    {
        $objectId = spl_object_id($this);
        syslog(LOG_DEBUG,"object $objectId was destroyed");
    }
```

The **syslog** function writes a message to the system log, identifying the priority, in this case, **LOG_DEBUG**. Each time an **Author** class object is destroyed, a message will be written to the system log.

Private attributes cannot be read or written outside of an object of the class where they were defined. However, there are a couple of magical methods that allow you to simulate direct access to private attributes.

Let us illustrate the use of these methods by creating the **AuthorTest->testAttributeReadingAndWriting** test, as follows:

```
public function testAttributeReadingAndWriting()
{
    $author = new Author();
    $author->firstName = 'Sarat';
    $author->middleName = 'Chandra';
    $author->lastName = 'Chattopadhyay';
    $this->assertEquals('Sarat', $author->firstName);
    $this->assertEquals('Chandra', $author->middleName);
    $this->assertEquals('Chattopadhyay', $author->lastName);
}
```

If you run this test, the result will be as follows:

1) AuthorTest::testAttributeReadingAndWriting

Error: Cannot access private property Librarian\Model\Author::$firstName

As we said before, private attributes cannot be read or written outside the object. That is why we define public methods to read and write the private attributes. However, we can use a magic method in PHP, which is public, to pretend that private attributes are public.

There is a magic method in PHP that, when implemented, is invoked whenever there is an attempt to write a private attribute. It is the **__set** method. Let us implement it in the **Author** class, as follows:

```
public function __set($name, $value)
{
    $this->$name = $value;
}
```

The **__set** method receives the name and value of the private attribute that is trying to be modified. We will use the attribute name as a variable to access the attribute and assign the value to it.

If you run the test again, you will see the same error message, but pointing to a different line. The test can write to the three private attributes through the **__set** method, but cannot read their values. There is another magic method in PHP that, when implemented, is invoked whenever there is an attempt to read a private attribute. It is the **__get** method.

Let us implement it in the Author class, as follows:

```
public function __get($name)
{
    return $this->$name;
}
```

The **__get** method receives the name of the private attribute that is trying to be read. We use the attribute name as a variable to access the attribute and return it.

You could argue that these two magic methods (**__set** and **__get**) are useless, as declaring attributes as public has the same effect with fewer lines of code and still avoids method invocations. If there is no processing of the data read or written, these methods are really useless, if you want to maintain attribute protection and perform filters or data conversions, they become very useful.

Objects cannot be printed or concatenated by default. There is a magical method that can define a textual representation of an object.

Let us create the **AuthorTest->testAuthorPrinting** test to illustrate as follows:

```
public function testAuthorPrinting()
{
    $author = new Author('Yahya','Taher','Abdullah');
    $sentence = $author . ' is the author of The Collar and the
Bracelet';
    $this->assertStringContainsString('Yahya Taher Abdullah',
$sentence);
}
```

When running this test, you will receive the following error:

1) AuthorTest::testAuthorPrinting

Error: Object of class Librarian\Model\Author could not be converted to string

As we see in the error message, PHP does not automatically convert objects to text. We can implement the **__toString** method in the Author class to define this conversion, as follows:

```
public function __toString()
{
    return "{$this->firstName} {$this->middleName} {$this->lastName}";
}
```

With this implementation, the test will pass successfully. Note that we use curly braces to delimit the object's attributes within the string. The use of braces is necessary to convert attribute names and array elements to their respective values within a string. Without curly braces, the PHP interpreter knows where variables begin, but not where they end.

We have learned in *Chapter 2, PHP Foundations,* that a variable can be used as a function if it contains the name of a function. It is the variable function. A variable that contains a reference to an object can also be used as a function if the object's class implements the **invoke** magic method. This method can allow, for example, the population of the object's attributes after its creation without having to call each of the writer methods.

Let us illustrate this with the **AuthorTest->testAuthorInvoker** method, as follows:

```
public function testAuthorInvoker()
{
    $author = new Author();
    $author('Ahmet', 'Hamdi', 'Tanpinar');
    $this->assertEquals('Ahmet', $author->getFirstName());
    $this->assertEquals('Hamdi', $author->getMiddleName());
    $this->assertEquals('Tanpinar', $author->getLastName());
}
```

This test, when run, will produce the following error:

```
1) AuthorTest::testAuthorInvoker
Error: Object of type Librarian\Model\Author is not callable
```

The test tries to assign values to the attributes of the **Author** class object in a call that looks like a late constructor. The error message says that the variable **$author** cannot be called as a function. This is because the **Author** class does not implement the **__invoke** magic method. Let us implement this method, as follows:

```
public function __invoke(string $firstName = '', string $middleName =
'', string $lastName = '')
{
    $this->firstName = $firstName;
    $this->middleName = $middleName;
    $this->lastName = $lastName;
}
```

There are still other magical methods, as follows:

- **__call**: This method is invoked when an attempt is made to call a non-existent method of the object. It receives as arguments the name of the non-existent method and the values of the arguments of the non-existent method.

- **__callStatic**: This method is similar to the **__call** method but is only invoked for calls to static methods, or class methods.

- **__isset**: This method is invoked if the object is used as an argument in a call to the **isset** function.

- **__unset**: This method is invoked if the object is used as an argument in a call to the **unset** function.

- **__sleep**: This method is invoked if the object is used as an argument in a call to the **serialize** function. Serialization is the process of converting the object in memory into a textual representation that can be persisted, preserving the state data of the object.

- **__wakeup**: This method is invoked if the object is used as an argument in a call to the **unserialize** function. Unserialization is the process of restoring a persisted textual representation of the object to the memory.

- **__serialize**: This method is invoked if the object is used as an argument in a call to the **serialize** function and must return an associative array of key-value pairs that represent the serialized form of the object. If **__serialize** and **__sleep** is both implemented in the same class, only **__serialize** will be called.

- **__unserialize**: This method is invoked if the object is used as an argument in a call to the **unserialize** function and receives as argument the array generated by **__serialize** method. If **__unserialize** and **__wakeup** is both implemented in the same class, only **__unserialize** will be called.

- **__set_state**: This method is invoked if the object is used as an argument in a call to the **var_export** function. The **var_export** function creates a string representation of a variable. Therefore, the **__set_state** method must return an object.

- **__clone**: This method is invoked if the object is created with the **clone** operator.

- **__debugInfo**: This method is invoked if the object is used as an argument in a call to the **var_dump** function. The **var_dump** function shows all public, protected and private attributes of an object. You can restrict the attributes to be showed implementing **__debugInfo** and returning an array with the attributes which you want to expose.

Magic methods must be declared as public, with the exception of **__construct()**, **__destruct()**, and **__clone()**. This means that you can prevent the creation or destruction of objects of a class. When we cover design patterns, we will illustrate this by implementing a private constructor.

Note: Methods names starting with double underline are reserved for magic methods. Magic methods cannot be invoked directly.

Handling databases with PHP Data Objects

A part of building a software system involves deciding which database management systems to use. It may be that initially a single database vendor meets your system requirements and your team writes data persistence code specific to that database. However, what if, for example, your software system is installed by your customers and they want to choose which database to use. This is a scenario that requires a database abstraction layer. This means that your application should not communicate directly with the database. This approach leaves the application decoupled from the database and allows the system administrator to choose which database to use from a configuration file.

PHP has an extension that provides a data abstraction layer. It is the PDO extension. Let us learn how to use the PDO extension to decouple the Librarian application from the MySQL database using classes.

Let us create a test class called **PDOTest** to test writing and reading records in the relational database using PDO. This class will be very similar to **DatabaseTest**. It will implement the same methods, although only two (**setUpBeforeClass** and **tearDownAfterClass**) are exactly the same. So, before to create **PDOTest**, let us create an abstract class to isolate what is exactly the same between the two classes. This class will be **AbstractDabataseTest**, will inherit from **PHPUnit\Framework\TestCase** and will be in the **Librarian\Test** namespace, as follows:

```
abstract class AbstractDatabaseTest extends TestCase
```

The **AbstractDatabaseTest** class will implement the static methods **setUpBeforeClass** and **tearDownAfterClass** exactly as they were defined in **DatabaseTest**. The other **DatabaseTest** methods will not be implemented in **AbstractDabaseTest**, only their signatures will be declared. Abstract classes can define abstract methods, which are methods without implementation. It is similar to what interfaces do. When a class inherits abstract methods from an abstract class, it is required to implement them unless it is also abstract.

Abstract methods are preceded by the **abstract** keyword. The abstract methods for manipulating author records in the **AbstractDatabaseTest** class will be as follows:

```
abstract  public function testSaveAuthorInDatabase();

abstract  public function testReadAuthorInDatabase();

abstract  public function testReadAuthorsInDatabase();

abstract  public function testUpdateAuthorInDatabase();

abstract  public function testDeleteAuthorInDatabase();
```

Now, we can create the **PDOTest** class, as follows:

```
class PDOTest extends AbstractDatabaseTest
```

When a non-abstract class inherits abstracted methods from an abstract class, it must implement them. We will fully reuse the **setUpBeforeClass** and **tearDownAfterClass** methods from **AbstractDatabaseTest**, but we will implement the other methods.

First, let us implement the **testSaveAuthorInDatabase** method, as follows:

```
public function testSaveAuthorInDatabase()
{
    $authorPDO = new AuthorPDO();
    $this->assertTrue($authorPDO→save('George', 'Herbert', 'Wells'));
    truncateTable('authors');
}
```

Of course, the test will fail, because the **AuthorPDO** class does not exist. Before complaining about the absence of **AuthorPDO**, PHP will complain about the unimplemented abstract methods, as follows:

PHP Fatal error: Class PDOTest contains 4 abstract methods and must therefore be declared abstract or implement the remaining methods

You cannot run any tests until you implement the abstract methods. So, for now, let us create the bodyless methods, as follows:

```
public function testReadAuthorInDatabase() {}


public function testReadAuthorsInDatabase() {}


public function testUpdateAuthorInDatabase() {}


public function testDeleteAuthorInDatabase() {}
```

With the method bodies implemented, **PHPUnit** will run, although it issues a warning due to the absence of assertions, as follows:

This test did not perform any assertions

Now that we have met the requirement for abstract methods, let us create **AuthorPDO** class in the **Librarian\Model\PDO** namespace, as follows:

```
<?php
namespace Librarian\Model\PDO;
class AuthorPDO
{
}
```

Let us add an attribute to this class to store an instance of the **PDO** class, as follows:

```
private \PDO $pdo;
```

The descending slash before the **PDO** class represents the root namespace. If a file does not have a defined namespace, it is not necessary to put the slash, but as the **AuthorPDO** class file has a namespace, it is necessary to put the slash, otherwise the **PDO** class will be interpreted as **Librarian\Model\PDO\PDO**.

An object of the **PDO** class requires an identifier called a **data source name** (**DSN**), a user name, and a password. The username and password are already defined in the configuration. Let us add a key for the DSN to the database configuration array, in the **book.config.php** file, as follows:

```
'dsn' => 'mysql:dbname=librarian;host=localhost',
```

As you can see, the DSN informs the database provider (MySQL, in this case), the database name and the server address. Next, let us implement a constructor in **AuthorPDO** that creates an instance of the **PDO** class, as follows:

```
    public function __construct()
    {
        $db = getConfig()['db'];
        $this->pdo = new \PDO($db['dsn'], $db['username'],
$db['password']);
    }
```

We cannot forget to change the DSN to use the test bench when running the tests. To do this, we will have to add the following statement to the **AbstractDatabaseTest::setUpBeforeClass** method:

```
    replaceConfigFileContent('dbname=librarian','dbname=librarian_test');
```

We also will have to add the following statement to the **AbstractDatabaseTest::tearDownAfterClass** method:

```
    replaceConfigFileContent('dbname=librarian_test','dbname=librarian');
```

Since the **AuthorPDO** object has a **PDO** instance, it can read and write from the database using the **PDO** interface. As we are dealing with the author creation test, we will implement the **AuthorPDO->save** method, as follows:

```
    public function save(string $firstName, string $middleName, string
$lastName): bool
    {
        $sql = 'INSERT INTO authors(first_name,middle_name,last_name) values
(:firstname,:middlename,:lastname)';
        $statement = $this->pdo->prepare($sql);
        $statement->bindParam(':firstname', $firstName);
        $statement->bindParam(':middlename', $middleName);
        $statement->bindParam(':lastname', $lastName);
        $statement->execute();
        return $statement->rowCount() == 1;
    }
```

In the **AuthorPDO->save** method, we do the following:

- We set up a SQL **INSERT** command with placeholders for the values to be included, placeholders are preceded by a colon.

- We create a **PDOStatement** object with the **PDO->prepare** method. This object stores the command for later execution.

- We use the **PDOStatement->bindParam** method to bind values to placeholders.

- We execute the query with the **PDOStatement->execute** method. This method returns true if the SQL command was executed successfully. The **PDOStatement->rowCount** method returns the number of rows affected by the command.

- We return true if a row was included.

We could avoid creating a **PDOStatement** object using and calling the **bindParam** method using the **PDO->exec** method. With **PDO->exec** we can directly pass the SQL **INSERT** command as an argument, concatenating the values to be included. The price of ease is the lack of processing of input data and the possibility of injecting malicious SQL commands into field values. Using **PDOStatement->bindParam**, we have the opportunity to process the input data before executing the SQL command. For now, we will not do any treatment, as, as we promised previously, we will deal with this in the section *Handling exceptions and errors*.

Note: When using PDO, information about the database supplier is encapsulated in the configuration in the DSN string. If any other database that can be used as an adapter for PDO is used, the AuthorPDO->save method does not need to be modified.

Our next step in using **PDO** is to test reading an included author retrieved by your code. Let us implement **PDOTest->testReadAuthorInDatabase,** as follows:

```
public function testReadAuthorInDatabase()
{
    $authorPDO = new AuthorPDO();
    $authorPDO->save('Johann', 'Wolfgang', 'Von Goethe');
    $authorPDO->save('Francis', 'Scott', 'Fitzgerald');
    $authorPDO->save('Arthur', 'Conan', 'Doyle');
    $author = $authorPDO->readByCode(2);
    $this->assertEquals('Scott',$author['middle_name']);
    truncateTable('authors');
}
```

Of course, the test will fail, because the **AuthorPDO->readByCode** method does not exist. Let us implement it as follows:

```
public function readByCode(int $code): array
{
```

```
        $sql = 'SELECT * FROM authors WHERE code = :code';
        $statement = $this->pdo->prepare($sql);
        $statement->bindParam(':code', $code);
        $statement->execute();
        return $statement->fetch(\PDO::FETCH_ASSOC);
    }
```

The **PDOStatement->execute** method does not return records retrieved by a SQL **SELECT** command. It just stores the resource that points to those records. To retrieve a record, we use the **PDOStatement->fetch** method. The default is to return an indexed array, but when passing the **PDO::FETCH_ASSOC** argument, the method returns an associative array.

After testing reading a single record, let us create the test to read a set of records. Let us implement the **PDOTest->testReadAuthorsInDatabase**, as follows:

```
    public function testReadAuthorsInDatabase()
    {
        $authorPDO = new AuthorPDO();
        $authorPDO->save('Mary', 'Wollstonecraft', 'Shelley');
        $authorPDO->save('Agatha', 'Mary', 'Christie');
        $authorPDO->save('Chaya', 'Pinkhasivna', 'Lispector');
        $authors = $authorPDO->readAuthors();
        $this->assertCount(3,$authors);
        $this->assertEquals('Agatha',$authors[1]['first_name']);
        truncateTable('authors');
    }
```

You may have guessed that the test will fail because the **AuthorPDO->readAuthors** method does not exist. You are right, so let us create this method, as follows:

```
    public function readAuthors(): array
    {
        $sql = 'SELECT * FROM authors';
        $statement = $this->pdo->prepare($sql);
        $statement->execute();
        return $statement->fetchAll(\PDO::FETCH_ASSOC);
    }
```

The only new thing here is the use of the **PDOStatement->fetchAll** method. While fetch method returns just one record, **fetchAll** method returns them all, as the name suggests.

The next step is updating authors with PDO. Let us implement the **PDOTest->testUpdateAuthorInDatabase** method, as follows:

```php
    public function testUpdateAuthorInDatabase()
    {
        $authorPDO = new AuthorPDO();
        $authorPDO->save('Guy', 'de', 'Maupassant');
        $authorPDO->save('Antoine', 'de', 'Saint-Exupéry');
        $authorPDO->save('Honoré', 'de', 'Balzac');
        $author = $authorPDO->readByCode(1);
        $this->assertEquals('Guy',$author['first_name']);
        $authorPDO->update(1,['first_name' =>'Rudolf','middle_name'=>'Erich','last_name' =>'Raspe']);
        $author = $authorPDO->readByCode(1);
        $this->assertEquals('Rudolf',$author['first_name']);
        truncateTable('authors');
    }
```

As incredible as this may sound, this test will fail because the **AuthorPDO->update** method does not exist. Let us not waste time lamenting this. Let us create it as follows:

```php
    public function update(int $code, array $data)
    {
        $placeholders = '';
        $fields = [];
        foreach($data as $field => $value){
            $placeholder = str_replace('_','',$field);
            $placeholders .= $field . " = :$placeholder,";
            $fields[$placeholder] = $value;
        }
        $placeholders = substr($placeholders,0,strlen($placeholders)-1);
        $sql = 'UPDATE authors SET ' . $placeholders . ' WHERE code = :code';
        $statement = $this->pdo->prepare($sql);
        foreach($fields as $field => &$value){
            $statement->bindParam(":$field", $value);
        }
        $statement->bindParam(':code', $code);
        $statement->execute();
        return $statement->rowCount() == 1;
    }
```

Note: If you want to see the SQL expression produced by `PDOStatement`, **you can use** `debugDumpParams` **method. For example, considering the** `AuthorPDO->save` **method, you can save the SQL expression into the system log like this:** `syslog(LOG_DEBUG,$statement->debugDumpParams());`.

The `AuthorPDO->update` method has two for each structure. The first is to define the placeholders in the SQL **UPDATE** command. The second serves to assign values to these placeholders. Note that the `$value` variable, in the second `foreach`, is preceded by an **&**. This means that the `$value` variable is receiving the reference to the array element and not its value. This is necessary because the `PDOStatement->bindParam` method takes the reference of the variable used as the second argument and not its value. Thus, without using the **&** operator, at the end of `foreach` execution, all placeholders will be associated with the last value read from the array.

At each iteration, the `$value` variable receives the value of the current element of the `$fields` array. The `PDOStatement->bindParam` method uses the address of this variable, not its value. So, as it changes value, the placeholder values automatically change as well. For example, our test will assign to the `$value` variable, in sequence, the values **'Rudolf'**, **'Erich'**, and **'Raspe'**. Without using the **&** operator, each time the `$value` variable is changed in `foreach`, the value of the placeholder that received it will also change. When passing the address of the array element, the placeholder is linked to the array element, which does not change, and not the foreach variable, which changes with each iteration.

You can experiment to see what happens if you remove the **&** on the left of the `$value` variable. **Spoiler**: the test will fail.

Passing by reference in PHP is something roughly similar to using pointers in the C language. In the C language you can declare a variable that contains a memory address in place of a value. This type of variable is called a **pointer**. In PHP, we do not need to declare variables, but we can assign a reference to another variable to a variable, so that one variable points to another.

This is the moment when *Linus Torvalds* would say: *talk is cheap, show me the code*. Well, let us show an example of difference between variables passed by value and by reference, as follows:

```php
<?php
$value = 42;
$copyOfValue = $value;
$referenceOfValue = &$value;
$value = 13;
echo "\$value = $value\n";
echo "\$copyOfValue = $copyOfValue\n";
echo "\$referenceOfValue = $referenceOfValue\n";
```

After running, the output of this file will be as follows:

$value = 13

$copyOfValue = 42

$referenceOfValue = 13

The **$copyOfValue** variable retained the value that **$value** had when it was assigned. This happened because it received a value.

The variable **$referenceOfValue** changed value after **$value** changed value. This happened because she received a reference to a variable. Thus, when the referenced variable changes, the referencing variable also changes.

After we have clarified the passing of references to variables, let us implement the last author test of the **PDOTest** class, the **testDeleteAuthorInDatabase** method, as follows:

```php
public function testDeleteAuthorInDatabase()
{
    $authorPDO = new AuthorPDO();
    $authorPDO->save('Machado', 'de', 'Assis');
    $authorPDO->save('José', 'de', 'Alencar');
    $authorPDO->save('Rachel', 'de', 'Queiroz');
    $author = $authorPDO->readByCode(2);
    $this->assertEquals('Alencar',$author['last_name']);
    $authorPDO->delete(2);
    $author = $authorPDO->readByCode(2);
    $this->assertEmpty($author);
    truncateTable('authors');
}
```

As you might suspect, the test will fail because the **AuthorPDO** method does not exist. Let us create it as follows:

```php
public function delete(int $code)
{
    $sql = 'DELETE FROM authors WHERE code = :code';
    $statement = $this->pdo->prepare($sql);
    $statement->bindParam(':code', $code);
    $statement->execute();
    return $statement->rowCount() == 1;
}
```

Comparing this method with the previous ones, there seems to be nothing new. When you happily try to run the **PDOTest** class, you are surprised by this error, as follows:

1) PDOTest::testDeleteAuthorInDatabase

TypeError: Librarian\Model\PDO\AuthorPDO::readByCode(): Return value must be of type array, false returned

This error happens because the **AuthorPDO->readByCode** method is returning false instead of an integer. It returns false because the query found no records. The **PDOStatement->fetch** method returns an array if there is a record, but returns false if there is not. Several PHP functions and methods return more than one type, usually with false being the response for a value not found.

Therefore, we need to modify the **Author PDO->readByCode** method, so that it checks the return of **PDOStatement->fetch**. The changed method will be as follows:

```
public function readByCode(int $code): array
{
    $sql = 'SELECT * FROM authors WHERE code = :code';
    $statement = $this->pdo->prepare($sql);
    $statement->bindParam(':code', $code);
    $statement->execute();
    $record = $statement->fetch(\PDO::FETCH_ASSOC);
    return (is_array($record) ? $record : []);
}
```

Following the same reasoning, we need to change the **AuthorPDO->readAuthors** method, as follows:

```
public function readAuthors(): array
{
    $sql = 'SELECT * FROM authors';
    $statement = $this->pdo->prepare($sql);
    $statement->execute();
    $records = $statement->fetchAll(\PDO::FETCH_ASSOC);
    return (is_array($records) ? $records : []);
}
```

Now, the **PDOTest** class will run successfully.

Handling exceptions and errors

Building tests helps us deal with two inevitable facts of building software: exceptions and errors. If there are tests and they are run with each software change, you will discover exceptions and errors at development time and be able to handle them. Occasionally, some exceptions and errors may only occur in production, due to differences in the environment, either way, the code needs to be robust to continue working if something goes wrong.

A good development process should document alternative paths when gathering requirements. Naturally, we are interested in the happy path, the sequence of steps that achieves our goal. We need to think about everything that could go wrong in this sequence. This is why use case documents have a main flow and alternative flows, to document errors and exceptions and how to deal with them.

Some situations where an error may occur can be anticipated by the programming language or software component you are using (class or library). This anticipation in OOP is done with exception classes. An exception class instance stores an error code, an error message, and the execution trace until the error occurred. The exception class does not solve the problem, it provides a way to handle the problem. Exception objects are captured by the try...catch structure, which we learned about in *Chapter 2, PHP Foundations*. Exception objects allow you to handle errors, preventing the program from ending abruptly. Exception handling is part of the software continuity plan. Robust software handles all possible exceptions.

PHP provides the **Exception** class and several subclasses to handle common exceptions, but you can also extend **Exception** and create exception classes for the specific cases of your applications.

Let us copy **PDOTest** class as **PDOExceptionTest** and let us modify it to test some exceptions when handling the database with **PDO**. The class will be **PDOExceptionTest**. Let us start with the **testSaveAuthorInDatabase** method. First, let us change the author data, passing a last name with more than twenty characters, as follows:

```
public function testSaveAuthorInDatabase()
{
    $authorPDO = new AuthorPDO();
    $this->assertTrue($authorPDO->save('Karl', 'Philipp',
'Hottentottenstottertrottelmutter'));
    truncateTable('authors');
}
```

The result will be the throwing of an exception by the **PDO** extension, as follows:

1) PDOExceptionTest::testSaveAuthorInDatabase

PDOException: SQLSTATE[22001]: String data, right truncated: 1406 Data too long for column 'first_name' at row 1

The table rejected the inclusion because the data exceeds the limit of one of the fields. This behavior is correct and expected. So, our test should check if this exception is thrown and not if the record was included.

Let us modify **PDOTest->testSaveAuthorInDatabase** for the following:

```
public function testSaveAuthorInDatabase()
{
```

```
    $authorPDO = new AuthorPDO();
    try {
        $authorPDO->save('Karl', 'Philipp',
'Hottentottenstottertrottelmutter');
    } catch (\Throwable $th) {
        $this->assertInstanceOf(\PDOException::class,$th);
    }
    truncateTable('authors');
}
```

The **assertInstanceOf** method is equivalent to using the **instanceof** operator, which checks whether an object is an instance of a given class. It returns true if the object is an instance of the given class or any of its subclasses.

Now, the test will pass because a **PDOException** exception will be thrown when we execute **AuthorPDO->save**, and it will be caught by the catch of the try...catch structure, which, in this case, captures objects from classes that implement the **Throwable** interface.

Note: Exception class is the base class for all user exceptions. This class implements Throwable interface. You can create your own exception classes implementing Throwable or you can use any of the PHP predefined exception classes.

In the book *Clean Code, Robert Martin* states that with tests the *fear virtually disappears. The higher your test coverage, the less your fear*. If you test the happy path and the unhappy paths, you know that your code is prepared to maintain application continuity. Tests help us, for example, to understand that we must always guarantee a valid return, so that the application is not interrupted because it does not know what to do with an unexpected or missing type of data. We have already done this in part of our implementation, for example, when reading authors. If an author code is not found, the method returns an empty array, but returns something.

However, we cannot implement the treatment in an unfortunate way and fail to create the test that verifies that this treatment really works. More precisely, whether it continues to work after any change to the application. To illustrate this, let us implement the **PDOExceptionTest->testReadAuthorInDatabase** method to check whether the **AuthorPDO->readByCode** method returns an empty array for non-existent code, as follows:

```
    public function testReadAuthorInDatabase()
    {
        $authorPDO = new AuthorPDO();
        $author = $authorPDO->readByCode(2);
        $this->assertIsArray($author);
        $this->assertThat($author,$this->logicalNot($this-
>arrayHasKey('first_name')));
```

```
        truncateTable('authors');
    }
```

We will discuss the **assertThat** method. This method allows you to construct assertions with expressions from methods that encapsulate operators. In this case, we check that the **$author** array does not have the key **'first_name'**.

The author reading test in case there is no author is simple, as it is enough to check whether the returned array has no elements, as follows:

```
    public function testReadAuthorsInDatabase()
    {
        $authorPDO = new AuthorPDO();
        $authors = $authorPDO->readAuthors();
        $this->assertCount(0,$authors);
        truncateTable('authors');
    }
```

The author updating test in case there is no author is simple too, as it is enough to check whether **authorPDO->update** returns false, as follows:

```
    public function testUpdateAuthorInDatabase()
    {
        $authorPDO = new AuthorPDO();
        $this->assertFalse($authorPDO->update(1,['first_name'
=>'Rudolf','middle_name'=>'Erich','last_name' =>'Raspe']));
        truncateTable('authors');
    }
```

The principle of always returning a value helps you know if the operation worked. It may be that a function or method executes the instructions without producing an error, but without doing what we want. In the case of database operations, SQL writing commands may be valid and not generate errors in the database, but they may also not modify any record. When programming, you must play the role of manager, do not just order something done, check that it has been done.

So, we conclude testing alternative paths for operations on authors with the implementation of **PDOExceptionTest ->testDeleteAuthorInDatabase,** as follows:

```
    public function testDeleteAuthorInDatabase()
    {
        $authorPDO = new AuthorPDO();
        $this->assertFalse($authorPDO->delete(2));
        truncateTable('authors');
    }
```

The **PDOExceptionTest** class is just an introduction to exception handling. Over the next few chapters, we will do several refactoring that will make our code more robust and we will deal with throwing and exception handling.

Conclusion

In this chapter, we covered how to define classes and their members and how to use them to program with maximum code reuse. We covered the access implementation to a relational database without creating technology lock-in with a specific vendor. Finally, we covered the exception handling.

In the next chapter, we are going to learn about the refactoring of the function driven registration with file storage for object-oriented implementation.

Points to remember

- PHP supports OOP and allows you to create classes and their respective attributes and methods.

- The main reuse mechanism in object-orientation is inheritance. PHP has simple inheritance, allowing you to inherit from a single class.

- It is possible to reuse more than one code block in a class through traits.

- PHP has magic methods, which are triggered by events, such as the creation and destruction of class instances.

- The PDO extension allows you to use different databases with the same interface, which allows you to decouple the application from a specific database vendor.

Exercises

1. Start PHP in interactive mode, import the autoload.php file and try to create an instance of the AbstractCode class. Observe what happens.

2. Based on the AuthorTest->testAuthorDestructor method, create a test that writes a message to the system log when an object of the Author class is cloned.

3. Remove setUpBeforeClass and tearDownAfterClass methods from DatabaseTest, change its parent class for AbstractDatabaseTest and run the tests for checking if they keep working.

CHAPTER 7

Object-oriented Registration with File System Storage

Introduction

This chapter of the book will cover how to refactor a function driven registration with file system storage for an object-oriented implementation. We will learn how to create classes and their methods from functions initially by converting the author recording in a plain text file to object-oriented mode. After this experience, we will refactor the recording in other file system formats. We will continue converting read, update and remove operations from functions to class methods.

Structure

The chapter covers the following topics:

- Refactoring functions into classes
- Saving data to file system with classes
- Reading data from file system with classes
- Updating and deleting data from the file system with classes

Objectives

By the end of this chapter, you will be able to convert functions into methods and group them into classes. You will learn how to think about call semantics by having an actor performing an action rather than an action occurring without someone responsible for it. Long function names will give way to more concise method names.

Refactoring functions into classes

We started the Librarian application with the registration of authors and books with storage in a plain text file. So, let us start converting function-based code to object-oriented code via the **txt.functions.php** functions file.

Following our test-driven approach, we begin by creating the **PlainTextTest** class, which will inherit from **AbstractBackupTest** to preserve the text file if it already exists. At each step of our implementation, you can compare the **PlainTextTest** methods with the **TxtTest** methods. The initial structure of **PlainTextTest**, as follows:

```php
<?php
use Librarian\Test\AbstractBackupTest;
use PHPUnit\Framework\Attributes\CoversClass;
/**
 * @covers AuthorPlainText
 */
#[CoversClass(AuthorPlainText::class)]
class PlainTextTest extends AbstractBackupTest
{
}
```

Note: The TxtTest class did not cover anything, but the PlainTextTest method covers a class. This will make a difference in the coverage report. Remember we are using annotations because of backward compatibility.

Let us implement the **testSaveAuthor** test method, as follows:

```php
    public function testSaveAuthor()
    {
        $authorPlainText = new AuthorPlainText();
        $this->assertTrue($authorPlainText->save('Wells','Herbert','George'));
        $filepath = Config::get('author_plaintext_filepath');
        unlink($filepath);
    }
```

The **PlainTextTest->testSaveAuthor** method is similar to the **TxtTest->testSaveAuthorInPlainText** method. The **saveAuthorInPlainText** and **getConfig** functions have been replaced, respectively, by the **AuthorPlainText->save** and **Config::get** methods.

This test will fail because the **AuthorPlainText** class does not exist. To fix this, let us create a new subdirectory in **src/Model** called **Filesystem**.

In this new subdirectory, we will create a class called **AuthorPlainText**, as follows:

```php
<?php
namespace Librarian\Model\Filesystem;
class AuthorPlainText
{
}
```

Next, let us implement the **AuthorPlainText->save**, as follows:

```php
    public function save($lastName, $middleName, $firstName): bool
    {
        $filepath = Config::get('author_plaintext_filepath');
        $handle = fopen($filepath,'a+');
        fseek($handle, -self::ROW_LENGTH, SEEK_END);
        $row = fread($handle, self::ROW_LENGTH);
        $code = (int) substr($row, 0, self::CODE_LENGTH);
        $code++;
        $row = $this->formatField($code, self::CODE_LENGTH) . $this->formatField($lastName, self::NAME_LENGTH) .
        $this->formatField($middleName, self::NAME_LENGTH) . $this->formatField($firstName, self::NAME_LENGTH) . "\n";
        fwrite($handle,$row);
        fclose($handle);
        $handle = fopen($filepath,'r');
        $found = false;
        fseek($handle, -self::ROW_LENGTH, SEEK_END);
        $currentRow = fread($handle, self::ROW_LENGTH);
        $found = ($currentRow == $row);
        fclose($handle);
        return $found;
    }
```

As you can see, this method is similar to **saveAuthorInPlainText** function, but there some different details, as follows:

- The use of **Config::get** method for getting the path of the plain text file.
- The use of the **ROW_LENGTH**, **CODE_LENGTH** and **NAME_LENGTH** class constants.

Note: Replacing numbers with constants is a good programming practice, because if the value of the constant changes, simply change the line that declares the constant.

These details require implementing the **Config::get** method and declaring the constants. The **Config** class will be created in the **Librarian\Util** namespace, which means we have to create the **Util** subdirectory in the **src** folder, which is the directory mapped as **Librarian** by Composer.

We are trying to separate classes into namespaces according to their responsibilities. The classes that refer to our application entities (author and book) or their data storage sources are in the model namespace because they are a part of our business model. The **Config** class is not a part of the business model, but it is useful for any other class that needs configuration data. So, we put it in a utility namespace.

Let us implement the **Config** class and it **get** method, as follows:

```php
<?php
namespace Librarian\Util;
class Config
{
    private static ?array $config = null;

    public static function get(string $key)
    {
        if (self::$config == null){
            self::$config = require __DIR__ . '/../../book.config.php';
        }
        return self::$config[$key];
    }
}
```

The question mark (**?**) to the left of an attribute's type acts as a nullable operator. This means that the attribute accepts null as an alternative to a value of the declared type, without this operator, assigning null to an array variable result in an error.

Once we have created the **Config** class, the next step is to declare the constants used in the **AuthorPlainText->save** method. The immediate and seemingly obvious thought will be to declare them in the **AuthorPlainText** class itself, since we already use the **self** keyword to refer to these constants but we have to think that these constants are not only used for plain text files, but for files in CSV and JSON formats. Therefore, to avoid repetition, it is more appropriate to create an abstract class that declares these functions and make **AuthorPlainText** inherit from that class.

Let us then create the **AbstractAuthorFilesystem** class, as follows:

```php
<?php
namespace Librarian\Model\Filesystem;
abstract class AbstractAuthorFilesystem
{
    const ROW_LENGTH = 65;
    const CODE_LENGTH = 4;
    const NAME_LENGTH = 20;

    public function formatField($field, int $length)
    {
        return str_pad($field, $length, ' ', STR_PAD_LEFT);
    }
}
```

As you can see, we encapsulated the **formatField** function as a method of the **AbstractAuthorFileSystem** class. Since this function is used for various text file formats, it is convenient for it to be in an abstract class for reuse.

Now, we will go back to the **AuthorPlainText** class and modify it so that it inherits from **AbstractAuthorFilesystem**, as follows:

```php
class AuthorPlainText extends AbstractAuthorFilesystem
```

After this change, **PlainTextTest->testSaveAuthor** will run successfully. Now that we have presented the path for converting functions into class methods, with identification of reuse opportunities, let us reimplement the recording of text files in other formats using objects.

Saving data to file system with classes

In this section, we will learn how to save author data in CSV and JSON formats.

Saving as CSV

Let us implement recording authors in CSV format by creating the **CSVTextTest** class, which will inherit from **AbstractBackupTest**, as follows:

```php
class CSVTextTest extends AbstractBackupTest
```

Next, let us implement the **CSVTextTest->saveAuthor** method, as follows:

```php
    public function testSaveAuthor()
    {
        $authorCSV = new AuthorCSV();
```

```
        $this->assertTrue($authorCSV->save('Wells','Herbert','George'));
        $filepath = Config::get('author_csv_filepath');
        unlink($filepath);
    }
```

You know this test will fail because the **AuthorCSV** class does not exist. Let us create it in the **Librarian\Model\Filesystem** namespace, as follows:

```
class AuthorCSV extends AbstractAuthorFilesystem
```

Let us encapsulate the **saveAuthorInCSV** function from the **csv.functions.php** file as the **AuthorCSV->save** method, as follows:

```
    public function save($lastName, $middleName, $firstName): bool
    {
        $filepath = Config::get('author_csv_filepath');
        $handle = fopen($filepath,'a+');
        $code = 0;
        while (!feof($handle)){
            $row = fgetcsv($handle, null, ';');
            $code = $row[0] ?? $code;
        }
        $code++;
        $fields = [
            $this->formatField($code, 4),
            $this->formatField($lastName, 20),
            $this->formatField($middleName, 20),
            $this->formatField($firstName, 20)
        ];
        fputcsv($handle, $fields, ';');
        fclose($handle);
        $handle = fopen($filepath,'r');
        $found = false;
        $currentCode = 0;
        while (!feof($handle)) {
            $currentRow = fgetcsv($handle, null, ';');
            $currentCode = $currentRow[0] ?? $currentCode;
        }
        $found = ((int) $currentCode == $code);
        fclose($handle);
        return $found;
    }
```

In addition to replacing the **getConfig** function with the **Config::get** method, we replaced the **formatField** function with the inherited **$this->formatField** method. As incredible as it may seem, this is enough for the **CSVTextTest->testSaveAuthor** test to pass.

Saving as JSON

Let us implement recording authors in JSON format by creating the **JSONTextTest** class, which will inherit from **AbstractBackupTest**, as follows:

```
class JSONTextTest extends AbstractBackupTest
```

Next, let us implement the **JSONTextTest->saveAuthor** method, as follows:

```
public function testSaveAuthor()
{
    $authorJSON = new AuthorJSON();
    $this->assertTrue($authorJSON->save('Wells','Herbert','George'));
    $filepath = Config::get('author_json_filepath');
    unlink($filepath);
}
```

You know this test will fail because the **AuthorJSON** class does not exist. Let us create it in the **Librarian\Model\Filesystem** namespace, as follows:

```
class AuthorJSON extends AbstractAuthorFilesystem
```

Let us encapsulate the **saveAuthorInJSON** function from the **json.functions.php** file as the **AuthorJSON->save** method, as follows:

```
public function save($lastName, $middleName, $firstName): bool
{
    $filepath = Config::get('author_json_filepath');
    $handle = fopen($filepath,'a');
    fclose($handle);
    $json = json_decode(file_get_contents($filepath));
    if ($json == NULL){
        $json = [];
    }
    $code = 0;
    foreach ($json as $row) {
        $code = $row->code;
    }
    $code++;
    $dict = [
```

```
                    'code' => $code,
                    'last_name'  => $lastName,
                    'middle_name' => $middleName,
                    'first_name' =>  $firstName
            ];
            $json[] = $dict;
            $text = json_encode($json);
            file_put_contents($filepath, $text);
            $json = json_decode(file_get_contents($filepath));
            $found = false;
            $currentCode = 0;
            foreach ($json as $row) {
                $currentCode = $row->code;
            }
            $found = ($currentCode == $code);
            return $found;
    }
```

This time we just need to replace the **getConfig** function with the **Config::get** method. As incredible as it may seem, this is enough for the **JSONTextTest->testSaveAuthor** test to pass.

Reading data from file system with classes

We now have test classes to test reading and writing data in plain text (**PlainTextTest**), CSV (**CSVTextTest**) and JSON (**JSONTextTest**) formats. In the section, *Saving data to file system with classes*, we implemented the author inclusion tests in these three formats. Now, let us implement the reading tests.

Note: We have a reading of a single record and a reading of the set of records.

Reading from Plain Text

For beginning, let us create the **PlainTextTest->testReadAuthor** method based on the **TxtTest->testReadAuthorInPlainText** method.

Note: When we refactor the methods, we not only change the implementation but we also revise the names to eliminate redundancies.

Object-orientation helps us organize names into sentences, because we have an actor, the object and an action, the method. The method will be as follows:

```php
public function testReadAuthor()
{
    $authorPlainText = new AuthorPlainText();
    $authorPlainText->save('Von Goethe','Wolfgang','Johann');
    $authorPlainText->save('Fitzgerald','Scott','Francis');
    $authorPlainText->save('Doyle','Arthur','Conan');
    $author = $authorPlainText->readByCode(2);
    $this->assertEquals('Scott',$author['middle_name']);
    $filepath = Config::get('author_plaintext_filepath');
    unlink($filepath);
}
```

The test will fail because the **readByCode** method does not exist in the **AuthorPlainText** class. So let us implement it from the **readAuthorInPlainTextByCode** function, as follows:

```php
public function readByCode(int $code): array
{
    $filepath = Config::get('author_plaintext_filepath');
    $handle = fopen($filepath,'r');
    $author = [];
    while(!feof($handle)){
        $row = fread($handle, self::ROW_LENGTH);
        $readCode = (int) substr($row,0,self::CODE_LENGTH);
        if ($readCode == $code){
            $author = [
                'code' => $code,
                'last_name' => trim(substr($row, self::CODE_LENGTH,
self::NAME_LENGTH)),
                'middle_name' => trim(substr($row, self::CODE_LENGTH +
self::NAME_LENGTH + 1, self::NAME_LENGTH)),
                'first_name' => trim(substr($row, self::CODE_LENGTH + (2
* self::NAME_LENGTH) + 1, self::NAME_LENGTH))
            ];
            break;
        }
    }
    fclose($handle);
    return $author;
}
```

Unlike the function, we are now only using constants to format the record fields. This makes the code more robust to changes if the field size change. If the length of a field is changed, it is enough to change the value of the corresponding constant in the **AbstractAuthorFilesystem** class, avoiding an audit in the **AuthorPlainText->readByCode** method. By implementing this method, you can successfully run **PlainTextTest->testReadAuthor**.

Now, let us implement the record set reading test, with **PlainTextTest->testReadAuthors**, as follows:

```
public function testReadAuthors()
{
    $authorPlainText = new AuthorPlainText();
    $authorPlainText->save('Shelley','Wollstonecraft','Mary');
    $authorPlainText->save('Christie','Mary','Agatha');
    $authorPlainText->save('Lispector','Pinkhasivna','Chaya');
    $authors = $authorPlainText->readAll();
    $this->assertCount(3,$authors);
    $this->assertEquals('Agatha',$authors[1]['first_name']);
    $filepath = Config::get('author_plaintext_filepath');
    unlink($filepath);
}
```

This test will fail because the **readAll** method does not exist in the **AuthorPlainText** class. Let us implement it from the **readAuthorsInPlainText** function, as follows:

```
public function readAll(): array
{
    $filepath = getConfig()['author_plaintext_filepath'];
    $handle = fopen($filepath,'r');
    $authors = [];
    while(!feof($handle)){
        $row = fread($handle, self::ROW_LENGTH);
        $author = [
            'code' => (int) substr($row,0,self::CODE_LENGTH),
            'last_name' => trim(substr($row, self::CODE_LENGTH,
self::NAME_LENGTH)),
            'middle_name' => trim(substr($row, self::CODE_LENGTH +
self::NAME_LENGTH + 1, self::NAME_LENGTH)),
            'first_name' => trim(substr($row, self::CODE_LENGTH + (2 *
self::NAME_LENGTH) + 1, self::NAME_LENGTH))
        ];
```

```
        if ($author['code'] != 0) {
            $authors[] = $author;
        }
    }
    fclose($handle);
    return $authors;
}
```

By implementing this method, you can successfully run **PlainTextTest->testReadAuthors**.

Reading from CSV

Let us create the **CSVTextTest->testReadAuthor** method based on the **CSVTTest->testReadAuthorInCSV** method, as follows:

```
public function testReadAuthor()
{
    $authorCSV = new AuthorCSV();
    $authorCSV->save('Von Goethe','Wolfgang','Johann');
    $authorCSV->save('Fitzgerald','Scott','Francis');
    $authorCSV->save('Doyle','Arthur','Conan');
    $author = $authorCSV->readByCode(2);
    $this->assertEquals('Scott',$author['middle_name']);
    $filepath = Config::get('author_csv_filepath');
    unlink($filepath);
}
```

This test will fail because the **AuthorCSV->readByCode** method does not exist. Let us implement it, using the **readAuthorInCSVByCode** function, as follows:

```
public function readByCode(int $code): array
{
    $filepath = Config::get('author_csv_filepath');
    $handle = fopen($filepath,'r');
    $author = [];
    while(!feof($handle)){
        $row = fgetcsv($handle, null, ';');
        $readCode = (int) is_array($row) && isset($row[0]) ? $row[0] : 0;
        if ($readCode == $code){
            $author = [
                'code' => $code,
```

```
                'last_name' => trim($row[1]),
                'middle_name' => trim($row[2]),
                'first_name' => trim($row[3]),
            ];
            break;
        }
    }
    fclose($handle);
    return $author;
}
```

The difference between the function and the method is the use of the **Config** class to read the configuration file.

Now, let us implement the record set reading test with **CSVTextTest->testReadAuthors** method, based on the **CSVTest->testReadAuthorsInCSV** method, as follows:

```
public function testReadAuthors()
{
    $authorCSV = new AuthorCSV();
    $authorCSV->save('Shelley','Wollstonecraft','Mary');
    $authorCSV->save('Christie','Mary','Agatha');
    $authorCSV->save('Lispector','Pinkhasivna','Chaya');
    $authors = $authorCSV->readAll();
    $this->assertCount(3,$authors);
    $this->assertEquals('Agatha',$authors[1]['first_name']);
    $filepath = Config::get('author_csv_filepath');
    unlink($filepath);
}
```

The test will fail because the **AuthorCSV->readAll** method does not exist. Let us implement it from the **readAuthorsInCSV** function, as follows:

```
public function readAll(): array
{
    $filepath = Config::get('author_csv_filepath');
    $handle = fopen($filepath,'r');
    $authors = [];
    while(!feof($handle)){
        $row = fgetcsv($handle, null, ';');
        if (!is_array($row) || count($row) != self::CODE_LENGTH)
continue;
```

```
            $author = [
                'code' => (int) $row[0],
                'last_name' => trim($row[1]),
                'middle_name' => trim($row[2]),
                'first_name' => trim($row[3]),
            ];
            $authors[] = $author;
        }
        fclose($handle);
        return $authors;
    }
```

By implementing this method, you can successfully run **CSVTextTest->testReadAuthors**.

Reading from JSON

The last step of refactoring file system reading is with the JSON format. Let us create the **JSONTextTest->testReadAuthor** method based on the **JSONTest->testReadAuthorInCSV** method, as follows:

```
    public function testReadAuthor()
    {
        $authorJSON = new AuthorJSON();
        $authorJSON->save('Von Goethe','Wolfgang','Johann');
        $authorJSON->save('Fitzgerald','Scott','Francis');
        $authorJSON->save('Doyle','Arthur','Conan');
        $author = $authorJSON->readByCode(2);
        $this->assertEquals('Scott',$author['middle_name']);
        $filepath = Config::get('author_json_filepath');
        unlink($filepath);
    }
```

This test will fail because the **AuthorJSON->readByCode** method does not exist. Let us implement it using the **readAuthorInJSONByCode** function, as follows:

```
    public function readByCode(int $code): array
    {
        $filepath = Config::get('author_json_filepath');
        $content = file_get_contents($filepath);
        $authors = json_decode($content);
        $authors = is_null($authors) ? [] : $authors;
        foreach($authors as $author) {
```

```
        if ((int) $author->code == $code) {
            return (array) $author;
        }
    }
    return [];
}
```

Now, **JSONTextTest->readAuthor** will run successfully. We can proceed by implementing the **testReadAuthors** method, based on **JSONTest->testReadAuthorsInJSON**, as follows:

```
public function testReadAuthors()
{
    $authorJSON = new AuthorJSON();
    $authorJSON->save('Shelley','Wollstonecraft','Mary');
    $authorJSON->save('Christie','Mary','Agatha');
    $authorJSON->save('Lispector','Pinkhasivna','Chaya');
    $authors = $authorJSON->readAll();
    $this->assertCount(3,$authors);
    $this->assertEquals('Agatha',$authors[1]['first_name']);
    $filepath = Config::get('author_json_filepath');
    unlink($filepath);
}
```

You know this test will fail because the **readAll** method does not exist in the **AuthorJSON** class. Let us implement it using the **readAuthorsInJSON** function, as follows:

```
public function readAll(): array
{
    $filepath = Config::get('author_json_filepath');
    $content = file_get_contents($filepath);
    $authors = json_decode($content);
    $authors = is_null($authors) ? [] : $authors;
    foreach($authors as $index => $author) {
        $authors[$index] = (array) $author;
    }
    return $authors;
}
```

Now, all reading tests refactored using objects will run successfully.

Updating and deleting data from file system with classes

In the previous section, we implemented tests for writing and reading authors in plain text, CSV and JSON formats running successfully. Now, let us implement the updating and deleting tests.

Updating and deleting from plain text

For beginning, let us create the **PlainTextTest->testUpdateAuthor** method based on the **TxtTest->testUpdateAuthorInPlainText** method, as follows:

```
public function testUpdateAuthor()
{
    $authorPlainText = new AuthorPlainText();
    $authorPlainText->save('Maupassant','de','Guy');
    $authorPlainText->save('Saint-Exupéry','de','Antoine');
    $authorPlainText->save('Balzac','de','Honoré');
    $author = $authorPlainText->readByCode(1);
    $this->assertEquals('Guy',$author['first_name']);
    $authorPlainText->update(1,[
        'last_name' => 'Raspe',
        'middle_name' => 'Erich',
        'first_name' => 'Rudolf'
    ]);
    $author = $authorPlainText->readByCode(1);
    $this->assertEquals('Rudolf',$author['first_name']);
    $filepath = Config::get('author_plaintext_filepath');
    unlink($filepath);
}
```

This test will fail because the **AuthorPlainText** class does not have the **update** method. Let us implement it, as follows:

```
public function update(int $code, array $data): bool
{
    $sourcePath = Config::get('author_plaintext_filepath');
    $targetPath = str_replace('.txt','.tmp',$sourcePath);
    $sourceHandle = fopen($sourcePath,'r');
    $targetHandle = fopen($targetPath,'w');
    $changed = false;
```

```php
        while(!feof($sourceHandle)){
            $row = fread($sourceHandle, self::ROW_LENGTH);
            $readCode = (int) substr($row,0,self::CODE_LENGTH);
            if ($readCode == $code){
                $author = [
                    'code' => $code,
                    'last_name' => trim(substr($row, self::CODE_LENGTH,
self::NAME_LENGTH)),
                    'middle_name' => trim(substr($row, self::CODE_LENGTH +
self::NAME_LENGTH + 1, self::NAME_LENGTH)),
                    'first_name' => trim(substr($row, self::CODE_LENGTH + (2
* self::NAME_LENGTH) + 1, self::NAME_LENGTH))
                ];
                foreach($data as $key => $value){
                    $author[$key] = $value;
                }
                $row = $this->formatField($code,self::CODE_LENGTH) . $this-
>formatField($author['last_name'], self::NAME_LENGTH) .
                $this->formatField($author['middle_name'], self::NAME_
LENGTH) . $this->formatField($author['first_name'], self::NAME_LENGTH) .
"\n";
                $changed = true;
            }
            fwrite($targetHandle,$row,self::ROW_LENGTH);
        }
        fclose($sourceHandle);
        fclose($targetHandle);
        unlink($sourcePath);
        copy($targetPath,$sourcePath);
        unlink($targetPath);
        return $changed;
    }
```

Since the update test runs successfully, let us create the **PlainTextTest->testDeleteAuthor** method based on the **TxtTest->testDeleteAuthorInPlainText** method, as follows:

```php
    public function testDeleteAuthor()
    {
        $authorPlainText = new AuthorPlainText();
```

```
$authorPlainText->save('Assis','de','Machado');
$authorPlainText->save('Alencar','de','José');
$authorPlainText->save('Queiroz','de','Rachel');
$author = $authorPlainText->readByCode(2);
$this->assertEquals('Alencar',$author['last_name']);
$authorPlainText->delete(2);
$author = $authorPlainText->readByCode(2);
$this->assertEmpty($author);
$filepath = Config::get('author_plaintext_filepath');
unlink($filepath);
    }
```

This test will fail because the **AuthorPlainText** class does not have the **delete** method. Let us implement it, as follows:

```
public function delete(int $code): bool
{
    $sourcePath = Config::get('author_plaintext_filepath');
    $targetPath = str_replace('.txt','.tmp',$sourcePath);
    $sourceHandle = fopen($sourcePath,'r');
    $targetHandle = fopen($targetPath,'w');
    $changed = false;
    while(!feof($sourceHandle)){
        $row = fread($sourceHandle, self::ROW_LENGTH);
        $readCode = (int) substr($row,0,4);
        if ($readCode == $code) {
            $changed = true;
            continue;
        }
        fwrite($targetHandle,$row,self::ROW_LENGTH);
    }
    fclose($sourceHandle);
    fclose($targetHandle);
    unlink($sourcePath);
    copy($targetPath,$sourcePath);
    unlink($targetPath);
    return $changed;
}
```

Now, the plain text author removal test using objects will run successfully.

Updating and deleting from CSV

Let us create the **CSVTextTest->testUpdateAuthor** method based on the **CSVTTest->testUpdateAuthorInCSV** method, as follows:

```
public function testUpdateAuthor()
{
    $authorCSV = new AuthorCSV();
    $authorCSV->save('Maupassant','de','Guy');
    $authorCSV->save('Saint-Exupéry','de','Antoine');
    $authorCSV->save('Balzac','de','Honoré');
    $author = $authorCSV->readByCode(1);
    $this->assertEquals('Guy',$author['first_name']);
    $authorCSV->update(1,[
        'last_name' => 'Raspe',
        'middle_name' => 'Erich',
        'first_name' => 'Rudolf'
    ]);
    $author = $authorCSV->readByCode(1);
    $this->assertEquals('Rudolf',$author['first_name']);
    $filepath = Config::get('author_csv_filepath');
    unlink($filepath);
}
```

As you might guess, this test will fail because the **AuthorCSV->update** method does not exist. Let us implement it, using the **updateAuthorInCSV** function, as follows:

```
public function update(int $code, array $data): bool
{
    $sourcePath = Config::get('author_csv_filepath');
    $targetPath = str_replace('.csv','.tmp',$sourcePath);
    $sourceHandle = fopen($sourcePath,'r');
    $targetHandle = fopen($targetPath,'w');
    $changed = false;
    while(!feof($sourceHandle)){
        $row = fgetcsv($sourceHandle, null, ';');
        if (!is_array($row) || count($row) != self::CODE_LENGTH)
continue;
        $readCode = (int) $row[0];
        if ($readCode == $code){
```

```
        $author = [
            'code' => $code,
            'last_name' => trim($row[1]),
            'middle_name' => trim($row[2]),
            'first_name' => trim($row[3]),
        ];
        foreach($data as $key => $value){
            $author[$key] = $value;
        }
        $row = [
            $this->formatField($code,self::CODE_LENGTH),
            $this->formatField($author['last_name'],self::CODE_
LENGTH,self::NAME_LENGTH),
            $this->formatField($author['middle_name'],self::NAME_
LENGTH),
            $this->formatField($author['first_name'],self::NAME_
LENGTH)
        ];
        $changed = true;
    }
    fputcsv($targetHandle,$row,';');
}
fclose($sourceHandle);
fclose($targetHandle);
unlink($sourcePath);
copy($targetPath,$sourcePath);
unlink($targetPath);
return $changed;
}
```

Since the update test runs successfully, let us create the **CSVTextTest->testDeleteAuthor** method based on the **CSVTest->testDeleteAuthorInPlainText** method, as follows:

```
public function testDelete()
{
    $authorCSV = new AuthorCSV();
    $authorCSV->save('Assis','de','Machado');
    $authorCSV->save('Alencar','de','José');
    $authorCSV->save('Queiroz','de','Rachel');
    $author = $authorCSV->readByCode(2);
```

```
$this->assertEquals('Alencar',$author['last_name']);
$authorCSV->delete(2);
$author = $authorCSV->readByCode(2);
$this->assertEmpty($author);
$filepath = Config::get('author_csv_filepath');
unlink($filepath);
    }
```

This test will fail because the **AuthorCSV** class does not have the **delete** method. Let us implement it as follows:

```
public function delete(int $code): bool
{
    $sourcePath = Config::get('author_csv_filepath');
    $targetPath = str_replace('.csv','.tmp',$sourcePath);
    $sourceHandle = fopen($sourcePath,'r');
    $targetHandle = fopen($targetPath,'w');
    $changed = false;
    while(!feof($sourceHandle)){
        $row = fgetcsv($sourceHandle, null, ';');
        if (!is_array($row) || count($row) != self::CODE_LENGTH)
continue;
        $readCode = (int) $row[0];
        if ($readCode == $code){
            $changed = true;
            continue;
        }
        fputcsv($targetHandle,$row,';');
    }
    fclose($sourceHandle);
    fclose($targetHandle);
    unlink($sourcePath);
    copy($targetPath,$sourcePath);
    unlink($targetPath);
    return $changed;
}
```

Now, the CSV author removal test using objects will run successfully.

Updating and deleting from JSON

Let us create the **JSONTextTest->testUpdateAuthor** method based on the **JSONTest->testUpdateAuthorInJSON** method, as follows:

```php
public function testUpdateAuthor()
{
    $authorJSON = new AuthorJSON();
    $authorJSON->save('Maupassant','de','Guy');
    $authorJSON->save('Saint-Exupéry','de','Antoine');
    $authorJSON->save('Balzac','de','Honoré');
    $author = $authorJSON->readByCode(1);
    $this->assertEquals('Guy',$author['first_name']);
    $authorJSON->update(1,[
        'last_name' => 'Raspe',
        'middle_name' => 'Erich',
        'first_name' => 'Rudolf'
    ]);
    $author = $authorJSON->readByCode(1);
    $this->assertEquals('Rudolf',$author['first_name']);
    $filepath = Config::get('author_json_filepath');
    unlink($filepath);
}
```

This test will fail because the **AuthorJSON->update** method does not exist. Let us implement it using the **updateAuthorInJSON** function, as follows:

```php
public function update(int $code, array $data): bool
{
    $sourcePath = Config::get('author_json_filepath');
    $content = file_get_contents($sourcePath);
    $authors = json_decode($content);
    $authors = is_null($authors) ? [] : $authors;
    $changed = false;
    foreach($authors as $index => $author) {
        if ((int) $author->code == $code) {
            foreach($data as $key => $value){
                $author->$key = $value;
            }
            $authors[$index] = $author;
```

```
                    $changed = true;
                }
            }
            $targetPath = str_replace('.json','.tmp',$sourcePath);
            file_put_contents($targetPath,json_encode($authors));
            unlink($sourcePath);
            copy($targetPath,$sourcePath);
            unlink($targetPath);
            return $changed;
        }
```

Since the **update** test runs successfully, let us create the **JSONTextTest->testDeleteAuthor** method based on the **JSONTest->testDeleteAuthorInJSON** method, as follows:

```
        public function testDeleteAuthor()
        {
            $authorJSON = new AuthorJSON();
            $authorJSON->save('Assis','de','Machado');
            $authorJSON->save('Alencar','de','José');
            $authorJSON->save('Queiroz','de','Rachel');
            $author = $authorJSON->readByCode(2);
            $this->assertEquals('Alencar',$author['last_name']);
            $authorJSON->delete(2);
            $author = $authorJSON->readByCode(2);
            $this->assertEmpty($author);
            $filepath = Config::get('author_json_filepath');
            unlink($filepath);
        }
```

You know this test will fail because the **delete** method does not exist in the **AuthorJSON** class. Let us implement it using the **deleteAuthorInJSON** function, as follows:

```
        public function delete(int $code): bool
        {
            $sourcePath = Config::get('author_json_filepath');
            $content = file_get_contents($sourcePath);
            $authors = json_decode($content);
            $changed = false;
            foreach($authors as $index => $author) {
                if ((int) $author->code == $code) {
                    unset($authors[$index]);
```

```
            $changed = true;
        }
    }
    $targetPath = str_replace('.json','.tmp',$sourcePath);
    file_put_contents($targetPath,json_encode($authors));
    unlink($sourcePath);
    copy($targetPath,$sourcePath);
    unlink($targetPath);
    return $changed;
}
```

Now, the JSON author removal test using objects will run successfully and with this method, we have finished converting the entire implementation of CRUD operations in the file system to an object-oriented structure.

They claim that one of the rewards of the work of programming is the pleasure of a feeling of continuous improvement. This pleasure will only come if you effectively try to continually improve your work.

Not all functions had a return type and this is not a good practice, as the return type prevents an error from propagating to the person who called the function, or method. From now on, all methods we implement will have a return type.

Although, we only covered the refactoring of the author read and write functions in the file system for classes in this chapter, you will also find the implementation for the books in *chapter 07* directory in our source code repository.

Conclusion

In this chapter, we covered how to refactor a function driven registration with file system storage for an object-oriented implementation. We covered the creation of classes and their methods from implemented functions.

In the next chapter, we will convert the driven function registration with relational database to an object-oriented implementation and we are going to learn about patterns for object relational mapping.

Points to remember

- Class methods have the same structure as functions, but they have a visibility identifier. Most of the time, a method uses the public identifier because it needs to be called from outside the class.

- Methods of a class can call other methods of the same class using the word $this for instance context and self for class context.

Exercise

1. You should notice that in the new test classes for the file system, we have created a class instance for each method. For example, in the PlainTextTest class, each test method creates an instance of AuthorPlainText. We could create a single instance and use it in all methods. Using the setUp method and a private attribute, eliminate repeated and unnecessary instance creation in the PlainTextTest, CSVTextTest, and JSONTextTest classes.

Join our book's Discord space

Join the book's Discord Workspace for Latest updates, Offers, Tech happenings around the world, New Release and Sessions with the Authors:

https://discord.bpbonline.com

CHAPTER 8

Object-oriented Registration with Relational Database Storage

Introduction

This chapter will cover how to refactor a function driven registration with relational database storage for an object-oriented implementation. In this chapter, we will replace the use of the native MySQL driver with the **PHP Data Objects** (**PDO**) driver. We will learn what **object-relational mapping** (**ORM**) is, the architectural patterns of this approach and how to implement the two of them and using them to refactor the Librarian application.

Structure

The chapter covers the following topics:

- Using PDO
- Object-relational mapping
- Architecture patterns of ORM
- Refactoring application with ORM architecture patterns

Objectives

By the end of this chapter, you will be able to understand how to replace the use of native MySQL driver with the PDO driver. You will be able to understand ORM and ORM architectural patterns and how to use them for refactoring an application using a relational database.

Using PDO

In *Chapter 6, PHP OOP*, we learned about PDO abstraction layer. We created classes to read and write data to tables using PDO and the respective test classes, but the Librarian application continues to use the native MySQL driver, with functions that are tightly coupled with this database. In this section, we will decouple the Librarian application from the MySQL database using PDO.

Refactoring database functions

Let us modify the database functions in the **database.functions.php** file, to use the PDO classes we created in *Chapter 6, PHP OOP*. As we discussed in the previous chapters, we will show how to do this refactor to authors. The implementation for books can be found in the **Chapter 08** directory of our code repository.

An alternative definition for **object-oriented programming** (**OOP**) could be the art of avoiding work delegating to someone else. This meaning will be evident after we redo the reading and recording methods of authors, as they will basically delegate the work to the **AuthorPDO** class.

Let us start with the **saveAuthorInDatabase** function, which will be refactored, as follows:

```php
function saveAuthorInDatabase($lastName, $middleName, $firstName)
{
    $authorPDO = new AuthorPDO();
    return $authorPDO->save($firstName, $middleName, $lastName);
}
```

The function receives the arguments in a different order from the **authorPDO->save** method. Then, let us refactor the **readAuthorInDatabaseByCode** function, as follows:

```php
function readAuthorInDatabaseByCode(int $code)
{
    $authorPDO = new AuthorPDO();
    return $authorPDO->readByCode($code);
}
```

The next function to be refactored is **readAuthorInDatabase**. This function, which returns all the authors is as follows:

```php
function readAuthorsInDatabase()
{
    $authorPDO = new AuthorPDO();
```

```
    return $authorPDO->readAuthors();
}
```

The delegation to the **AuthorPDO** class is making database functions very short. This is an intermediate step in the overall refactoring of the application. When we finish refactoring the persistence in MongoDB to fully object-oriented mode, we can completely discard the functions and use directly the methods of our classes. Continuing the refactoring, let us modify the **UpdateAuthorInDatabase** function, as follows:

```
function updateAuthorInDatabase(int $code, array $data)
{
    $authorPDO = new AuthorPDO();
    return $authorPDO->update($code, $data);
}
```

Finally, let us refactor the **deleteAuthorInDatabase** function, as follows:

```
function deleteAuthorInDatabase(int $code)
{
    $authorPDO = new AuthorPDO();
    return $authorPDO->delete($code);
}
```

This summarizes the refactoring of database functions for authors. We know that the PDO classes work because we created the tests for it but now, we need to modify the database-related dependencies and tests that were based on using the native driver.

Refactoring dependencies and tests

In the **database.functions.php** file there is a **truncateTable** function that deletes the contents of a table and resets the auto-increment counter. Let us modify it to use a PDO object instead of the native MySQL driver, as follows:

```
function truncateTable(string $table)
{
    $pdo = getConnection();
    $sql = 'DELETE FROM ' . $table;
    $statement = $pdo->prepare($sql);
    $statement->execute();
    $sql = 'ALTER TABLE ' . $table . ' AUTO_INCREMENT = 1';
    $statement = $pdo->prepare($sql);
    $statement->execute();
}
```

This change requires the **getConnection** function to return a **PDO** object. This is done with two lines, as follows:

```
function getConnection(): \PDO
{
    $db = Config::get('db');
    return new \PDO($db['dsn'], $db['username'], $db['password']);
}
```

So far, we have been working with a single configuration file that we can modify while running the tests. It is not good to mix production data with test data or another environment. So, let us decouple the test configuration, creating a specific configuration file for this environment. First, copy the **book.config.php** file as **book.config.test.php**. In this new file, we must change the database name from librarian for **librarian_test** both times it occurs. Then, we will change the **Config::get** method, as follows:

```
public static function get(string $key)
{
    $configFileName = 'book.config.php';
    if ((defined('LIBRARIAN_TEST_ENVIRONMENT') && LIBRARIAN_TEST_
ENVIRONMENT) ||
        getenv('LIBRARIAN_TEST_ENVIRONMENT')){
            $configFileName = 'book.config.test.php';
    }
    if (self::$config == null){
        self::$config = require __DIR__ . '/../../' . $configFileName;
    }
    return self::$config[$key];
}
```

Modifying the **Config::get** method consists of checking the existence of the **LIBRARIAN_TEST_ENVIRONMENT** constant or the environment variable of the same name. If either exists and is equal to true, then the environment is test and the test configuration file must be selected. The constant is defined in the **PHPUnit** configuration file, **phpunit.xml**, in the **php** section, as follows:

```
<php>
    <const name="LIBRARIAN_TEST_ENVIRONMENT" value="true"/>
</php>
```

The **LIBRARIAN_TEST_ENVIRONMENT** constant works for PHP code called directly by test classes, because it is executed by **PHPUnit** but in web interface testing, we load a PHP web server, and this constant is not created. This is why, we use the **LIBRARIAN_TEST_ENVIRONMENT** environment variable, so that the code called by the server knows that it is running in a test environment. This environment variable must be configured for all test classes that test the web interface: **ViewCollectionTest**, **ViewCSVTest**, **ViewDatabaseTest**, **ViewJSONTest** and **ViewTxtTest**. In the **setUpBeforeClass** method of these classes, we will add a call to the **putenv** function as the first instruction, as follows:

```
putenv('LIBRARIAN_TEST_ENVIRONMENT=true');
```

With this statement, we can remove the following line from the method:

```
replaceConfigFileContent("'database' => 'librarian'","'database' =>
'librarian_test'");
```

In the **tearDownAfterClass** method of these same classes, to revert the change, we will add a call to the putenv function as the last instruction, as follows:

```
putenv('LIBRARIAN_TEST_ENVIRONMENT=false');
```

With this statement, we can remove the following line from the method:

```
replaceConfigFileContent("'database' => 'librarian_test'","'database' =>
'librarian'");
```

As our system is not yet fully object-oriented, the **Config** class is not used throughout the code. So, for now, we need to adapt the **getConfig** function in the **book.functions.php** file, so that it checks the **PHPUnit** constant and the environment variable and selects the correct configuration file. The **getConfig** function will be as follows:

```
function getConfig()
{
    $configFileName = 'book.config.php';
    if ((defined('LIBRARIAN_TEST_ENVIRONMENT') && LIBRARIAN_TEST_
ENVIRONMENT) ||
    getenv('LIBRARIAN_TEST_ENVIRONMENT')){
        $configFileName = 'book.config.test.php';
    }
    $config = require $configFileName;
    return $config;
}
```

As the configuration file already has the correct database name for each environment, we can remove the **setUpBeforeClasse** and **tearDownAfterClass** methods from the **AbstractDatabaseTest** class, as it will no longer be necessary to change the database name.

At the end of these changes, the tests will run successfully. Now, the relational database implementation only uses PDO to access the MySQL database, which allows for a simple switch to another database vendor.

Object-relational mapping

We are gradually transforming our function-oriented application into an object-oriented application, but this object-oriented application accesses a relational database, which has a table structure. In an ideal world, an object-oriented information system would access an object-oriented database, so that communication between the system and the database would be via objects.

Relational databases are mature and well-established in the market, and they use a powerful query language, SQL. This language follows standards documented by the *American National Standards Institute* (*ANSI*), which ensures that its core is the same for different vendors. This reduces the risk of vendor lock-in, as it prevents commands from having to be rewritten if the database is changed.

Even using a standard query language, the way queries are organized within an application can make system maintenance complicated. In his book, *Patterns of Enterprise Application Architecture*, *Martin Fowler* states that it is best to access databases using mechanisms that fit with the application development language. If the language is object-oriented, the way to access the database must be object-oriented. For an object-oriented application to be able to manipulate relational databases using objects, a mapping between classes and tables is necessary, an ORM.

The practice of ORM involves encapsulating SQL commands in specific classes rather than writing SQL everywhere. This approach keeps the programmer focused on using objects while allowing the database administrator to have a specific place to examine and improve database queries.

There is more than one way to implement ORM. We will look at two ORM patterns in the next section.

Architecture patterns of ORM

The object relational mapping patterns can be used to populate an object with a single table record or with a set of records. Let us start with this last approach.

Table Data Gateway

In the Table Data Gateway pattern, an object acts as a gateway to a database table. In this pattern, an object manipulates all the rows in a table. A gateway is a base architectural pattern. It defines an object that encapsulates access to an external system or resource. In the case of ORM, the external system is the relational database management system.

In fact, without realizing it, you have already implemented the Table Data Gateway pattern. The **AuthorPDO** and **BookPDO** classes act as a gateway to their respective tables, manipulating all records.

In the next section, we will refactor the application and adopt the names of the ORM patterns for the classes that implement them. Therefore, we will prepare a transition by copying and adjusting some classes.

Following are the steps:

1. Copy the **AuthorPDO** and **BookPDO** classes as **AuthorTableGateway** and **BookTableGateway** respectively.

2. Change the namespace of these two new classes to **Librarian\Model\ORM**.

3. Copy the **PDOTest** class as **TableGatewayTest**.

4. In the **TableGatewayTest** class, replace the inheritance from **AbstractDatabaseTest** with **PHPUnit\Framework\TestCase**.

5. Remove the **InDatabase** suffix from all **TableGatewayTest** methods.

6. Replace the **AuthorPDO** and **BookPDO** classes in **TableGatewayTest** with **AuthorTableGateway** and **BookTableGateway**, respectively.

7. Replace the **$authorPDO** and **$bookPDO** variables in **TableGatewayTest** with **$authorTableGateway** and **$bookTableGateway**, respectively.

8. Run the **TableGatewayTest** class.

The new test class will run successfully. For now, we have not created anything really new, just more suitable names for the refactoring we will do later.

Row Data Gateway

In the Row Data Gateway pattern, an object acts as a gateway to a single record in a table. Each instance of Row Data Gateway corresponds to a record. While the Table Data Gateway implementation is a class that only has methods, Row Data Gateway implementation is a class with attributes and methods. In fact, there is a separation of responsibilities with the Row Data Gateway pattern. There is one class responsible for write operations, that is, the **Gateway** class and one class responsible for read operations, that is, the **Finder** class. Let us demonstrate this according to our test-driven approach.

The first step in test-driven development, as you already know, is to create a failing test. Let us create the **RowGatewayTest** class, which inherits from **PHPUnit TestCase** class, as follows:

```
class RowGatewayTest extends TestCase
```

Let us create a method in this class to test an author's recording using the Data Row Gateway pattern, as follows:

```
    public function testSaveAuthor()
    {
        $this->assertTrue((new AuthorRowGateway(0,'George', 'Herbert',
```

```
'Wells'))->save());
        truncateTable('authors');
    }
```

We are not binding the **AuthorRowGateway** class object to a variable. We will create the object and then execute a method, using parentheses to access the newly created instance. This syntax is useful when you will not use the object more than once in a method.

> **Note: Remember that you are not required to associate an object with a variable. The variable is used to retrieve the reference to the object to use it in different instructions. Even without being associated with a variable, the object will be destroyed at the end of the PHP script where it was created.**

Well, we saved a line of code by dispensing with creating a variable, but despite this, the test will fail, because the **AuthorRowGateway** class does not exist. So, let us create it in the **Librarian\Model\ORM**, as follows:

```
class AuthorRowGateway
```

This class will have the following attributes:

```
    public int $code;
    public string $firstName;
    public string $middleName;
    public string $lastName;
    private \PDO $pdo;
```

The four **public** attributes refer to fields in the **authors** table. The **private** attribute is the database connection object.

Let us create a constructor for the class that receives the attribute values, as expected in the test, as follows:

```
    public function __construct(int $code = 0, string $firstName = '',
string $middleName = '', string $lastName = '')
    {
        $this->code = $code;
        $this->firstName = $firstName;
        $this->middleName = $middleName;
        $this->lastName = $lastName;
        $db = getConfig()['db'];
        $this->pdo = new \PDO($db['dsn'], $db['username'],
$db['password']);
    }
```

In addition, the constructor establishes the database connection, which is necessary for the class methods to write to the table. After the constructor, we will implement the save method, as follows:

```
public function save(): bool
{
    $sql = 'INSERT INTO authors(first_name,middle_name,last_name) values
(:firstname,:middlename,:lastname)';
    $statement = $this->pdo->prepare($sql);
    $statement->bindParam(':firstname', $this->firstName);
    $statement->bindParam(':middlename', $this->middleName);
    $statement->bindParam(':lastname', $this->lastName);
    $statement->execute();
    return $statement->rowCount() == 1;
}
```

Now, **RowGatewayTest->testSaveAuthor** will pass. Let us continue implementing the test for reading an author, as follows:

```
public function testReadAuthor()
{
    (new AuthorRowGateway(0,'Johann', 'Wolfgang', 'Von Goethe'))-
>save();
    (new AuthorRowGateway(0, 'Francis', 'Scott', 'Fitzgerald'))-
>save();
    (new AuthorRowGateway(0, 'Arthur', 'Conan', 'Doyle'))->save();
    $author = (new AuthorFinder())->readByCode(2);
    $this->assertEquals('Scott',$author->middleName);
    truncateTable('authors');
}
```

This test will fail because the **AuthorFinder** class does not exist. Let us implement it in the **Librarian\Model\ORM** namespace, as follows:

```
class AuthorFinder
```

This class will have a **private** attribute **$pdo,** the same as the **AuthorRowGateway** class, as follows:

```
private \PDO $pdo;
```

AuthorFinder will also have a constructor to initialize this attribute, as follows:

```
public function __construct()
{
    $db = Config::get('db');
```

```
        $this->pdo = new \PDO($db['dsn'], $db['username'],
$db['password']);
    }
```

From this attribute and constructor, we can implement the **AuthorFinder->readByCode** method, as follows:

```
    public function readByCode(int $code): AuthorRowGateway
    {
        $sql = 'SELECT * FROM authors WHERE code = :code';
        $statement = $this->pdo->prepare($sql);
        $statement->bindParam(':code', $code);
        $statement->execute();
        $record = $statement->fetch(\PDO::FETCH_ASSOC);
        $author = new AuthorRowGateway();
        if (is_array($record)){
            $author->code = $record['code'];
            $author->firstName = $record['first_name'];
            $author->middleName = $record['middle_name'];
            $author->lastName = $record['last_name'];
        }
        return $author;
    }
```

Now, **RowGatewayTest->testReadAuthor** will pass. Let us continue implementing the test for reading all the authors, as follows:

```
    public function testReadAuthors()
    {
        (new AuthorRowGateway(0, 'Mary', 'Wollstonecraft', 'Shelley'))-
>save();
        (new AuthorRowGateway(0, 'Agatha', 'Mary', 'Christie'))->save();
        (new AuthorRowGateway(0, 'Chaya', 'Pinkhasivna', 'Lispector'))-
>save();
        $authors = (new AuthorFinder())->readAll();
        $this->assertCount(3,$authors);
        $this->assertEquals('Agatha',$authors->get(1)->firstName);
        truncateTable('authors');
    }
```

This test will fail because the **AuthorFinder** class does not have the **readAll** method. Let us implement it in the **Librarian\Model\ORM** namespace, as follows:

```php
    public function readAll(): AuthorRowSet
    {
        $sql = 'SELECT * FROM authors';
        $statement = $this->pdo->prepare($sql);
        $statement->execute();
        $records = $statement->fetchAll(\PDO::FETCH_ASSOC);
        $authors = new AuthorRowSet();
        if (is_array($records)) {
            foreach($records as $record){
                $authors->add(new AuthorRowGateway(
                    $record['code'],
                    $record['first_name'],
                    $record['middle_name'],
                    $record['last_name']
                    )
                );
            }
        }
        return $authors;
    }
```

As you can see, the **AuthorFinder->readAll** method adds the **AuthorRowGateway** instances to an object of the **AuthorRowSet** class. This class does not exist, so we need to create it, as follows:

```php
<?php
namespace Librarian\Model\ORM;
class AuthorRowSet extends AbstractRowSet
{
    public function add(AuthorRowGateway $row): void
    {
        $this->rows[] = $row;
    }
}
```

The **AuthorRowSet** class defines only one method, to add an **AuthorRowGateway** instance to an array. but it does not have just this one method, because it inherits from **AbstractRowSet,** an abstract class that defines generic methods for a collection of Row Data Gateways. Let us create **AbstractRowSet** as an implementation of the **Iterator** interface, as follows:

```php
abstract class AbstractRowSet implements \Iterator
```

This class will define two attributes, as follows:

```
protected array $rows;
protected int $key = 0;
```

The **AbstractRowSet->current** method will return the element from **$this->rows** whose key is equal to the **$this->key** attribute, as follows:

```
public function current(): mixed
{
    return $this->rows[$this->key];
}
```

The **AbstractRowSet->key** method returns the attribute of the same name, as follows:

```
public function key(): mixed
{
    return $this->key;
}
```

The **AbstractRowSet->next** method increments the value of the **$this->key** attribute, as follows:

```
public function next(): void
{
    $this->key++;
}
```

The **AbstractRowSet->rewind** method sets **the $this->key** attribute to zero, as follows:

```
public function rewind(): void
{
    $this->key = 0;
}
```

The **AbstractRowSet->valid** method returns true if there is an element in **$this->rows** with the key **$this->key**, as follows:

```
public function valid(): bool
{
    return isset($this->rows[$this->key]);
}
```

The **AbstractRowSet->get** method returns the element in **$this->rows** with the key **$this->key**, as follows:

```
public function get(int $key): mixed
{
    return $this->rows[$key];
}
```

Now, we can successfully run the **RowGatewayTest->testReadAuthors** method. The next step is to implement the **RowGatewayTest->testUpdateAuthor** method, as follows:

```php
public function testUpdateAuthor()
{
    (new AuthorRowGateway(0, 'Guy', 'de', 'Maupassant'))->save();
    (new AuthorRowGateway(0, 'Antoine', 'de', 'Saint-Exupéry'))-
>save();
    (new AuthorRowGateway(0, 'Honoré', 'de', 'Balzac'))->save();
    $finder = new AuthorFinder();
    $author = $finder->readByCode(1);
    $this->assertEquals('Guy',$author->firstName);
    $author->firstName = 'Rudolf';
    $author->middleName = 'Erich';
    $author->lastName = 'Raspe';
    $author->update();
    $author = $finder->readByCode(1);
    $this->assertEquals('Rudolf',$author->firstName);
    truncateTable('authors');
}
```

Of course, this test will not work because the **AuthorRowGateway->update** method does not exist. Let us implement it, as follows:

```php
public function update(): bool
{
    $data = ['code' => $this->code];
    $data['first_name'] = $this->firstName;
    $data['middle_name'] = $this->middleName;
    $data['last_name'] = $this->lastName;
    $placeholders = '';
    $fields = [];
    foreach($data as $field => $value){
        $placeholder = str_replace('_','',$field);
        $placeholders .= $field . " = :$placeholder,";
        $fields[$placeholder] = $value;
    }
    $placeholders = substr($placeholders,0,strlen($placeholders)-1);
    $sql = 'UPDATE authors SET ' . $placeholders . ' WHERE code =
:code';
```

```
    $statement = $this->pdo->prepare($sql);
    foreach($fields as $field => &$value){
        $statement->bindParam(":$field", $value);
    }
    $statement->bindParam(':code', $this->code);
    $statement->execute();
    return $statement->rowCount() == 1;
}
```

To finish testing with the author data gateway, let us create the **RowGatewayTest->testDeleteAuthor** method, as follows:

```
public function testDeleteAuthor()
{
    (new AuthorRowGateway(0, 'Machado', 'de', 'Assis'))->save();
    (new AuthorRowGateway(0, 'José', 'de', 'Alencar'))->save();
    (new AuthorRowGateway(0, 'Rachel', 'de', 'Queiroz'))->save();
    $finder = new AuthorFinder();
    $author = $finder->readByCode(2);
    $this->assertEquals('Alencar',$author->lastName);
    $author->delete();
    $author = $finder->readByCode(2);
    $this->assertTrue($author->isEmpty());
    truncateTable('authors');
}
```

You know this test will not work because the **AuthorRowGateway->delete** method does not exist. Let us implement it as follows:

```
public function delete(): bool
{
    $sql = 'DELETE FROM authors WHERE code = :code';
    $statement = $this->pdo->prepare($sql);
    $statement->bindParam(':code', $this->code);
    $statement->execute();
    return $statement->rowCount() == 1;
}
```

You may have noticed that the **AuthorRowGateway->delete** method is not enough for the author removal test to work. The **RowGateway->testDeleteAuthor** method makes an assertion by invoking the **AuthorRowGateway->isEmpty** method. This method does not exist, so we must create it as follows:

```
public function isEmpty(): bool
{
    return empty($this->code) &&
    empty($this->firstName) &&
    empty($this->middleName) &&
    empty($this->lastName);
}
```

Refactoring application with ORM architecture patterns

In our journey to convert the Librarian application from a function-oriented application to an object-oriented application, we made a refactoring in the first section so that the functions in the **database.functions.php** file use the **AuthorPDO** and **BookPDO** classes. We saw that these classes implement the Table Data Gateway pattern and created classes with a name that clearly identifies this pattern. We can now replace the use of the **AuthorPDO** and **BookPDO** classes respectively with the **AuthorTableGateway** and **BookTableGateway** classes. This change will be restricted to the **database.functions.php** file, since the methods will continue to return the same types of values.

However, we can choose to replace the **AuthorPDO** and **BookPDO** classes with the **AuthorRowGateway** and **AuthorFinder** and **BookRowGateway** and **BookFinder** pairs. The reason for doing this is that in the Row Data Gateway implementation, the read methods return objects instead of arrays, which is more in line with an object-oriented structure. The problem is that the web interface expects arrays, and the other storage classes continue to return arrays.

Therefore, to adopt the Row Data Gateway implementation in the **database.functions. php** functions, we will have to refactor the file system and document-oriented database functions so that they return objects instead of arrays.

Returning objects for file system storage

In the previous chapter, we created an object-oriented implementation for manipulating authors and books stored in the file system, but we did not connect it to the application. If you review the implementation we created, you will see that it resembles the Table Data Gateway pattern approach, where one class does all the reading and writing. Let us modify this implementation so that the responsibilities are split and the class responsible for reading records from text files returns objects instead of arrays.

Let us start with plain text files. Let us start with plain text files. In the **PlainTextTest->testReadAuthor** method, we will replace these lines, as follows:

```
$author = $authorPlainText->readByCode(2);
$this->assertEquals('Scott',$author['middle_name']);
```

For these ones will be as follows:

```
$author = (new AuthorPlainTextFinder())->readByCode(2);
$this->assertEquals('Scott',$author->middleName);
```

This change requires us to implement an **AuthorPlainTextFinder** class. This class is not the same as the one used for the relational database. We will create it in the **Librarian\ Model\Filesystem** namespace.

Following are the steps:

1. Copy the **AuthorPlainText** class as **AuthorPlainTextFinder**. Remove all methods from the new class except **readByCode** and **readAll**.

2. Replace this instruction in **readByCode** method, as follows:

```
$author = [
    'code' => $code,
    'last_name' => trim(substr($row, self::CODE_
LENGTH, self::NAME_LENGTH)),
    'middle_name' => trim(substr($row, self::CODE_
LENGTH + self::NAME_LENGTH + 1, self::NAME_LENGTH)),
    'first_name' => trim(substr($row, self::CODE_
LENGTH + (2 * self::NAME_LENGTH) + 1, self::NAME_LENGTH))
];
```

For this one, as follows:

```
$author = new Author(
    $code,
    trim(substr($row, self::CODE_LENGTH + (2 *
self::NAME_LENGTH) + 1, self::NAME_LENGTH)),
    trim(substr($row, self::CODE_LENGTH +
self::NAME_LENGTH + 1, self::NAME_LENGTH)),
    trim(substr($row, self::CODE_LENGTH, self::NAME_
LENGTH))
);
```

Note: That the reading order is different, because the name is written first to the text file, but it is the last argument of the Author class constructor.

3. Change the return type of **readByCode** method and **$author** variable to **Author**.

4. Import the namespace for **Author** class, as follows:

```
use Librarian\Model\Author;
```

We created the **Author** class in *Chapter 6, PHP OOP*. Now it is time to integrate it into the application.

Remove **readByCode** and **readAll** methods from **AuthorPlainText** class. If you run the **PlainTextTest** class now, the **testReadAuthor** method will fail, saying that the middle name it received is not the one it expected. This is because the **Author** class constructor does not expect the code as its first argument. So, we need to make some changes to the **Author** class, add an integer attribute named **$code**, change all the attributes from private to public and add a **$code** argument to the constructor, as follows:

```
public int $code;
public string $firstName;
public string $middleName;
public string $lastName;

public function __construct(int $code = 0, string $firstName = '',
string $middleName = '', string $lastName = '')
{
    $this->code = $code;
    $this->firstName = $firstName;
    $this->middleName = $middleName;
    $this->lastName = $lastName;
}
```

With this change, **PlainTextTest->testReadAuthor** will run successfully again.

The approach we use, with a class that only stores data manipulated by another class that only performs operations, is an adaptation of the Data Mapper architectural pattern. Although it is a pattern originally recommended for ORM, the truth is that, like other patterns, it can be adapted to work with other forms of storage.

Now, let us change the **PlainTextText->testReadAuthors** method, replacing the following lines:

```
$authors = $authorPlainText->readAll();
$this->assertCount(3,$authors);
$this->assertEquals('Agatha',$authors[1]['first_name']);
```

For these ones, as follows:

```
$authors = (new AuthorPlainTextFinder())->readAll();
$this->assertCount(3,$authors);
$this->assertEquals('Agatha',$authors->get(1)->firstName);
```

If you run the **PlainTextTest** class now, the **testReadAuthors** method will fail, because **$authors** is not an object, but an array. So, we need to make some changes to the **AuthorPlainTextFinder->readAll** method, as follows:

```
            $author = [
                'code' => (int) substr($row,0,self::CODE_LENGTH),
                'last_name' => trim(substr($row, self::CODE_LENGTH,
self::NAME_LENGTH)),
                'middle_name' => trim(substr($row, self::CODE_LENGTH +
self::NAME_LENGTH + 1, self::NAME_LENGTH)),
                'first_name' => trim(substr($row, self::CODE_LENGTH + (2 *
self::NAME_LENGTH) + 1, self::NAME_LENGTH))
            ];
            if ($author['code'] != 0) {
                $authors[] = $author;
            }
```

For these ones, as follows:

```
            $author = new Author(
                (int)trim(substr($row, 0, self::CODE_LENGTH)),
                trim(substr($row, self::CODE_LENGTH + (2 * self::NAME_
LENGTH) + 1, self::NAME_LENGTH)),
                trim(substr($row, self::CODE_LENGTH + self::NAME_LENGTH +
1, self::NAME_LENGTH)),
                trim(substr($row, self::CODE_LENGTH, self::NAME_LENGTH))
            );
            if ((int) $author->code != 0) {
                $authors->add($author);
            }
```

The **$authors** variable is no longer an array but an object. It should be created as follows:

```
        $authors = new AuthorRowSet();
```

The **AuthorRowSet** class we use here is not the same as the one in the database. It must be created in the **Librarian\Model\Filesystem** namespace, as follows:

```
<?php
namespace Librarian\Model\Filesystem;
use Librarian\Model\ORM\AbstractRowSet;
use Librarian\Model\Author;
class AuthorRowSet extends AbstractRowSet
{
    public function add(Author $row): void
    {
        $this->rows[] = $row;
    }
}
```

We need some final adjustments to get the **PlainTextTest** class running successfully again, as follows:

- The return type of **AuthorPlainTextFinder::readAll** should be changed to **AuthorRowSet**.

- In the **PlainTextTest->testUpdateAuthor** and **PlainTextTest->testDeleteAuthor** methods, the **readByCode** and **readAll** methods must be called from an **AuthorPlainTextFinder** instance.

- In the **PlainTextTest->testUpdateAuthor** and **PlainTextTest->testDeleteAuthor** methods, we must replace the array key of **$author** variable with the equivalent attribute.

With this change, **PlainTextTest->testReadAuthors** will run successfully again. Now, you should reproduce what was done in the **PlainTextTest** class in the **CSVTextTest** and **JSONTextTest** classes, following the applied patterns. At the end of the changes, we will have a file system class implementation that returns objects in read operations.

Returning objects for document database storage

Let us now create the object-oriented implementation to read and write data in the document-oriented database. We will modify the **CollectionTest** class and, based on the changes in the tests, we will create the classes for this implementation. Let us start with the **CollectionTest->testSaveAuthorInCollection** method, which we will rename to **CollectionTest->testSaveAuthor**. This method will look as follows:

```
public function testSaveAuthor()
{
    $this->assertTrue((new AuthorCollection())->save('Wells','Herbert',
'George'));
    dropCollection('authors');
}
```

Of course, for the test to work, the **AuthorCollection** class must exist, as well as the **save** method. Let us create the **AuthorCollection** class in the **Librarian\Model\ODM** namespace and implement the **save** method, as follows:

```
public function save($lastName, $middleName, $firstName)
{
    $insertOneResult = $this->database->authors->insertOne([
        'code' => $this->database->authors->countDocuments() + 1,
        'last_name' => $lastName,
        'middle_name' => $middleName,
        'first_name' => $firstName
```

```
        ]);
        return $insertOneResult->getInsertedCount() == 1;
    }
```

As you can see, the **AuthorCollection->save** method uses a **$this->database** attribute. Let us declare this attribute in the class and initialize it in the constructor method, as follows:

```
    private $database;

    public function __construct()
    {
        $database = Config::get('db')['database'];
        $mongo = new \MongoDB\Client("mongodb://localhost:27017");
        $this->database = $mongo->$database;
    }
```

The second test to be refactored is **CollectionTest->testReadAuthorInCollection**, which will now be called **testReadAuthor**. Its implementation will be as follows:

```
    public function testReadAuthor()
    {
        $authorCollection = new AuthorCollection();
        $authorCollection->save('Von Goethe','Wolfgang','Johann');
        $authorCollection->save('Fitzgerald','Scott','Francis');
        $authorCollection->save('Doyle','Arthur','Conan');
        $author = (new AuthorCollectionFinder())->readByCode(2);
        $this->assertEquals('Scott',$author->middleName);
        dropCollection('authors');
    }
```

As you can see, this test will not work because the **AuthorCollectionFinder** class does not exist, nor does the **readByCode** method. Let us create this class in the **Librarian\ Model\ODM** namespace. The **readByCode** method in this class will be as follows:

```
    public function readByCode(int $code)
    {
        $result = $this->database->authors->findOne(['code' => $code]);
        if (is_null($result)){
            return new Author();
        }
        return new Author($code, $result['first_name'],$result['middle_
name'],$result['last_name']);
    }
```

As you can see, the **AuthorCollectionFinder->readByCode** method uses a **$this->database** attribute. So, we need to declare this attribute in this class and initialize it in the constructor method, exactly the same way we did in the **AuthorCollection** class.

The third method to be refactored is **CollectionTest->testReadAuthorsInCollection**, which will now be called **testReadAuthors**. The implementation of this method will be as follows:

```
public function testReadAuthors()
{
    $authorCollection = new AuthorCollection();
    $authorCollection->save('Shelley','Wollstonecraft','Mary');
    $authorCollection->save('Christie','Mary','Agatha');
    $authorCollection->save('Lispector','Pinkhasivna','Chaya');
    $authors = (new AuthorCollectionFinder())->readAll();
    $this->assertCount(3,$authors);
    $this->assertEquals('Agatha',$authors->get(1)->firstName);
    dropCollection('authors');
}
```

As you can see, this test requires the **AuthorCollectionFinder** class to have the **readAll** method. Let us implement it as follows:

```
public function readAll()
{
    $result = $this->database->authors->find();
    if (is_null($result)){
        return new AuthorRowSet();
    }
    return new AuthorRowSet($result->toArray());
}
```

You may have noticed that we passed the **MongoDB** result array to the **Librarian\Model\ODM\AuthorRowSet** constructor. This will have no effect unless you implement the constructor to receive the array and populate the collection's **$this->rows** attribute, creating the **Author** class objects. The constructor will be as follows:

```
public function __construct(array $rows = [])
{
    foreach($rows as $row){
        $this->rows[] = new Author(
            (int)$row['code'],
            $row['first_name'],
```

```
                $row['middle_name'],
                $row['last_name']
            );
        }
    }
```

The fourth method to be refactored is **CollectionTest->updateAuthorInCollection**, which will now be called **testUpdateAuthor**. The implementation of this method will be as follows:

```
    public function testUpdateAuthor()
    {
        $authorCollection = new AuthorCollection();
        $authorCollection->save('Maupassant','de','Guy');
        $authorCollection->save('Saint-Exupéry','de','Antoine');
        $authorCollection->save('Balzac','de','Honoré');
        $authorCollectionFinder = new AuthorCollectionFinder();
        $author = $authorCollectionFinder->readByCode(1);
        $this->assertEquals('Guy',$author->firstName);
        $authorCollection->update(1,[
            'last_name' => 'Raspe',
            'middle_name' => 'Erich',
            'first_name' => 'Rudolf'
        ]);
        $author = $authorCollectionFinder->readByCode(1);
        $this->assertEquals('Rudolf',$author->firstName);
        dropCollection('authors');
    }
```

For this test to work, it is necessary to implement the **AuthorCollection->update** method, as follows:

```
    public function update(int $code, array $data)
    {
        $result = $this->database->authors->updateOne(
            ['code' => $code],
            ['$set' => $data]
        );
        return $result->getModifiedCount() == 1;
    }
```

The fifth method to be refactored is **CollectionTest->deleteAuthorInCollection**, which will now be called **testDeleteAuthor**. The implementation of this method will be as follows:

```php
public function testDeleteAuthor()
{
    $authorCollection = new AuthorCollection();
    $authorCollection->save('Assis','de','Machado');
    $authorCollection->save('Alencar','de','José');
    $authorCollection->save('Queiroz','de','Rachel');
    $authorCollectionFinder = new AuthorCollectionFinder();
    $author = $authorCollectionFinder->readByCode(2);
    $this->assertEquals('Alencar',$author->lastName);
    $authorCollection->delete(2);
    $author = $authorCollectionFinder->readByCode(2);
    $this->assertEmpty($author->code);
    dropCollection('authors');
}
```

As you can notice, for this test to work, it is necessary to implement the **AuthorCollection->delete** method, as follows:

```php
public function delete(int $code)
{
    $result = $this->database->authors->deleteOne(['code' => $code]);
    return $result->getDeletedCount() == 1;
}
```

With this change, the author test methods of **CollectionTest** class will run successfully again. At the end of the changes, we will have a document database class implementation that returns objects in read operations.

Refactoring web interface

We now have classes with methods that return objects for storage in a file system, relational database, and document-oriented database. This will allow us to change the functions in **book.functions.php** that return one or more authors but before we change any functions, let us generalize our application's collections implementation. Let us copy the **AbstractRowSet** class from the **Librarian\Model\ORM** namespace to **Librarian\Model** and copy the **AuthorRowSet** and **BookRowSet** classes from the **Librarian\Model\ODM** namespace to **Librarian\Model**. These classes were born from specific storage scenarios, but they deal with the generic entity model that is independent of the type of storage used.

Keeping with our test-driven approach, let us refactor the web interface by refactoring the web interface tests. Let us start with the **ViewTxtText** class. The first test, **testIndex**, does not change, because it only tests for the existence of the title. The second test, **testListAuthors**, does not change either, but the page it tests generates the list of authors based on the **listAuthorsInTable** function from the **book.functions.php** file, which manipulates **authors** in array format. Let us modify this function so that it uses the objects created by the classes we defined in the previous sections. The **listAuthorsInTable** function will be as follows:

```php
function listAuthorsInTable()
{
    try {
        $authors = getAuthorFinder()->readAll();
    } catch(\Exception $e) {
        $authors = new AuthorRowSet();
    }
    $html = '';
    foreach($authors as $author){
        $html.='<tr>';
        $html.='<td><a href="author.edit.php?code=' . $author->code . '">'
. $author->code . '</a><td>';
        $html.="<td>{$author->firstName} {$author->middleName} {$author->lastName}<td>";
        $html.='<td><a href="author.delete.php?code=' . $author->code .
'">remove</a><td>';
        $html.='</tr>';
    }
    return $html;
}
```

listAuthorsInTable gets the object instance that returns collection of authors through the **getAuthorFinder** function, which is implemented as follows:

```php
function getAuthorFinder()
{
    $storageFormat = Config::get('storage_format');
    switch($storageFormat){
        case 'txt':
            prepareFile('author');
            return new AuthorPlainTextFinder();
        case 'csv':
```

```
            prepareFile('author');
            return new AuthorCSVFinder();
        case 'json':
            prepareFile('author');
            return new AuthorJSONFinder();
        case 'rdb':
            return new AuthorFinder();
        case 'ddb':
            return new AuthorCollectionFinder();
    }
    throw new \Exception('invalid storage format');
}
```

If **getAuthorFinder** throws an exception, **listAuthorsInTable** returns an instance of **Librarian\Model\AuthorRowSet**. This class does not exist, so we need to create it. Create this class as a copy of **Librarian\Model\ODM\AuthorRowSet** and copy **Librarian\ Model\ORM\AbstractRowSet** as **Librarian\Model\AbstractRowSet**.

The next test to refactor is **ViewTxtText->testUpdateAuthor**. The following is the assertion:

```
$this->assertEquals('Neigauz',$author['last_name']);
```

It should be replaced, as follows:

```
$this->assertEquals('Neigauz',$author->lastName);
```

Moving on, the next test to refactor is **ViewTxtText->testDeleteAuthor**. The following is the assertion:

```
$this->assertEmpty($author['last_name']);
```

It should be replaced, as follows:

```
$this->assertEmpty($author->lastName);
```

To make the **ViewTxtTest->testNewAuthor** and **ViewTxtTest->testEditAuthor** tests work again, you need to replace the following lines in the **author.edit.php file**:

```
<input type="text" name="first_name" value="<?=$author['first_name']?>"><br/>
<label for="middle_name">Middle name:</label>
<input type="text" name="middle_name" value="<?=$author['middle_
name']?>"><br/>
<label for="last_name">Last name:</label>
<input type="text" name="last_name" value="<?=$author['last_name']?>"><br/>
```

For this one, it is as follows:

```
<input type="text" name="first_name" value="<?=$author->firstName?>"><br/>
<label for="middle_name">Middle name:</label>
<input type="text" name="middle_name" value="<?=$author->middleName?>"><br/>
<label for="last_name">Last name:</label>
<input type="text" name="last_name" value="<?=$author->lastName?>"><br/>
```

Observe that arrays were replaced by objects.

With this, we have completed the necessary changes so that **ViewTxtTest** can run again, testing with objects instead of arrays.

Let us now refactor the **ViewCSVTest** class. In the **ViewCSVTest->testUpdateAuthor** method, we will replace the line, as follows:

```
$this->assertEquals('Neigauz',$author['last_name']);
```

For this one, is as follows:

```
$this->assertEquals('Neigauz',$author->lastName);
```

In the **ViewCSVTest->testDeleteAuthor** method, we will replace the line, as follows:

```
$this->assertEmpty($author['last_name']);
```

For this one, as follows:

```
$this->assertEmpty($author->lastName);
```

With this, we have completed the necessary changes so that **ViewCSVTest** can run again, testing with objects instead of arrays.

Let us now refactor the **ViewJSONTest** class. It is easy. You will change the **ViewJSONTest->testUpdateAuthor** and **ViewJSONText->testDeleteAuthor** methods, according to the changes that we made for the same methods in **ViewCSVTest**.

The next step is to refactor the **ViewDatabaseTest** class. **ViewDatabaseTest->testUpdateAuthor** and **ViewDatabaseTest->testDeleteAuthor**. The change will seem like the same as you did the changes with **ViewJSONTest**.

However, this time the changes in the test class are not enough, because we need to change the database functions. Existing functions return arrays, but the tests and web interface now expect objects.

In the **database.functions.php** file, we will replace the PDO classes in the functions with the **Finder** and **TableGateway** classes from the ORM implementation. Let us start with the **saveAuthorInDatabase** function, which will be as follows:

```
function saveAuthorInDatabase($lastName, $middleName, $firstName)
{
```

```
    return (new AuthorTableGateway())->save($firstName, $middleName,
$lastName);
}
```

Observe that we have a function with only one line. This function follows the object-oriented approach to delegate a work for someone else.

The second function to be refactored will be **readAuthorInDatabase** function, which will be as follows:

```
function readAuthorInDatabaseByCode(int $code)
{
    return (new AuthorFinder())->readByCode($code);
}
```

The third function to be refactored will be **readAuthorsInDatabase,** which will be as follows:

```
function readAuthorsInDatabase()
{
    return (new AuthorFinder())->readAll();
}
```

The fourth function to be refactored will be **updateAuthorsInDatabase**, which will be as follows:

```
function updateAuthorInDatabase(int $code, array $data)
{
    return (new AuthorTableGateway())->update($code, $data);
}
```

The fifth function to be refactored will be **deleteAuthorsInDatabase,** which will be as follows:

```
function deleteAuthorInDatabase(int $code)
{
    return (new AuthorTableGateway())->delete($code);
}
```

Now, the **ViewDatabaseTest** class will run successfully again. With this, every view interface test class is using objects instead of arrays for handling the entities of our application.

Note: Although, we do not show the implementation for books, this implementation is available in our code repository but it is desirable that you try to implement the classes and functions for handling books according to the example of authors.

Refactoring database tests

Well, the tests with web interface using the several types of storage are working, but, if you try running the classes **DatabaseTest** and **CollectionTest**, you will discover that they are not working anymore. The reason is simple, these classes still expect entities as arrays and not as objects. Therefore, we need to refactor them too.

Let us start removing the suffix **InDatabase** from the **DatabaseTest** method. Do you agree that it is redundant to have this suffix in a class named **DatabaseTest**. Remember to remove the suffix from the methods in the parent class too.

After this change, let us refactor the **DatabaseTest->testReadAuthor**, replacing the following line:

```
$this->assertEquals('Scott',$author['middle_name']);
```

For this one, is as follows:

```
$this->assertEquals('Scott',$author->middleName);
```

Next, let us refactor the **DatabaseTest->testReadAuthors**, replacing the following line:

```
$this->assertEquals('Agatha',$authors[1]['first_name']);
```

For this one, is as follows:

```
$this->assertEquals('Agatha',$authors->get(1)->firstName);
```

In the **DatabaseTest->testUpdateAuthor,** we will replace the following line:

```
$this->assertEquals('Agatha',$authors[1]['first_name']);
```

For this one, is as follows:

```
$this->assertEquals('Agatha',$authors->get(1)->firstName);
```

Also, in the **DatabaseTest->testUpdateAuthor**, we will replace the following line:

```
$this->assertEquals('Rudolf',$author['first_name']);
```

For this one, is as follows:

```
$this->assertEquals('Rudolf',$author->firstName']);
```

Next, in the **DatabaseTest->testDeleteAuthor,** we will replace the following line:

```
$this->assertEquals('Alencar',$author['last_name']);
```

For this one, is as follows:

```
$this->assertEquals('Alencar',$author->lastName);
```

Also, in the **DatabaseTest->testDeleteAuthor**, we will replace the following line:

```
$this->assertEmpty($author);
```

For this one, is as follows:

```
$this->assertEmpty($author->code);
```

After these changes, you can run **DatabaseTest** class successfully again. As **CollectionTest** inherits **DatabaseTest**, you do not need to change it and can run it successfully too.

However, as you changed the methods of **AbstractDatabaseTest** class, removing the suffix **InDatabase**, you must remove it from the methods of **PDOTest** and **PDOExceptionTest** classes too. So, these two classes will run successfully again.

Using ORM objects for saving and deleting

We have changed the reading functions in the **book.functions.php** file to use objects from the mapping classes we created throughout this chapter. Now, let us modify the functions for writing and removing records so that they also use objects.

Let us start with the **saveAuthor** function. We will explore the function calls with the equivalent method calls. We will have classes with a **save** method for each storage type. All **save** methods take the same arguments in the same order except that in the **Librarian\Model\ORM\AuthorTableGateway** class. Let us establish a pattern, which is the first step to using an interface later on. All **save** methods for the **Author** entity must have the same arguments in the same order. Let us change only the one that is the exception, **AuthorTableGateway->save**. The order for the arguments must be: **$lastName**, **$middleName** and **$firstName**.

After changing **AuthorTableGateway->save**, you will need to revisit the **TableGatewayTest** class, changing all calls to the modified method.

It is also necessary to change the order in which the **AuthorTableGateway->save** arguments are called in the **saveAuthorInDatabase** function in the **database.functions.php** file. This function is called by the **DatabaseTest** class.

After the adjustments, **saveAuthor** function in **book.functions.php** file should be as follows:

```
function saveAuthor($lastName, $middleName, $firstName)
{
    $storageFormat = Config::get('storage_format');

    $saved = false;
    switch($storageFormat){
        case 'txt':
            $saved = (new AuthorPlainText())->save($lastName, $middleName,
$firstName);
            break;
```

```
        case 'csv':
            $saved = (new AuthorCSV())->save($lastName, $middleName,
$firstName);
            break;
        case 'json':
            $saved = (new AuthorJSON())->save($lastName, $middleName,
$firstName);
            break;
        case 'rdb':
            $saved = (new AuthorTableGateway())->save($lastName,
$middleName, $firstName);
            break;
        case 'ddb':
            $saved = (new AuthorCollection())->save($lastName, $middleName,
$firstName);
    }
    return $saved;
}
```

Refactoring is the third step in the **test-driven development** (TDD) cycle. It is the time to review what is working, with the goal of making it work better. This does not necessarily mean an improvement in performance. The improvement may refer to a reorganization of the source code, which makes it more readable, easier to understand and, as a result, easier to maintain.

The creator of the C++ language, *Bjarne Stroustrup*, stated that he liked his code to be both elegant and efficient. Efficiency refers to how well the code runs, and it should be immediately noticeable but elegance seems to suggest that the code should be a kind of work of art. In fact, Stroustrup explains that elegant code should make it difficult for bugs to hide. Elegance here refers to organization, to a place where you know where things are, so that it is not easy to miss something.

With each refactoring we try to make our code more elegant, more organized, easier to modify to improve and correct if necessary.

Code elegance also helps us notice patterns, which help us make the code even more elegant. You should notice some pattern when you change the **updateAuthor** function, which is as follows:

```
function updateAuthor($code, $lastName, $middleName, $firstName)
{
    $storageFormat = Config::get('storage_format');

    $data = [
```

```
        'last_name' => $lastName,
        'middle_name' => $middleName,
        'first_name' => $firstName
    ];

    $saved = false;
    switch($storageFormat){
        case 'txt':
            $saved = (new AuthorPlainText())->update($code, $data);
            break;
        case 'csv':
            $saved = (new AuthorCSV())->update($code, $data);
            break;
        case 'json':
            $saved = (new AuthorJSON())->update($code, $data);
            break;
        case 'rdb':
            $saved = (new AuthorTableGateway())->update($code, $data);
            break;
        case 'ddb':
            $saved = (new AuthorCollection())->update($code, $data);
    }
    return $saved;
}
```

You may have noted that the case lines in both the **saveAuthor** and **updateAuthor** functions are very similar. The only thing that changes is the class name.

A pattern is something that repeats itself but it is something that has to repeat itself more than twice. When something happens once, it could be a coincidence. When it happens twice in the same way, it could be a coincidence but after three times, we can already consider that we have a pattern. This is what you can conclude after changing the **deleteAuthor** function, as follows:

```
function deleteAuthor($code)
{
    $storageFormat = Config::get('storage_format');

    $deleted = false;
    switch($storageFormat){
```

```
        case 'txt':
            $deleted = (new AuthorPlainText())->delete($code);
            break;
        case 'csv':
            $deleted = (new AuthorCSV())->delete($code);
            break;
        case 'json':
            $deleted = (new AuthorJSON())->delete($code);
            break;
        case 'rdb':
            $deleted = (new AuthorTableGateway())->delete($code);
            break;
        case 'ddb':
            $deleted = (new AuthorCollection())->delete($code);
    }
    return $deleted;
}
```

By refactoring these three functions, we have reduced the dependency of the **book. functions.php** file on the **database.functions.php** file. Now, there is really only one dependency, which is the **truncateTable** function, which is also used by the database test classes. Let us create a class to perform generic operations on tables and wrap the **truncateTable** function as a method.

We will create a class named **Table** in the **Librarian\Model\ORM** namespace. This class will have two attributes that will be configured by the constructor method, as follows:

```
private $table;
private \PDO $connection;

public function __construct(string $table)
{
    $this->table = $table;
    $db = Config::get('db');
    $this->connection = new \PDO($db['dsn'], $db['username'],
$db['password']);
}
```

The **Table** class will implement the **truncate** method, as follows:

```
public function truncate()
{
```

```
    $sql = 'DELETE FROM ' . $this->table;
    $statement = $this->connection->prepare($sql);
    $statement->execute();
    $sql = 'ALTER TABLE ' . $this->table . ' AUTO_INCREMENT = 1';
    $statement = $this->connection->prepare($sql);
    return $statement->execute();
}
```

The **truncateTable** function is used in the **book.functions.php** file by the **clearEntity** function. To replace the function with the method, you should replace the following line in **clearEntity**:

```
        truncateTable($entity . 's');
```

With this one, as follows:

```
        (new Table($entity . 's'))->truncate();
```

With this change, the **book.functions.php** file is completely decoupled from the **database.functions.php** file, so it is possible to remove the **require_once** command that imports the second file into the first but now, we have two new problems, that is, the relational database test classes will not run because they use the **truncateTable** function and other functions from the **database.functions.php** file. So, let us review all the relational database test classes, replacing the **truncateTable** function with the **Table->truncate** method and the record reading and writing functions with the equivalent methods from the **AuthorTableGateway** and **AuthorFinder** classes. The test classes to be refactored are as follows:

- **DatabaseTest**
- **PDOTest**
- **PDOExceptionTest**
- **TableGatewayTest**
- **RowGatewayTest**

Now, database access in our application no longer needs the functions in the **database.functions.php** file. It can be removed.

Conclusion

In this chapter, we covered how to refactor a function driven registration with relational database storage for an object-oriented implementation. In this chapter we covered the use of the native MySQL driver with the PDO driver. We covered the explanation about ORM, about the architectural patterns of this approach and we covered the implementation of two of them, which were used to refactor the Librarian application.

In the next chapter, we are going to complete the conversion of the driven function registration with document database to an object-oriented implementation and we are going to refactor the application with the help of quality assurance tools.

Points to remember

- ORM allows you to deal with relational database tables and their records in the form of objects.

- The Table Data Gateway pattern allows you to manipulate a table, or a set of records from a table, as an object.

- The Row Data Gateway pattern allows you to manipulate a record in a table as an object.

Exercise

1. Refactor the saveAuthor, updateAuthor and deleteAuthor functions in the book.functions.php file, extracting the common code for a new function and, so, eliminating the replicated code.

Join our book's Discord space

Join the book's Discord Workspace for Latest updates, Offers, Tech happenings around the world, New Release and Sessions with the Authors:

https://discord.bpbonline.com

CHAPTER 9

Object-oriented Registration with Document Database Storage

Introduction

In this chapter, we will cover how to refactor a function-oriented database implementation from a document-oriented database to an object-oriented implementation using the Row Data Gateway design pattern. We will identify duplications and eliminate them, generalizing with abstract classes and enforcing patterns with interfaces. We will review the models we created, the user interface, and the request handling.

Structure

The chapter covers the following topics:

- From object to object
- Reviewing model layer
- Reviewing user interface
- Reviewing controlling layer

Objectives

By the end of this chapter, readers will be able to understand how to use Row Data Gateway pattern for document-oriented databases. You will be able to perform refactoring to eliminate duplication using abstract classes and enforce communication patterns using interfaces.

From object to object

In the previous chapter, we implemented the Table Data Gateway pattern to read and write records from MongoDB. Now, we will implement the Row Data Gateway pattern. We have already implemented this pattern for relational database tables. However, you will notice that an architectural pattern can be leveraged for scenarios other than the one it was designed for, as long as the scenario is compatible with the core idea of the pattern.

Since we are developing from tests, let us start, as always, with the test class. Your first task is to copy the **CollectionTest** class as **CollectionRowGatewayTest**. This new class will inherit from the first, so the class declaration will be as follows:

```
class CollectionRowGatewayTest extends CollectionTest
```

With inheritance, we can delete the **setUpBeforeClass** and **tearDownAfterClass** methods in the new class. Next, let us refactor the **testSaveAuthor** method, as follows:

```
public function testSaveAuthor()
{
    $this->assertTrue((new AuthorCollectionRowGateway(0,'George','Herbert','Wells'))->save());
    (new Collection('authors'))->drop();
}
```

Of course, this test will fail because the **AuthorCollectionRowGateway** class does not exist. Let us create this class in the **Librarian\Model\ODM** namespace. This class will inherit from **Librarian\Model\Author**, so the class declaration will be as follows:

```
class AuthorCollectionRowGateway extends Author
```

The constructor of the **Author** class receives the attributes of that class as arguments. The inheriting class must maintain the signature of the inherited method. The constructor of the **AuthorCollectionGateway** class will inherit the implementation of the parent class and add the initialization of the attribute that maintains the connection to the MongoDB database, as follows:

```
public function __construct(int $code = 0, string $firstName = '',
string $middleName = '', string $lastName = '')
{
    parent::__construct($code, $firstName, $middleName, $lastName);
    $database = Config::get('db')['database'];
    $mongo = new \MongoDB\Client("mongodb://localhost:27017");
    $this->database = $mongo->$database;
}
```

As you may recall, the parent keyword makes the inheriting class reuse the implementation of the inherited class's method. Thus, we overload the constructor method as we reuse generic code and add specific code.

Of course, this constructor requires the class to declare the **$this->database** attribute, as follows:

```
private $database;
```

Having a connection to the database and knowing that the field values are in class attributes, we can implement the **AuthorCollectionRowGateway->save** method, as follows:

```
public function save()
{
    $insertOneResult = $this->database->authors->insertOne([
        'code' => $this->database->authors->countDocuments() + 1,
        'last_name' => $this->lastName,
        'middle_name' => $this->middleName,
        'first_name' => $this->firstName
    ]);
    return $insertOneResult->getInsertedCount() == 1;
}
```

This is enough to satisfy the test assertion but there will be an error because the **Collection** class does not exist, nor does its **drop** method. Let us create the **Collection** class in the **Librarian\Model\ODM** namespace. It will have an attribute for the collection name and a constructor to initialize that attribute, as follows:

```
private string $name;

public function __construct(string $name)
{
    $this->name = $name;
}
```

The **Collection->drop** method will be implemented similarly to the **dropCollection** function, as follows:

```
public function drop()
{
    $database = $this->getConnection();
    $name = $this->name;
    $collection = $database->$name;
    $collection->drop();
}
```

This change requires a refactoring in some methods. We will achieve the following in five steps:

1. It is necessary to implement a **Collection->getConnection** method. We will implement it as a **private** method, since its use is restricted to the **Collection** class. It will be as follows:

```
private function getConnection()
{
    $database = Config::get('db')['database'];
    $mongo = new \MongoDB\Client("mongodb://localhost:27017");
    return $mongo->$database;
}
```

2. Refactor the **CollectionRowGatewayTest->testReadAuthor** method so that it is as follows:

```
public function testReadAuthor()
{
    (new AuthorCollectionRowGateway(0,'Johann','Wolfgang','Von
Goethe'))->save();
    (new AuthorCollectionRowGateway(0,'Francis','Scott','Fitzger
ald'))->save();
    (new AuthorCollectionRowGateway(0,'Arthur','Conan','Doy
le'))->save();
    $author = (new AuthorCollectionFinder())->readByCode(2);
    $this->assertEquals('Scott',$author->middleName);
    (new Collection('authors'))->drop();
}
```

3. There is no need for changes because this test uses what already exists. Refactor the **CollectionRowGatewayTest->testReadAuthors** method so that it is as follows:

```
public function testReadAuthors()
{
    (new AuthorCollectionRowGateway(0,'Mary','Wollstonecraft','S
helley'))->save();
    (new AuthorCollectionRowGateway(0,'Agatha','Mary','Christ
ie'))->save();
    (new AuthorCollectionRowGateway(0,'Chaya','Pinkhasivna','Lis
pector'))->save();
    $authors = (new AuthorCollectionFinder())->readAll();
    $this->assertCount(3,$authors);
    $this->assertEquals('Agatha',$authors->get(1)->firstName);
```

```
        (new Collection('authors'))->drop();
    }
```

4. As per the previous test, there is no need for changes because this test uses what already exists. So, let us goto refactor the **CollectionRowGatewayTest->testUpdateAuthor** method so that it is as follows:

```
    public function testUpdateAuthor()
    {
        (new AuthorCollectionRowGateway(0,'Guy','de','Maupassant'))-
>save();
        (new AuthorCollectionRowGateway(0,'Antoine','de','Saint-
Exupéry'))->save();
        (new AuthorCollectionRowGateway(0,'Honoré','de','Balzac'))-
>save();
        $authorCollectionFinder = new AuthorCollectionFinder();
        $author = $authorCollectionFinder->readByCode(1);
        $this->assertEquals('Guy',$author->firstName);
        (new AuthorCollectionRowGateway(1,'Rudolf','Erich','Ras
pe'))->update();
        $author = $authorCollectionFinder->readByCode(1);
        $this->assertEquals('Rudolf',$author->firstName);
        (new Collection('authors'))->drop();
    }
```

Of course, this test will fail because **AuthorCollectionRowGateway->update** method does not exist. Let us create this method, as follows:

```
    public function update()
    {
        $result = $this->database->authors->updateOne(
            ['code' => $this->code],
            ['$set' => [
                'last_name' => $this->lastName,
                'middle_name' => $this->middleName,
                'first_name' => $this->firstName]
            ]
        );
        return $result->getModifiedCount() == 1;
    }
```

5. Refactor **CollectionGatewayTest->testDeleteAuthor** method as follows:

```
public function testDeleteAuthor()
{
    (new AuthorCollectionRowGateway(0,'Machado','de','Assis'))-
>save();
    (new AuthorCollectionRowGateway(0,'José','de','Alencar'))-
>save();
    (new AuthorCollectionRowGateway(0,'Rachel','de','Queiroz'))-
>save();
    $authorCollectionFinder = new AuthorCollectionFinder();
    $author = $authorCollectionFinder->readByCode(2);
    $this->assertEquals('Alencar',$author->lastName);
    (new AuthorCollectionRowGateway(2))->delete();
    $author = $authorCollectionFinder->readByCode(2);
    $this->assertEmpty($author->code);
    (new Collection('authors'))->drop();
}
```

As you can see, it is necessary to implement **AuthorCollectionRowGateway->**delete method. We will implement it as follows:

```
public function delete()
{
    $result = $this->database->authors->deleteOne(['code' => $this-
>code]);
    return $result->getDeletedCount() == 1;
}
```

With this, we can finally run the **CollectionRowGatewayTest** class successfully.

Reviewing model layer

In *Chapter 6, PHP OOP*, we created models for our application, from there we created several helper classes to read and write records, until we implemented classes that returned models as results. It is time to review the several classes which we have created into the **src\Model** folder. Let us install a tool that generates metrics for PHP applications. The **phploc** tool, created by *Sebastian Bergmann*, the same creator of PHPUnit, allows you to measure the size of PHP application based on a series of indicators.

Following instructions download the current version of **phploc**, move it to a directory in the operating system's search path, and grants it permission to run:

```
$ wget https://phar.phpunit.de/phploc.phar
$ sudo mv phploc.phar /usr/bin/phploc
$ sudo chmod 755 /usr/bin/phploc
```

After these steps, we can run **phploc** . inside the **librarian** folder as follows:

```
$ phploc .
```

You will end up with a report with several metrics. In the class metrics section, it should be as follows:

```
Structure
  Namespaces                                  148
  Interfaces                                  157
  Traits                                       16
  Classes                                    1499
    Abstract Classes                       54 (3.60%)
    Concrete Classes                     1445 (96.40%)
      Final Classes                       443 (30.66%)
      Non-Final Classes                  1002 (69.34%)
```

You might be surprised by the report, because even though we created several classes, it is not possible that we create more than a thousand classes. The issue is that **phploc** . is counting all the classes in the current directory and its subdirectories, which includes Composer dependencies. Delete the **vendor** directory and run **phploc** . again. Then, you will get a report that looks more like the following:

```
Structure
  Namespaces                                    7
  Interfaces                                    1
  Traits                                        1
  Classes                                      70
    Abstract Classes                        7 (10.00%)
    Concrete Classes                       63 (90.00%)
      Final Classes                         1 (1.59%)
      Non-Final Classes                    62 (98.41%)
```

Now, we have a view of the classes we created and we can see that we practiced a bit of reuse by having abstract classes but we can improve this practice.

Making models leaner

During software development, we may inadvertently create duplicate structures or create them in inappropriate places, this is why we need to stop every now and then to review our code and make sure there are no duplications that need to be eliminated or classes that are not in the right place. Let us start with the **Author** and **Book** models.

In *Chapter 6, PHP OOP*, we created an abstract class **AbstractCode** to define the common code between the **Author** and **Book** classes. When we created this class, we defined a protected attribute and public methods to access it but later we changed the visibility of this attribute to public in the inherited classes and stopped using methods to read and write the attributes. We can now make the **AbstractCode** class leaner with the following changes:

- Change the visibility of the **$code** attribute to public.

- Remove the implementation of the **CodeInterface** interface and remove the interface itself, which is now useless.

- Remove the **getCode** and **setCode** methods.

Now, the **Author** and **Book** classes do not need to define the **$code** attribute, as they will inherit it in the required visibility. We can remove it from these two classes. We can also remove all methods from these classes with the exception of the constructor method. These changes will cause the **AuthorTest** and **BookTest** test classes to break. You will need to refactor these classes, removing the eliminated method tests and replacing the use of getters and setters with their own attributes.

The **TraitUser** class and the **CodeTrait** trait can be removed, because our application does not use them. They served well as examples and they are available in our repository code for the previous chapters. Since they are removed, the **TraitTest** class must be removed too.

We do not need the classes from **Librarian\PDO** namespace because they are not used by the application anymore. So, you can remove the **src/Model/PDO** folder and the **PDOTest** and the **PDOExceptionTest** classes.

As the functions in **book.functions.php** are using classes for reading and writing object, we can remove some function files and their test classes. You can remove the following files:

- **collection.functions.php**
- **csv.functions.php**
- **json.functions.php**
- **txt.functions.php**

You can remove the **require_once** commands which import these files in **book.functions.php** file. In fact, you must remove it, because it is not possible to require something that does not exist.

We do not need the classes **TxtTest**, **CSVTest** and **JSONTest** anymore. They can be removed.

Of course, after these removals, a test class might stop working. We are talking about **CollectionTest** and **ViewCollectionTes** and not **collection.functions.php** or **dropCollection** function. So, we need to replace the calls to this function with **Collection->drop** method.

Creating single AbstractRowSet

If you review the classes which read the several storages and return the entities as objects, you can observe the following:

- We have three **AuthorRowSet** and three **BookRowSet** classes in three different namespaces.

- All of these classes extend **AbstractRowSet**, however there are two classes with this name.

The only difference among the children of **AbstractRowSet** are the argument of the add method and the existence of a constructor method. We can reduce the number of duplicates by creating a single and more generic implementation for **AbstractRowSet**. Along this refactoring, we can remove the **AuthorRowSet** and **BookRowSet** classes from the specific storage namespaces, keeping one single copy of each one in **Librarian\Model** namespace. We will make it with 8 steps, as follows:

1. We will remove the following classes:

   a. **AbstractRowSet** in **Librarian\Model\ORM** namespace.

   b. **AuthorRowSet** and **BookRowSet** in **Librarian\Model\Filesystem** namespace.

   c. **AuthorRowSet** and **BookRowSet** in **Librarian\Model\ODM** namespace.

   d. **AuthorRowSet** and **BookRowSet** in **Librarian\Model\ORM** namespace.

   Of course, this will break several test classes, but we will fix this step by step.

2. We will add the following method to **Librarian\Model\AbstractRowSet**:
   ```
   public function add(object $row): void
   {
       $this->rows[] = $row;
   }
   ```

3. We will remove the **add** method from **AuthorRowSet** and **BookRowSet** classes in **Librarian\Model** namespace.

4. We will run **PlainTextTest** class. The test report will show you that you must change the namespace of **RowSet** classes in the **AuthorPlainTextFinder** and **BookPlainTextFinder** classes.

5. We will run **CSVTextTest** class. The test report will show you that you must change the namespace of **RowSet** classes in the **AuthorCSVFinder** and **BookCSVFinder** classes.

6. We will run **JSONTextTest** class. The test report will show you that you must change the namespace of **RowSet** classes in the **AuthorJSONFinder** and **BookJSONFinder** classes.

7. We will run **DatabaseTest** class. The test report will show you that you must change the namespace of **RowSet** classes in the **AuthorFinder** and **BookFinder** classes.

8. We will run **CollectionTest** class. The test report will show you that you must change the namespace of **RowSet** classes in the **AuthorCollectionFinder** and **BookCollectionFinder** classes.

After these 8 steps, we have a leaner **RowSet** implementation, which works for any existing storage and for new ones that we might add to our application.

Eliminating duplicate code with inheritance and traits

We need to make an adjustment to the **Librarian\Model\ODM** classes. If you look at the constructors of all the classes in this namespace, you will see that there is a lot of code that is repeated to establish the connection to the MongoDB database. Let us extract this code into a **trait** so that we can use it in the constructor of an **abstract class** and in custom constructors of inheriting classes. Let us create the class, as follows:

```
abstract class AbstractCollection
{
    protected $database;

    public function __construct()
    {
        $this->initDatabase();
    }

    protected function initDatabase(): void
    {
        $database = Config::get('db')['database'];
        $mongo = new \MongoDB\Client("mongodb://localhost:27017");
        $this->database = $mongo->$database;
    }
}
```

Following classes must inherit **AbstractCollection**:
- **AuthorCollection**
- **AuthorCollectionFinder**
- **BookCollection**
- **BookCollectionFinder**

With inheritance, you can eliminate the **$database** attribute and constructor in these classes.

The **AuthorCollectionRowGateway** and **BookCollectionRowGateway** classes also have a **$database** attribute and a constructor with some common code with **AbstractCollection**. The problem is that these classes already inherit from their respective models and PHP does not have multiple inheritance.

In *Chapter 6, PHP OOP*, you learned how traits can be used to solve the problem of a piece of code that needs to be shared between classes that inherit from different superclasses. Let us create a trait by extracting the most generic code from the **AbstractCollection** class. We will create it in the **Librarian\Model\ODM** namespace with the name **CollectionTrait**. It will be defined as follows:

```
trait CollectionTrait
{
    protected $database;

    protected function initDatabase()
    {
        $database = Config::get('db')['database'];
        $mongo = new \MongoDB\Client("mongodb://localhost:27017");
        $this->database = $mongo->$database;
    }
}
```

Having created this **trait**, we can refactor the **AbstractCollection** class, as follows:

```
abstract class AbstractCollection
{
    use CollectionTrait;

    public function __construct()
    {
        $this->initDatabase();
    }
}
```

Using the same trait in the **AuthorCollectionRowGateway** and **BookCollectionRowGateway** classes, we can remove the **$database** attribute from them and shorten their constructors. The **AuthorCollectionRowGateway** constructor will be as follows:

```
    public function __construct(int $code = 0, string $firstName = '',
string $middleName = '', string $lastName = '')
    {
        parent::__construct($code, $firstName, $middleName, $lastName);
        $this->initDatabase();
    }
```

As we progress through the chapters, we assume that you have already grasped a few concepts. A trait is incorporated into a class by using the **use** keyword within the class declaration. We demonstrate this in the refactoring of the **AbstractCollection** class.

The **BookCollectionRowGateway** constructor will be as follows:

```
    public function __construct(int $code =0 , string $title = '', Author
$author = null)
    {
        parent::__construct($code, $title, $author);
        $this->initDatabase();
    }
```

Thus, by combining inheritance and traits, we were able to eliminate code repetition in the **Librarian\Model\ODM** namespace.

Let us use this same approach to eliminate duplication in the **Librarian\Model\ORM** namespace. You can see that all classes in this namespace have the same code snippet to establish connection to MySQL database using **PDO**.

First, let us create the **DatabaseTrait** trait, in the **Librarian\Model\ORM** namespace, as follows:

```
trait DatabaseTrait
{
    protected \PDO $pdo;

    public function initDatabase()
    {
        $db = Config::get('db');
        $this->pdo = new \PDO($db['dsn'], $db['username'],
$db['password']);
    }
}
```

Next, we will create an abstract class that will use this trait. This class will be called **AbstractDatabase** and its concise implementation will be as follows:

```
abstract class AbstractDatabase
{
    use DatabaseTrait;

    public function __construct()
    {
        $this->initDatabase();
    }
}
```

You can remove the **$pdo** attribute declaration from all classes in the **Librarian\Model\ORM** namespace, and you can also remove all constructors except from the **AuthorRowGateway** and **BookRowGateway** classes.

After this cleaning, let us extend the **AbstractDatabase** class to the following classes:

- **AuthorFinder**
- **AuthorTableGateway**
- **BookFinder**
- **BookTableGateway**

For example, for **AuthorFinder**, the class opening will be as follows:

```
class AuthorFinder extends AbstractDatabase implements FinderInterface
```

A class can extend another reusing its methods, and at the same time it can implement an interface, committing to implement the methods defined by it.

Let us change the **AuthorRowGateway** class so that it extends the **Author** class and uses the **DatabaseTrait** trait. With this change you can eliminate all the attributes of the **AuthorRowGateway** class and modify its constructor so that it is as follows:

```
    public function __construct(int $code = 0, string $firstName = '',
string $middleName = '', string $lastName = '')
    {
        parent::__construct($code, $firstName, $middleName, $lastName);
        $this->initDatabase();
    }
```

The **BookRowGateway**, in turn, must extend the **Book** class. After making the inheritance, **BookRowGateway->__construct** method will be as follows:

```
    public function __construct(int $code = 0, string $title = '', Author
$author = null)
    {
        parent::__construct($code, $title, $author);
        $this->initDatabase();
    }
```

Here, we have a detail that can cause errors in the tests. The **$author** argument is optional and if it is omitted its value is **null**. However, in the reading methods it is necessary that the **$this->author** attribute be an instance of **Author**. So, we need to change the constructor of the **Book** class so that it guarantees that the **$this->author** attribute is always an object. The **Book->__construct** method will be as follows:

```
    public function __construct(int $code = 0, string $title = '', Author
$author = null)
    {
      $this->code = $code;
      $this->title = $title;
      $this->author = is_null($author) ? new Author() : $author;
    }
```

The inheritance from **Book** class also requires that **BookFinder->readAll** method be modified. Following line from the code:

```
              $record['author_code']
```

It should be replaced, as follows:

```
              new Author($record['author_code'])
```

For the same reason, we will need to change all the test methods of the **RowGatewayTest** class, replacing the third argument in the call to the **BookRowGateway** constructor with an instance of the **Author** class. For example, following line from the code:

```
(new BookRowGateway(0, 'Fausto', 1))->save();
```

It must be as follows:

```
(new BookRowGateway(0, 'Fausto', new Author(1)))->save();
```

Thus, by combining inheritance and traits, we were able to eliminate code repetition in the **Librarian\Model\ORM** namespace.

Standardizing finder classes

We already know what can happen if we do not establish rules for defining the same method signature for different classes. You have noticed that all **Finder** classes implement the same **readByCode** and **readAll** methods. You might have noticed that some classes define return type, other ones do not define. Let us make sure, in two steps, that these methods have the same arguments and return type across all classes in the **Librarian\ Model** namespace refer to the following steps:

1. We will create the **FinderInterface** interface in the **Librarian\Model** namespace. This interface will be as follows:

```
interface FinderInterface
{
    public function readByCode(int $code): AbstractCode;

    public function readAll(): AbstractRowSet;
}
```

Note that the return type of the methods are abstract classes. Each **Finder** class can return specific type objects, but the interface ensures that these objects have a minimal set of attributes and methods.

2. Implement this interface in the following classes:
   a. **Librarian\Model\Filesystem\AuthorCSVFinder**
   b. **Librarian\Model\Filesystem\AuthorJSONFinder**
   c. **Librarian\Model\Filesystem\AuthorPlainTextFinder**
   d. **Librarian\Model\Filesystem\BookCSVFinder**
   e. **Librarian\Model\Filesystem\BookJSONFinder**
   f. **Librarian\Model\Filesystem\BookPlainTextFinder**
   g. **Librarian\Model\ODM\AuthorCollectionFinder**
   h. **Librarian\Model\ODM\BookCollectionFinder**
   i. **Librarian\Model\ORM\AuthorFinder**
   j. **Librarian\Model\ORM\BookFinder**

Of course, implementing the interface means modifying the signature of the class methods so that they are compatible with the interface.

With this change, we have just applied the Liskov Substitution Principle, one of the five principles known by the acronym **Single, Open-closed, Liskov Substitution, Interface Segregation, Dependency Inversion (SOLID)**.

By this principle, code written in terms of a supertype specification continues to work correctly when we use objects of a subtype.

Note: The FinderInterface methods return abstract class types, but the classes that implement these methods return objects of classes that extend these abstract classes.

For example, **AuthorFinder** implements the **FinderInterface** interface, whose **readByCode** method should return **AbstractCode** but **AuthorFinder->readByCode** actually returns an object of class **AuthorRowGateway**. By the Liskov Substitution Principle, this is valid because **AuthorRowGateway** is a subtype of **AbstractCode**, since **AuthorRowGateway** extends **Author** which extends **AbstractCode**.

Standardizing RowGateway classes

You also have noticed that all **RowGateway** classes implement the same save, update and delete methods. You also might have noticed that some classes define return type, other ones do not define. Let us make sure, in two steps, that these methods have the same arguments and return type across all classes in the **Librarian\Model** namespace.

1. We will create the **RowGatewayInterface** interface in the **Librarian\Model** namespace. This interface will be as follows:

```
interface RowGatewayInterface
{
    public function save(): bool;
    public function update(): bool;
    public function delete(): bool;
}
```

2. Implement this interface in the following classes:

- **Librarian\Model\ODM\AuthorCollectionRowGateway**
- **Librarian\Model\ODM\BookCollectionRowGateway**
- **Librarian\Model\ORM\AuthorRowGateway**
- **Librarian\Model\ORM\BookRowGateway**

Now, these classes follow the same standard for their common methods.

Reviewing user interface

The model layer of our application seems to be converted to object-oriented style but we still have several script files which depends on functions for rendering the user interface. We can replace these script files with classes which are responsible for creating the user interface, applying two architecture patterns, as follows:

- Front controller
- Page controller

Until now, the access to our application is made through several files. You request a file for adding an author, you request another file for listing the author, and so we have to request different files for different purposes. The front controller pattern defines one single access point for an application. It is useful for ensuring that all requests will have the same treatment and it will be very necessary for applying a centralized data input treatment in the *Chapter 11, Refactoring the Application with Secure Development*.

The single access point for our application will be the **index.php** file. This file will receive all HTTP requests and instantiate the class responsible for handling each one of them. Let us establish a protocol so that the request designates which class will be responsible and which action that class will execute. We will use URL arguments, which can be retrieved by the superglobal variable **$_GET**. Let us define that the **c** argument will designate the class and the **a** argument will designate the method to be executed. The letter **c** in this context means controller and the letter **c** means action, which are terms from the page controller pattern.

We will also modify the structure of the HTML pages. We will create a **view** folder, at the same level as the **src** folder, to store the files with the content of the application pages. In the **src** folder, we will create a **Controller** subfolder, which will store the classes that will control the pages, that is the page controllers.

After these definitions, we will refactor the page implementation, starting with the **index. php** file, which will be as follows:

```php
<?php
require 'vendor/autoload.php';


$c = isset($_GET['c']) ? $_GET['c'] : 'index';
$action = isset($_GET['a']) ? $_GET['a'] : 'index';


$controller = 'Librarian\Controller\\' . ucfirst($c);


(new $controller())->run($action);
```

Following is what the PHP script does:

- It tries to read an argument **c** sent by the URL. If it does not exist, it assumes that the value is **index**.

- It tries to read an argument a sent by the URL. If it does not exist, it assumes that the value is **index**. The value is assigned to a variable **$action**.

- From the variable **c**, it assembles the namespace of a class and assigns it to the variable **$controller**.

- An object is instantiated using the variable function technique and a **run** method is invoked from this object, sending the variable **$action** as an argument.

From now on, the **index.php** file does not generate HTML content. It delegates this responsibility to an object, whose class is determined by the request arguments.

We need to understand how this will work and how the pages will be displayed. Let us start with the homepage. We have assumed that the class responsible for the homepage is the **Index** class. More specifically, the index method of the Index class is responsible for generating the homepage.

We need to create the **Index** class but before that, let us create an abstract class for all the page controllers in our application. As you can see from the **index.php** file, all controllers will have a **run** method that will receive a string. This already indicates that the definition of this method is in the abstract class. The abstract class will connect the processing of the received data with the display of a page with the results.

A page controller can control multiple pages. In principle, each public method of a page controller will be associated with an HTML page. This is the rule but there is an exception, when a method is executed, it needs to redirect to another page. This requires the possibility of the page controller method doing a redirection instead of requiring a page.

We will adopt some conventions to regulate the functioning of page controllers. Each page controller will have a subfolder within the **view** with its name, but all in lowercase letters. **User interface** folders and files will, from now on, have only lowercase letters in their names. Uppercase letters will be used only for classes and folders that represent class namespaces.

Let us create the **AbstractControllerPage** class in **the Librarian\Controller** namespace. It will be as follows:

```php
abstract class AbstractPageController
{
    public function run(string $action): void
    {
        $this->$action();
        $tokens = (explode('\\',get_class($this)));
        $controller = lcfirst(end($tokens));
        require __DIR__ . '/../../view/' . $controller . '/' . $action . '.phtml';
    }


    protected function redirect(string $controller, string $action, array $args = [])
    {
        $parameters = '';
        foreach($args as $arg => $value){
            $parameters .= "&$arg=$value";
        }
        header("Location: index.php?c=$controller&a=$action" . $parameters);
        exit;
    }
}
```

The **run** method needs to be public because it is called externally in **index.php**. The **redirect** method will only be used by **AbstractControllerPage** extensions, so it can be protected.

Once the abstract class is defined, let us create its first extension, the **Index** class. It will be a very simple class initially, because the homepage only displays links to the records. The **Index** class, which will also be created in the **Librarian\Controller** namespace, will be as follows:

```
class Index extends AbstractPageController
{
    public function index(): void
    {


    }
}
```

When the **index.php** file is invoked without any arguments, it will instantiate the **Index** class and invoke the **index** method via the **run** method. The **run** method will then import the **index.phtml** file, which must be created inside the **view/index** folder. It will have the following content:

```
<!doctype html>
<html>
<head>
<title>Librarian</title>
</head>
<body>
<h1>Librarian</h1>
<ul>
<li><a href="index.php?c=author&a=list">Authors</a></li>
<li><a href="index.php?c=book&a=list">Books</a></li>
</ul>
</body>
</html>
```

This is almost the content that was there previously in the **index.php** file. We are adopting, from now on, a convention to differentiate files that have only PHP code from files that have a lot of HTML code and some PHP. The former will continue to use the **.php** extension. The latter will adopt the **.phtml** extension.

If you run any user interface tests at this point, they will still work, because the homepage is still generated by the **index.php** file. We have not changed the request address. From now on, however, we will break the tests because we will change the way we invoke our application's services.

As you may have noticed in the **index.phtml** file, to call the author listing page, we will call the **index.php** file, passing **c=author** and **a=list** as arguments. This means that we have to create a controller class called **Author** that has a method called **list**. Initially, therefore, the **Author** class will be as follows:

```
class Author extends AbstractPageController
{
    public function list(): void
    {

    }
}
```

As you may have already understood, as soon as the **Author->list** method is closed, the inherited run method will try to import a file called **list.phtml**, which should be in the **view/author** folder.

You can copy the **author.list.php** file, which is in the application **root** directory, as **list.phtml**. You can remove the initial PHP code snippet that imports the **vendor/autoload.php** file. You will no longer need to import this file for each HTML page, since all of them will be displayed by classes, which will be invoked by the **index.php** file, which will centralize the import of the **Composer** class loading file.

The **list.phtml** file will be as follows:

```
<!doctype html>
<html>
<head>
<title>Librarian</title>
</head>
<body>
<h1>Authors</h1>
<a href="index.php?c=author&a=edit">Add an author</a>
<table>
<thead>
<tr>
<th>code</th><th>name</th><th>action</th>
</tr>
</thead>
<tbody>
<?=$this->listAuthorsInTable()?>
</tbody>
</table>
<a href="index.php">Homepage</a>
</body>
</html>
```

You noticed that there is a call to a method using the **$this** keyword. Remember that the **list.phtml** file is being imported inside a method of the **Author** class. So, this file has access to all the methods and attributes of the class. The **Author->listAuthorsInTable** method will have the following implementation:

```
protected function listAuthorsInTable(): string
{
    try {
        $authors = $this->getAuthorFinder()->readAll();
    } catch(\Exception $e) {
        $authors = new AuthorRowSet();
    }
    $html = '';
    foreach($authors as $author){
        $html.='<tr>';
        $html.='<td><a href="index.php?c=author&a=edit&code=' .
$author->code . '">' . $author->code . '</a><td>';
        $html.="<td>{$author->firstName} {$author->middleName} {$author-
>lastName}<td>";
        $html.='<td><a href="index.php?c=author&a=delete&code=' .
$author->code . '">remove</a><td>';
        $html.='</tr>';
    }
    return $html;
}
```

As you can see, this method will override the **listAuthorsInTable** function from the **book. functions.php** file. Additionally, this method calls another **method, getAuthorFinder**, which will be implemented in the **Author** class, as follows:

```
protected function getAuthorFinder(): FinderInterface
{
    $storageFormat = Config::get('storage_format');
    switch($storageFormat){
        case 'txt':
            return new AuthorPlainTextFinder();
        case 'csv':
            return new AuthorCSVFinder();
        case 'json':
            return new AuthorJSONFinder();
        case 'rdb':
```

```
                return new AuthorFinder();
        case 'ddb':
                return new AuthorCollectionFinder();
    }
    throw new \Exception('invalid storage format');
}
```

If you run any user interface tests at this point, they will still work, but the server will show warnings for filesystem storage tests. The reason is that text files are not created before reading operations. The solution is simple, you must change all the **readByCode** and **readAll** methods of the **Finder** classes in the **Librarian\Model\Filesystem** namespace, ensuring that the file exists before it is read.

Following is a snippet from the **AuthorPlainTextFinder->readByCode** method:

```
$filepath = Config::get('author_plaintext_filepath');
$handle = fopen($filepath,'r');
```

It should be replaced with the following snippet:

```
$filepath = Config::get('author_plaintext_filepath');
if (!file_exists($filepath)){
    $handle = fopen($filepath,'w');
    fclose($handle);
}
$handle = fopen($filepath,'r');
```

After applying this change to all **Finder** classes, those classes become responsible for ensuring that these files exist before reading them and you can delete the **author.list. php** file. As a consequence, the user interface test classes will fail again. You need to replace the following URL:

http://localhost:8000/author.list.php

Replace it with the following:

http://localhost:8000/index.php?c=author&a=list

The list of authors has now been transferred to the **Author controller** class. The next action we will encapsulate in this controller will be the editing of the author. Let us implement the **Author->edit** method, as follows:

```
public function edit(): void
{
    $code = $_GET['code'] ?? 0;
    $this->author = $this->getAuthorByCode($code);
}
```

When reading this method you should notice two things. The first is that we need to declare a **$this->author** attribute in the class, as follows:

```
protected AuthorModel $author;
```

You might wonder why the attribute is of a type **AuthorModel** that does not exist. In fact, **AuthorModel** is an alias for the **Librarian\Model\Author** namespace. Since the controlling class is also called **Author**, we need to use an alias to differentiate one from the other. The alias is given by the use statement, as follows:

```
use Librarian\Model\Author as AuthorModel;
```

Note: If you want an attribute of a subclass to be non-public but visible to the superclass, you must declare it as protected. Superclasses do not have access to private attributes of subclasses, because private means only to the class where it is declared.

The second thing we need to do in the **AuthorController** class is to implement the **getAuthorByCode** method, which is called by the **edit** method. Its implementation will be as follows:

```
    protected function getAuthorByCode($code): AuthorModel
    {
        try {
            $author = $this->getAuthorFinder()->readByCode($code);
        } catch(\Exception $e) {
            $author = new AuthorModel();
        }
        return $author;
    }
```

The editing part in the controller is finished. Now, we have to create the editing view, which is the **edit.phtml** file inside **view/author**. You already understood that the header of our pages is always the same, so we will just show the body of the document, which will be as follows:

```
<body>
<h1>Author</h1>
<form method="post" action="index.php?c=author&a=save">
<label for="first_name">First name:</label>
<input type="text" name="first_name" value="<?=$this->author-
>firstName?>"><br/>
<label for="middle_name">Middle name:</label>
<input type="text" name="middle_name" value="<?=$this->author-
>middleName?>"><br/>
<label for="last_name">Last name:</label>
<input type="text" name="last_name" value="<?=$this->author-
```

```
>lastName?>"><br/>
<input type="hidden" name="code" value="<?=$this->author->code?>"><br/>
<input type="submit" value="save">
</form>
</body>
```

Now, you can remove the **author.edit.phtml** file. As a consequence, the edit tests in the user interface test classes will fail. You need to replace the following URL:

http://localhost:8000/author.edit.php

Replace with the following URL:

http://localhost:8000/index.php?c=author&a=edit

So, the tests will run successfully again for a short break.

After the edit page, we will implement the method responsible for saving the author record. The **Author->save** method will be as follows:

```php
public function save(): void
{
    $code = $_POST['code'] ?? 0;
    $firstName = $_POST['first_name'] ?? null;
    $middleName = $_POST['middle_name'] ?? null;
    $lastName = $_POST['last_name'] ?? null;
    $message = 'The record has not been recorded';
    if ($firstName == null || $middleName == null || $lastName == null){
        $message = 'No data, no recording';
    }
    if ($code == 0 && $this->insert($lastName,$middleName,$firstName)) {
        $message = 'Record saved successfully!';
    }
    if ($code <> 0 && $this->update($code,$lastName,$middleName,$firstName)) {
        $message = 'Record updated successfully!';
    }
    $this->redirect('author','message',['message' => base64_encode($message)]);
}
```

As you can see, the **Author->save** method can call an **insert** or **update** method. The **Author->insert** method will be as follows:

```
    protected function insert($lastName, $middleName, $firstName): bool
    {
        $storageFormat = Config::get('storage_format');
        $dataGateway = 'Librarian\Model\\' . match($storageFormat){
            'txt' => 'Filesystem\AuthorPlainText',
            'csv' => 'Filesystem\AuthorCSV',
            'json' => 'Filesystem\AuthorJSON',
            'rdb' => 'ORM\AuthorTableGateway',
            'ddb' => 'ODM\AuthorCollection'
        };
        try {
            return (new $dataGateway())->save($lastName, $middleName,
$firstName);
        } catch (\Exception $e){
            return false;
        }
    }
```

The **Author->update** method, in turn, will be as follows:

```
    protected function update($code, $lastName, $middleName, $firstName):
bool
    {
        $storageFormat = Config::get('storage_format');

        $data = [
            'last_name' => $lastName,
            'middle_name' => $middleName,
            'first_name' => $firstName
        ];
        $dataGateway = 'Librarian\Model\\' . match($storageFormat){
            'txt' => 'Filesystem\AuthorPlainText',
            'csv' => 'Filesystem\AuthorCSV',
            'json' => 'Filesystem\AuthorJSON',
            'rdb' => 'ORM\AuthorTableGateway',
            'ddb' => 'ODM\AuthorCollection'
        };
        try {
            return (new $dataGateway())->update($code, [
```

```
                    'last_name' => $lastName,
                    'middle_name' => $middleName,
                    'first_name' => $firstName]
            );
        } catch (\Exception $e){
            return false;
        }
    }
}
```

Now, you can delete the **author.save.php** file. As a consequence, the user interface test classes will fail again. You need to replace the following URL:

http://localhost:8000/author.save.php

Replace it with the following:

http://localhost:8000/index.php?c=author&a=save

The tests, however, will continue to fail after this replacement. The problem is that the tests check if the redirected page has a message and we have not implemented the method in the controller class that displays the message. Let us implement the **Author->message** method, as follows:

```
public function message(): void
{


}
```

This method does not need content because the message is in the **$_GET** superglobal variable. So, to display the message, we need to create the **message.phtml** file in **view/author** with the following document body:

```
<body>
<p><?=base64_decode($_GET['message'] ?? 'no message')?></p>
<a href="index.php?c=author&a=list">Authors</a>
</body>
```

Now, you can delete the **author.message.php** file.

After the message page, we will implement the method responsible for deleting the authors. The **Author->delete** method will be as follows:

```
public function delete()
{
    $code = $_GET['code'] ?? 0;
    $message = 'The record has not been deleted';
```

```
    if ($code == 0){
        $message = 'It cannot delete what does not exist';
    }
    if ($code <> 0 && $this->remove($code)) {
        $message = 'Record deleted successfully!';
    }
    $this->redirect('author','message',['message' => base64_
encode($message)]);
    }
```

As you can see, the **Author->delete** method invokes a **remove** method. The latter will be implemented, as follows:

```
    public function remove($code)
    {
        $storageFormat = Config::get('storage_format');

        $deleted = false;
        $dataGateway = 'Librarian\Model\\' .  match($storageFormat){
            'txt' => 'Filesystem\AuthorPlainText',
            'csv' => 'Filesystem\AuthorCSV',
            'json' => 'Filesystem\AuthorJSON',
            'rdb' => 'ORM\AuthorTableGateway',
            'ddb' => 'ODM\AuthorCollection'
        };

        try {
            return (new $dataGateway())->delete($code, [
                'last_name' => $lastName,
                'middle_name' => $middleName,
                'first_name' => $firstName]
            );
        } catch (\Exception $e){
            return false;
        }
    }
```

Now, you can delete the **author.delete.php** file. As a consequence, the user interface test classes will fail again. You need to replace the following URL:

http://localhost:8000/author.delete.php

Replace it with the following:

http://localhost:8000/index.php?c=author&a=delete

Now, the author registry is managed by the **AuthorController** class. A single PHP file controls all requests for this registration. Now, the pages related to authors are subordinate to a class, a page controller.

The book registry, however, continues with the previous user interface structure, generated from files with HTML content independent of the processing scripts. Based on the changes we made for authors, you should create the book controller class and move the page files for this registry to the corresponding subfolder in view.

Reviewing controller layer

Now, the Librarian application has a single access point, which is the **index.php** file. You can refute this claim by saying that you can access any page directly, without going through the **index.php** file, if you request the following address:

http://localhost:8008/view/index/index.phtml

You will see the same page displayed when you request the **index.php** file. It is like having a gatehouse for a piece of land that has no fences or walls.

For the front controller pattern to work effectively, we must limit public access to files that can be directly requested. Web servers can restrict access to folders via configuration. PHP's built-in server is not a production web server, but it does have a way to set access restrictions by defining a router. A router is a PHP script that is called by the server before processing the HTTP request. This way, we can prevent the client from accessing resources that are not public. Let us create the **router.php** file, as follows:

```php
<?php
$uri = $_SERVER['REQUEST_URI'];
$parts = explode('/',$uri);
if ($parts[1] == ''){
    return false;
}
$fileName = explode('?',$parts[1])[0];
if ($fileName !== 'index.php'){
    header("HTTP/1.1 404 Not Found");
    echo "404 Not Found";
    exit;
}
return false;
```

If the router script returns false, it means that the embedded server can process the request normally. Our script checks whether the request is for the **index.php** file. If it is not, it returns an HTTP 404 response. It is not true that the resource was not found. Perhaps a 403 (forbidden) code would be more appropriate but it is safer to report that the resource was not found, since this way the user will not have information about the structure of the application. You do not know if the person accessing the application is an attacker, so do not provide unnecessary information with details about the application.

To use the router with PHP's built-in server, you will put the router filename after the address and port, as follows:

```
$ php -S localhost:8008 router.php
```

Try making a request for a file in the **view** folder, as follows:

http://localhost:8008/view/index/index.phtml

You will see that the answer will be as follows:

404 Not Found

You can try to request any other file from the **view** folder or the **src** folder, or even the **vendor** folder. The router prevents access to these folders. On a production web server, the same effect is achieved through configuration. Thus, the front controller pattern is fully implemented.

There is no need to change the requests in the existing test classes because they are made to valid addresses but we can create a class to test the router requesting an invalid route.

Let us create the **RouterTest** class, as follows:

```
class RouterTest extends TestCase
{
    /**
     * @coversNothing
     */
    #[CoversNothing()]
    public function testInvalidRoute()
    {
        $rest = new Rest();
        $response = $rest->doGet([],'localhost:8008/view/index/index.
phtml',200);
        $this->assertStringContainsString('404 Not Found',$response);
    }
}
```

If you run this class, you will see that the test fails with an **ERROR ON REQUEST** message. The failure occurs because the request is made without a web server to respond. We need to start a web server to make this request. We have already done this in the classes that test the user interface, and you may have noticed that there is some code that is repeated in several classes. Let us make the **RouterTest** class work while eliminating the replication of code that starts and stops the web server.

Let us create the **PHPServer** class in the **Librarian\Test** namespace, as follows:

```
final class PHPServer
```

The class will have the final modifier so that it cannot be extended. Final classes cannot be inherited and therefore cannot be modified by other classes. The **PHPServer** class will have two private attributes, as follows:

```
private $process;
private static $instance = null;
```

The **$process** attribute will store the resource for the web server process. The **$instance** attribute will store an object of the **PHPServer** class. We will have a single object of this class in use, so we will block public use of the constructor by defining a private constructor, as follows:

```
private function __construct()
{}
```

Without a public constructor, we need another way to generate an instance of the class. We will do this with a **static** method, which creates an instance and stores it in a **static** attribute, ensuring that there is only one instance of the class. This method, which we will call **getInstance**, will be as follows:

```
public static function getInstance()
{
    if (self::$instance == null){
        self::$instance = new PHPServer();
    }
    return self::$instance;
}
```

The **PHPServer** class will have a method to start the server. The **PHPServer->start** method should be implemented, as follows:

```
public function start(): bool
{
    $path = realpath(__DIR__ . '/../../');
    $descriptorspec = array(
        0 => ["pipe", "r"],
        1 => ["pipe", "w"],
        2 => ["file", "/dev/null", "a"]
```

```
        );
        $process = proc_open('nohup php -S localhost:8008 router.php
&',$descriptorspec,$path);
        sleep(1);
        if (is_bool($process)){
            return false;
        }
        $this->process = $process;
        return true;
    }
```

To shut down the server, we will implement the **stop** method, as follows:

```
    public function stop(): bool
    {
        return proc_terminate($this->process);
    }
```

After creating the **PHPServer** class, we will use it to start the web server by implementing the **RouterTest::setUpBeforeClass** class, as follows:

```
    public static function setUpBeforeClass(): void
    {
        PHPServer::getInstance()->start();
    }
```

Let us stop the server by implementing the **RouterTest::tearDownAfterClass** method, as follows:

```
    public static function tearDownAfterClass(): void
    {
        PHPServer::getInstance()->stop();
    }
```

Now, the **RouterTest** class will run successfully.

If you observed well, we can remove the repetitive code that starts and stops PHP's built-in web server in user interface test classes by centralizing the responsibility in the **PHPServer** class. We will make the following changes to these classes:

- We will remove the static **$process** attribute
- We will remove the static **startPHPServer** method
- We will replace the following instruction:

```
        self::$process = self::startPHPServer();
```

with this:

```
PHPServer::getInstance()->start();
```

- We will replace the following instruction:

```
proc_terminate(self::$process);
```

- with this:

```
PHPServer::getInstance()->stop();
```

This eliminates the replication of an attribute and method in multiple test classes.

Before we wrap up this section, let us make another improvement to the test classes that manipulate the file system. These classes inherit from **AbstractBackupTest** to make copies of the production text files during testing and restore them at the end. This might have been necessary when we had just one configuration file, but now we have separate files for each environment. We can name the text files with different names in the test environment configuration file so that the tests do not manipulate the production files. This way, we can eliminate the inheritance from the **AbstractBackupTest** class and the **AbstractBackupTest** class itself in three steps, as follows:

1. First, let us modify the name of the text files in the **book.config.test.php** file by adding a **.test** before the file extension. So, for example, **authors.txt** will become **authors.test.txt**.

2. Next, we remove the inheritance of the **AbstractBackupTest** class from the UI test classes which handle the filesystem. This means removing the **extends** keyword and the method calls from the inherited class.

3. The third step is to make these classes inherit from **PHPUnit\Framework\ TestCase**.

4. Finally, the last step is to delete the **AbstractBackupTest** class.

Conclusion

In this chapter, we covered how to refactor a function-oriented database implementation from a document-oriented database to an object-oriented implementation using the Row Data Gateway design pattern. We covered the identification of duplications and the elimination of them, generalizing with abstract classes and enforcing patterns with interfaces.

In the next chapter, we are going to learn about the creation of a new layer for decoupling the model layer from the storage paradigm.

Points to remember

- The refactoring of the persistence implementation in MongoDB required changes in the classes that work with other persistence paradigms.

- To make changes in many classes is a consequence of a tightly coupled implementation.

- When building an application, we have to avoid this type of coupling, to reduce the amplitude of change in software maintenance.

Exercises

1. In this chapter, we have eliminated duplication using traits and abstract classes. However, we did not eliminate a bad practice in the implementation for document-based databases. You have noticed that we get the data for relational database connection from the configuration file, but the same data for document-based database are hard coded. This is not recommended, because connection data are mutable data and mutable data must be in configuration files. Refactor the relational database classes of Librarian application extracting the hard coded data to configuration file.

2. We are converting a function-based application to an object-oriented application. So, we have to replace functions with methods as a rule. We already have a class for handling the configuration file. It is time to replace the occurrences of getConfig function by Config::get method. After that, you must remove getConfig function from the book.functions.php file.

Join our book's Discord space

Join the book's Discord Workspace for Latest updates, Offers, Tech happenings around the world, New Release and Sessions with the Authors:

https://discord.bpbonline.com

CHAPTER 10

Abstracting the Application Storage

Introduction

This chapter of the book will cover the refactoring of the previous version of the book registration application and the creation of a new layer for decoupling the model layer from the storage paradigm. This change is justified to avoid vendor lock-in and reduce migration costs. This chapter will start covering what design patterns are and how to use them. Next, we will learn how to create a **Representational State Transfer (REST) application programming interface (API)** for our application. After having implemented an API, we will learn how to generate a code coverage report. Then, we will follow with changes in the handling of the web pages, introducing an architecture pattern to separate the layout from the content. Finally, we will refactor the application with the **Model-View-Controller (MVC)** pattern.

Structure

Following is the structure of the chapter:

- Design patterns
- Making REST API
- Code coverage
- Handling web pages with classes
- Refactoring application with MVC architecture pattern

Objectives

By the end of this chapter, readers will be able to understand what design patterns are and how to use them to solve recurring problems in **object-oriented programming** (**OOP**). You will learn to implement a REST API in your PHP application. You will also learn how to generate a code coverage report with **PHPUnit** and will know if you are writing enough tests for your application. Finally, you will be able to apply the MVC pattern for dividing responsibilities in a web application.

Design patterns

A design pattern in software development is a concept borrowed from architecture. A design pattern is a solution that has been applied to a recurring problem in OOP and has been shown to be effective. Thus, a design pattern is the reuse of an idea. A design pattern is like a recipe, with the ingredients and how to make it. This last analogy is interesting to say what a design pattern is not. Just as the recipe is not the finished dish, but the way to make it, the design pattern is the way to solve a problem and not its implementation. Design patterns can be implemented in any object-oriented or object-oriented-supporting programming language.

Just as recipes can be collected in a cookbook, design patterns are collected in design pattern catalogues. When you have a problem in OOP, you can consult one or more catalogues and see if it has already been solved and how, in the same way that someone who wants to make an apple cake opens a cookbook and looks for the cake recipe.

> **Note: Design patterns are well-documented solutions to recurring problems in object-oriented software.**

Let us introduce the use of design patterns by addressing a problem in our tests. You know that some test classes need to start the built-in PHP server to make HTTP requests. In the last chapter, we encapsulated the server start and stop in a class to avoid code repetition. As we only use one server, we used only one object of this class.

In object orientation, you have two scenarios for a class, that is, generating multiple instances or none. If a class is abstract, it is not possible to instantiate an object from it. Only inherited classes will be able to generate objects but if they can generate objects, they can generate multiple objects, up to the limit of computational capacity.

Thus, the default implementation of classes does not provide a mechanism to limit the number of instances if we want to do so.

However, the catalog of design patterns by *Erich Gamma* and his fellows provides a pattern whose stated intention is the following:

Ensure a class only has one instance, and provide a global point of access to it.

This means that at some point someone has already had this problem, solved it and documented the solution. Design patterns have names to facilitate memorization and communication between developers. The problem of limiting the creation of instances of a class to just one is documented under the name **Singleton**.

Before implementing the Singleton pattern in our application, let us review the algorithm for using design patterns, as follows:

1. We have a problem.

2. We want to know if anyone has already solved this problem.

3. Search a catalog of design patterns.

4. We read the intents of the patterns until we find one that matches our problem.

5. We study the structure of the documented solution and implement it.

You already implemented the Singleton design pattern in the previous chapter. It is implemented in the **PHPServer** class, which we created to centralize the starting and stopping of the web server used for testing. We mentioned that this class only allowed one instance to be created, but that may not have been clear. Let us create a test class that will demonstrate that the **PHPServer** class can only create one instance. We cannot, however, forget that we are working with **test-driven development** (**TDD**). Let us create the **ServerTest** class and implement the **testServer** method, as follows:

```
class ServerTest extends TestCase
{
    public function testServer()
    {
        $server = PHPServer::getInstance();
        $this->assertInstanceOf(PHPServer::class, $server);
        $anotherServer = PHPServer::getInstance();
        $this->assertEquals(spl_object_id($server),spl_object_
id($anotherServer));
    }
}
```

Note: We omitted the CodeNothing annotation and attribute, but they exist. This annotation specifies that no code coverage information will be recorded for the annotated test case.

The **ServerTest->testServer** method checks whether the variable **$server** is an object of the **PHPServer** class and whether the variables **$server** and **$anotherServer** are pointing to the same object.

Note that we are not using the **new** or **clone** operator to generate an instance of the **PHPServer** class. Instead, we are using the static **getInstance** method. Well, the test suggests that the **getInstance** method should return an object of the **PHPServer** class.

The static **PHPServer->getInstance** method returns the static attribute **self::$instance.** If it is **null**, it receives an instance of **PHPServer**. This means that this method will always return the same object but what stops the programmer from creating other instances using the **new** operator is a private constructor:

```
private function __construct()
{}
```

If the constructor is private, the **new** operator cannot be used for the class, because the **new** operator invokes the constructor method. Only the class itself can use the **new** operator if the constructor is private. Therefore, the only way to get a **PHPServer** instance is to use the **getInstance** method. This strategy is the solution described as Singleton. Now, you can run **ServerTest** successfully.

It is important to note that a design pattern may present a solution to a particular case of a broader problem. The description of the Singleton pattern (and its name) suggest that it only serves to limit the creation of instances of a class to a single instance but the solution strategy can be applied to limit creation to any number of instances.

Imagine you are creating software to play chess. Chess has two players. In object-oriented modeling, you will define a **Player** class and this class can only have two instances. To ensure this, you will define a private constructor for the **Player** class and create two attributes to guard the only two instances of the class. Each instance can be retrieved by a specific method such as **getPlayerOne** and **getPlayerTwo**) or by a parameterized method such as **getPlayer(playerNumber)**.

Design patterns are lessons learned about object-oriented software development. They should not limit our thinking, as we will not always find problems that perfectly fit the scenario described by the patterns. However, they can show the way.

In addition to the Singleton pattern, we implemented the page controller and front controller patterns in the previous chapter. By the end of this chapter, we will implement one more pattern. However, before that, let us implement an API.

Making REST API

Applications can be used by humans or by other applications. The use of one application by another can be motivated by task automation or system integration. Therefore, it is necessary to provide the application with an interface to offer its services to other applications. This is the purpose of the API.

In principle, a web application can provide an API from endpoints that can be invoked by HTTP requests. The structure of the endpoints, their names, and the accepted HTTP methods are design decisions. The model that has become the standard for the structure of endpoints and the discipline of HTTP methods in APIs is REST.

According to the REST model, we must create endpoints in which operations on the same resource are identified by HTTP methods. Thus, the same URL can be used to perform different operations. In the REST standard, HTTP methods are used as follows:

- **POST**: It creates a new resource
- **PUT**: It replaces data from a given resource
- **PATCH**: It partially updates a given resource
- **GET**: It gets data from a resource
- **DELETE**: It deletes a specific resource

Let us implement a REST API for the Librarian application. As we are developing with tests, let us start by creating the **RESTTest** class, as follows:

```
class RESTTest extends TestCase
```

Since **RESTTest** will make HTTP requests, it requires a PHP server. Good thing we created a **PHPServer** class. To have the server start before any tests are run, we will create the **PHPServer** instance in the static **RESTTest::se tUpBeforeClass** method, as follows:

```
public static function setUpBeforeClass(): void
{
    putenv('LIBRARIAN_TEST_ENVIRONMENT=true');
    PHPServer::getInstance()->start();
}
```

As you can see, we also change the environment variable for using the test configuration. We already have done this before, in classes that test the user interface. and as you may recall, we need to stop the server after the last test in the class has run. We do this in the **RESTTest::tearDownAfterClass** method, as follows:

```
public static function tearDownAfterClass(): void
{
    PHPServer::getInstance()->stop();
    putenv('LIBRARIAN_TEST_ENVIRONMENT=false');
}
```

The object returned by **PHPServer** in both static methods is the same, because we are using the Singleton design pattern, which guarantees the existence of a single instance of the class.

Now, we can start to implement our API from the tests. Let us create the **RESTTest->testSaveAuthor** method, as follows:

```
[REFAZER]
public function testSaveAuthor()
{
```

```
$url = 'http://localhost:8008/index.php?api=author';
$rest = new Rest();
$data = [
    'first_name' => 'George',
    'middle_name' => 'Herbert',
    'last_name' => 'Wells'
];
$response = $rest->doPost($data, [], $url, 200);
$json = json_decode($response);
$this->assertIsObject($json);
$this->assertObjectHasProperty('included',$json);
$this->assertTrue($json->included);
Entity::clear('author');
}
```

Let us explain what the **testSaveAuthor** method does, as follows:

- It creates an instance of the **Rest** class, from the **Fgsl\Rest** namespace, and makes a POST request to the **index.php** script. This script must return content in JSON format.

- It decodes the JSON and checks if it is an object, if it has the included attribute and if this attribute is true.

The test will fail, because the **index.php** file does not know how to handle the **api** argument passed by the URL. Let us modify this file so that it handles this argument in order to direct **REST** requests to a specific set of **controller** classes. The source code of this file after importing the **Composer** class loader will be as follows:

```
if (isset($_GET['api'])){
    $api = $_GET['api'];
    $controller = 'Librarian\Controller\\REST\\' . ucfirst($api) . 'REST';
    $action = 'index';
} else {
    $c = isset($_GET['c']) ? $_GET['c'] : 'index';
    $action = isset($_GET['a']) ? $_GET['a'] : 'index';

    $controller = 'Librarian\Controller\\' . ucfirst($c);
}

(new $controller())->run($action);
```

As you can see, now when the **index.php** file receives the api argument, it uses its contents to instantiate a class from the **Librarian\Controller\REST** namespace with the REST suffix. In the case of the failing test, the class to be instantiated is **AuthorREST**. Let us implement it as an inheritor of **AbstractRESTController**, as follows:

```
class AuthorREST extends AbstractRESTController
```

You might object to this by saying that the **AbstractRESTController** class does not exist. It does not, but we will create it to ensure a common implementation and interface for the controller classes that will handle REST requests from our API, as follows:

```
abstract class AbstractRESTController
{
    public function run(string $action)
    {
        $response = '';
        switch ($_SERVER['REQUEST_METHOD']) {
            case 'POST':
                $response = $this->post($_POST);
                break;
            case 'PUT':
                $response = $this->put($this->getPutData());
                break;
            case 'GET':
                $response = $this->get((int)($_GET['code'] ?? 0));
                break;
            case 'DELETE':
                $response = $this->delete((int)($_GET['code'] ?? 0));
                break;
            default:
                $response = ['error' => 'METHOD NOT ALLOWED'];
                http_response_code(405);
        }
        header('Content-Type: application/json');
        echo json_encode($response);
        exit;
    }

    abstract public function post(array $data): array;

    abstract public function get(int $code): mixed;
```

```
abstract public function put(array $data): array;

abstract public function delete(int $code): array;
}
```

As you can see, the **AbstractRESTController->run** method calls another method of the instance, according to the HTTP method. The return from the called methods is encoded in JSON format and sent as an HTTP response. If a method outside the list is used, the script will return a response with status code 405.

The role of the **AbstractRESTController** subclasses is to serve as an intermediary between REST requests and the object that will process the data from these requests. The **run** method will check which HTTP method was called and direct the request to a specialist method of the object responsible for REST requests. The responsible class, in this case, is **AuthorREST**, which will have a private attribute and a constructor to initialize that attribute, as follows:

```
private AuthorProxy $authorProxy;

public function __construct()
{
    $this->authorProxy = new AuthorProxy();
}
```

AuthorProxy is a class that abstracts the type of storage used for the application data. The control layer does not need to know where the data comes from and where it goes. This is determined by the configuration and can be decided by the model layer. Therefore, it is in the **Librarian\Model** namespace that we will create the **AuthorProxy** class.

For dealing with HTTP POST requests, **AuthorREST** must implement the **post** method, as follows:

```
public function post(array $data): array
{
    $firstName = $data['first_name'];
    $middleName = $data['middle_name'];
    $lastName = $data['last_name'];

    $response = ['included' => false];

    if ($this->authorProxy->save($lastName, $middleName, $firstName))
    {
        $response = ['included' => true];
    }
    return $response;
}
```

Note: You must implement all the abstract methods of an abstract class in an heir class, even they method do not have any code line. If you do not implement any method, the class will throw a fatal error. You can initially create all the methods with only a void body and gradually fill them.

As you can see, **AuthorREST->post** calls a **AuthorProxy->save** method. This last method will be implemented as follows:

```
public function save($lastName, $middleName, $firstName): bool
{
    try {
        $saved = ($this->getDataGateway())->save($lastName,
$middleName, $firstName);
    } catch (\Throwable $th) {
        $saved = false;
    }


    return $saved;
}
```

You must have noticed that the **AuthorProxy->save** method depends on an **AuthorProxy->getDataGateway** method. Let us implement the latter, as follows:

```
private function getDataGateway(): object
{
    $storageFormat = Config::get('storage_format');

    try {
        $dataGateway = match($storageFormat){
            'txt' => 'Librarian\Model\Filesystem\AuthorPlainText',
            'csv' => 'Librarian\Model\Filesystem\AuthorCSV',
            'json' => 'Librarian\Model\Filesystem\AuthorJSON',
            'rdb' => 'Librarian\Model\ORM\AuthorTableGateway',
            'ddb' => 'Librarian\Model\ODM\AuthorCollection'
        };
    } catch (\Throwable $th) {
        throw $th;
    }
    return new $dataGateway();
}
```

Now we have the **AuthorProxy** class, which is called by **AuthorREST**, which is indirectly invoked by the HTTP POST request to the **index.php** file with the api argument. This means that the assertions of **RESTTest->testSaveAuthor** must be satisfied but there is a detail in the last statement of the test method: A call to the static clear method of the **Entity** class. This class does not exist. Let us create it along with its clear method in the **Librarian\Model** namespace, as follows:

```php
final class Entity
{
    public static function clear(string $entity)
    {
        $storageFormat = Config::get('storage_format');

        $path = '';
        switch($storageFormat){
            case 'txt':
            case 'csv':
            case 'json':
                $path = getPathForFile($entity);
                if (file_exists($path)) { unlink($path) };
                break;
            case 'rdb':
                (new Table($entity . 's'))->truncate();
                break;
            case 'ddb':
                (new Collection($entity . 's'))->drop();
        }
    }
}
```

Replace the **clearEntity** function with the **Entity::clear** method in all the test classes. Now, **RESTTest->testSaveAuthor** will pass successfully. Once that we have tested the inclusion, let us test the reading, implementing the **RESTTest->testReadAuthor** method, as follows:

```php
    public function testReadAuthor()
    {
        $url = 'http://localhost:8008/index.php?api=author';
        $rest = new Rest();
        $data = [
            'first_name' => 'Johann',
```

```
            'middle_name' => 'Wolfgang',
            'last_name' => 'Von Goethe'
        ];
        $rest->doPost($data, [], $url, 200);
        $data = [
            'first_name' => 'Francis',
            'middle_name' => 'Scott',
            'last_name' => 'Fitzgerald'
        ];
        $rest->doPost($data, [], $url, 200);
        $data = [
            'first_name' => 'Arthur',
            'middle_name' => 'Conan',
            'last_name' => 'Doyle'
        ];
        $rest->doPost($data, [], $url, 200);
        $response = $rest->doGet([], $url . '&code=2', 200);
        $author = json_decode($response);
        $this->assertEquals('Scott',$author->middleName);
        Entity::clear('author');
    }
```

An HTTP GET request will trigger the **AuthorREST->get** method to be called. Let us implement this method, as follows:

```
    public function get(int $code): mixed
    {
        if ($code == 0) {
            return $this->authorProxy->getFinder()->readAll();
        }
        return $this->authorProxy->getByCode($code);
    }
```

The GET request can return one author or a list of authors. This is determined by passing the author's code. You may notice that to return a single author, the **AuthorREST** class calls a getByCode method. Let us implement it, as follows:

```
    public function getByCode($code): Author
    {
        try {
            $author = $this->getFinder()->readByCode($code);
```

```
    } catch(\Exception $e) {
        $author = new Author();
    }
    return $author;
}
```

The **getByCode** method depends on a **getFinder** method. Let us implement it, as follows:

```
public function getFinder(): FinderInterface
{
    $storageFormat = Config::get('storage_format');

    try {
        $finder = match($storageFormat){
            'txt' => 'Librarian\Model\Filesystem\
AuthorPlainTextFinder',
            'csv' => 'Librarian\Model\Filesystem\AuthorCSVFinder',
            'json' => 'Librarian\Model\Filesystem\AuthorJSONFinder',
            'rdb' => 'Librarian\Model\ORM\AuthorFinder',
            'ddb' => 'Librarian\Model\ODM\AuthorCollectionFinder'
        };
    } catch (\Throwable $th) {
        throw $th;
    }
    return new $finder();
}
```

Now **RESTTest->testReadAuthor** will pass successfully. Once that we have tested the reading of one single author, let us test the reading of several authors, implementing the **RESTTest->testReadAuthors** method, as follows:

```
public function testReadAuthors()
{
    $url = 'http://localhost:8008/index.php?api=author';
    $rest = new Rest();
    $data = [
        'first_name' => 'Mary',
        'middle_name' => 'Wollstonecraft',
        'last_name' => 'Shelley'
    ];
    $rest->doPost($data, [], $url, 200);
```

```
        $data = [
            'first_name' => 'Agatha',
            'middle_name' => 'Mary',
            'last_name' => 'Christie'
        ];
        $rest->doPost($data, [], $url, 200);
        $data = [
            'first_name' => 'Chaya',
            'middle_name' => 'Pinkhasivna',
            'last_name' => 'Lispector'
        ];
        $rest->doPost($data, [], $url, 200);
        $response = $rest->doGet([], $url, 200);
        echo $response;
        $authors = json_decode($response);
        $this->assertCount(3,$authors);
        $this->assertEquals('Agatha',$authors[1]->firstName);
        Entity::clear('author');
    }
```

The test will indirectly call the **AuthorProxy->getFinder** method, which in turn will call the **readAll** method of the active data gateway object for the current configuration. This will throw an error, because the **realAll** method returns an **AbstractRowSet** instance, which will be converted to a JSON object, and the test assertion expects a JSON list. We need a way to extract a list from the **AbstractRowSet** instance. We can do this by implementing a method in this class that returns the wrapped list, as follows:

```
public function getRows(): array
{
    return $this->rows;
}
```

The next step is to refactor the **AuthorREST->get** method to return an array when the author code is not specified, as follows:

```
public function get(int $code): mixed
{
    if ($code == 0) {
        return $this->authorProxy->getFinder()->readAll()->getRows();
    }
    return $this->authorProxy->getByCode($code);
}
```

Now, you should have understood why we defined the return of this method as mixed in the abstract class. This method can return an object or an array. From this change **RESTTest->testSaveAuthor** will pass successfully. Once that we have tested the reading, let us test the updating, implementing the **RESTTest->testUpdateAuthor** method, as follows:

```php
public function testUpdateAuthor()
{
    $url = 'http://localhost:8008/index.php?api=author';
    $rest = new Rest();
    $data = [
        'first_name' => 'Guy',
        'middle_name' => 'de',
        'last_name' => 'Maupassant'
    ];
    $rest->doPost($data, [], $url, 200);
    $data = [
        'first_name' => 'Antoine',
        'middle_name' => 'de',
        'last_name' => 'Saint-Exupéry'
    ];
    $rest->doPost($data, [], $url, 200);
    $data = [
        'first_name' => 'Honoré',
        'middle_name' => 'de',
        'last_name' => 'Balzac'
    ];
    $rest->doPost($data, [], $url, 200);
    $response = $rest->doGet([], $url . '&code=1', 200);
    $author = json_decode($response);
    $this->assertEquals('Guy',$author->firstName);
    $data = $this->getAuthorArray('Rudolf','Erich','Raspe');
    $data['code'] = $author->code;
    $rest->doPut($data,[], $url, 200);
    $response = $rest->doGet([], $url . '&code=1', 200);
    $author = json_decode($response);
    $this->assertEquals('Rudolf',$author->firstName);
    Entity::clear('author');
}
```

An HTTP PUT request will trigger the **AuthorREST->put** method to be called. Let us implement this method, as follows:

```
    public function put(array $data): array
    {
        $code = (int) $data['code'];
        unset($data['code']);
        $response = ['updated' => false];
        if ($this->authorProxy->update($code, $data))
        {
            $response = ['updated' => true];
        }
        return $response;
    }
```

You may have noticed that the **$data** argument injected by **AbstractRESTController->run** is provided by a **getPutData** method, but we did not implement it yet. The **getPutData** method retrieves data sent via HTTP PUT and it must be implemented in the **AbstractRESTController** class, as follows:

```
protected function getPutData()
{
    $stdin = fopen('php://input', 'r');
    $putData = '';
    while($data = fread($stdin, 1024))
        $putData .= $data;
    fclose($stdin);
    $rows = explode('&',$putData);
    $fields = [];
    foreach($rows as $row)
    {
        $tokens = explode('=', $row);
        $fields[$tokens[0]] = $tokens[1];
    }
    return $fields;
}
```

The **AuthorREST->put** method requires the **AuthorProxy->update** method. Let us implement it, as follows:

```php
public function update($code, $data): bool
{
    try {
        $saved = ($this->getDataGateway())->update($code, $data);
    } catch (\Throwable $th) {
        $saved = false;
    }
    return $saved;
}
```

Now, **RESTTest->testUpdateAuthor** will pass successfully. Once that we have tested the updating, let us test the deleting, implementing the **RESTTest->testDeleteAuthor** method, as follows:

```php
public function testDeleteAuthor()
{

    $url = 'http://localhost:8008/index.php?api=author';
    $rest = new Rest();
    $data = [
        'first_name' => 'Machado',
        'middle_name' => 'de',
        'last_name' => 'Assis'
    ];
    $rest->doPost($data, [], $url, 200);
    $data = [
        'first_name' => 'José',
        'middle_name' => 'de',
        'last_name' => 'Alencar'
    ];
    $rest->doPost($data, [], $url, 200);
    $data = [
        'first_name' => 'Rachel',
        'middle_name' => 'de',
        'last_name' => 'Queiroz'
    ];
    $rest->doPost($data, [], $url, 200);
    $response = $rest->doGet([], $url . '&code=2', 200);
    $author = json_decode($response);
```

```
$this->assertEquals('Alencar',$author->lastName);
$rest->doDelete([], $url . '&code=2', 200);
$response = $rest->doGet([], $url . '&code=2', 200);
$author = json_decode($response);
$this->assertEquals(0, $author->code);
Entity::clear('author');
    }
```

An HTTP DELETE request will trigger the **AuthorREST->delete** method to be called. Let us implement this method, as follows:

```
public function delete(int $code): array
{
    $response = ['deleted' => false];
    if ($this->authorProxy->delete($code))
    {
        $response = ['deleted' => true];
    }
    return $response;
}
```

Regarding the return of the **AuthorREST->delete** method, we apply the second principle of *Object Calisthenics*: Do not use the **else** Keyword. Object Calisthenics is a set of nine rules created by *Jeff Bay* to improve the maintainability, readability, testability, and comprehensibility of object-oriented software.

Well, the **AuthorREST->delete** method requires the **AuthorProxy->delete** method. Let us implement it, as follows:

```
public function delete($code): bool
{
    try {
        $deleted = ($this->getDataGateway())->delete($code);
    } catch (\Throwable $th) {
        $deleted = false;
    }
    return $deleted;
}
```

Now, **RESTTest->testDeleteAuthor** will pass successfully. With this last method, we can successfully run all the author tests of the **RESTTest** class. It is worth remembering that, although we do not present the tests and implementation for registering books in this chapter, they are available in the code repository. But the idea is that you try to implement it yourself first, based on what you learned here, before rushing to copy the source code. Then, before to read the next section about code coverage, you can practice what you have learned here exposing the books through the API that you have created.

Code coverage

We have been trying to follow the TDD methodology, although so far, we have been limiting ourselves to the first two steps: Creating a test that fails and implementing code that passes the test. However, there is no mechanism that guarantees that will follow at least these two steps in our development process. There is nothing prevent us, after creating a class, from continuing the implementation without testing.

So, we do not know if we are testing enough. We implemented a class to test for exceptions when using PDO, but exceptions can occur throughout the rest of our system. There is nothing, at this moment, that makes us pay attention to this and implement the missing tests.

For solving this issue, we need to check code coverage. We need a tool that shows us how much of our code is covered by tests so we know if we have created enough tests. In PHP, this tool is **PHPUnit**. You can generate a code coverage report as long as you have the **xdebug** extension installed and the **php.ini** file has the following directive:

```
xdebug.mode=coverage
```

The code coverage report can be generated in several formats, but you must define a directory to store it. Let us create the **coverage** directory in our project to store this report.

In addition to requiring a **writable** directory to write the report, **PHPUnit** must be configured to know exactly which files it should inspect to see if they are covered by tests. This configuration is done in the **phpunit.xml** file. In addition to requiring a **writable** directory to write the report, **PHPUnit** must be configured to know exactly which files it should inspect to see if they are covered by tests. We will modify the source tag of this file, so that it only inspects files with the **.php** extension within the Librarian application directory, excluding the **tests** and **vendor** subdirectories. The **source** tag excerpt will be as follows:

```
    <source ignoreIndirectDeprecations="true" restrictNotices="true"
restrictWarnings="true">
        <include>
            <directory suffix=".php">./</directory>
        </include>
        <exclude>
            <directory>./tests/</directory>
            <directory>./vendor/</directory>
        </exclude>
    </source>
```

Note: If you misconfigure the code coverage target, `PHPUnit` may throw an error in the `RecursiveDirectoryIterator` class when trying to read files from directories to which it does not have access.

After creating the **coverage** directory, we will generate a code coverage report in HTML format, with the following command:

```
vendor/bin/phpunit --coverage-html coverage
```

When the report is finished generating, there will be an **index.html** file inside the **coverage** directory. You can open it with your favorite web browser. The page displayed will be as shown in *Figure 10.1*:

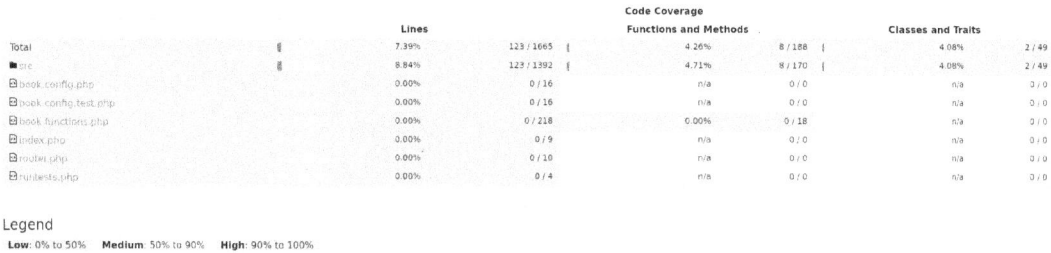

	Lines		Code Coverage Functions and Methods		Classes and Traits	
Total	7.39%	123 / 1665	4.26%	8 / 188	4.08%	2 / 49
src	8.84%	123 / 1392	4.71%	8 / 170	4.08%	2 / 49
book_config.php	0.00%	0 / 16	n/a	0 / 0	n/a	0 / 0
book_config.test.php	0.00%	0 / 16	n/a	0 / 0	n/a	0 / 0
book_functions.php	0.00%	0 / 218	0.00%	0 / 18	n/a	0 / 0
index.php	0.00%	0 / 9	n/a	0 / 0	n/a	0 / 0
router.php	0.00%	0 / 10	n/a	0 / 0	n/a	0 / 0
runtests.php	0.00%	0 / 4	n/a	0 / 0	n/a	0 / 0

Legend
Low: 0% to 50% **Medium:** 50% to 90% **High:** 90% to 100%

Figure 10.1: Code coverage homepage

The code coverage report works with the traffic light model, where three different colors represent three levels of coverage. Red is low (0 to 50% coverage), yellow is medium (50 to 90% coverage), and green is high (90 to 100% coverage). You may be disappointed to see that after writing so many tests, the report states that the code coverage is low. Well, knowing and changing this is what a code coverage tool is for.

You can browse your application's directories and files and see code coverage by lines, by functions and methods, and by classes and traits. Furthermore, on the home page there is a link to a dashboard as shown in *Figure 10.2*. On the dashboard, it is possible to view coverage indicators by class and method:

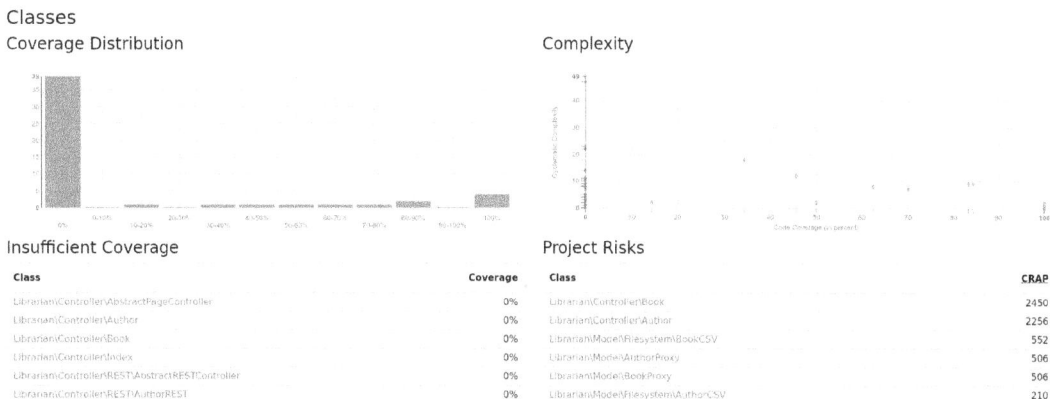

Classes
Coverage Distribution

Complexity

Insufficient Coverage

Project Risks

Class	Coverage
Librarian\Controller\AbstractPageController	0%
Librarian\Controller\Author	0%
Librarian\Controller\Book	0%
Librarian\Controller\Index	0%
Librarian\Controller\REST\AbstractRESTController	0%
Librarian\Controller\REST\AuthorREST	0%

Class	CRAP
Librarian\Controller\Book	2450
Librarian\Controller\Author	2256
Librarian\Model\Filesystem\BookCSV	552
Librarian\Model\AuthorProxy	506
Librarian\Model\BookProxy	506
Librarian\Model\Filesystem\AuthorCSV	210

Figure 10.2: Code coverage dashboard

One of our goals in the next chapters is to increase our code coverage and the **PHPUnit** report will help us with this. Converting a function-oriented application to an object-oriented application is the first step to improve the code coverage. We can declare code coverage for functions, but this will make control more complex. It is more convenient to control by class, since a class groups several functions in the form of methods.

The second step is to declare what should be covered by each test class. So, we will review all the test classes and declare which classes of our application should be covered by the tests. Since we are working in compatibility mode with different versions of **PHPUnit**, we will follow a model that uses annotations and attributes. These declarations should be placed only once before the class declaration. Therefore, you should make, for each class to be covered by the tests, a pair of statements, as follows:

```
/**
 * @covers Author
 */
#[CoversClass(Author::class)]
```

> **Note: As of PHPUnit 12 there are no more annotations, so if you are using PHPUnit 12 you do not need to write annotations, just attributes. As we said in Chapter 3, Function Driven Registration with File System Storage, we are using both ways of declaring code coverage for compatibility reasons.**

You should remove all **CoversNothing** annotations and attributes from the test methods, because now you are telling which classes the tests should cover. After removing **CoverNothing**, if there are classes or functions that are called by tests but are not covered in annotations and attributes, **PHPUnit** will list them after the following message:

This test executed code that is not listed as code to be covered or used.

You will see that **PHPUnit** will show you several functions that are not marked to be covered by the tests, but are called by them. We will not mark these functions, but replace them with classes and cover classes only.

One of the functions listed as uncovered code is the **getPathForFile** function. This function is called indirectly several times, but is only called directly by the **Entity** class. Thus, it makes sense to incorporate the **getPathForFile** function as a private static method of the **Entity** class. This way, the **Entity::clear** method starts calling another method of the same class and no longer an external function.

In the user interface test classes, we use the **saveAuthor** function to include an author. Let us replace the call to this function with the **AuthorProxy->save** method. Following is an example:

```
saveAuthor('Márquez','García','Gabriel');
```

It will be replaced as follows:

```
(new AuthorProxy())->save('Márquez','García','Gabriel');
```

Next, let us replace the call to **getAuthorByCode** function with the **AuthorProxy->getByCode** method. Following is an example:

```
$author = getAuthorByCode(1);
```

It will be replaced, as follows:

```
$author = (new AuthorProxy())->getByCode(1);
```

You must make the same changes for the functions that write and read books.

There is another function that we often call in the **setUpBeforeClass** and **tearDownAfterClass methods: replaceConfigFileContent**. There is an OOP principle called the **Single Responsibility Principle**. It is the letter *S* in the set of principles known as **SOLID**. According to this principle, each class should have a single responsibility, and a responsibility should be assigned to a single class. We have a class responsible for configuration, which is the **Config** class. Changing the configuration file is part of the responsibility of this class.

Before copying the function and pasting it as a method of the **Config** class, we need to consider whether what the function does will still be appropriate when converted to a method. A function is an isolated block of code that depends only on the arguments it receives. A method, on the other hand, has access to all the attributes of the class where it is defined.

Therefore, analyzing the structure of the **Config** class and it **get** method, we can see that it is not necessary to change the file in the file system, since we can overwrite the configuration value in memory. To do this, we need to create an attribute in the **Config** class that stores the values to be overwritten. Let us create the **$overridedValues** attribute, as follows:

```
private static array $overridedValues = [];
```

We will use this attribute to modify the **Config::get** method, as follows:

```
public static function get(string $key)
{
    if (isset(self::$overridedValues[$key])){
        return self::$overridedValues[$key];
    }
    $configFileName = 'book.config.php';
    if ((defined('LIBRARIAN_TEST_ENVIRONMENT') && LIBRARIAN_TEST_
ENVIRONMENT) ||
        getenv('LIBRARIAN_TEST_ENVIRONMENT')){
            $configFileName = 'book.config.test.php';
    }
    if (self::$config == null){
        self::$config = require __DIR__ . '/../../' . $configFileName;
```

```
        }
        return self::$config[$key];
    }
```

Of course, this change will only work if the programmer has a method to pass the values to be overridden. So let us implement the **Config::override** method, as follows:

```
    public static function override($key, $value)
    {
        self::$overridedValues[$key] = $value;
    }
```

With this change, you can replace calls to the **replaceConfigFileContent** function with calls to **Config::override.** For example, the following call:

```
replaceConfigFileContent("'storage_format' => 'txt'","'storage_format' =>
'csv'");
```

It should be replaced, as follows:

```
Config::override('storage_format','csv');
```

After replacing the last remaining functions in our application with class methods, you can delete the **book.functions.php** file. Since the **book.functions.php** file is loaded by Composer, you should also remove the following line from the **composer.json** file:

```
        "files": ["book.functions.php"],
```

To update the **autoload** files, you must run the following Composer command:

$ composer dumpautoload

The **Config::override** method, however, will not work in user interface tests. This method changes the value in memory, but the memory used by **PHPUnit** is not shared by the PHP application running on the embedded server. In the case of user interface tests, we need to change the **configuration** file. To do this, we will create the **Config:change** function, as follows:

```
    public static function change($current, $new)
    {
        $configFileName = __DIR__ . '/../../' . self::getConfigFileName();
        $content = file_get_contents($configFileName);
        $content = str_replace($current, $new, $content);
        file_put_contents($configFileName, $content);
    }
```

As you can see, **Config::change** calls the **Config::getConfigFileName** method. This method should be implemented as follows:

```php
    private static function getConfigFileName(): string
    {
        $configFileName = 'book.config.php';
        if ((defined('LIBRARIAN_TEST_ENVIRONMENT') && LIBRARIAN_TEST_
ENVIRONMENT) ||
            getenv('LIBRARIAN_TEST_ENVIRONMENT')){
            $configFileName = 'book.config.test.php';
        }
        return $configFileName;
    }
```

You can use the **Config::getConfigFileName** method to refactor the **Config::get** method, reducing the number of lines of the latter.

In the user interface test classes, the classes that start with the **View** prefix, you can replace calls to the **replaceConfigFileContent** function with calls to **Config::change**. For example, the following call:

```php
replaceConfigFileContent("'storage_format' => 'txt'","'storage_format' =>
'csv'");
```

It should be replaced, as follows:

```php
Config::change("'txt'","'csv'");
```

After these changes, you can run **PHPUnit** again to generate the code coverage report. However, a problem that must have been occurring since *Chapter 8, Object-oriented Registration with Relational Database Storage*, will still occur, failures when all the tests are run together.

If you run each test class separately, they run successfully, but together they fail. This is because we are using **PHPUnit** to perform integration tests in a way that interferes with **PHPUnit** operation.

As you know, interface tests start a web server to make HTTP requests and then stop it. This works fine when only one class is executed, but when several classes start and stop a PHP server together with other test classes, there is a process interference, because **PHPUnit** runs the tests out of order.

To eliminate this problem, we will separate the interface tests from the other tests. We will create a **uitests** directory in the **root** of the Librarian application and move all the test classes that have **View** as a prefix to there. Now you can run **PHPUnit** without arguments and you will see that it runs all the test classes in the **test** directory successfully. Do not forget to exclude the **uitests** directory of the coverage in the **phpunit.xml** file.

Note: If tests are interrupted during execution and a text file is not deleted, you must manually delete it before running the tests again, as this may interfere with the functioning of the tests.

From now on, we will run the user interface tests separately and one at a time, so that the web server processes of one test class do not interfere with the other. However, the user interface test classes may present the following warning when executed:

```
DOMDocument::loadHTML(): htmlParseEntityRef: expecting ';' in Entity
```

This is because the pages now have links with multiple arguments connected with the **&** character and the **DOMDocument::loadHTML** method initially tries to match this character with an HTML symbol, so it looks for a semicolon. Since this is a false alarm, we can inhibit this warning by using the warning inhibition operator, the **@** character, before calling the method. Thus, all lines with the following instruction:

```
$doc->loadHTML($response);
```

It should be as follows:

```
@$doc->loadHTML($response);
```

Now, we have concluded the separation of general tests, from which we generate the code coverage report, from the integration tests of the user interface with the application backend. With the code coverage report, you know what is being tested and which tests still need to be created. You can generate the code coverage report again and verify that, after the changes we made to the attributes and annotations, we have an average code coverage of the **src** folder.

Handling web pages with classes

In the previous chapter, we implemented the page controller design pattern, so that the web pages of our application are not accessed directly by the user. The controller classes display the pages according to the request data. The pages of our application have one thing in common that all the HTML page headers are the same. In fact, the headers of the pages must be the same because they determine the visual identity of the website or web application. Maintaining this identity, however, can become difficult as the number of pages increases. Imagine that there will be a change in the look of the application and you will have to modify more than forty different files so that all the pages have the same appearance. To avoid this effort, we can separate the layout of the pages, which is the common part, from their content, which is the specific part. To do this, we will use an architectural pattern called **Two-Step View**.

First, let us create a layout file containing the generic part of our HTML pages. Let us create the **layout.phtml** file in the **views** directory with the following content:

```
<!doctype html>
<html>
<head>
<title>Librarian</title>
</head>
```

```
<body>
<?php
require __DIR__ . '/' . $controller . '/' . $action . '.phtml';
?>
</body>
</html>
```

This file will import another **.phtml** file to define the body of the HTML document. The file name and directory are defined by the **$controller** and **$action** variables. These variables come from the **AbstractPageController::run** method, which we will modify to look, as follows:

```
public function run(string $action): void
{
    $this->$action();
    $tokens = (explode('\\',get_class($this)));
    $controller = lcfirst(end($tokens));
    require __DIR__ . '/../../view/layout.phtml';
}
```

From now on, the **AbstractPageController** instance imports the layout file, and the layout file imports the file with the document body content. There are two steps to building the web page, which is why the pattern is called the **Two-Step View**.

If you navigate through the application and view the source code of the pages, you will see that the header and footer of the HTML document appear duplicated. It is necessary to review all the page files and remove the header and footer, leaving these code blocks only in the layout file.

In addition to modifying the **.phtml** files that define the body of your pages, you can remove files that you no longer use. When we implemented the page controller pattern, redirection was built-into the **AbstractPageController** class. This made the **delete. phtml** files unnecessary. You can remove these files from the **view/author** and **view/book** directories.

With this change, the maintenance of the visual identity of the pages can be done in a single location, in the layout file. It makes no difference whether there are four or forty pages, the maintenance effort will be the same.

The purpose of the Two-Step View pattern can be summarized in the following sentence: Change one line, change all pages.

Refactoring application with MVC architecture pattern

In 1979, computer scientist *Trygve Reenskaug* wrote a report in which he proposed a solution to the general problem of giving users control over their information as seen from multiple perspectives. The first note about his solution was a metaphor he called **thing-model-view-editor**. The elements of this metaphor are described by *Reenskaug*, as follows:

- **Thing**: something that is of interest to the user.
- **Model**: an active representation of an abstraction in the form of data.
- **View**: one or more pictorial representations of the model on the screen.
- **Editor**: an interface between a user and one or more views.

After this proposed discussion with some people, *Reenskaug* wrote a second note, in which he reformulated his proposal for an architectural pattern called **MVC**. The three constituent elements of the pattern were defined by *Reenskaug*, as follows:

- **Model**: A representation of knowledge
- **View**: Visual representation of its model
- **Controller**: The link between a user and the system

As you can see, the original concept of editor has been transformed into controller. The Thing element, from the initial proposal, refers to the purpose of the system, the business that the application is automating. This purpose, in the MVC pattern, is in the model element, which is responsible for the system's business rules.

The MVC pattern was originally designed to help create desktop applications, but it has become popular for creating web applications. Today, there are several frameworks available in various programming languages that implement the MVC pattern.

MVC addresses the broad problem of how to separate responsibilities in an application. It is like an expanded view of the Single Responsibility Principle from SOLID. In MVC, classes are separated into three categories and each category has a specific responsibility, according to the definitions given by *Reenskaug*.

Martin Fowler, in his book *Patterns of Enterprise Application Architecture*, states that it is easy to separate the view of an application from the rest, because developers can distinguish what is the user interface and what is not. However, *Fowler* states that separating the controller from the model is not an easy task and can therefore lead to erroneous implementations.

Pádraic Brady, when talks about MVC, gives some fundamental guidelines for trying to successfully divide responsibilities between model and controller, as follows:

- Models are discrete classes that can be tested in isolation from the presentation layer (View).
- Controllers are the exact opposite of the models.

These guidelines are vital because a mistake in implementing MVC can occur from the belief that models should be minimal, and controllers are all important. It is the opposite of that, actually. The Model is so important that it was the first part of MVC that we implemented, in *Chapter 6, PHP OOP*. You may recall that it was in that chapter that we created the `Model` subdirectory within `src`. The responsibilities of the view and controller were separated later in *Chapter 9, Object-oriented Registration with Document Database Storage*.

The view and controller exist for the model. The model is the core of an information system. The view displays data from the model, and the controller controls the flow of data between the model and the view.

Reenskaug calls MVC notions, but you will find authors calling these elements layers. A layer in software is analogous to a layer of a pie or cake made in layers. A wedding cake, for example, is made of several cakes of different sizes, stacked on top of each other. In this analogy, one layer supports another. The lower the layer, the higher it is, because it has to support more weight. In the case of software, the more responsibility and importance the layer has the larger the implementation (more lines of code, more methods, more classes).

As you may have noticed, we have already implemented the MVC architectural pattern in our application. We did it slowly, gradually, and safely, almost naturally. What helped us do this was that we started the right way, implementing the model first.

Let us review our MVC implementation by first learning how to document a PHP application. In the previous chapter we learned about **phploc**, a tool that generates metrics for PHP projects. With **phploc** we can find out how many classes there are, and what category they belong to (abstract, concrete, final) but this is a quantitative view to measure the complexity of the project. There is another tool that generates a more detailed description of the project structure in HTML format: **phpDocumentor**.

In this book, we use **phpDocumentor** *version 3.5.3*. It can be downloaded from the following address:

https://github.com/phpDocumentor/phpDocumentor/releases/download/v3.5.3/phpDocumentor.phar

To generate the documentation, copy the **phpDocumentor** file to the root of the librarian project and run the following command:

```
$ php phpDocumentor.phar -d src/ -t docs
```

In the **docs** folder, there will be an **index.html** file that you can open in your web browser. This file will display the page as shown in *Figure 3.10*. The documentation is generated from the class namespaces and annotations. If the **@package** annotation is not used to separate classes into packages, **phpDocumentor** will group all classes into the default application package.

In the **Documentation** side menu, we have four items as follows: **Namespaces**, **Packages**, **Reports** and **Indices**.

Mastering Test-Driven Development with PHP 8

In the **Namespaces** item, you can navigate from the most generic namespace (**Librarian**) to the classes contained in the most specific namespace. For each class, a page is generated with the description of its attributes and methods, as well as information about the annotations used in the class, such as authorship and license. In the **Indices** item, you will find a list of classes in alphabetical order.

In the **Reports** item, you can see if there are any classes or methods marked as deprecated.

Refer to the following figure:

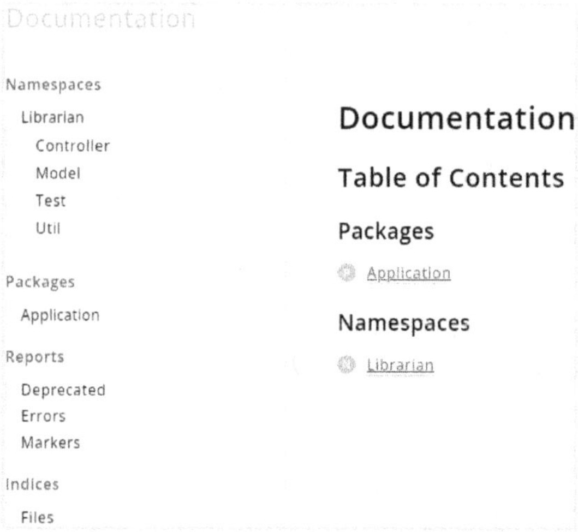

Figure 10.3: Documentation homepage code coverage dashboard

The pages generated by **phpDocumentor** help us understand the general structure of an application and have a quick reference on the interface of the classes but besides having an overview of the structure, we need to continually analyze the application for problems. For this there is a tool called **PHP Mess Detector** (**PHPMD**).

In this book, we use **phpmd** version 2.15.0. It can be downloaded from the following address:

https://github.com/phpmd/phpmd/releases/download/2.15.0/phpmd.phar

Let us create an **analysis** directory to contain the report generated by **phpmd**. The clutter detection report can be generated from several rules, documented at **https://phpmd.org/rules/index.html**. Let us generate the report with all available rules, as follows:

```
$ php phpmd.phar src/ html
cleancode,codesize,controversial,design,naming,unusedcode > analysis/index.html
```

After the generation, you can open the **index.html** file in **analysis** folder with your web browser. The result will be a page similar to *Figure 10.4*.

The **PHPMD Report** groups detected issues **By priority**, **namespace**, **rule set** and **rule name**.

PHPMD Report

Generated at ~~~~~~~~~ *10:12* with PHP Mess Detector on **PHP 8.3.10** on ~~~~~~~~~~~

92 problems found

Summary

By priority

Count	%	Priority
79	85.9 %	**Top (1)**
12	13.0 %	**Moderate (3)**
1	1.1 %	**High (2)**

By namespace

Count	%	PHP Namespace
12	70.6 %	**Librarian\Controller**
4	23.5 %	**Librarian\Controller\REST**
1	5.9 %	**Librarian\Test**

By rule set

Count	%	Rule set
62	67.4 %	**Clean Code Rules**
16	17.4 %	**Controversial Rules**
8	8.7 %	**Unused Code Rules**
3	3.3 %	**Design Rules**
3	3.3 %	**Naming Rules**

Figure 10.4: *PHPMD report*

The **PHPMD Report** initially displays a summary that groups the detected issues **By priority**, **namespace**, **rule set** and **rule name**. This provides an overview of the quantity, quality and severity of the issues. To view each of the detected issues, you can click the show details link below the summary. The page will open to a list like the one in *Figure 10.5*:

#1 Avoid unused local variables such as '*$controller*'. *(help)*   Moderate (3)

File: ~~~~~~~~~~/masteringtestdrivenphp/chapter10/librarian/src/Controller/**AbstractPageController.php** *Show code* ▼

#2 The *method redirect()* contains an exit expression. *(help)*   Top (1)

File: ~~~~~~~~~~/masteringtestdrivenphp/chapter10/librarian/src/Controller/**AbstractPageController.php** *Show code* ▼

#3 edit accesses the super-global variable *$_GET*. *(help)*   Top (1)

File: ~~~~~~~~~~/masteringtestdrivenphp/chapter10/librarian/src/Controller/**Author.php** *Show code* ▼

#4 save accesses the super-global variable *$_POST*. *(help)*   Top (1)

File: ~~~~~~~~~~/masteringtestdrivenphp/chapter10/librarian/src/Controller/**Author.php** *Show code* ▼

#5 save accesses the super-global variable *$_POST*. *(help)*   Top (1)

File: ~~~~~~~~~~/masteringtestdrivenphp/chapter10/librarian/src/Controller/**Author.php** *Show code* ▼

#6 save accesses the super-global variable *$_POST*. *(help)*   Top (1)

File: ~~~~~~~~~~/masteringtestdrivenphp/chapter10/librarian/src/Controller/**Author.php** *Show code* ▼

#7 save accesses the super-global variable *$_POST*. *(help)*   Top (1)

File: ~~~~~~~~~~/masteringtestdrivenphp/chapter10/librarian/src/Controller/**Author.php** *Show code* ▼

#8 Avoid using static access to class '\Librarian\Util\Config' in *method 'insert'*. *(help)*   Top (1)

File: ~~~~~~~~~~/masteringtestdrivenphp/chapter10/librarian/src/Controller/**Author.php** *Show code* ▼

Figure 10.5: *PHPMD report details*

For each item highlighted in the details list, there is a source file name followed by a **Show code** link. When you click on it, you see the code snippet that causes the detected problem, with the line numbers. For example, the first message in the list, as shown in *Figure 10.5*:

Avoid unused local variables such as '$controller'.

If you do not understand exactly what the problem is, you can click the **help** link to the right of the message, and a PHPMD documentation page will open with an explanation of the message.

Continuing with the example, the code snippet displayed highlights the following line as the cause of the error:

$controller= lcfirst(end($tokens));

This line is in the **AbstractPageController->run** method. If you reread the error message and look at the highlighted line, you will see that the **$controller** variable is not actually used. In other words, it appears not to be used.

You should understand that PHPMD analyzes each block of code statically. In this case, PHPMD cannot verify that the **layout.phtml** file will use the **$controller** variable, because when the method is executed, the **layout.phtml** file will be imported and its code will be part of the **AbstractPageController->run** method. If we removed the **$controller** variable based only on the PHPMD message, we would be causing an error in the application.

In this case, where a file imported by a method uses a variable created by the method, to prevent **phpmd** from reporting a false error, it is preferable to use an attribute instead of a variable. Let us create the private attribute **$controller** in the **AbstractPageController** class as follows:

```
private string $controller;
```

Next, we will replace the following line in the **run** method:

```
$controller = lcfirst(end($tokens));
```

By this other line, as follows:

```
$this->controller = lcfirst(end($tokens));
```

Finally, we will change the following line in the **layout.phml** file:

```
require __DIR__ . '/' . $controller . '/' . $action . '.phtml';
```

To this one, as follows:

```
require __DIR__ . '/' . $this->controller . '/' . $action . '.phtml';
```

After this change, if you run **phpmd** again, the report will no longer display the message about not using the **$controller** variable.

phpmd notes are not necessarily bugs. They are observations of details that can make it difficult to maintain a system and, eventually, contribute to the emergence of bugs.

To effectively detect bugs, you can use the **phpstan** tool. This tool can be installed by Composer as follows:

```
$ composer require --dev phpstan/phpstan
```

To search for bugs in the librarian project classes, we run the following command:

```
$ vendor/bin/phpstan analyse src/
```

If there are bugs, they will be listed, with a straightforward message indicating the source of the bug.

There is another tool that provides a global view of the complexity of our application, **pdepend**.

In this book we use **pdepend** *version 2.16.2*. It can be downloaded from the following address:

https://github.com/pdepend/pdepend/releases/download/2.16.2/pdepend.phar

One of the products generated by **pdepend** is a graph of dependencies between packages (namespaces, for PHP). To generate this graph, we use the following command:

```
$ php pdepend.phar --jdepend-chart=librarian.depend.svg src/
```

The file is generated in **Scalable Vector Graphics** (**SVG**) format with a transparent background. You can open the file in a web browser to view it with a white background without having to edit the image.

Figure 10.6 shows the contents of the **librarian.depend.svg** file. It is a graph that relates **Abstractness** (X axis) to **Instability** (Y axis).

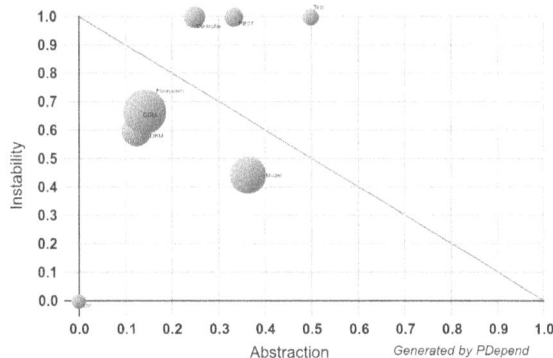

Figure 10.6: The librarian inters package dependencies

- **Abstractness** is the ratio between abstract classes and the total of all classes. If the abstractness is zero, all classes in this package (namespace) are non-abstract. In other hand, if abstractness is one, the package only consists of abstract classes and interfaces. The more abstract a package has, the more generic it is and therefore more reusable.

- **Instability** is the ratio between efferent coupling and the total package coupling. If the instability is zero, there is a maximally stable package that depends upon nothing. In other hand, if instability is one, there is a total instable package that has no incoming dependencies but depends upon other packages. The more dependencies a package has, the more unstable it is, because dependencies are points of failure.

We see in *Figure 10.6*, for example, that the **Controller** package has maximum instability. This package depends on the **Model** and **Util** packages. The **Model** package, in turn, does not depend on **Controller**, but only on **Util** and, thus, has an intermediate instability. The **Util** package, in turn, does not depend on any other package and, therefore, has zero instability.

The descending diagonal that divides the graph into two parts is a reference to what would be the best compromise between instability and abstraction or rather, a system that offers the best combination of decoupling and reuse.

Other of the products generated by **pdepend** is a pyramid that shows a visual summary of the analyzed project source code. To generate this graph, we use the following command:

```
$ php pdepend.phar --overview-pyramid=librarian.pyramid.svg src/
```

The file is generated in SVG format with a transparent background, as the previous file. You can also open the file in a web browser to view it.

Figure 10.7 shows the contents of the **librarian.pyramid.svg** file. It is a graph with several metrics.

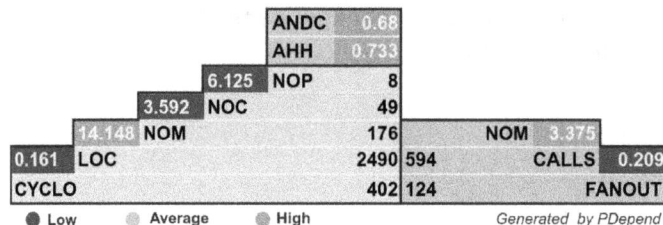

Figure 10.7: Visual summary of the analyzed source code of the librarian project

The metrics displayed in this pyramid are as follows:

- **Average Number of Derived Classes (ANDC)**: The average of direct subclasses of a class.

- **Average Hierarchy Height (AHH)**: The average of the maximum length from a root class to its deepest subclass.

- **FANOUT**: Number of fanouts referenced classes.

- **Number of Packages (NOP)**: Total packages declared.

- **Number of Classes (NOC)**: Total classes declared.

- **Number of Methods (NOM)**: Total methods declared.

- **Lines of Code (LOC)**: Total instructions.

- **Cyclomatic Complexity Number (CYCLO)**: A metric that counts the available decision paths in a software fragment to determine its complexity.

The values that appear on the rungs of the pyramid are the ratios of the value of the metric in the row beneath to the value of the metric in the current row. For example, in the LOC row, we see a value of 0.161. This is the ratio of the CYCLO metric, 402, to the LOC metric, 2490. These ratios fall into one of three categories: **Low**, **Average**, and **High**. In the example, the ratio of LOC to NOM is high, which means that there are too few methods for the amount of code. This could be an indication that there are large methods that could be broken down into smaller methods.

The **pdepend** documentation contains a detailed explanation of the cyclomatic complexity calculation and the reference for this metric. The page is as follows:

https://pdepend.org/documentation/software-metrics/cyclomatic-complexity.html

While some metrics can be interpreted based on the current state of a system, the cyclomatic complexity number should be observed comparatively between different versions of the same system. This metric is used to determine whether a new version of a system is more or less complex than the previous one.

As you can see, with simple commands it is possible to generate several analyses of the source code of a PHP application, in addition to creating documentation about the classes and methods. However, we do not generate a visual representation of the application classes. This can be done with the combination of two tools: **php-class-diagram** and **PlantUML**. The first one generates a script so that the second one creates the image of a **Unified Modeling Language** (UML) class diagram.

You can install **php-class-diagram** using Composer. We will do this one directory above the **librarian** directory, to avoid dependency conflicts with the components used by the application. The installation command is as follows:

```
$ composer require smeghead/php-class-diagram
```

In the same directory above **librarian**, we will download the **PlantUM.jar** file. In this book, we will use version 1.2024.7, available at the following address:

https://github.com/plantuml/plantuml/releases/download/v1.2024.7/plantuml-1.2024.7.jar

Rename the file to **plantuml.jar**. Remember that you need to have Java installed to run JAR files.

Let us generate the UML class diagram of the **Controller** package, as an example. The first step is to generate the script with the following command:

```
$ vendor/bin/php-class-diagram librarian/src/Controller/ > librarian.
controller.plantuml
```

The second step is to use the generated script to create the diagram image, with the following command:

```
$ java -jar plantuml.jar librarian.controller.plantuml
```

This command will create a file named **class-diagram.png**, the contents of which is shown in *Figure 10.8*. With the combination of **php-class-diagram** and **PlantUML** you can have up-to-date class diagrams of your application with a couple of simple commands. You can generate diagrams of specific packages or of the entire application and thus quickly visualize the dependencies between classes and interfaces.

You can use Markdown files to group the class diagrams generated by **PlantUML**. In a CI process, with each change in the source code, you can update the diagrams and always have a real view of the application structure.

MVC architectural pattern is a high-level pattern. An application that implements it may have a complex class structure. That is why it is important to have a set of tools that help developers control this complexity, preventing bugs from reaching the production environment and helping developers reduce the effort of implementing changes.

Refer to the following figure:

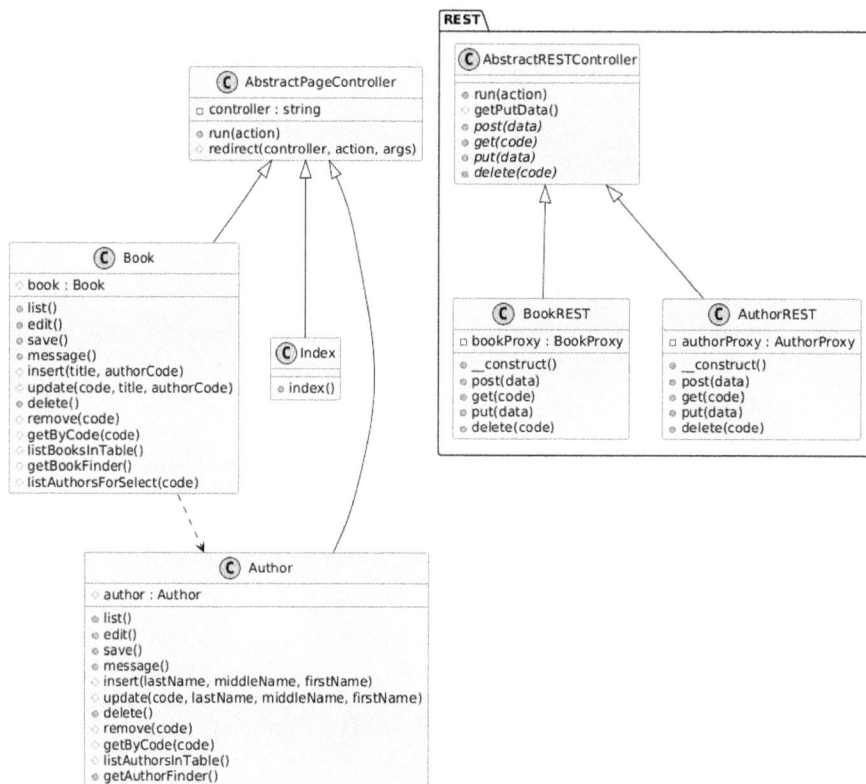

Figure 10.8: Class diagram for the Controller namespace

Conclusion

In this chapter, we covered the refactoring of the previous version of the book registration application and the creation of a new layer for decoupling the model layer from the storage paradigm. We covered what design patterns are and how to use them. We covered how to create a REST API for our application and how to generate a code coverage report. We also covered the handling of the web pages, introducing an architecture pattern to separate the layout from the content. Finally, we covered the refactoring of the application with the MVC pattern, which actually occurred throughout the previous chapters.

In the next chapter, we are going to learn about secure development.

Points to remember

- Design patterns are documented solutions to recurring problems in OOP.

- It is very simple to implement a REST API with PHP.

- It is possible to know how much code is covered with tests using PHPUnit.

- It is possible to know the complexity of a PHP project with PDepend.

- It is possible to generate UML Class diagrams from PHP code using PlantUML and php-class-diagram.

Exercises

1. Create new tests until the code coverage report shows coverage above 90%.

2. Read the PHPMD Report messages and try to change the application code until all the messages disappear.

Join our book's Discord space

Join the book's Discord Workspace for Latest updates, Offers, Tech happenings around the world, New Release and Sessions with the Authors:

https://discord.bpbonline.com

CHAPTER 11
Refactoring the Application with Secure Development

Introduction

This chapter of the book will cover how to refactor PHP application by applying techniques to let it secure to reduce an attacker's chance of success. We will start talking about the relationship between secure development and secure code. We will learn about information resources about web application vulnerabilities and PHP vulnerabilities. After understanding these fundamentals, we will review the application's inputs, introducing filters and data validators. Next, we will review the data outputs, analyzing whether the application does not expose data that it should not. Finally, we will talk about the automated code analysis as a tool to help discover vulnerabilities.

Structure

The chapter covers the following topics:

- Secure development producing secure code
- Reviewing inputs
- Reviewing outputs
- Vulnerability scanning

Objectives

By the end of this chapter, you will be able to understand the fundamentals of secure code development as applied to PHP. You will be able to create filters and validators to handle data input to your application. You will also be able to prevent sensitive data from being exposed at the application view layer. Also, you will be able to perform vulnerability scanning in an automated way.

Secure development producing secure code

In their book *Writing Secure Code*, *Michael Howard* and *David LeBlanc* present four principles that software developers should observe when building applications, as follows:

- The defender must defend all points; the attacker can choose the weakest point.

- The defender can defend only against known attacks; the attacker can probe for unknown vulnerabilities.

- The defender must be constantly vigilant; the attacker can strike at will.

- The defender must play by the rules; the attacker can play dirty.

You should not program with the belief that the application will be secure because there is a firewall, an **intrusion detection system** (**IDS**), and an encrypted connection. You should program with the belief that everything will fail and that the application must take care of its own security.

Sometimes, security flaws can be costly; prevention is cheaper than remediation. That is why it is important to focus on development of producing secure code. If you develop with test-driven approaches, you are at an advantage because you already have a framework in place to help you detect security flaws. In secure development, we do not just test the application's functionality but also its security aspects.

Sometimes, in our eagerness to make something work, we implement something that meets the functional requirement but leaves room for inappropriate actions. We may implement code that does what was defined in the requirement and more. A part of developing secure code is ensuring that each class or method does only what it is supposed to do and nothing more.

Let us look at an example of code in the Librarian application that can do more than it should. You may recall that in the *Chapter 10, Abstracting the Application Storage*, we implemented a change method in the **Config** class. We did it because we needed to change the configuration file for user interface testing. The tests worked but the **Config::change** method left a hole in the code for failure if not used correctly.

The method searches for a string in the configuration file and replaces it with another string. We know that the string **txt** exists only once and that it will be the only one found because we are controlling everything on our development machine but, if a change in the configuration file causes more than one **txt** string to exist, the test will probably fail.

We will present a real case report on this type of approach in which the search for a string of characters assumes that its occurrence in the file is unique. Around 2004, one of the biggest Brazilian banks generated a report to identify the largest exporters and importers in the country that took out loans from that bank. To generate this report, the foreign trade finance team needed to collect data from several external systems. One of the systems consulted was the Brazilian central bank system, which reported the currency rates valid for bank transactions. It was a system with a text-mode interface, accessed by a 3270-Terminal emulator. A program read the screen, converted it into a text file and extracted the value of the rate to be used in the report conversions. To locate the US dollar rate in the text file, the program needed to know from which position it should read. This position was determined by the screen code, which appeared before the rate. The process worked well until one day the program stopped because it could not read the quote value. When it tried to convert the string, it had read into a number, the result was zero. The team was desperate because the report was supposed to be generated and delivered that day. The employee who had created the extraction system was on vacation and they were about to call him when another employee, recently hired, noticed a detail on the bank's quote screen. Before the code on the screen, there was a date which was displayed without separators between day, month and year. That day, part of the date coincided with the code on the screen, and the program read the part of the screen that preceded the dollar quote, which was not a number, so the conversion resulted in zero.

If someone adds a setting before the **storage_format** key with the value **txt**, the test classes will change this key, the storage will not be changed, and the tests for the other storage formats will fail. The cause may or may not be immediately apparent. We cannot rely on luck or people's memory. We need to try to be as precise as possible as inaccuracy leaves room for failure.

A better approach to changing the configuration file is to change the format of the file. Currently, it is a file containing a PHP array. This is an easy format to read, as it does not require parsing but it is a bad format to write. The **print_r** function can convert an array into text that looks like the way we declare an array, but without the string delimiters. So, we cannot reconstruct the array declaration. JSON format is better because it is easy to read and write. Therefore, let us change the files **book.config.php** and **book.config.test.php** to **book.config.json** and **book.config.test.json**.

The contents of the **book.config.json** file, for example, will be as follows:

```json
{
    "author_plaintext_file": "authors.txt",
    "author_csv_file":"authors.csv",
    "author_json_file":"authors.json",
    "book_plaintext_file":"books.txt",
```

```
"book_csv_file": "books.csv",
"book_json_file": "books.json",
"storage_format": "txt",
"db": {
    "dsn": "mysql:dbname=librarian;host=localhost",
    "username": "root",
    "password": "",
    "database": "librarian",
    "host": "localhost"
}
}
```

In order for the application to be able to read this new configuration file format, we need to change the **Config::get** method so that it reads the file in JSON format and converts its contents to an array.

Note: The book.config.json file defines a JSON object and the application handles the configuration as an array. It is important to remember that the type conversion from object to array only works at the level.

It means that the object attributes are converted to array elements but if the values of the elements are also objects, they remain as objects. Therefore, it is necessary to convert the values as well. Once we are aware of these issues, we should change the **Config::get** method to the following:

```
public static function get(string $key): mixed
{
    if (isset(self::$overridedValues[$key])){
        return self::$overridedValues[$key];
    }
    if (self::$config == null){
        $json = file_get_contents(__DIR__ . '/../../' .
self::getConfigFileName());
        $config = (array) json_decode($json);
        self::$config = $config;
    }
    $value = self::$config[$key];
    return is_object($value) ? (array) $value : $value;
}
```

However, the **Config::get** method is no longer useful for providing full path to text files.

Note: We changed the configuration keys that ended with `filepath` to file because they now only contain the filenames. In PHP format, we could use file constants to determine the path to text files, but we cannot do that in JSON format.

To get the full path to the files we will need to implement a **new** method, **Config::getPathFile**, which will be as follows:

```php
public static function getPathFile(string $key): mixed
{
    $file = self::get($key);
    return __DIR__ . '/../../' . $file;
}
```

We need to replace occurrences of **Config::get** with **Config::getPathFile** in all methods where the path to files needs to be read. These files are as follows:

- **src/Model/Entity**
- **src/Model/Filesystem/AuthorPlainText**
- **src/Model/Filesystem/AuthorCSV**
- **src/Model/Filesystem/AuthorJSON**
- **src/Model/Filesystem/BookPlainText**
- **src/Model/Filesystem/BookCSV**
- **src/Model/Filesystem/BookJSON**
- **src/Model/Filesystem/AuthorPlainTextFinder**
- **src/Model/Filesystem/AuthorCSVFinder**
- **src/Model/Filesystem/AuthorJSONFinder**
- **src/Model/Filesystem/BookPlainTextFinder**
- **src/Model/Filesystem/BookCSVFinder**
- **src/Model/Filesystem/BookJSONFinder**
- **tests/ConfigTest**

Now, let us change the **Config::change** method, which has a loophole.

Let us change it so that it is as follows:

```php
public static function change($key, $value)
{
    $configFileName = self::getConfigFileName();
    $json = file_get_contents(__DIR__ . '/../../' . $configFileName);
    $config = (array) json_decode($json);
    $config[$key] = $value;
    $object = (object) $config;
    $json = json_encode($object);
    file_put_contents($configFileName, $json);
}
```

> **Note: The method now looks not for the value to replace, but for the key. This makes it more accurate but requires us to refactor the use of this method in all test classes that call it.**

Do not forget to change the name of the configuration files in the **Config::getConfigFileName** method, so that it is as follows:

```php
private static function getConfigFileName(): string
{
    $configFileName = 'book.config.json';
    if ((defined('LIBRARIAN_TEST_ENVIRONMENT') && LIBRARIAN_TEST_
ENVIRONMENT) ||
        getenv('LIBRARIAN_TEST_ENVIRONMENT')){
            $configFileName = 'book.config.test.json';
    }
    return $configFileName;
}
```

With these changes, tests will continue to run successfully and you will no longer see a warning, as follows:

This test executed code that is not listed as code to be covered or used:

- /masteringtestdrivenphp/chapter11/librarian/book.config.test.php:10

This message was caused because the test configuration file, imported during test execution, was mistaken for a test.

The Brazilian bank study case and the code-switching exercise show how we can easily create loopholes for failures in our applications. The configuration file case may not exactly seem like a security flaw but rather a system failure that makes it unavailable without necessarily allowing an attacker to access the system. However, information security is a concept that defines some basic properties, such as confidentiality, integrity, availability, authenticity, and legality. If a system stops working, the information becomes unavailable to those who need access to it.

Reviewing inputs

In his book, *Exploiting Software*, *Greg Hoglund* and *Gary McGraw* state that one very common assumption made by developers and architects is that the users of their software will never be hostile. They also claim that this belief is terribly wrong. You should not trust the user, as they may eventually act maliciously.

Let us see an example of how a data entry that trusts the user can allow unwanted actions. We will start the Librarian application and access the author registry.

Let us register an author by filling in the fields with the following content:

- **First name: \José**
- **Middle name: \<i>do\</i>**
- **Last name: \<h1>Telhado\</h1>**

Including this record will result in the listing page, as shown in *Figure 11.1*:

Figure 11.1: Registration with injected HTML

Note: The author's listing allows the user to enter HTML tags into the fields that make up the author's name, changing the way it is displayed in the listing.

This example shows that the user can inject tags that are interpreted by the browser. Instead of using HTML tags, the user places a block of JavaScript code. For example, in a book title, the user might type the following script:

```
<script>for(var i=0;i<10;i++){window.alert('hi');}</script>
```

This script will open 10 alert windows in sequence but an unreachable condition can cause it to open infinitely. This will not actually crash the system because the browser will ask if you want to block the window, but it shows how it is possible to inject commands into a register using JavaScript.

Michael Howard and *David LeBlanc* have two rules about data entry into software, as follows:

- All input is evil until proven otherwise.
- Data must be validated as it crosses the boundary between untrusted and trusted environments.

No data can be persisted by the system, if it contains unwanted content which includes malicious content. The first step of the input data treatment is to filter the data that enters our application.

Creating filter

Let us create a test to verify a filtering of data from author names that removes tags. The test class will be **FilterTest** and the test method will be **testAuthorNamesWithTags**, as follows:

```php
/**
 * @covers TagFilter
 */
#[CoversClass(TagFilter::class)]
class FilterTest extends TestCase
{
    public function testAuthorNamesWithTags()
    {
        $filter = new TagFilter();
        $firstName = '<b>José</b>';
        $middleName = '<i>do</i>';
        $lastName = '<h1>Telhado</h1>';
        list($firstName, $middleName, $lastName) =
[$filter($firstName),$filter($middleName),$filter($lastName)];
        $this->assertEquals('José',$firstName);
        $this->assertEquals('do',$middleName);
        $this->assertEquals('Telhado',$lastName);
    }
}
```

The **list** function allows us to assign values from an array to a list of variables, avoiding having to create an instruction for each assignment. As you can see, we are reproducing the tag injection as discussed at the beginning of this section and checking if a filter object eliminates those tags. When running this class, you will get the following error:

Error: Class "TagFilter" not found

Let us create the **TagFilter** class in the **Librarian\Filter** namespace, as follows:

```php
<?php
namespace Librarian\Filter;
class TagFilter
{
    public function __invoke($value)
    {
        return $this->filter($value);
    }

    public function filter(mixed $value): mixed
    {
        return strip_tags($value);
    }
}
```

Note: The `TagFilter` class implements the __invoke magic method to allow the `filter` method to be invoked when the `TagFilter` instance is used as a function. After creating the class, the test passes successfully.

Let us add a test to the **TagTest** class to test the removal of tags from the book title. This test will as follows:

```
public function testBookTitleWithTags()
{
    $filter = new TagFilter();
    $title = "<script>for(var i=0;i<10;i++){window.alert('hi');}</
script>";
    $title = $filter($title);
    $this->assertEquals('for(var i=0;i',$title);
}
```

As you can see from the assertion, the filter will remove everything after a greater than sign, so even the instruction between the **<script>** and **</script>** tags will not be preserved in its entirety.

Note: The function `strip_tags` does not normalize Unicode input. For improving input filtering efficiency, you can use `HTMLPurifier` component, which prevents malformed encoding exploits and XSS bypass techniques. `HTMLPurifier` can be installed with Composer.

Now that we have tested the **filter**, let us incorporate it into the application. The **filter** must be used before the data is persisted. Currently, the objects that forward the data for persistence are the proxy classes. The **AuthorProxy->save** method, for example, is responsible for including author data. We could use the **filter** in this method, before it instantiates the specific storage class.

The **AuthorProxy** class, as the name suggests, is an intermediary. The responsibility for the data should lie with the model class, which in this case is the **Author** class.

So, let us incorporate the **filter** into this class. We will change the **FilterTest->testAuthorNamesWithTags** method to the following implementation:

```
public function testAuthorNamesWithTags()
{
    $firstName = '<b>José</b>';
    $middleName = '<i>do</i>';
    $lastName = '<h1>Telhado</h1>';

    $author = new Author(0,$firstName,$middleName,$lastName);
    $this->assertEquals('José',$author->firstName);
```

```
        $this->assertEquals('do',$author->middleName);
        $this->assertEquals('Telhado',$author->lastName);
    }
```

The test will fail because the **Author** class does not filter its attributes. We need to modify the constructor of this class so that it applies the **TagFilter** filter to the name attributes. The **__construct** method will be as follows:

```
    public function __construct(int $code = 0, string $firstName = '',
string $middleName = '', string $lastName = '')
    {
        $filter = new TagFilter();
        $this->code = $code;
        $this->firstName = $filter($firstName);
        $this->middleName = $filter($middleName);
        $this->lastName = $filter($lastName);
    }
```

With this, the test passes again. Now that the test assures us that the **filter** works incorporated into the model, let us modify the recording methods so that they use the model. The **save** method will be as follows:

```
    public function save($lastName, $middleName, $firstName): bool
    {
        $author = new Author(0,$firstName,$middleName,$lastName);
        try {
            $saved = ($this->getDataGateway())->save($author);
        } catch (\Throwable $th) {
            $saved = false;
        }


        return $saved;
    }
```

This will require us to change all classes that can be instantiated by the **getDataGateway** method to receive an instance of **Author**. The **save** method will be as follows:

```
    public function save(Author $author): bool
    {
        $filepath = Config::getPathFile('author_plaintext_file');
        $handle = fopen($filepath,'a+');
        fseek($handle, -self::ROW_LENGTH, SEEK_END);
        $row = fread($handle, self::ROW_LENGTH);
```

```
        $code = (int) substr($row, 0, self::CODE_LENGTH);
        $code++;
        $row = $this->formatField($code, self::CODE_LENGTH) . $this-
>formatField($author->lastName, self::NAME_LENGTH) .
        $this->formatField($author->middleName, self::NAME_LENGTH) . $this-
>formatField($author->firstName, self::NAME_LENGTH) . "\n";
        fwrite($handle,$row);
        fclose($handle);
        $handle = fopen($filepath,'r');
        $found = false;
        fseek($handle, -self::ROW_LENGTH, SEEK_END);
        $currentRow = fread($handle, self::ROW_LENGTH);
        $found = ($currentRow == $row);
        fclose($handle);
        return $found;
    }
```

Notice that we changed the method argument and replaced the local variables with the **Author** instance attributes. With this approach, we then change the **AuthorCSV->save** method, as follows:

```
    public function save(Author $author): bool
    {
        $filepath = Config::getPathFile('author_csv_file');
        $handle = fopen($filepath,'a+');
        $code = 0;
        while (!feof($handle)){
            $row = fgetcsv($handle, null, ';');
            $code = $row[0] ?? $code;
        }
        $code++;
        $fields = [
            $this->formatField($code, 4),
            $this->formatField($author->lastName, 20),
            $this->formatField($author->middleName, 20),
            $this->formatField($author->firstName, 20)
        ];
        fputcsv($handle, $fields, ';');
        fclose($handle);
        $handle = fopen($filepath,'r');
```

```
        $found = false;
        $currentCode = 0;
        while (!feof($handle)) {
            $currentRow = fgetcsv($handle, null, ';');
            $currentCode = $currentRow[0] ?? $currentCode;
        }
        $found = ((int) $currentCode == $code);
        fclose($handle);
        return $found;
    }
```

The **AuthorJSON->save** method, in turn, will be as follows:

```
    public function save(Author $author): bool
    {
        $filepath = Config::getPathFile('author_json_file');
        $handle = fopen($filepath,'a');
        fclose($handle);
        $json = json_decode(file_get_contents($filepath));
        if ($json == NULL){
            $json = [];
        }
        $code = 0;
        foreach ($json as $row) {
            $code = $row->code;
        }
        $code++;
        $dict = [
            'code' => $code,
            'last_name'  => $author->lastName,
            'middle_name' => $author->middleName,
            'first_name' =>  $author->firstName
        ];
        $json[] = $dict;
        $text = json_encode($json);
        file_put_contents($filepath, $text);
        $json = json_decode(file_get_contents($filepath));
        $found = false;
        $currentCode = 0;
```

```
        foreach ($json as $row) {
            $currentCode = $row->code;
        }
        $found = ($currentCode == $code);
        return $found;
    }
```

The **AuthorTableGateway->save** method, in turn, will be as follows:

```
    public function save(Author $author): bool
    {
        $sql = 'INSERT INTO authors(first_name,middle_name,last_name) values
(:firstname,:middlename,:lastname)';
        $statement = $this->pdo->prepare($sql);
        $statement->bindParam(':firstname', $author->firstName);
        $statement->bindParam(':middlename', $author->middleName);
        $statement->bindParam(':lastname', $author->lastName);
        $statement->execute();
        return $statement->rowCount() == 1;
    }
```

Note: For parameters that are not strings, you can use the method bindValue, which prevents type juggling attacks where attackers try to bypass numeric filters. If we are handling the author ID, for example, we could write something like: $statement->bindValue(':author_id', (int) $authorId, PDO::PARAM_INT);

Finally, the **AuthorCollection->save** method, will be as follows:

```
    public function save(Author $author)
    {
        $insertOneResult = $this->database->authors->insertOne([
            'code' => $this->database->authors->countDocuments() + 1,
            'last_name' => $author->lastName,
            'middle_name' => $author->middleName,
            'first_name' => $author->firstName
        ]);
        return $insertOneResult->getInsertedCount() == 1;
    }
```

Note: The method countDocuments() can be inefficient to generate author codes in a system with many simultaneous users. For preventing race conditions when multiple users create records simultaneously, you can replace countDocuments() with a MongoDB ObjectId, like this: new \MongoDB\BSON\ObjectId().

After modifying the **save** method in the classes that handle storage and their invocations, as in the controllers, for instance, we need to change all the test classes where this method is invoked. After this task, the tests will run successfully again but converting or removing content from the input data is not enough. We need to know if, after this operation, the data is valid.

Creating validator

When gathering application requirements, we discover the business rules of the system to be implemented. From the business rules, we define data validation rules. The business owner knows what type of data they want to store and can therefore define what values are acceptable.

Let us assume that the business owner of our application has established the following rule for author names:

Each name must be at least two characters long with a maximum of 20 characters.

Let us create a test class called **ValidationTest**. In this class, we will implement the **testAuthorNames** method to test the name validation rule. The method will be as follows:

```
public function testAuthorNames()
{
    $firstName = 'a';
    $middleName = 'bad';
    $lastName = 'author';

    $author = new Author(0,$firstName,$middleName,$lastName);
    $this->assertFalse($author->isValid());

    $firstName = 'one';
    $middleName = 'author';
    $lastName = 'with more words than this field can support';

    $author = new Author(0,$firstName,$middleName,$lastName);
    $this->assertFalse($author->isValid());

    $firstName = 'this';
    $middleName = 'is';
    $lastName = 'valid';

    $author = new Author(0,$firstName,$middleName,$lastName);
```

```php
        $this->assertTrue($author->isValid());
    }
```

The test will fail because the **Author** class does not have the **isValid** method. Let us implement it as follows:

```php
    public function isValid(): bool
    {
        $validated = new NameValidator();
        return $validated($this->firstName) && $validated($this->middleName)
&& $validated($this->lastName);
    }
```

Validation methods always return Boolean types because the data is either valid or not.

The test will continue to fail because the **NameValidator** class does not exist. Let us implement it in the namespace **Librarian\Validator**, as follows:

```php
<?php
namespace Librarian\Validator;
class NameValidator
{
    public function __invoke($value)
    {
        return $this->isValid($value);
    }

    public function isValid(mixed $value): bool
    {
        $length = strlen($value);
        return $length>=2 && $length<=20;
    }
}
```

Now, the **ValidationTest->testAuthorNames** method will pass. With this test ensuring that validation works, let us incorporate validation into the author recording process.

We will do this by creating a new test first. Let us implement the **ValidationTest->testSaveInvalidAuthor** method, as follows:

```php
    public function testSaveInvalidAuthor()
    {
        $authorProxy = new AuthorProxy();
```

```
        $this->assertFalse($authorProxy->save('o','this is','invalid'));
        Entity::clear('author');
    }
```

This test will fail because the **AuthorProxy->save** method does not validate the data. Let us change it as follows:

```
    public function save($lastName, $middleName, $firstName): bool
    {
        $author = new Author(0,$firstName,$middleName,$lastName);
        if (!$author->isValid()){
            return $false;
        }
        try {
            $saved = ($this->getDataGateway())->save($author);
        } catch (\Throwable $th) {
            $saved = false;
        }

        return $saved;
    }
```

Now, the **ValidationTest** class will run successfully again. No author with invalid data, according to the validation rules, will be included from now on but remember that authors can be edited, so you need to apply both validators and filters in the update operation.

Reviewing outputs

If you do not filter and validate the input data to your application, the output data can be used for an attack. For example, if an application receives email but does not process its content, it can expose the user to a **cross-site scripting** (**XSS**) attack. This name refers to the case in which a malicious user uses a vulnerable application to transport malicious code, usually written in JavaScript, to another user's browser. Since the same-origin policy is respected, the victim's browser understands that the received code is legitimate and, therefore, sensitive information, such as the user's session identifier, for example, can be accessed programmatically.

Since, you are filtering and validating the data submitted via forms to your application, it seems like there is no reason to have concern about the data output. In fact, you need to make sure that you are handling all of the input because your application may be receiving data from sources other than forms filled out manually by humans. For example, if your application consumes data from another application's API, you should not trust any data that you have not personally handled. If your application reads data from a database fed by other applications, it must sanitize that data before displaying it.

In the section, *Reviewing inputs*, we delegate the responsibility of filtering and validating author data to the author model class. The model is responsible for the data and the business rules associated with it, including rules that ensure data security. Since the model performs data sanitization, it is appropriate for it to be used to provide data to the view layer.

In fact, we are already using models to provide the data to the view layer since we have adopted the MVC architecture pattern. You can see that the author and book listings are generated from collections of objects of the model classes of these entities.

Note: It is strongly recommended that only the model sends data to the view layer, since it is responsible for the data and its filtering and validation.

In addition to the use of filters and validators mediated by models, we should observe a type of eventual output that we do not really want, that is, error messages from the programming language. These messages are of interest only to developers and support technicians. It is desirable that the error messages be verbose enough to allow good observability of the application, but users should not have access to this information, as it can reveal details about the architecture and infrastructure and thus provide input for a more elaborate attack attempt.

It is important that you verify that two directives in the PHP configuration file are set to Off in the production environment, as follows:

`display_errors` and `xdebug.force_display_errors` (if Xdebug is installed).

The best advice about output is to always expect the unexpected. If an operation that will inevitably generate output is likely to fail, then provide exception handling that ensures that the information needed for support is forwarded to log files and that the user receives an appropriate message that does not expose any data they do not need to know.

Vulnerability scanning

Implementing and using filters and validators is just one part of developing secure code. They can help defend against injection attacks, such as SQL injection but these are not the only types of attacks. We need to keep in mind *Howard* and *LeBlanc's* second principle, as follows:

The defender can defend only against known attacks; the attacker can probe for unknown vulnerabilities.

The attacker is like a predator who watches the prey patiently, waiting for the moment when it is most vulnerable to then attack. They can make multiple attack attempts and learn from them, making each attempt more elaborate and closer to success.

The attacker has time to think and try to deduce information about your application. They might think as: A system called **librarian** should have tables called **authors** and **books**.

I can try injecting a **DROP TABLE** command with either of those names and see if the system stops working.

You can try injecting a **DROP TABLE** into the fields of both records in your application to see if an attacker would be successful with this type of injection attack.

Just as the attacker continually studies to make his attacks more efficient, we must continually study to keep our applications as secure as possible.

One of the recommended sources for this is the **Open Web Application Security Project** (**OWASP**) website. OWASP provides a wealth of information about vulnerabilities in web applications and guidance on how to reduce the risk of successful attack attempts. One of the highlights of the OWASP website is the Top 10 page, which presents the ten most critical security risks for web applications. Each risk is described in detail, as well as how to avoid it. Examples of attacks, references about the risk, and lists of mapped vulnerabilities are also presented.

You can find the OWASP Top 10 in the following link:

https://owasp.org/Top10

OWASP project provides information on web application security in general. *Zend*, the company created by the duo who introduced **object-oriented programming** (**OOP**) to PHP, maintains a page listing the vulnerabilities of each PHP version: **https://www.zend. com/php-security-center**.

Implementing secure code is not easy. Typically, the mind is focused on making the code work, or more precisely, on implementing the functional requirements of the system. You are usually thinking about how the user will be able to perform the operations successfully and not about how someone will try to hack or break the application, that is why we need tools that help us locate vulnerabilities.

Using SonarQube to detect security issues

One tool that can help you locate vulnerabilities is SonarQube. SonarQube is a static code analysis software that can detect bugs and basic vulnerabilities in code and review security hotspots. Let us download the community version of SonarQube from the following link: **https://www.sonarsource.com/products/sonarqube/downloads**.

SonarQube has three components, that is, a scanner, a server and a database. You can use Microsoft SQL Server, Oracle, or PostgreSQL as the database manager. We will use PostgreSQL because it is free and open source.

> **Note: You can use SonarQube from a Docker container, which avoids manual database configuration.**

PostgreSQL can be obtained from **https://www.postgresql.org/download**. On Debian system distributions, like the one we are using in our virtual machine, you can install the PostgreSQL server and client with the following commands:

```
$ sudo apt install postgresql
$ sudo apt install postgresql-client
```

To use the PostgreSQL client on a Debian system, you must switch to the **postgres** user. To switch to the **postgres** user, you must switch to the root user.

The sequence for accessing the PostgreSQL client on Debian is therefore, as follows:

```
# sudo su
# su postgres
# psql
```

You must create a SonarQube user and an empty schema in the PostgreSQL. Grant the SonarQube user permissions to create, update, and delete objects for this schema. Let us do this in five steps:

1. Let us to create the SonarQube user. We will do this with the following command:

   postgres=# CREATE USER sonarqube;

2. Next, let us define a password for this user with the following command:

   postgres=# ALTER USER sonarqube WITH ENCRYPTED PASSWORD 'sonarqube';

3. Create a database whose owner is the user SonarQube, with the following command:

   postgres=# CREATE DATABASE sonarqube WITH OWNER = sonarqube;

4. In this book, we downloaded SonarQube 10.6. Let us move the downloaded file to the **/opt** directory and grant it read, write, and execute permissions with the following sequence of commands:

   ```
   $ sudo mv ~/Downloads/sonarqube-10.6.0.92116.zip /opt/
   $ cd /opt
   $ sudo unzip sonarqube-10.6.0.92116.zip
   $ sudo chmod -R a+wrx sonarqube-10.6.0.92116
   ```

5. Configure the SonarQube server connection to the database. To do this, we will edit the **sonar.properties** file in the **conf** directory of the SonarQube installation.

   Let us locate the following commented lines:

   ```
   #sonar.jdbc.username=
   #sonar.jdbc.password=
   ```

The character **#** means a comment in this kind of file. Let us preserve these lines and add the following under them:

```
sonar.jdbc.username=sonarqube
sonar.jdbc.password=sonarqube
```

Next, let us locate the following commented line:

```
#sonar.jdbc.url=jdbc:postgresql://localhost/sonarqube?currentSchema=my_
schema
```

Let us preserve this line and add the following under it:

```
sonar.jdbc.url=jdbc:postgresql://localhost/sonarqube?currentSchema=public
```

Note: We will use the default public schema, but if you want to use another schema, you need to make the user who created it the owner of that schema and configure the user to use that schema as the default path for creating tables.

You can check anytime if there are any errors related to the database configuration by reading the **web.log** file in the SonarQube **logs** directory.

To start the SonarQube server, we use a script inside the **bin** folder, as per the following example:

```
$ ./sonarqube-10.6.0.92116/bin/linux-x86-64/sonar.sh start
```

The SonarQube administration page is available at **http://localhost:9000**. If this page is unavailable, you will need to open the **nohup.log** file inside the **logs** folder of your SonarQube installation.

One possible problem is the version of the Java virtual machine installed. It may be lower than the version used to compile SonarQube. In this case, the message in the **log** file should be as follows:

```
java.lang.UnsupportedClassVersionError: org/sonar/application/App has been
compiled by a more recent version of the Java Runtime
```

You will then need to install a newer version of Java. For the version we downloaded in this book, we needed to use the following Debian Java package, with Java 17:

```
$ sudo apt install openjdk-17-jre
```

Since, we can have multiple versions of Java on a machine, we need to tell SonarQube which one it should use. We do this by setting the **SONAR_JAVA_PATH** environment variable. In the example in this book, we set it as follows:

```
$ export SONAR_JAVA_PATH=/usr/lib/jvm/java-1.17.0-openjdk-amd64/bin/java
```

It may be that even after configuring an updated Java for SonarQube, the server still does not start. When reading the **nohup.log** file, you may find error messages as follows:

```
ERROR: Elasticsearch did not exit normally
ERROR: Elasticsearch died while starting up, with exit code 78
```

In this case, if you open the **es.log** file inside the **logs** folder, you should see a message as follows:

```
bootstrap check failure [1] of [1]: max virtual memory areas vm.max_map_
count [65530] is too low, increase to at least [262144]
```

You can increase this virtual memory setting with the **sysctl** command, as follows:

sudo sysctl -w vm.max_map_count=524288

This will resolve the issue for the current terminal session. For the change to be persistent, you must change the value of the **vm.max_map_count** directive in the **/etc/sysctl.conf** file, adding the following line:

vm.max_map_count=524288

After fixing any issue, you should be able to access the SonarQube admin interface at **http://localhost:9000**. The page will be as shown *Figure 11.2*:

Figure 11.2: SonarQube login page

The username is admin and the initial password is admin. However, SonarQube does not allow that you continue to use the default password. After entering the password for the first time, you will be prompted to change it on the next page, as shown in *Figure 11.3*:

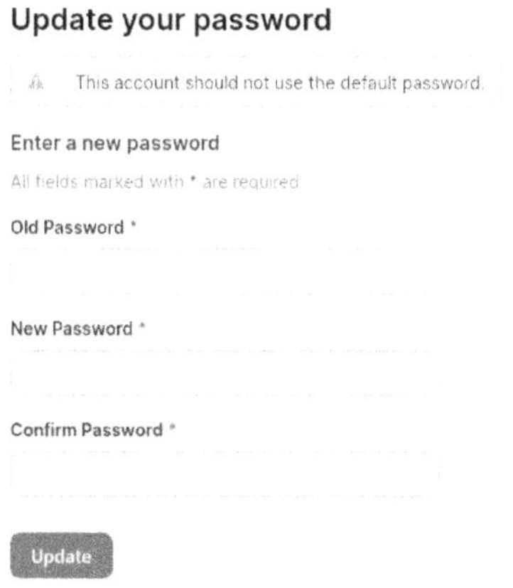

Figure 11.3: Password update page

After changing the password, you will be presented with the project creation page. SonarQube allows to import a project from several cloud repositories like Bitbucket and GitHub. As our project is local, let us create a local project by clicking the **Create a local project** button at the bottom right of the page, as shown in *Figure 11.4*:

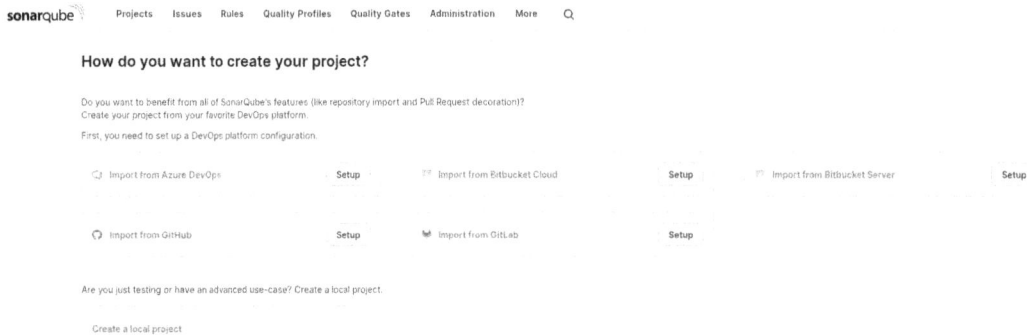

Figure 11.4: Options to create a project

Once you have chosen your project source, there are two steps to creating it. The first step in creating a SonarQube project is to define the **Project display name** and **Project key**, as shown in *Figure 11.5*. At this point we are not pointing to the source code but just creating an identifier. If the project was imported from a remote repository, you must define which branch is the main branch. In the local project, this is not necessary.

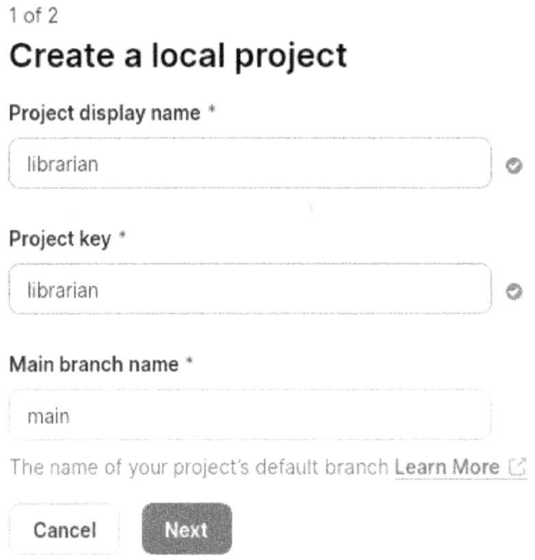

Figure 11.5: Defining the name and key for the project

The second step is to define which part of your code will be considered new code. We will choose the **Use the global setting**, as shown in *Figure 11.6*. In this option, any code that has changed since the previous version is considered new code:

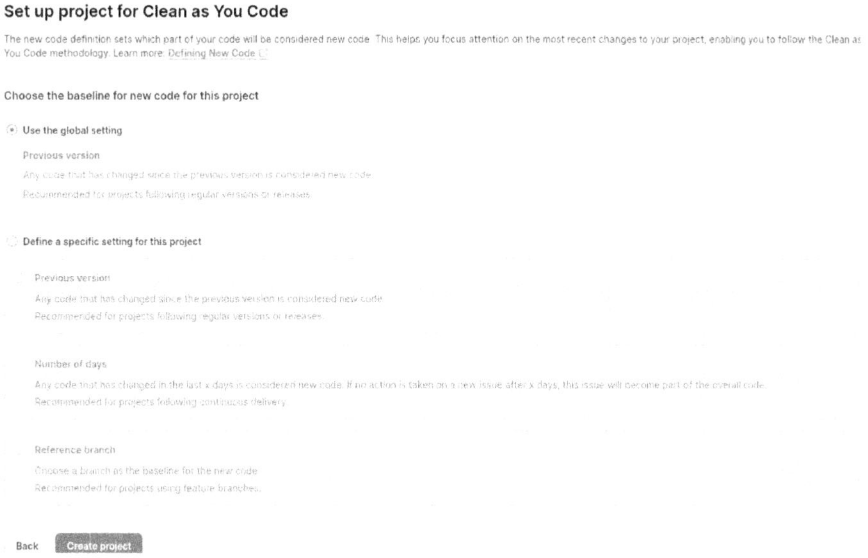

Set up project for Clean as You Code

The new code definition sets which part of your code will be considered new code. This helps you focus attention on the most recent changes to your project, enabling you to follow the Clean as You Code methodology. Learn more: Defining New Code

Choose the baseline for new code for this project

◉ Use the global setting

Previous version

Any code that has changed since the previous version is considered new code.
Recommended for projects following regular versions or releases.

◯ Define a specific setting for this project

Previous version

Any code that has changed since the previous version is considered new code.
Recommended for projects following regular versions or releases.

Number of days

Any code that has changed in the last x days is considered new code. If no action is taken on a new issue after x days, this issue will become part of the overall code.
Recommended for projects following continuous delivery.

Reference branch

Choose a branch as the baseline for the new code.
Recommended for projects using feature branches.

Back **Create project**

Figure 11.6: *Choosing the baseline for new code*

After clicking the **Create project** button, you will see a page as shown in *Figure 11.7*. At this page, you must click on **Locally** section, at the bottom left of the page:

Analysis Method

Use this page to manage and set-up the way your analyses are performed.

How do you want to analyze your repository?

◴ With Jenkins   ◯ With GitHub Actions   ▨ With Bitbucket Pipelines

◔ With GitLab CI   ◁ With Azure Pipelines   Other CI

SonarQube integrates with your workflow no matter which CI tool you're using.

Locally

Use this for testing an unversioned source code. Other modes are recommended to help you set up your CI checks in time.

Figure 11.7: *SonarQube Analysis methods*

The first step in configuring local analysis is generating a token as shown in *Figure 11.8*:

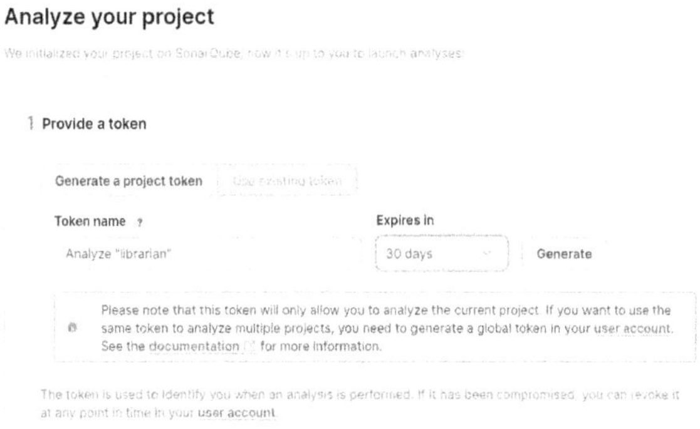

Analyze your project

We initialized your project on SonarQube; now it's up to you to launch analyses.

1 **Provide a token**

Generate a project token   Use existing token

Token name ?   Expires in

Analyze "librarian"   30 days ⌄   Generate

ℹ Please note that this token will only allow you to analyze the current project. If you want to use the same token to analyze multiple projects, you need to generate a global token in your user account. See the documentation for more information.

The token is used to identify you when an analysis is performed. If it has been compromised, you can revoke it at any point in time in your user account.

Figure 11.8: *Generating project token*

After clicking the **Generate a project token** button, the generated token is displayed. Keep this token as you will need it to analyze the code. You will see that this section will have a new **Continue** button. Click this button and a new section will open, as shown in *Figure 11.9*:

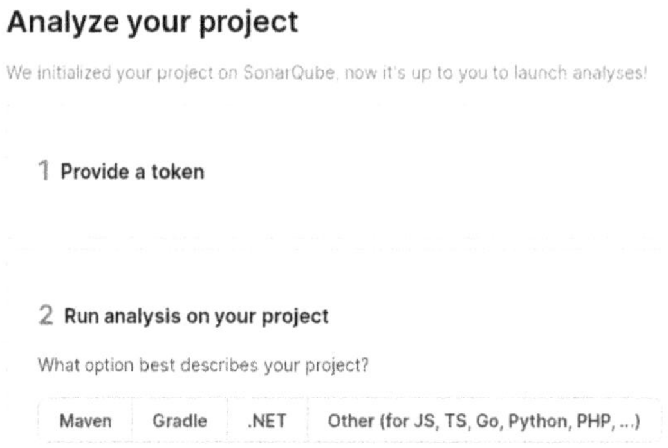

Analyze your project

We initialized your project on SonarQube, now it's up to you to launch analyses!

1 **Provide a token**

2 **Run analysis on your project**

What option best describes your project?

| Maven | Gradle | .NET | Other (for JS, TS, Go, Python, PHP, ...) |

Figure 11.9: Describing the project structure

Since our project is PHP, let us click on the **Other** button. SonarQube will present the full sonar-scanner code analyzer call for you to copy and run but the code analyzer is a separate component of the SonarQube server. You need to download it from the following address:**https://docs.sonarsource.com/sonarqube/latest/analyzing-source-code/ scanners/sonarscanner**.

In this book, we downloaded SonarScanner CLI 6.2.0. Let us move the downloaded file to the **/opt** directory and grant it read, write, and execute permissions with the following sequence of commands:

```
$ sudo mv ~/Downloads/sonar-scanner-cli-6.2.0.4584-linux-x64.zip /opt/
$ cd /opt
$ unzip sonar-scanner-cli-6.2.0.4584-linux-x64.zip
$ sudo chmod -R a+wrx sonar-scanner-cli-6.2.0.4584-linux-x64
```

The next step is to configure the SonarScanner connection to the SonarQube server. To do this, we will edit the **sonar-scanner.properties** file in the **conf** directory of the SonarScanner installation. Let us locate the following commented line:

```
#sonar.host.url=https://mycompany.com/sonarqube
```

Let us preserve this line and add the following:

```
sonar.host.url=http://localhost:9000
```

After saving the file, goto our project directory in the terminal and run the following command:

```
$ /opt/sonar-scanner-6.2.0.4584-linux-x64/bin/sonar-scanner    -Dsonar.
projectKey=librarian    -Dsonar.sources=.    -Dsonar.host.url=http://
localhost:9000    -Dsonar.token=[TOKEN]
```

Note: You do not need to use the complete path to sonar-scanner script if you add the SonarScanner installation directory to the operating system path.

When the scanner is finished running, the project page in SonarQube will change to a page like the one in *Figure 11.10*:

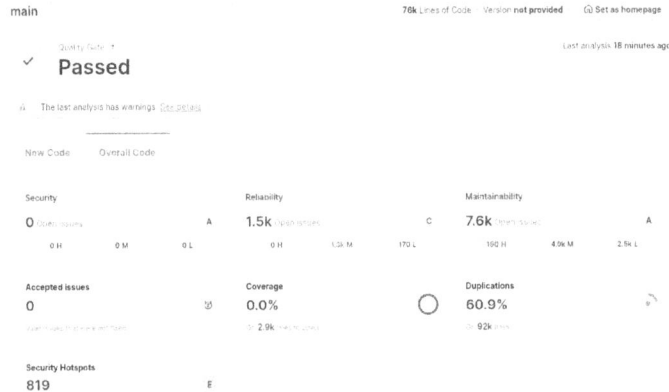

Figure 11.10: *SonarQube analysis report*

You can verify that there are no security issues, according to the first section of the page in the upper left corner. SonarQube's rating for the project in this regard is A (maximum score). This is the result of an architecture that makes invasions difficult, plus the adoption of some security techniques, such as filters and validators.

If there is a security problem, the procedure is to open the section and check which file and lines are responsible for the problem, locate them and make the correction according to SonarQube's guidance.

However, not everything is perfect in our project. SonarQube warns that there are hundreds of Security Hotspots. For understanding the difference between security issues and Security Hotspot issues, we need to understand what a Security Hotspot is. A Security Hotspot is a highlighted security-sensitive piece of code which may or not impact the overall application security. It is something that depends on the developer's review. In this case, when we open the Security Hotspots item, we see that the first problem listed point to files in the **analysis** directory, which were generated by **phpmd**. These files should not be analyzed because they are development artifacts. They will not be part of the application deployment.

So, we have to run the scanner excluding everything that is not part of the application that will be put into production. The exclusions directive allows us to exclude directories and subdirectories from the scan. Let us use it to re-run the **sonar-scanner** script as follows:

```
$ /opt/sonar-scanner-6.2.0.4584-linux-x64/bin/sonar-scanner
-Dsonar.projectKey=librarian    -Dsonar.sources=.    -Dsonar.
host.url=http://localhost:9000    -Dsonar.token=[TOKEN] -Dsonar.
exclusions=analysis/**,coverage/**,docs/**
```

After refreshing our project page (**http://localhost:9000/dashboard?id=librarian**), we see that there are no more hotspot security issues, as shown in *Figure 11.11*:

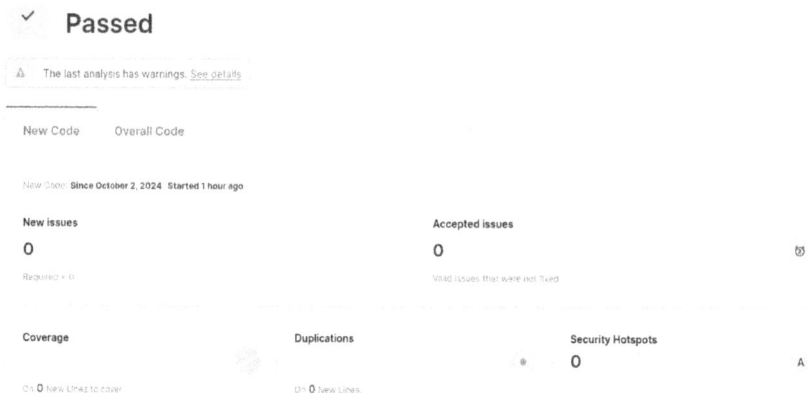

Figure 11.11: *SonarQube analysis report without Security Hotspots*

NOTE: **There are two tabs on the SonarQube overview page, that is, New Code and Overall Code. The New Code page is displayed by default and shows what has changed between the last scan and the current one.**

To know that, there really are no security issues, we need to open the **Overall Code** tab.

As we can see in *Figure 11.12*, the **Overall Code** tab confirms that there are no security issues. but the SonarQube does more than just perform security analysis. There is a **Coverage** section, which shows the test coverage of the application. It is zero, as if there were no tests, which we know is not true. What happens is that SonarQube is not aware of the test coverage unless we tell it.

First, we need to generate an XML file with the test coverage. We do this with the following command in the root project directory:

```
$ vendor/bin/phpunit --coverage-clover=coverage/coverage.xml
```

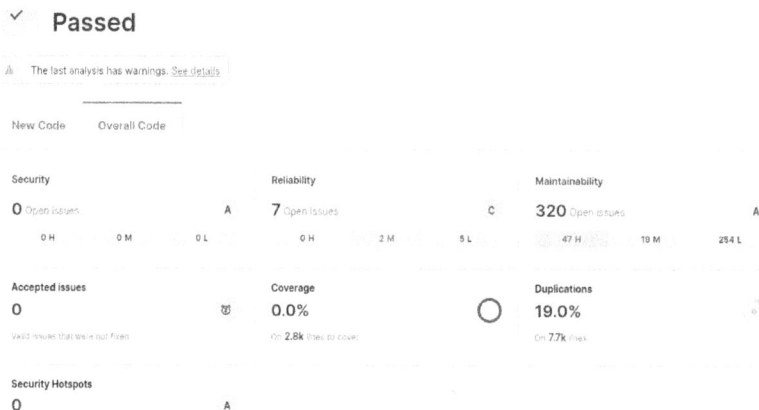

Figure 11.12: *SonarQube analysis report without Security Hotspots*

As you can see, the **coverage.xml** file will be saved in the **coverage** directory, the same as used to store test coverage in HTML format. Once this file is created, we can re-run the **sonar-scanner** script, adding the PHP test **coverage** directive, as follows:

```
$ /opt/sonar-scanner-6.2.0.4584-linux-x64/bin/sonar-scanner
-Dsonar.projectKey=librarian    -Dsonar.sources=.    -Dsonar.
host.url=http://localhost:9000    -Dsonar.token=[TOKEN] -Dsonar.
exclusions=analysis/**,coverage/**,docs/** -Dsonar.php.coverage.
reportPaths=coverage/coverage.xml
```

After refreshing the SonarQube page, we will see the code coverage percentage as shown in *Figure 11.13*:

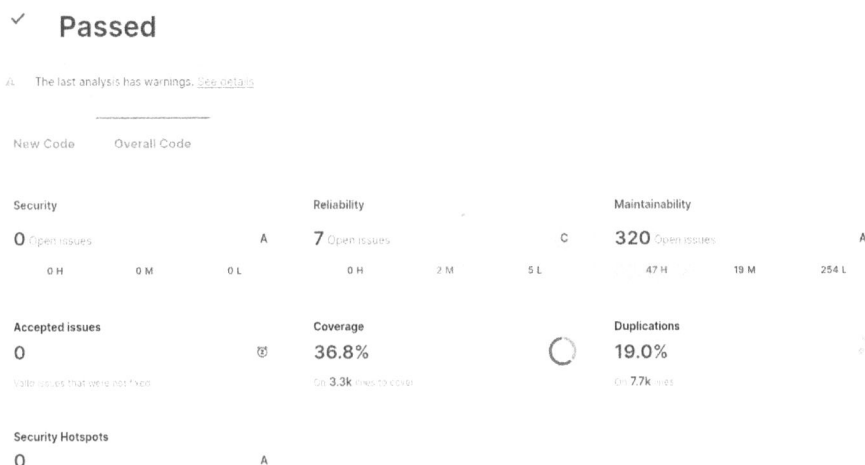

Figure 11.13: SonarQube analysis report with code coverage

Covering penetration testing

Scanning tools like SonarQube help detect vulnerability points, but we cannot limit application security verification to static code analysis. Some problems only manifest themselves when the code is being executed that is why it is recommended to create tests that simulate intrusion attempts.

Code injection attacks remain one of the top ten security risks for web applications, according to OWASP. Earlier, we mentioned one of the attacks included in this category, the SQL injection attack. This type of attack can be executed in very simple ways, such as filling a form field with SQL command. You may recall that we said earlier to always expect the unexpected. Having a student with SQL command in their name is something like that.

In the librarian system, it would not be possible to perform a similar attack on the **authors** table because the author's name is separated into three fields, each of which has 20 characters. The expression **DROP TABLE Students;**—has 25 characters but the **title** field of the **authors** table has 80 characters. Let us create a test to see if it would be possible to perform a SQL injection attack on the **books** table.

Create the **SQLInjectionTest** class in the **tests** directory and within this class we will implement the **testDropTableInjection** method, as follows:

```php
public function testDropTableInjection()
{
    $authorProxy = new AuthorProxy();
    $authorProxy->save('Roberts','of','Son');
    $title = '); DROP TABLE books;-';
    $bookProxy = new BookProxy();
    $bookProxy->save($title,1);

    $this->initDatabase();
    $stmt = $this->pdo->query("select * from information_schema.tables
where table_schema = 'librarian' and table_name = 'books' limit 1");
    $rows = $stmt->fetchAll();
    $this->assertEquals(1,count($rows));

    Entity::clear('book');
    Entity::clear('author');
}
```

This test attempts to inject a command to delete the **books** table and checks whether it was deleted. If it was not, the attack was unsuccessful. It is important to remember that tests should be run every time a change occurs, to ensure that the software continues to do what we expect it to do. This attack is now repelled but it is possible that a change could eventually open a loophole for it, so the test should exist and run continuously. If at some point someone changes the system in a way that allows this attack, we will know before a new version is released.

It is recommended to look at OWASP Top 10 list and try to create tests that cover all the security risks on that list.

Although, we have covered security after several implementations for the sake of pedagogy, security checks should be done in practice all the time, starting with the first implementation. Each test should consider both the functionality requirements and the security requirements.

To close this chapter, we will quote OWASP recommendation, recorded in risk *A04 Insecure Design*: Secure design is a culture and methodology that constantly evaluates threats and ensures that code is robustly designed and tested to prevent known attack methods. Threat modelling should be integrated into refinement sessions or similar activities; look for changes in data flows and access control or other security controls.

Conclusion

In this chapter, we covered how to refactor PHP application by applying techniques to let enough secure to turn the life of an attacker a little difficult. At first, we covered the relationship between secure development and secure code. Then, we learned about information resources about web application vulnerabilities and PHP vulnerabilities. After understanding these fundamentals, we covered the review the application's inputs, introducing filters and data validators. Next, we covered the review the data outputs, analyzing whether the application does not expose data that it should not. Finally, we learned about automated code analysis as a tool to help discover vulnerabilities.

In the next chapter, we will learn about authentication and authorization.

Points to remember

- In this chapter we saw that application security must be part of the development process and that scanning tools are important to help us detect vulnerabilities.

- We learned that data input and output from a web application needs to be handled.

Exercises

1. Change the BookProxy class so that it uses the Book model for recording and make the necessary changes to all related classes, according to the example of the AuthorProxy class.

2. Create a filter and a validator for title books, according to the example of the Author class. Validate the maximum length of the book title according to the field length in the database table.

3. Apply the filters and validators through the models in the update operations.

Join our book's Discord space

Join the book's Discord Workspace for Latest updates, Offers, Tech happenings around the world, New Release and Sessions with the Authors:

https://discord.bpbonline.com

CHAPTER 12
Authentication and Authorization

Introduction

This chapter of the book will cover two more topics of secure development. We will learn how to authenticate users using authentication based on session and based on token using the **JSON Web Token** (**JWT**) specification. We also will learn how to authorize users to perform specific operations within an application, using two different approaches, **access control list** (**ACL**) and **role-based authorization control** (**RBAC**). In the latest version of the Librarian application, users will only be able to manipulate authors and books if they are authenticated and have permission to perform the operations.

Structure

The chapter covers the following topics:

- Authentication based on session
- Authentication based on token
- Authorization based on access control list
- Authorization based on roles
- Authentication and authorization for APIs

Objectives

By the end of this chapter, you will be able to implement authentication and authorization in PHP applications. You will be able to authenticate users and persist the authentication data in the session or use a token in the JWT standard and use the application control layer to ensure that all non-public pages are only accessed by authenticated users. You will be able to control user permissions with ACLs or roles and use the application control layer to ensure that an operation can only be performed by a user who has permission to do so.

Authentication based on session

In this section, we will initially review the architecture of our system to prepare the ground and to understand what the authentication process should address and then we will implement authentication with user data storage in the session. In fact, it is good practice to perform an architectural review of the application before introducing a new feature. The pressure to deliver can lead to inadequate implementations that create maintenance problems. The review at the beginning of a new development task is the time to identify if there is anything to be improved. The third step of **test-driven development** (**TDD**) consists of improving what is working.

Reviewing system architecture

We will use the **php-class-diagram** and **plantuml** tools that we learned about in *Chapter 10, Abstracting the Application Storage,* to generate UML diagrams of the three layers of our application, according to the MVC pattern. Let us start by generating the model layer diagram. In the directory before the application, we will execute the following command:

```
$ vendor/bin/php-class-diagram librarian/src/Model/ > librarian.model.
plantuml
```

Next, we will use **plantuml** to turn the script generated by **php-class-diagram** into an image, with the following command:

```
$ java -jar plantuml.jar librarian.model.plantuml
```

PlantUML will generate an image named **class-diagram.png** by default. Let us rename it to **model-class-diagram.png**, as follows:

```
$ mv class-diagram.png model-class-diagram.png
```

Let us start with file system storage, by running the following sequence of commands:

```
$ vendor/bin/php-class-diagram librarian/src/Model/Filesystem/ > librarian.
model.filesystem.plantuml
$ java -jar plantuml.jar librarian.model.filesystem.plantuml
$ mv class-diagram.png model-filesystem-class-diagram.png
```

The filesystem class diagram will still be too large to be readable on a single page. In *Figure 12.1,* we can have a partial view of this diagram, but it is enough to observe some interesting details:

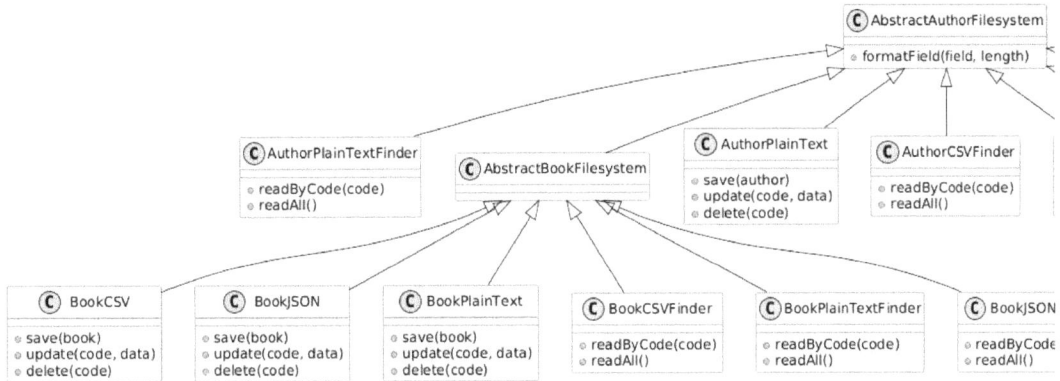

Figure 12.1: Partial view of class diagram of the filesystem classes of the model layer

Filesystem classes can be divided into two groups according to the methods they implement. There is a group of reader classes, which implements the **readByCode** and **readAll** methods, and a group of writer classes, which implement the save, update and delete methods. If it is necessary to implement classes for another text file format, they must follow this same pattern. To formalize this, we need to define interfaces, so that it is clear that the classes are fulfilling a contract.

We have already created an interface for the reading methods, **FinderInterface**. This interface is implemented by all classes in the model layer with the **Finder** suffix. We need to complete the standardization with the recording methods.

There is a detail, however, that prevents us from creating just one interface for saving. The **save** method of the **Author** classes receives an object of the **Author** class and the **save** method of the **Book** classes receives an object of the **Book** class. Apparently, we will have to create two interfaces repeating the **update** and **delete** methods because of a single different method.

We will not need to repeat the code, even if we have more than one interface because just like classes, interfaces can inherit from another interfaces. Let us create a generic interface with the common methods for the **Author** and **Book** classes, called **WriterInterface**. It will be defined as follows:

```php
<?php
namespace Librarian\Model;

interface WriterInterface
{
```

```php
    public function update(int $code, array $data): bool;
    public function delete(int $code): bool;
}
```

Next, let us create two interfaces that inherit from **WriterInterface**: **AuthorWriterInterface** and **BookWriterInterface**. They will be respectively defined, as follows:

```php
<?php
namespace Librarian\Model;

interface AuthorWriterInterface extends WriterInterface
{
    public function save(Author $author): bool;
}
```

```php
<?php
namespace Librarian\Model;

interface BookWriterInterface extends WriterInterface
{
    public function save(Book $book): bool;
}
```

After creating the interfaces, you should review all the classes in the model layer that implement their methods and establish the contract. When running the tests, you may get messages warning that some methods do not declare the return type, which is defined in the interfaces. This is an advantage of using interfaces. They act as a police force, ensuring that the classes actually follow communication standards.

Another detail that we can notice in the filesystem class diagram is the dependency between the **AbstractAuthorFileSystem** and **AbstractBookFileSystem** classes. This dependency was created to avoid repeating the **CODE_LENGTH** constant and the **formatField** method but it is an inappropriate dependency. The **Book** classes are inheriting code related to **Author** that is not used. We have learned a more elegant way to deal with this, traits.

Let us extract the common code between the two abstract classes into a trait and make them use it, decoupling one from the other at the same time.

First, let us create the **FilesystemTrait** trait, as follows:

```php
<?php
namespace Librarian\Model\Filesystem;
trait FilesystemTrait
```

```
{
    const CODE_LENGTH = 4;

    public function formatField($field, int $length)
    {
        return str_pad($field, $length, ' ', STR_PAD_LEFT);
    }
}
```

Next, let us refactor the **AbstractAuthorFilesystem** and **AbstractBookFilesystem** classes, as follows:

```
<?php
namespace Librarian\Model\Filesystem;
abstract class AbstractAuthorFilesystem
{
    const ROW_LENGTH = 65;
    const NAME_LENGTH = 20;

    use FilesystemTrait;
}
```

```
<?php
namespace Librarian\Model\Filesystem;
abstract class AbstractBookFilesystem
{
    const ROW_LENGTH = 89;
    const TITLE_LENGTH = 80;

    use FilesystemTrait;
}
```

We now have a more suitable implementation, where the abstract **Author** and **Book** classes share common code but are not tightly coupled to each other.

After reviewing the filesystem classes, let us generate the class diagram for ORM classes, with the following commands:

```
$ vendor/bin/php-class-diagram librarian/src/Model/ORM/ > librarian.model.
orm.plantuml
$ java -jar plantuml.jar librarian.model.orm.plantuml
$ mv class-diagram.png model-orm-class-diagram.png
```

As shown in *Figure 12.2*, the classes with the **TableGateway** suffix have reading methods as in the classes with the **Finder** suffix. In our application modeling, we delegated the responsibility for reading to the **Finder** classes, so the **TableGateway** classes should not have methods for this purpose.

We mentioned in *Chapter 10, Abstracting the Application Storage*, the Single Responsibility Principle. According to this principle, each class should have a single responsibility. We will leave the **TableGateway** classes with the responsibility for writing data and remove the responsibility for reading from them, because the latter belongs to the **Finder** classes.

Let us remove the **readByCode** and **readAuthors** methods from **AuthorTableGateway** and **readByCode** and **readBooks** from **BookTableGateway**.

The tests should be run after each change, right after removing the mentioned methods, you should run the tests. They will show that the **TableGatewayTest** class now fails because it calls the removed methods. You should refactor the test class, replacing the calls to the removed methods with the methods from the **Finder** classes. Do not forget that the **read** methods of the **Finder** classes return objects and not arrays refer to the following figure:

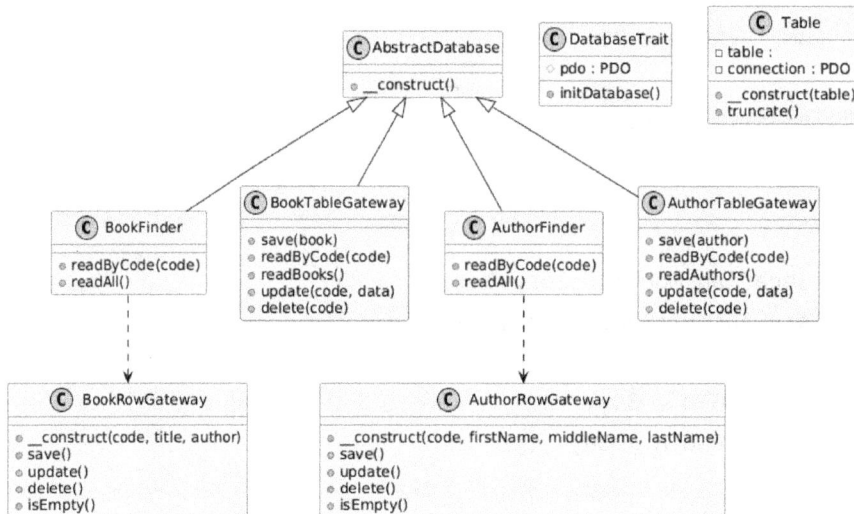

Figure 12.2: Class diagram of the ORM classes of the model layer

After reviewing ORM classes, let us generate the class diagram for the ODM classes, with the following commands:

```
$ vendor/bin/php-class-diagram librarian/src/Model/ODM/ > librarian.model.
odm.plantuml
$ java -jar plantuml.jar librarian.model.odm.plantuml
$ mv class-diagram.png model-odm-class-diagram.png
```

The reading and writing responsibilities are already separated in ODM classes, as shown in *Figure 12.3*:

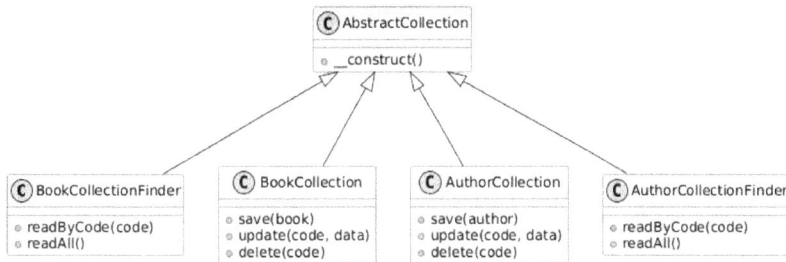

Figure 12.3: *Partial view of the class diagram of the ODM classes of the model layer*

We generate UML diagrams of the classes in each sub-namespace of the model. We can also generate a diagram that only shows the classes in the root namespace, excluding the sub-namespaces. To do this, we use the **--exclude** argument of **php-class-diagram**, defining which directories or files we want to exclude. Let us run the following commands:

```
$ vendor/bin/php-class-diagram --exclude='Filesystem' --exclude="ORM"
--exclude="ODM" librarian/src/Model > librarian.model.root.plantuml
$ java -jar plantuml.jar librarian.model.root.plantuml
$ mv class-diagram.png model-root-class-diagram.png
```

The result will be as shown in *Figure 12.4*, which shows the root classes of the model layer and their dependencies.

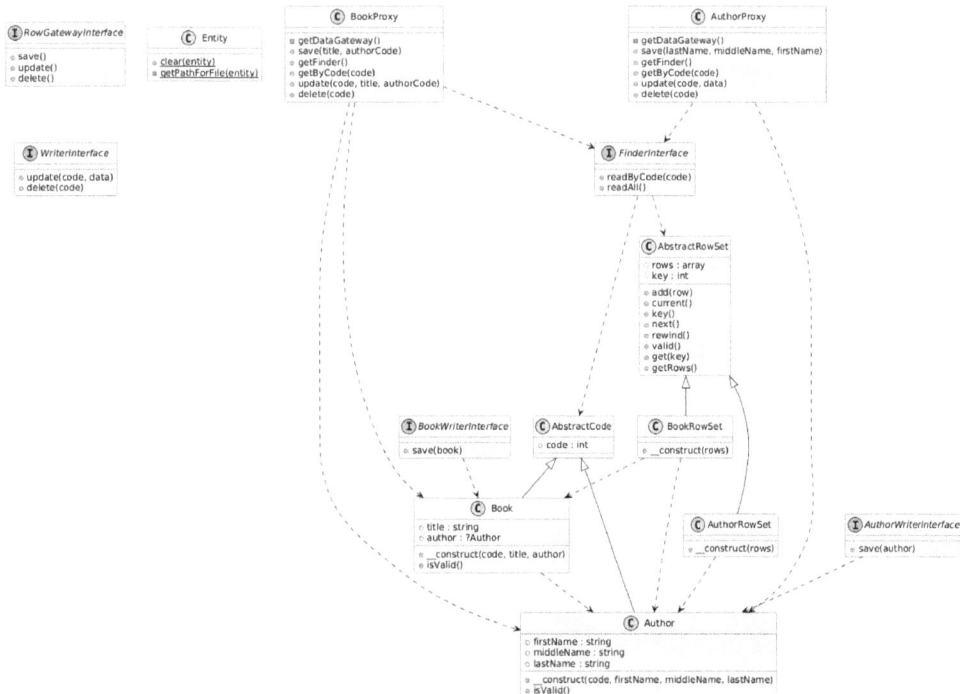

Figure 12.4: *Class diagram of the root classes of the model layer*

As you can see, the **AuthorProxy** and **BookProxy** classes have several methods in common and the implementation of most of these methods is the same. We can reduce this duplication by creating an abstract class that concentrates this common core of methods.

Let us create the **AbstractProxy** class, which will be declared, as follows:

```php
<?php
namespace Librarian\Model;
use Librarian\Util\Config;
abstract class AbstractProxy
```

This class will implement a protected method **getDataGateway**, which will use a variable to determine what the model is and thus choose the writer class associated with it. The **AbstractProxy->getDataGateway** method will be as follows:

```php
    protected function getDataGateway(): object
    {
        $storageFormat = Config::get('storage_format');
        $modelName = $this->getModelName();
        try {
            $dataGateway = match($storageFormat){
                'txt' => "Librarian\Model\Filesystem\\{$modelName}
PlainText",
                'csv' => "Librarian\Model\Filesystem\\{$modelName}CSV",
                'json' => "Librarian\Model\Filesystem\\{$modelName}JSON",
                'rdb' => "Librarian\Model\ORM\\{$modelName}TableGateway",
                'ddb' => "Librarian\Model\ODM\\{$modelName}Collection"
            };
        } catch (\Throwable $th) {
            throw $th;
        }
        return new $dataGateway();
    }
```

We use brackets to delimit variables because there is no space after them and PHP will not know where they end. We use a double descending slash before the opening of the brackets because a single slash neutralizes the effect of the curly braces as a metacommand.

You may have noticed that the **AbstractProxy->getDataGateway** method gets the model's name from a **getModelName** method. This method is implemented as follows:

```php
    protected function getModelName(): string
    {
        $fullClassName = get_class($this);
```

```
        $parts = explode('\\',$fullClassName);
        $className = end($parts);
        return str_replace('Proxy','',$className);
    }
```

We use the **get_class** function to get the name of the class instance that is running. The **$this** argument will cause it to return the name of the class that invoked the method, not the name of the class where the method is declared. The **get_class** function returns the fully qualified name of the class, with the namespace. This is why we exploded this name and extracted the last part, excluding the word proxy.

The **getModelName** method will also be used by the **AbstractProxy->getFinder** method, as shown in the following code snippet:

```
    public function getFinder(): FinderInterface
    {
        $storageFormat = Config::get('storage_format');
        $modelName = $this->getModelName();
        try {
            $finder = match($storageFormat){
                'txt' => "Librarian\Model\Filesystem\\{$modelName}
PlainTextFinder",
                'csv' => "Librarian\Model\Filesystem\\{$modelName}
CSVFinder",
                'json' => "Librarian\Model\Filesystem\\{$modelName}
JSONFinder",
                'rdb' => "Librarian\Model\ORM\\{$modelName}Finder",
                'ddb' => "Librarian\Model\ODM\\{$modelName}
CollectionFinder"
            };
        } catch (\Throwable $th) {
            throw $th;
        }
        return new $finder();
    }
```

We will also use the **getModelName** method in the **AbstractProxy->getByCode** method, as shown in the following code snippet:

```
    public function getByCode($code): AbstractCode
    {
        try {
            $object = $this->getFinder()->readByCode($code);
```

```
        } catch(\Exception $e) {
            $model = __NAMESPACE__ . '\\' . $this->getModelName();
            $object = new $model();
        }
        return $object;
    }
```

The **AuthorProxy** and **BookProxy** classes have different signatures for the **update** method. Let us create a single signature, receiving only two arguments, as follows:

```
    public function update($code, $data): bool
    {
        try {
            $saved = ($this->getDataGateway())->update($code, $data);
        } catch (\Throwable $th) {
            $saved = false;
        }
        return $saved;
    }
```

This change will require us to refactor the call to this method into the following methods:

- **Librarian\Controller\Book ->update**
- **Librarian\Controller\REST\BookREST->put**

Finally, the method **AbstractProxy->delete** is a exact copy of the same method in **AuthorProxy** and **BookProxy**. After implementing the **AbstractProxy** class, we remove the duplicate methods in the **AuthorProxy** and **BookProxy** classes and make them inherit from **AbstractProxy**.

The view layer has no classes, only scripts that generate parts of HTML pages. The next step is to generate diagrams for the control layer with the following commands:

$ vendor/bin/php-class-diagram librarian/src/Controller/ > librarian. controller.plantuml

$ java -jar plantuml.jar librarian.controller.plantuml

$ mv class-diagram.png controller-class-diagram.png

The result will be as shown in *Figure 12.5*:

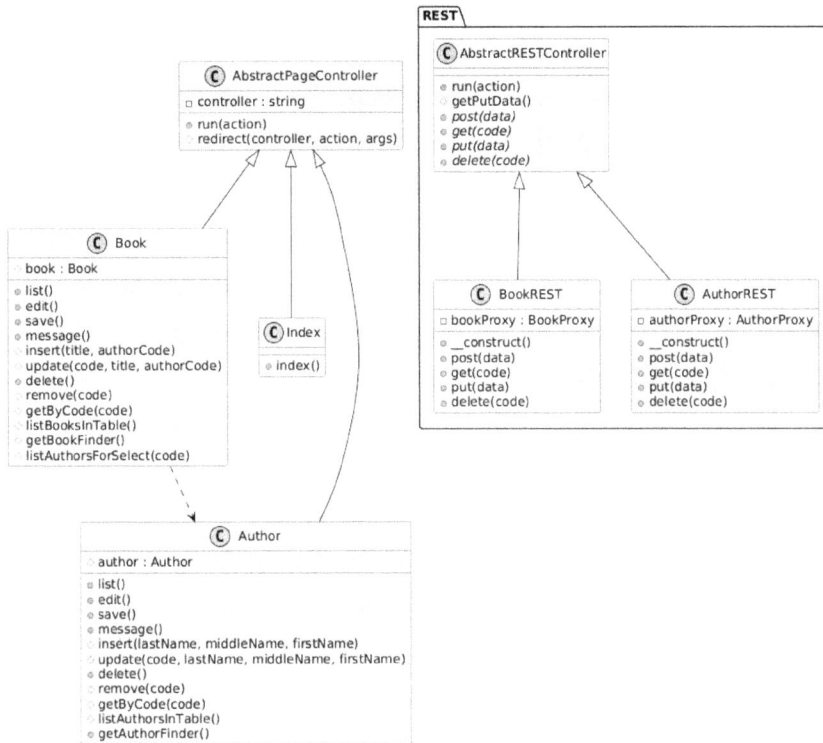

Figure 12.5: Class diagram of the controller layer

We can see that there are two abstractions that bring together common code between classes, but the **Author** and **Book** classes have more methods in common that are not generalized. Since they already inherit from a more generic abstract class, we will extract the duplicated code into a trait. Let us create a trait called **CRUDControllerTrait**, as follows:

```
<?php
namespace Librarian\Controller;
use Librarian\Util\Config;
use Librarian\Model\AbstractCode;

trait CRUDControllerTrait
```

Initially, we will bring the empty methods list and message to this trait. Next, let us create a method to return the data gateway object, as follows:

```
    protected function getDataGateway()
    {
        $model = $this->getModel();
        $storageFormat = Config::get('storage_format');
```

```
    return 'Librarian\Model\\' .  match($storageFormat){
        'txt' => "Filesystem\\{$model}PlainText",
        'csv' => "Filesystem\\{$model}CSV",
        'json' => "Filesystem\\{$model}JSON",
        'rdb' => "ORM\\{$model}TableGateway",
        'ddb' => "ODM\\{$model}Collection"
    };
}
```

The **getModel** method, invoked by **getDataGateway**, will be implemented, as follows:

```
protected function getModel()
{
    $fullClassName = get_class($this);
    $parts = explode('\\',$fullClassName);
    return end($parts);
}
```

We will implement the generic delete method in the **CRUDControllerTrait**, as follows:

```
public function delete()
{
    $code = $_GET['code'] ?? 0;
    $message = 'The record has not been deleted';
    if ($code == 0){
        $message = 'It cannot delete what does not exist';
    }
    if ($code <> 0 && $this->remove($code)) {
        $message = 'Record deleted successfully!';
    }
    $route = lcfirst($this->getModel());
    $this->redirect('author','message',['message' => base64_
encode($message)]);
}
```

The **remove** method, invoked by delete, will be implemented as follows:

```
protected function remove(int $code)
{
    $storageFormat = Config::get('storage_format');

    $deleted = false;
```

```
    $dataGateway = $this->getDataGateway();


    try {
        return (new $dataGateway())->delete($code);
    } catch (\Exception $e){
        return false;
    }
}
```

Finally, let us implement the **getByCode** method in **CRUDControllerTrait**, as follows:

```
protected function getByCode($code): AbstractCode
{
    $model = $this->getModel();
    $finderMethod = "get{$model}Finder";
    $modelClass = "Librarian\Model\{$model}";
    try {
        $entity = $this->$finderMethod()->readByCode($code);
    } catch(\Exception $e) {
        $entity = new $modelClass();
    }
    return $entity;
}
```

After completing **CRUDControllerTrait**, we must refactor the **Author** and **Book** classes of **Librarian\Controller**, removing the methods defined by the trait and replacing the data gateway choice blocks with the call to the **getDataGateway** method. Run the tests after the refactoring to verify that everything still works.

Now, we are ready to implement authentication in our application.

Authenticating users and storing them in the session

Authentication is used to determine whether a user is who they say they are. According to *Michael Howard* and *David LeBlanc*, in their book *Writing Secure Code*, *authentication requires evidence in the form of credentials*. Credentials must be stored to be compared with the data provided by the user. Credential storage can be part of the same storage used for other system data or be separate from it. We will work with a separate storage, using XML to store credentials, in the form of passwords. Passwords will be associated with users through their names. We are not referring to the real names of the users, but to the identities they use in the system.

In this book you learned how to persist data in different formats, so we will not cover the persistence of authentication data but imagine that there is a subsystem that manages this data. We will assume that this subsystem exists and that the passwords were created through it.

Let us create a **data** directory in our project, to store the file with the users' passwords. The name of the file will be **users.xml**. Passwords will be stored encrypted. The encryption algorithm will be implemented by the **User** class, as follows:

```php
<?php
namespace Librarian\Model;

class User
{
    public function encrypt($text)
    {
        return md5(strrev(soundex($text))) . 'SH4Z4M';
    }
}
```

PHP has some encryption functions, based on well-known algorithms. It is precisely because they are well-known that they should not be used alone. In the **User->encrypt** method we discussed an example of using a well-known algorithm, MD5, together with two PHP text transformation functions. In addition, we combine the encrypted text with a salt, produced by the **time()** function. According to *Michael Howard* and *David LeBlanc*, *a salt is a value, selected at random, sent or stored unencrypted with the encrypted message*. It is important to know that, although we have used MD5 here, as an example, you must use password hashing best practices like the use of the function **password_hash**, which protects against rainbow table attacks.

Note: It is good practice to decouple the encryption function from the class that uses it, using the Strategy design pattern, and to use a different function in the development environment and in the production environment. Developers do not need to know which cryptographic algorithm is used in production.

We can use PHP's interactive mode to generate a password with the **User->encrypt** method, as follows:

```
$ php -a
Interactive shell

php > require 'vendor/autoload.php';
php > $user = new Librarian\Model\User();
php > echo $user->encrypt('Mysecret123@');
5f0ce9c7755668a58d6218185627c4f7SH4Z4M
php >
```

Let us register a user jack in the **users.xml** file, with the password we generated, as follows:

```
<?xml version="1.0" encoding="UTF-8"?>
<users>
    <user>
        <username>jack</username>
        <password>5f0ce9c7755668a58d6218185627c4f7SH4Z4M</password>
    </user>
</users>
```

We have a **username** and **password**, but we need our application to require this data to display any of its pages. From now on, the rule is that every page is private. The exception will be the login page, which will become the application's home page if the user has not yet authenticated.

Let us rename the **index.phtml** file in **view/index** as **menu.phtml** and create a new **index.phtml** file, with this content, as follows:

```
<!doctype html>
<html>
<head>
<title>Librarian</title>
</head>
<body>
<h1>Librarian</h1>
<form action="index.php?a=login" method="post">
<label for="username">Username:</label>
<input type="text" name="username" autofocus="autofocus"/>
<label for="password">Password:</label>
<input type="password" name="password"/>
<input type="submit" value="login"/>
</form>
</body>
</html>
```

As you can see, the HTML form in the new **index.phtml** page submits the data to a **login** method in the **Index** class (the default class in the **Controller** namespace).

Let us implement this method, as follows:

```
    public function login(): void
    {
        $username = $_POST['username'] ?? '';
```

```
    $password = $_POST['password'] ?? '';

    $authAdapter = new Adapter();
    $authAdapter->setIdentity($username)
    ->setCredential($password);
    $authAdapter->authenticate();
    $action = 'index';
    if ($authAdapter->isValid()){
        $action = 'menu';
    }
    $this->redirect('index',$action);
}
```

The **Index->login** method receives the users' name and password sent via HTTP POST and passes them to the **Adapter** class, which checks whether the data is valid. If it is, the user is directed to the **menu.phtml** page, it is because there needs to be an **Index->menu** method. Otherwise, the user returns to the login page. For the **Index->login** method to work, we need to create the **Adapter** class.

Note: It is a good practice to limit login attempts because it prevents brute-force attacks. You can use Redis or a database table to track failed attempts.

Let us create it in the **Librarian\Auth** namespace, as follows:

```php
<?php
namespace Librarian\Auth;
use Librarian\Util\Config;
class Adapter
{
    private $format;
    private string $identity;
    private string $credential;

    public function __construct()
    {
        $authFormat = Config::get("auth_format");
        $className = 'Librarian\Auth\\' . ucfirst($authFormat);
        $this->format = new $className();
    }
}
```

The **Adapter** class is named as **Adapter** because it implements the Adapter design pattern. We are storing the user's passwords in an XML file, but we could store the passwords in any other format, just as we did with the author and book data, rather than implementing a class that assumes the data will always be stored in XML format, we create a framework that allows us to switch formats from one configuration to another. In this way, the **Adapter** class delegates the task of reading the authentication data to another, more specialized class.

As you can see, we used the **Config** class to read a key **auth_format**, which is used to define the name of the expert class. Since we are going to use XML, we will create in both configuration files the key **auth_format** with the value **xml**, as follows:

```
"auth_format":"xml"
```

The **Adapter** class has private attributes to store the users' name (**identity**) and password (**credential**). This requires public methods to receive values for these attributes, as follows:

```
public function setIdentity(string $identity): Adapter
{
    $this->identity = $identity;
    return $this;
}


public function setCredential(string $credential): Adapter
{
    $this->credential = $credential;
    return $this;
}
```

Setter methods usually do not return values, but they do return the instance of the object itself. This allows us to call methods on the same object in sequence without having to repeat the name of the variable that references the object. This is what we did in the **Index->login** method.

In the **Index->login** method, we invoke the **Adapter->authenticate** and **Adapter->isValid** methods. These two methods will make use of the expert class, as follows:

```
public function authenticate(): void
{
    $this->format->authenticate($this->identity,$this->credential);
}


public function isValid(): bool
{
    return $this->format->isValid();
}
```

The object referenced by **$this->format**, according to our configuration, is an instance of **Librarian\Auth\Xml**. Before creating this class, however, let us declare the **Adapter** methods that will use the session to control the user's authentication state, as follows:

```php
public function hasIdentity(): bool
{
    return isset($_SESSION['USERNAME']);
}

public function getIdentity(): string
{
    return $_SESSION['USERNAME'] ?? '';
}

public function clearIdentity(): void
{
    unset($_SESSION['USERNAME']);
}
```

The **Adapter->hasIdentity** method checks whether the user is authenticated. The **Adapter->getIdentity** method returns the user's name if the user is authenticated. The Adapter->**clearIdentity** method removes the user's name from the session, ending the authentication state.

Now, let us create the **Xml** expert class that will be responsible for authenticating the user using the **users.xml** file. The **Xml** class declaration will be as follows:

```php
<?php
namespace Librarian\Auth;
use Librarian\Util\Config;
class Xml
{
    private $valid = false;
```

The **$valid** attribute stores the success or failure of the authentication. Its default value is false and is only modified by the authenticate method, which we will implement as follows:

```php
public function authenticate(string $identity, string $credential):
void
{
    $this->valid = false;
    $file = __DIR__ . '/../../data/users.xml';
    $xml = simplexml_load_file($file);
```

```
    $result = $xml->xpath('//user[username="' . $identity . '"]');
    if (!is_array($result) || count($result) == 0){
        return;
    }
    if (isset($result[0]->password) && $result[0]->password ==
$credential){
            $this->valid = true;
            $_SESSION['USERNAME'] = $identity;
    }
}
```

We use the **simplexml_load_file** function to read the **users.xml** file and create an object of the **SimpleXMLElement** class from it. This class implements the **xpath** method, which allows searching for XML elements using the XPath search language.

The other method of **Xml** class is **isValid**, which we will implement as follows:

```
public function isValid(): bool
{
    return $this->valid;
}
```

Now, you can test the authentication. You can see that if you do not enter a username and password that are in the **users.xml** file, you will be continually redirected to the login page. Only after entering valid data will the page with the registration menu be displayed.

Just as we created a way to login, we need a way to logout. Let us add a logout link to the **menu.phtml** page, as follows:

```
<a href="index.php?c=index&a=logout">Logout</a>
```

This link will trigger the invocation of the **Index->logout** method, which will be implemented as follows:

```
public function logout()
{
    $authAdapter = new Adapter();
    $authAdapter->clearIdentity();
    $this->redirect('index','index');
}
```

Now, we can login and out of the application. Everything seems to be working as expected but in accordance with secure development, you should be suspicious of everything and experiment with paths that a malicious user would try to take.

In the *Chapter 11, Refactoring the Application with Secure Development*, we said that one of the principles of secure development was that *the defender must play by the rules; the attacker can play dirty*. In the case of our application, the rule is that the user must first access the login page and then access the other pages but an attacker will try to access any page without going through the login page. Assume the role of the attacker and, without being authenticated, try to access the following address:

http://localhost:8000/index.php?c=author&a=list.

You will see that you can open the page with the list of authors without being authenticated.

The flaw that allowed this access is that it is not enough to authenticate the user. It is necessary to verify that authentication has been done before displaying any page. We can do this in the abstract class that our controllers inherit from. Let us modify the **AbstractPageController->run** method to check if the user is authenticated. The method will look as follows:

```php
public function run(string $action): void
{
    $tokens = (explode('\\',get_class($this)));
    $this->controller = lcfirst(end($tokens));

    $authAdapter = new Adapter();
    if (!$authAdapter->hasIdentity() &&
        $action != 'login' &&
        !($action == 'index' && $this->controller == 'index')
    )
    {
        $this->redirect('index','index');
    }

    $this->$action();
    require __DIR__ . '/../../view/layout.phtml';
}
```

The user does not need to be authenticated to access the login page and submit login data.

With this change, you can try to access any page without logging in and will be redirected to the login page. However, if you try to login to access your records, you will also find that you cannot leave the login page.

The reason for this is that authentication is based on data stored in the session. In PHP, the session needs to be created and maintained for each request made with the **session_ start** function. Since we do not use this function, the authentication data is being lost. The solution is simple. Add a call to the **session_start** function as the first statement of the **AbstractPageController** method, as follows:

```php
session_start();
```

With this simple instruction, you will be able to access your records again, but now only if you login.

Authentication based on token

An alternative approach to session-based authentication, where the authentication data is stored on the server, is to generate a token and validate it on each request. This approach has been implemented using the JWT standard, specified by *RFC 7519*. Since it is an open standard, anyone can read and implement it.

The JWT operating mode consists of three basic steps, as follows:

1. Generate the token, from authentication.

2. Store the token on the client machine, that is, the requesting machine.

3. Send the token with each request, to be validated.

We will use a free and open implementation, the Fgsl JWT component, installable by Composer. You can install it in Librarian application, as follows:

```
$ composer require fgsl/jwt
```

Let us refactor what we implemented so far for authentication so that we can choose the strategy for validating the users' identity.

First let us create a new key in our configuration files called **auth_strategy** with the value **token**, as follows:

```
"auth_strategy":"token"
```

Let us create a subfolder in **Librarian\Auth** called **Strategy** and inside it create an interface called **StrategyInterface**, as follows:

```php
<?php
namespace Librarian\Auth\Strategy;
interface StrategyInterface
{
    public function hasIdentity(): bool;
    public function getIdentity(): string;
    public function clearIdentity(): void;
    public function storeIdentity(string $identity, string $credential):
void;
}
```

You have already seen the first three methods in the **Adapter** class. The new one is the **storeIdentity** method.

The approach we are using is a documented solution. We are implementing the Strategy design pattern. According to *Erich Gamma* and his friends, the Strategy pattern defines *a family of algorithms, encapsulate each one, and make them interchangeable.* Through configuration, we will allow the authentication algorithm to be changed easily, without having to modify any lines of code in the classes later. These algorithms must be encapsulated in classes that follow the same communication patterns. That is why we created an interface for the authentication strategies. We will use this interface to encapsulate the session authentication strategy in the **Librarian\Auth\Strategy\Session** class, as follows:

```php
<?php
namespace Librarian\Auth\Strategy;

class Session implements StrategyInterface
{
    public function hasIdentity(): bool
    {
        return isset($_SESSION['USERNAME']);
    }

    public function getIdentity(): string
    {
        return isset($_SESSION['USERNAME']) ?? '';
    }

    public function clearIdentity(): void
    {
        unset($_SESSION['USERNAME']);
    }

    public function storeIdentity(string $identity, string $credential):
void
    {
        $_SESSION['USERNAME'] = $identity;
    }
}
```

To use this **Strategy** class, we need to refactor the **Adapter** class. The first change is to define an attribute to hold the strategy class instance, as follows:

```php
    private $strategy;
```

The second change is the creation of the **Strategy** class instance in the **Adapter** constructor, as follows:

```php
    public function __construct()
    {
```

```
    $authStrategy = Config::get("auth_strategy");
    $className = 'Librarian\Auth\\Strategy\\' . ucfirst($authStrategy);
    $this->strategy = new $className();
    $authFormat = Config::get("auth_format");
    $className = 'Librarian\Auth\\' . ucfirst($authFormat);
    $this->format = new $className($this->strategy);
}
```

Note that we inject the **Strategy** class instance into the format class instance. This is necessary because the format class needs to know where to store the identity.

The third change is the refactoring of the methods that manipulated the session, so that they delegate their tasks to the strategy class instance, as follows:

```
public function hasIdentity(): bool
{
    return $this->strategy->hasIdentity();
}

public function getIdentity(): string
{
    return $this->strategy->getIdentity();
}

public function clearIdentity(): void
{
    $this->strategy->clearIdentity();
}
```

Now, the **Xml** class needs to be refactored to receive the **Strategy** class instance. To do this, we need to declare a private attribute, as follows:

```
private StrategyInterface $strategy;
```

The instance will be assigned by the constructor method, as follows:

```
public function __construct(StrategyInterface $strategy)
{
    $this->strategy = $strategy;
}
```

In the **Xml->authenticate** method, we will replace the following statement:

```
        $_SESSION['USERNAME'] = $identity;
```

With a call to the **storeIdentity** method of the strategy instance, as follows:

```
        $this->strategy->storeIdentity($identity,$credential);
```

What we have done so far is adapt session-based authentication to a configurable implementation. This sets us up for the main goal of this section: implementing the strategy class for token-based authentication.

Let us create the **Token** class in the **Librarian\Auth\Strategy** namespace, as follows:

```php
<?php
namespace Librarian\Auth\Strategy;
use Fgsl\Jwt\Jwt;

class Token implements StrategyInterface
```

The **Token** class will use the **Fgsl\Jwt\Jwt** component to generate the JWT. As you can see, it implements **StrategyInterface**, which forces **Jwt** class to implement the following methods:

As you can see, it implements **StrategyInterface**, which requires it to implement the methods declared in this interface. The token must be delivered to the client, who must send it in every request to validate its authentication. In applications with a frontend implemented in JavaScript, the adopted practice is to send the token in an asynchronous response so that the frontend saves it in the browser local storage.

In our example, we are not using JavaScript. To store the token on the client's machine, we will use a cookie. In *Chapter 2, PHP Foundations,* we learned that cookies are created with the **setcookie** function and manipulated with the superglobal variable **$_COOKIE**. We will use these two elements to store the token in a cookie called **BEARER_TOKEN**, according to the following methods:

```php
public function hasIdentity(): bool
{
    if (!isset($_COOKIE['BEARER_TOKEN'])){
        return false;
    }
    return !Jwt::expired($_COOKIE['BEARER_TOKEN']);
}

public function getIdentity(): string
{
    if (!isset($_COOKIE['BEARER_TOKEN'])){
        return '';
    }
    $payload = Jwt::getPayload($_COOKIE['BEARER_TOKEN']);
    return $payload->sub;
```

```
    }

    public function clearIdentity(): void
    {
        setcookie('BEARER_TOKEN','',time()-3600);
    }

    public function storeIdentity(string $identity, string $credential):
void
    {
        $jwt = new Jwt(['RS256','sha256'], 'JWT', 'librarian.com', 'PT2H');
// 2 hours for expiring
        $bearerToken = $jwt->getBearerToken($identity,$credential);
        setcookie('BEARER_TOKEN',$bearerToken,time()+7200);
    }
```

As you can see, the **Token->storeIdentity** method generates a token with an expiration time of two hours, which is stored in a cookie that expires at the same time.

With this latest change, we now have a working implementation of token-based authentication. You can experiment with logging in and out and trying to access a page without being authenticated. You can also experiment with changing the authentication strategy in the configuration file to see how easily you can switch between the two without having to change any more lines of code.

Authentication works. To ensure it will continue to work, we need to create a test.

We failed to follow the TDD approach in this section by having a working implementation before the failing test. This can happen naturally due to the pressure to show something works. But before you perfect the working code, you can create the missing test. That is what we will do now.

Let us create the **AuthenticationTest** class, with a **test** method for each authentication strategy, as follows:

```
class AuthenticationTest extends TestCase
{
    public function testAuthenticationWithSession()
    {
        Config::override('auth_strategy','session');
        $this->doAuthentication();
    }
```

```
public function testAuthenticationWithToken()
{
    Config::override('auth_strategy','token');
    $this->doAuthentication();
}


private function doAuthentication()
{
    $username = 'jack';
    $password = 'MySecret123@';
    $authAdapter = new AuthAdapter();
    $authAdapter->setIdentity($username)
    ->setCredential($password);
    $authAdapter->authenticate();
    $this->assertTrue($authAdapter->hasIdentity());
    $authAdapter->clearIdentity();
}
}
```

Note: We avoid repeating code by creating a private method, doAuthentication, that is shared by both tests.

If you run this test class, you will see that the session test passes, but the token test fails. The failure occurs because we are not running the code in a web environment, where there is a browser to send the cookie to. So, the **setcookie** function throws the token value into the void, and the **$_COOKIE** variable is not populated because there is no HTTP request to read data from.

We need to retain the token value so that it is visible within the strategy class in the same request. This way, we can verify that it is being generated correctly, without exposing this data unnecessarily.

Let us implement an attribute in the **Token** class that can be either string or null, as follows:

```
private ?String $bearerToken = null;
```

We will modify the **Token->storeIdentity** method so that it stores the token in the private attribute before trying to send it to a cookie, as follows:

```
public function storeIdentity(string $identity, string $credential):
void
    {
        $jwt = new Jwt(['RS256','sha256'], 'JWT', 'librarian.com', 'PT2H');
// 2 hours for expiring
```

```
    $bearerToken = $jwt->getBearerToken($identity,$credential);
    $this->bearerToken = $bearerToken;
    setcookie('BEARER_TOKEN',$bearerToken,time()+7200);
}
```

The last step is to check the attribute value in the **Token->hasIdentity** method, as follows:

```
public function hasIdentity(): bool
{
    if (!isset($_COOKIE['BEARER_TOKEN']) && $this->bearerToken == null)
{
        return false;
    }
    $bearerToken = $_COOKIE['BEARER_TOKEN'] ?? $this->bearerToken;
    return !Jwt::expired($bearerToken);
}
```

With these changes, the test **AuthenticationTest->testAuthenticationWithToken** will pass successfully. The conciseness of the authentication test demonstrates the power of implementing the Strategy design pattern.

Authorization based on access control list

Howard and *Leblanc* define authorization as *an access check to see whether the authenticated principal [user] has access to the resource being requested*. Authentication determines whether a user can access the system and what the user can do in the system after gaining access.

Authorization can be more complicated to understand than authentication. Although, it can use data stored in different formats with different validation strategies, authentication is a well-defined process. Authorization is more complex because it depends more on the system's business rules, which must define what the system's resources are and how they should be controlled.

In this section, we will present an authorization approach based on an ACL. In this approach, we define a list of resources that a user can have access to. If the user tries to access a resource that is not on the list, access will be denied.

You may ask what a resource is. As we discussed, this depends on the system's business rules, it depends on the requirements defined by the system owner. Let us define two resources for the Librarian application: author and book. Once we have defined the resources, we must define the permissions for the resources, that is, what users can do with these resources. We will define the permissions as the actions that can be requested from the controllers, that is, list, edit, write and delete.

Authorization is the next step after authentication and should be checked for every request. The most appropriate place for this in our application is the abstract controller, the **AbstractPageController** class. Let us refactor the **AbstractPageController->run** method so that it checks authorization after checking authentication, as follows:

```php
public function run(string $action): void
{
    session_start();
    $tokens = (explode('\\',get_class($this)));
    $this->controller = lcfirst(end($tokens));

    $authAdapter = new AuthAdapter();
    if (!$authAdapter->hasIdentity() &&
        $action != 'login' &&
        !($action == 'index' && $this->controller == 'index')
    )
    {
        $this->redirect('index','index');
    }

    $permissionAdapter = new PermissionAdapter();
    if ($this->controller !== 'index' && !$permissionAdapter-
>isAllowed($this->controller,$action))
    {
        $this->redirect('index','menu');
    }

    $this->$action();
    require __DIR__ . '/../../view/layout.phtml';
}
```

As you can see, the **run** method now creates an instance of **PermissionAdapter**. This is an alias for the **Librarian\Permissions\Adapter** class, which will be created, as follows:

```php
<?php
namespace Librarian\Permissions;
use Librarian\Util\Config;
class Adapter
{
    private $strategy;

    public function __construct()
    {
        $permissionsStrategy = Config::get("permissions_strategy");
```

```
        $permissionsFormat = Config::get("permissions_format");
        $className = 'Librarian\Permissions\\Strategy\\' .
ucfirst($permissionsStrategy . '\\' . ucfirst($permissionsFormat));
        $format = new $className();
        $className = 'Librarian\Permissions\\Strategy\\' .
ucfirst($permissionsStrategy);
        $this->strategy = new $className($format);
    }


    public function isAllowed(string $resource, string $permission): bool
    {
        return $this->strategy->isAllowed($resource,$permission);
    }


}
```

As you can see, this **Adapter** class has a constructor that creates an object for the permission format and another object for the permission strategy. The format object is injected into the strategy object, which needs to know how to retrieve the permission data. The other method of the **Adapter** class is **isAllowed**, which delegates to the strategy object to respond whether there is permission to access the resource.

The **Adapter** constructor depends on two configuration keys: **permissions_format** and **permissions_strategy**. We will create these keys in the configuration files with the following values:

```
    "permissions_format":"xml",
    "permissions_strategy":"acl"
```

Let us create the **Xml** class in the **Librarian\Permissions\Strategy\Acl** namespace, with the **getPermissions** method, according to the following code:

```
<?php
namespace Librarian\Permissions\Strategy\Acl;
use Librarian\Auth\Adapter;

class Xml
{
    public function getPermissions(): array
    {
        $authAdapter = new Adapter();
        $identity = $authAdapter->getIdentity();
        $file = __DIR__ . '/../../../../data/acl.xml';
```

```
        $xml = simplexml_load_file($file);
        $result = $xml->xpath('//user[@name="' . $identity . '"]');
        $resources = [];
        foreach($result[0] as $resource){
            $permissions = (array)$resource->permission;
            $name = (string) $resource->attributes()->name;
            $resources[$name] = $permissions;
        }
        return $resources;
    }
}
```

The **Xml->getPermissions** method reads an **acl.xml** file in the **data** directory and retrieves the contents of the user tag whose name attribute equals the authenticated user identity. The **acl.xml** file must exist in the specified location, and its contents will be as follows:

```
<?xml version="1.0" encoding="UTF-8"?>
<acl>
    <user name="jack">
        <resource name="author">
            <permission>list</permission>
        </resource>
        <resource name="book">
            <permission>list</permission>
        </resource>
    </user>
</acl>
```

We defined that the user jack only has permission for the list action of the author and book registration. This means that he will not be able to edit, save or delete either authors or books.

As we discussed in the **AbstractPageController->run** refactoring, the strategy class instance is the one that responds whether there is permission for the requested resource. As we already defined in the configuration, the strategy class that we will implement will be **Acl**, whose code is presented as follows:

```php
<?php
namespace Librarian\Permissions\Strategy;

class Acl implements StrategyInterface
{
```

```
    private $permissionsFormat;
    private array $permissions;

    public function __construct($permissionsFormat)
    {
        $this->permissionsFormat = $permissionsFormat;
        $this->permissions = $this->permissionsFormat->getPermissions();
    }

    public function isAllowed(string $resource, string $permission): bool
    {
        if (!isset($this->permissions[$resource])){
            return false;
        }
        return in_array($permission, $this->permissions[$resource]);
    }
}
```

The **Acl** class is quite simple. The instance that reads the permissions file provides an array that the **isAllowed** method uses to determine whether the requested resource is allowed. The class implements an interface. This interface defines the **isAllowed** method as a pattern for authorization strategy classes, as shown in the following code:

```
namespace Librarian\Permissions\Strategy;
interface StrategyInterface
{
    public function isAllowed(string $resource, string $permission): bool;
}
```

Now, you can try to login and navigate the application. You will see that you can access the listing pages normally. However, if you try to, for example, add an author, you will be redirected to the menu page.

To grant a permission, simply add a **<permission>** tag inside the desired **<resource>**. For example, to allow author editing, we include the following line inside the resource tag with name equal to author, as follows:

```
            <permission>edit</permission>
```

Immediately after this change, you can try to open the form to add the author and this time you will see the page, but you will not be able to save the change because you do not have permission to save.

At this point, it is important to make an observation about performance. Reading the permissions file at each permission check is convenient for the user, since he or she can use a new permission without having to logout and log back in. However, this affects performance, since the system needs to access the disk to read the file at each request. This problem also occurs when checking authentication. Thus, we have two file reads occurring at each request.

An alternative would be to read only the first time and save the data in the session. In this case, if any permission were modified, the user would need to logout of the system, so that the session would be destroyed and restarted at a new login. We will leave this alternative as an exercise at the end of the chapter. Now that we have shown how to implement an authorization process with an ACL, let us explore another approach.

Authorization based on roles

In this section, we will implement an authorization approach that is less personal than ACLs and makes more sense for organizations where different people can perform the same role.

After implementing this approach, we need to pay off some technical debt by creating authorization tests, but this will not be enough, because authentication and authorization affect both control layer tests and user interface tests. Therefore, we will do a general overhaul, to deliver an application with all the tests running.

Implementing RBAC

Nelson Uto defines RBAC as a model in which each user is associated with one or more roles, which reflect the different functions that can be performed in the environment. RBAC model separates users from their roles, or functions. This model recognizes that people may play different roles over time and may even play more than one role at the same time. By separating the role from who performs it, RBAC makes it easier to associate a role with multiple people without having to define permissions for each person.

Since we are using the Adapter design pattern for authorization, we do not need to modify the **AbstractPageController** class nor the **Adapter** class, instantiated by the first one. This is one of the advantages of the decoupling that this pattern provides: it avoids changing existing lines of code. To add a new authorization strategy, we implement the **Adapter** class and provide its name in the **configuration** file. It is as simple as plugging an appliance into a wall outlet.

As you already know, the **Adapter** constructor depends on two configuration keys: **permissions_format** and **permissions_strategy**. We will change the strategy to RBAC by changing the following value in the configuration files:

```
"permissions_strategy":"rbac"
```

We will use XML as format to store RBAC data, so you do not need to change the configuration key for the format file but we need to create a **Xml** class in the **Librarian\ Permissions\Strategy\Rbac**, according to the following code:

```php
<?php
namespace Librarian\Permissions\Strategy\Rbac;
use Librarian\Auth\Adapter;

class Xml
{
    public function getPermissions(): array
    {
        $authAdapter = new Adapter();
        $identity = $authAdapter->getIdentity();

        $file = __DIR__ . '/../../../../data/rbac.xml';
        $xml = simplexml_load_file($file);
        $result = $xml->xpath('//user[@name="' . $identity . '"]');
        $role = $result[0]->role;
        $result = $xml->xpath('//role[@name="' . $role . '"]');
        $resources = [];
        foreach($result[0] as $resource){
            $permissions = (array)$resource->permission;
            $name = (string) $resource->attributes()->name;
            $resources[$name] = $permissions;
        }
        return $resources;
    }
}
```

The **Xml->getPermissions** method reads an **rbac.xml** file in the **data** directory. First, the method searches for the authenticated user's role. Then, the method searches for the permissions associated with that role. The **rbac.xml** file must exist in the specified location, and its contents will be as follows:

```xml
<?xml version="1.0" encoding="UTF-8"?>
<rbac>
    <role name="admin">
        <resource name="author">
            <permission>list</permission>
            <permission>edit</permission>
        </resource>
        <resource name="book">
            <permission>list</permission>
        </resource>
```

```
        </role>
        <user name="jack">
            <role>admin</role>
        </user>
</rbac>
```

Note: The structure of the `rbac.xml` file separates the definition of roles from the association between user and role. In our application, we are assuming that each user will have only one role, so the implementation of `Xml->getPermissions` reads only one role from the XML file. But as per the system requirements, a user can have more than one role.

It is important to clarify that the structure of the access control data that we adopted in our implementation is not standard. It was the choice we made to present a comprehensible structure. The structure of the data in the file will depend both on the authorization approach and on a study by the team's architect for the best implementation.

The instance of **Xml** class will be injected into the **Rbac** class, which will have the same implementation as the **Acl** class. To avoid duplicate code, we will extract the implementation of the **Acl** class into an abstract class, called **AbstractAuthorization**, as follows:

```php
<?php
namespace Librarian\Permissions\Strategy;

abstract class AbstractAuthorization implements StrategyInterface
{
    protected $permissionsFormat;
    protected array $permissions;

    public function __construct($permissionsFormat)
    {
        $this->permissionsFormat = $permissionsFormat;
        $this->permissions = $this->permissionsFormat->getPermissions();
    }

    public function isAllowed(string $resource, string $permission): bool
    {
        if (!isset($this->permissions[$resource])){
            return false;
        }
        return in_array($permission, $this->permissions[$resource]);
    }
}
```

Note: Remember that non-public methods of an abstract class must be protected in order for them to be inherited by child classes.

With the **AbstractAuthorization** class, we can refactor the **Acl** class, as follows:

```php
<?php
namespace Librarian\Permissions\Strategy;

class Acl extends AbstractAuthorization
{

}
```

We can create the **Rbac** class like this:

```php
<?php
namespace Librarian\Permissions\Strategy;

class Rbac extends AbstractAuthorization
{

}
```

You may question the need to maintain classes that inherit everything from one another without implementing any attributes or methods. Indeed, considering that the three classes in this hierarchy are sharing the same implementation, it seems that the correct approach would be to use only one class and eliminate the other two. However, we must consider that the authorization implementation may change in the future, so we are preparing for a change. It may be that the RBAC structure will change and no longer use the inherited **AbstractAuthorization** implementation. If this happens, we will modify a specific class for this approach, without interfering with the ACL authorization. A preventive and evolutionary architecture is aware of change and tries to prevent the change from having a greater impact than necessary.

You can navigate through the application and verify that the permissions defined by the RBAC strategy are checked. You can add and remove permissions and observe the effect immediately, since the application reads the file with each check, but we have a technical debt, as we did not create a test for authorization.

Let us create the **AuthorizationTest** class, with a **test** method for each authorization strategy, as follows:

```php
class AuthorizationTest extends TestCase
{
    public function testAuthorizationWithAcl()
    {
```

```php
        Config::override('permissions_strategy','acl');
        $this->doAuthorization();
    }

    public function testAuthorizationWithRbac()
    {
        Config::override('permissions_strategy','rbac');
        $this->doAuthorization();
    }

    private function doAuthorization()
    {
        Config::override('auth_strategy','session');
        $username = 'jack';
        $password = 'MySecret123@';
        $authAdapter = new AuthAdapter();
        $authAdapter->setIdentity($username)
        ->setCredential($password);
        $authAdapter->authenticate();
        $permissionAdapter = new PermissionAdapter();
        $this->assertTrue($permissionAdapter->isAllowed('author','list'));
        $this->assertTrue($permissionAdapter->isAllowed('book','list'));
        $authAdapter->clearIdentity();
    }
}
```

As you can see, we use the same approach as in the authentication test, creating a private method to contain the common piece of code between the two authorization strategies.

This test class does not cover all possible scenarios, with all combinations of permissions and absence of permissions, but from it you can build a more complete class.

With this, we can finish implementing authorization in our application.

Reviewing tests

Authentication and authorization created a limitation on access to the system and its resources. When we created most of the tests, these limitations did not exist, so some of them may require refactoring to continue working.

If you run the general tests, which are in the **tests** folder, they should pass successfully. These tests do not use the user interface and control layer, so they do not rely on authentication and authorization.

If we run the user interface test using plain text storage, with the following command:

```
$ vendor/bin/phpunit uitests/ViewTxtTest.php
```

The result will be as follows:

FAILURES!

Tests: 15, Assertions: 18, Failures: 14.

In other words, most assertions will fail, because most system actions require authentication and authorization.

For authentication testing, we will not adopt either of the two existing strategies. We have already tested these strategies in another class. Let us create an authentication simulation from a mock strategy.

Let us create the **Mock** class in the **Librarian\Auth\Strategy** namespace, as follows:

```
class Mock implements StrategyInterface
{
    public function hasIdentity(): bool
    {
        return true;
    }

    public function getIdentity(): string
    {
        return 'jack';
    }

    public function clearIdentity(): void
    {
    }

    public function storeIdentity(string $identity, string $credential):
void
    {
    }
}
```

Let us modify the **setUpBeforeClass** method of the **ViewTxtText** class, so that it changes the authentication strategy, but stores the previous strategy in a static attribute, as follows:

```
    private static $authStrategy;

    public static function setUpBeforeClass(): void
```

```
    {
        putenv('LIBRARIAN_TEST_ENVIRONMENT=true');
        PHPServer::getInstance()->start();
        self::$authStrategy = Config::get('auth_strategy');
        Config::change('auth_strategy','mock');
    }
```

Next, we modify the **ViewTxtTest::tearDownAfterClass** method so that it reverts to the previous authentication strategy, as follows:

```
    public static function tearDownAfterClass():void
    {
        Config::change('auth_strategy',self::$authStrategy);
        putenv('LIBRARIAN_TEST_ENVIRONMENT=false');
        PHPServer::getInstance()->stop();
        Entity::clear('book');
        Entity::clear('author');
    }
```

If you run the **ViewTxtTest** class again, it will still fail, but not all tests. This is because the user jack does not have full permissions. It only has access to the author and book listing pages.

So, we will modify the **rbac.xml** file, which is the strategy we left configured as default, so that the user has permissions for all actions defined for the controllers of the **author** and **book** models. The **rbac.xml** file will be as follows:

```
<?xml version="1.0" encoding="UTF-8"?>
<rbac>
    <role name="admin">
        <resource name="author">
            <permission>list</permission>
            <permission>edit</permission>
            <permission>save</permission>
            <permission>delete</permission>
            <permission>message</permission>
        </resource>
        <resource name="book">
            <permission>list</permission>
            <permission>edit</permission>
            <permission>save</permission>
            <permission>delete</permission>
```

```
            <permission>message</permission>
        </resource>
    </role>
    <user name="jack">
        <role>admin</role>
    </user>
</rbac>
```

You can run the **ViewTxtTest** class again and now there will only be a failure in the **testIndex** method. The failure occurs because the content of the old **index.php** page is now served by the **index.php?a=menu** request. So we have to add the **?a=menu** parameter to the request that the **testIndex** method makes.

After this last change, you can run the **ViewTxtTest** class successfully. We can apply the same approach to the rest of the user interface test classes but first, we need to make sure that the authorization strategy is RBAC, because the test assumes that. Let us create a static attribute to store the current authorization strategy and restore it at the end of the tests, as we did with authentication.

We will create the following attribute in the **ViewTxtTest** class:

```
private static $permissionsStrategy;
```

Now, let us add the following statements at the end of the **ViewTxtTest::setUpBeforeClass** method:

```
    self::$permissionsStrategy = Config::get('permissions_strategy');
    Config::change('permissions_strategy','rbac');
```

Finally, let us include the following statement as *line 2* of the **ViewTxtTest::tearDownAfterClass** method:

```
    Config::change('permissions_strategy', self::$permissionsStrategy);
```

These changes ensure that the test will run under the correct assumptions. We can now apply the approach to all user interface test classes.

After verifying that all of your user interface test run successfully using mock authentication, you may be concerned about security. You may wonder what would happen if someone changed the authentication strategy in the production environment to one that does not validade credentials. You are right, you must be concerned.

We need to find the best compromise between testing needs and security requirements. One way to prevent classes intended exclusively for testing from being used in production is to exclude these classes in the application build process.

Note: What belongs to the test environment stays in the test environment. This means that artifacts created just for testing should not be distributed to the production environment.

You might argue that this is not a suitable solution for secure development, where the application must protect itself without relying on the environment to protect it. You are right. We can take steps to prevent a mock class from being used in production by changing the class that reads the configuration files.

First, let us create the **Config::isTestEnvironment** method to know if we are in a test environment. The code of the method will be as follows:

```
public static function isTestEnvironment(): bool
{
    return (defined('LIBRARIAN_TEST_ENVIRONMENT') && LIBRARIAN_TEST_
ENVIRONMENT) ||
    getenv('LIBRARIAN_TEST_ENVIRONMENT');
}
```

Let us use this new method to refactor **Config::get** method, as follows:

```
public static function get(string $key): mixed
{
    if (isset(self::$overridedValues[$key])){
        return self::$overridedValues[$key];
    }
    if (self::$config == null){
        $json = file_get_contents(__DIR__ . '/../../' .
self::getConfigFileName());
        $config = (array) json_decode($json);
        self::$config = $config;
    }
    $value = self::$config[$key];
    if (!self::isTestEnvironment() && str_
contains(strtolower($value),'mock')){
        throw new \InvalidArgumentException('No mock out of the test
environment');
    }
    return is_object($value) ? (array) $value : $value;
}
```

You can observe that we are throwing an exception if the word mock is found inside the value of a configuration key.

After this change, you can run any test, and they keep running successfully. You also can browse without any problem. But if you change the **auth_strategy** configuration key to mock in the **book.config.json** file and try to access the application, the result will be a blank page and the following error message in the server log:

Uncaught InvalidArgumentException: No mock out of the test environment

This is an aggressive approach that prevents misuse of existing and future mocks.

Authentication and authorization for APIs

We have reached this last section with an application that authenticates and controls access to its users. We have run the tests, after some adjustments, and everything seems to be working but there is something to review: The application's API. The API is not fully covered by tests. We have tested the API backend but not the access to the API via HTTP protocol.

In fact, we left the API alone for a while and made several changes without testing it manually and without covering it with automated tests. If we now try to access an API endpoint, such as **http://localhost:8008/?api=author**, we will get an error in the **AbstractRowSet** class, as follows:

```
Uncaught Error: Typed property Librarian\Model\AbstractRowSet::$rows must
not be accessed before initialization
```

This error occurs because we are trying to get a list of authors from an empty file. The **read** method tries to read an attribute that is not initialized. The solution is to change the following line of **AbstractRowSet**:

```
    protected array $rows;
```

So that it has an empty array as its initial value, as follows:

```
    protected array $rows = [];
```

With this change, we will receive an empty JSON object as a response. This looks good, but it is not.

Note: We receive a result without authentication. This is because the API, unlike the visual web interface, is managed by the AbstractRESTController class, which does not implement authentication or authorization. Thus, we need to implement them, so that the API does not act as a backdoor to our application.

Let us change the **AbstractRESTController->run** method, adding the following lines at the beginning:

```
        $authAdapter = new AuthAdapter();
        if (!$authAdapter->hasIdentity())
        {
            $_SERVER['REQUEST_METHOD'] = 'INVALID';
        }
```

AuthAdapter is an alias for **Librarian\Auth\Adapter**. After adding these lines, if you try to request **http://localhost:8008/?api=author** again, you will receive the following JSON object as a response:

```
{"error":"METHOD NOT ALLOWED"}
```

Now, API gap is closed. However, we need a way to authenticate ourselves in order to consume the API services. We cannot use the web interface login method, because it stores the identity in the session or sends it to a cookie. We need an authentication strategy specific to the API. Let us create an authentication adapter class that stores a JWT token in a public attribute. The implementation of the class will be as follows:

```php
class Api implements StrategyInterface
{
    public static string $token = '';

    public function hasIdentity(): bool
    {
        if (!isset($_GET['token'])){
            return false;
        }
        return !Jwt::expired($_GET['token']);
    }

    public function getIdentity(): string
    {
        if (!isset($_GET['token'])){
            return '';
        }
        $payload = Jwt::getPayload($_GET['token']);
        return $payload->sub;
    }

    public function clearIdentity(): void
    {
        unset($_GET['token']);
    }

    public function storeIdentity(string $identity, string $credential):
void
    {
        $jwt = new Jwt(['RS256','sha256'], 'JWT', 'librarian.com', 'PT2H');
// 2 hours for expiring
        self::$token = $jwt->getBearerToken($identity,$credential);
    }
}
```

You can see that this class is very similar to the **Token** class but instead of reading the JWT token from a cookie, the new class reads the token from a URL argument. We implemented the **clearIdentity** method because the interface requires it, but, in fact, this is not necessary because the identity lasts only for a request.

Let us use the new class as the API's authentication strategy, replacing the current authentication code block in the **AbstractRESTController->run** method with the following:

```
$fullClassName = get_class($this);
$parts = explode('\\',$fullClassName);
$className = end($parts);

Config::override('auth_strategy','api');
$authAdapter = new AuthAdapter();
if (!$authAdapter->hasIdentity() && $className != 'IndexREST')
{
    $_SERVER['REQUEST_METHOD'] = 'INVALID';
}
```

As you can see, the identity check is not performed if the controller is the **IndexREST** class. This class does not exist yet, but we will create it now. The **IndexREST** class will be responsible for authenticating the API user and only for that, then we will implement only the method for HTTP POST request. The **IndexREST->post** method will be as follows:

```
public function post(array $data): array
{
    $username = $data['username'];
    $password = $data['password'];

    Config::override('auth_strategy','api');
    $authAdapter = new Adapter();
    $authAdapter->setIdentity($username)
    ->setCredential($password);
    $authAdapter->authenticate();
    $response = ['token' => 'invalid'];
    if ($authAdapter->isValid()){
        $response = ['token' => API::$token];
    }
    return $response;
}
```

The other methods, which are required by the **AbstractRESTController** class interface, do not need to be implemented, but they do need to return something. We will return error messages stating that the HTTP methods GET, PUT, and DELETE is invalid. So, the get, put and delete methods of the **IndexREST** class will be as follows:

```php
public function get(int $code): mixed
{
    return ['error' => 'invalid'];
}

public function put(array $data): array
{
    return ['error' => 'invalid'];
}

public function delete(int $code): array
{
    return ['error' => 'invalid'];
}
}
```

Now let us do what we should have done in the beginning, that is, create a test class to test the API with authentication. Let us create the **APITest** class in the **uitests** folder. It will have attributes to store the authentication and authorization strategies and the authentication token, as follows:

```php
class APITest extends TestCase
{
    private static $authStrategy;
    private static $permissionsStrategy;
    private static $token;
```

Let us authenticate the user in the **setUpBeforeClass** method, as follows:

```php
public static function setUpBeforeClass(): void
{
    putenv('LIBRARIAN_TEST_ENVIRONMENT=true');
    PHPServer::getInstance()->start();
    self::$authStrategy = Config::get('auth_strategy');
    Config::change('auth_strategy','api');
    self::$permissionsStrategy = Config::get('permissions_strategy');
    Config::change('permissions_strategy','rbac');
    $data = [
        'username' => 'jack',
        'password' => 'MySecret123@'
```

```
            ];
            $rest = new Rest();
            $headers = ['Content-type:application/x-www-form-urlencoded'];
            $response = $rest->doPost($data,$headers,'localhost:8008/index.
php?api=index',200);
            $object = json_decode($response);
            self::$token = $object->token;
    }
```

Next, we will implement a method that tests the return of a set of authors in the form of a JSON list, as follows:

```
    public function testListAuthors()
    {
        (new AuthorProxy())->save('Márquez','García','Gabriel');
        (new AuthorProxy())->save('Borges','Luis','Jorge');
        (new AuthorProxy())->save('Llosa','Vargas','Mario');
        $rest = new Rest();
        $response = $rest->doGet([],'localhost:8008/index.
php?api=author&token=' . self::$token,200);
        $list = json_decode($response);
        $this->assertEquals('Borges',$list[1]->lastName);
        Entity::clear('author');
    }
```

Note: The token returned in the authentication request is sent as an argument in the address of other requests.

We will also implement a test for the case where there is no registered author, as follows:

```
    public function testListNoAuthors()
    {
        $rest = new Rest();
        $response = $rest->doGet([],'localhost:8008/index.
php?api=author&token=' . self::$token,200);
        $authors = json_decode($response);
        $this->assertEmpty($authors);
        Entity::clear('author');
    }
```

Next, we will test the inclusion of an author, confirmed by the Boolean attribute of a JSON object, as follows:

```
public function testSaveAuthor()
{
    $data = [
        'first_name' => 'Fyodor',
        'middle_name' => 'Mikhailovich',
        'last_name' => 'Dostoevsky'
    ];
    $rest = new Rest();
    $response = $rest->doPost($data, [],'localhost:8008/index.
php?api=author&token=' . self::$token,200);
    $object = json_decode($response);
    $this->assertTrue($object->included);
    Entity::clear('author');
}
```

Then, we will test the change of a registered author, as follows:

```
public function testUpdateAuthor()
{
    $data = [
        'first_name' => 'Boris',
        'middle_name' => 'Leonidovich',
        'last_name' => 'Pasternak'
    ];
    (new AuthorProxy())->save($data['last_name'],$data['middle_
name'],$data['first_name']);
    $data['code'] = 1;
    $data['last_name'] = 'Neigauz';
    $rest = new Rest();
    $response = $rest->doPut($data, [],'localhost:8008/index.
php?api=author&token=' . self::$token,200);
    $object = json_decode($response);
    $this->assertTrue($object->updated);
    $author = (new AuthorProxy())->getByCode(1);
    $this->assertEquals('Neigauz',$author->lastName);
    Entity::clear('author');
}
```

Then, we test removing an author, as follows:

```
public function testDeleteBook()
{
    $data = [
```

```
                'first_name' => 'Vladimir',
                'middle_name' => 'Vladimirovich',
                'last_name' => 'Nabokov'
            ];
            (new AuthorProxy())->save($data['last_name'],$data['middle_
name'],$data['first_name']);
            (new BookProxy())->save('Lolita',1);
            $rest = new Rest();
            $response = $rest->doDelete([],'localhost:8008/index.
php?api=book&code=1&token=' . self::$token,200);
            $object = json_decode($response);
            $this->assertTrue($object->deleted);
            $book = (new BookProxy())->getByCode(1);
            $this->assertEmpty($book->title);
            Entity::clear('book');
            Entity::clear('author');
        }
```

Finally, we revert to the state before the tests started, restoring the authentication and authorization settings. This is done in the **tearDownAfterClass** method, as shown in the following code:

```
        public static function tearDownAfterClass():void
        {
            Config::change('auth_strategy',self::$authStrategy);
            Config::change('permissions_strategy', self::$permissionsStrategy);
            putenv('LIBRARIAN_TEST_ENVIRONMENT=false');
            PHPServer::getInstance()->stop();
            Entity::clear('book');
            Entity::clear('author');
        }
```

You can run the **APITest** class successfully and verify that the API works with authentication. As you can see, we implemented the tests for author registration, but you can create tests for book registration from them.

The authorization process can be implemented similarly to what was done in the **AbstractPageController** controller. You just need to remember to register the permissions for the REST class methods. The most important is that you now have enough knowledge to create authenticated and authorized APIs for PHP applications.

Conclusion

In this chapter, we covered two topics of secure development. We covered authentication based on session and authentication based on token using JWT specification. We also covered how to authorize users to perform specific operations within an application, using two different approaches, ACL and RBAC.

Points to remember

- While authentication is a well-defined operation that can be summarized as a confrontation of identity and credential values, authorization depends on the specific requirements of the system. The structure of the permissions files we used were just examples, as was the storage format.

- There is more than one approach to authorization and a configurable system allows you to easily switch from one approach to another.

Exercises

1. In this chapter, we used a data directory to store authorization and authentication data. Change the application configuration so that text files in plaintext, CSV, and JSON formats are also stored in the data directory.

2. Create a subsystem to register users and their passwords.

3. Refactor the classes that read the authentication and authorization files so that they store the data into session after the first reading.

4. Check the server log, searching for warnings generated by authorization classes. If they exist, implement a treatment for eliminate them.

Join our book's Discord space

Join the book's Discord Workspace for Latest updates, Offers, Tech happenings around the world, New Release and Sessions with the Authors:

https://discord.bpbonline.com

Index

www.ingramcontent.com/pod-product-compliance
Lightning Source LLC
Chambersburg PA
CBHW061741210326
41599CB00034B/6757